The State Higher Education Executive Officer and the Public Good

The State Higher Education Executive Officer and the Public Good

Developing New Leadership for Improved Policy, Practice, and Research

EDITED BY

David A. Tandberg
Brian A. Sponsler
Randall W. Hanna
Jason P. Guilbeau

Foreword by Robert E. Anderson

TEACHERS COLLEGE PRESS

TEACHERS COLLEGE | COLUMBIA UNIVERSITY
NEW YORK AND LONDON

Published by Teachers College Press, 1234 Amsterdam Avenue, New York, NY 10027

Library of Congress Cataloging-in-Publication Data is available at loc.gov

ISBN 978-0-8077-5934-9 (paper)
ISBN 978-0-8077-7673-5 (ebook)

Printed on acid-free paper
Manufactured in the United States of America

25 24 23 22 21 20 19 18   8 7 6 5 4 3 2 1

Contents

**PART III: WHAT'S NEXT:
NEW WAYS OF THINKING ABOUT THE SHEEO**

Foreword

When I embarked on my own college career at The Citadel many years ago, I majored in English literature with the intention of going to law school. My reasoning was that this preparation would equip me to communicate effectively, think critically, and develop an argument—all skills I knew would be needed as an attorney. Imagine choosing a major with the intention of preparing oneself to lead a state higher education system. The list of requirements would be extensive. One would need to develop a foundation in P–20 education, quantitative and qualitative research methods, public policy, political science, finance, communications, leadership, and a host of other skills. What is required of these chief executives is not available from any one field. State higher education executive officers (SHEEOs) arrive at these positions from many walks of life.

I have had the privilege to work for and with five SHEEOs in three states over a 12-year span in my career. Through this lens, I had the opportunity to witness the myriad challenges that must be addressed in meeting the needs of states and institutions and, most importantly, the students they serve. The decisions these executives make and the actions they take to achieve this balancing act affect us all. Most recently, SHEEOs have been charged with increasing the productivity of their systems by graduating a greater number of students in a more cost-efficient, time-efficient manner, often in the face of declining state support due to competing policy priorities. It is not far-fetched to posit that the ability of these chief executives to deliver these outcomes will have repercussions through our economy and society.

The job of a SHEEO is part art and part science. Finding the most effective policy solution to attain educational success efficiently and adopting it at scale can only follow from considering the perspectives of diverse actors and contexts, including those put forth by governors, state legislatures, taxpayers, higher education boards, college presidents, faculty, and students. Each entity has its own understanding of what success means.

Consider as just one example the popular policy topic of performance funding. Traditionally, state systems and colleges have been funded based on the number of students they enroll. The expectation is that these state-appropriated dollars would be used to run a higher education system effectively and efficiently, issuing meaningful credentials to graduating students who would go on to fulfill the needs of local, state, and national economies, resulting in returns to both graduates and taxpayers subsidizing their education.

Within the policy arena of performance funding, dollars are appropriated based on certain outcomes, such as retention and graduation rates, with emphasis on the success of target populations such as STEM (science, technology, engineering, and mathematics) majors, low-income students, and first-generation college students. These goals are formulated to reflect varied perspectives. Governors desire the most effective use of limited state funds to meet competing state interests. Legislators share similar concerns but are also keenly aware of how the schools in their districts gain or lose based on the formula and the impact of this outcome on their local economy. College presidents are mindful of effectively running their campus and ensuring that there are adequate resources to achieve this goal. Faculty are concerned with the impact of performance funding on educational quality and assuring that the integrity of the credentials is preserved. Finally, students are mindful of all that a college experience provides, including quality credentials, personal growth, and the development of critical analytic and communication skills that will be transferable in an ever-shifting economy.

The SHEEO is called on to conduct this symphony, whose instruments often seem at cross-purposes or at least tuned differently. Even as educational administrators gain a greater understanding of the types of policy interventions that seem to be most effective at efficiently graduating students, these mechanisms must be balanced with an understanding of the current political, economic, and social contexts that exist at any given time in their states. The most impactful decisions achieve this careful balance.

By recognizing the myriad challenges facing SHEEOs, we can begin to comprehend and appreciate the complexity of our higher education systems. The intention of this book is to take a large step forward in increasing this comprehension. The aim of the contributions assembled here is to build on a foundation of state governance and coordination to specifically focus on the position of the SHEEO. This volume includes practical advice, empirical investigations, and theoretical considerations, all about and directed to the SHEEO. I welcome this volume and consider it far past due.

Our future will demand a more unified education strategy and structure that is focused on outcomes and opportunity for all. Education is the avenue by which we have hope to advance our society and economy. We as a nation must seize on Aristotle's notion that the whole is greater than the sum of its parts. It will take unwavering focus and determination, and our states will lead the way.

—Robert E. Anderson

The State Higher Education Executive Officer and the Public Good

Introduction

David A. Tandberg, Brian A. Sponsler,
Randall W. Hanna, and Jason P. Guilbeau

The ancient Roman god Janus is known for his capability of looking in two directions at once: forward and backward or into the past and future. In that regard, he is often depicted as having two faces. Janus has traditionally presided over doorways, entries, passages, exchanges, duality, and transitions. Although far from yielding godlike powers in state capitals, the chief executives of statewide postsecondary education agencies, often referred to as state higher education executive officers (SHEEOs), would benefit from developing Janus-like capabilities. Undoubtedly, boundary-spanning SHEEOs have the complicated obligation of sitting in the doorway between their states' postsecondary institutions and legislatures, while also concerning themselves with other state agencies and boards, business leaders, intermediary organizations, and myriad constituents. Without the divine abilities of Janus, these educational executives nonetheless are continually attempting to look in multiple directions at once.

The obligation to serve a wide audience is weighty, and achieving this balance entails constant reconsideration, debate, and direction changes. Surprisingly, given this crucial range of responsibilities, the SHEEO remains a neglected figure in the higher education, public policy, public administration, and political science literatures. In this volume, scholars and practitioners have come together to explore the position of the SHEEO as a critical policy actor worthy of direct and intentional consideration, to detail the role of the SHEEO in the current policy environment, and to establish a research agenda for the study of the SHEEO and the influence of those who hold this position on policy.

WHAT IS A SHEEO?

At the outset, we must acknowledge that few outside of education policy circles have ever heard of a SHEEO and that most citizens would likely not be able to identify the SHEEO(s) in their own states. Therefore, it is important to begin with a definition. Tandberg, Fowles, and McLendon provide a simple definition of SHEEOs: "the individuals responsible for leading the agencies that oversee higher education in the 50 states" (2017, p. 110).

A role analogous could be the state's secretary of education, who focuses on K–12 education. In many ways, this comparison makes sense. Both administrators are state agency heads, and both have obligations to state lawmakers and to the schools in their states collectively and individually. Where the similarities end, however, is in how states configure postsecondary governance and coordination. While the K–12 governance systems share many similarities regardless of geography, factors such as academic freedom and deference, political history and policy orientation, and state size have allowed for wide variation in postsecondary governance across states. The national association of SHEEOs (appropriately named the State Higher Education Executive Officers Association, more commonly known as SHEEO) alluded to this diversity in its description of the national organization and its members: "chief executives of statewide governing, policy, and coordinating boards of postsecondary education" (State Higher Education Executive Officers Association, n.d.).

Aims McGuinness and colleagues have detailed these differential structures and powers on a continuum from coordinating agencies to governing boards (e.g., McGuinness, 2003; McGuinness, Epper, & Arredondo, 1997; McGuinness & Fulton, 2007). In some states, more than one agency exists and therefore more than one SHEEO. In others, powerful and centralized postsecondary systems entrench a single agency with tremendous authority. Still other states have opted for decentralized systems whereby individual campus leaders may yield the most significant voices. Each of these governance configurations imply different responsibilities and authority. However, even these divisions mask the incredible range in the ways statewide higher education governance and coordination are structured.

This scope is less about state governance frameworks (which have received far greater attention in the literature) and is instead focused more directly on the individuals holding the title of SHEEO. As President Emeritus of SHEEO Paul E. Lingenfelter (2012) rightfully noted, the lack of academic and applied literature about this state-level policy actor with vast responsibilities is concerning. In his early work on SHEEOs and state coordination, Lyman Glenny wrote:

> In [the SHEEO's] relationships with the agency he [*sic*] acts as secretary, as staff director, and as chief initiator of policy recommendations. . . . As initiator of recommendations, he can wield more power and exert more influence on policy than any other person in the system. . . . He not only enforces agency decisions but also interprets their intent and scope and supplements policy with necessary administrative directives. (1959, pp. 51–52)

Going into far more detail, Lingenfelter, Novak, and Legon (2008) list the roles and responsibilities of SHEEOs as generally including the following:

1. advising governors and legislators on higher education policy;
2. making recommendations to the state with respect to the allocation of resources;
3. overseeing regulatory systems designed to promote quality in the academic offerings of constituent campuses;
4. administering state grant programs to students or institutions; and
5. collecting, analyzing, interpreting, and sharing data and information.

In summary, SHEEOs generally have at a minimum a twofold responsibility. "On the one hand, the SHEEO is responsible for helping ensure accountability in public higher education, a role that entails the various duties named above. On the other hand, the SHEEO also bears responsibility to the colleges and universities in the SHEEO's state" (Tandberg et al., 2017, pp. 112–113). Lingenfelter and colleagues go further in explaining that SHEEOs serve a higher purpose in ensuring that "the state properly achieves two overarching goals: (1) excellence in instruction, research, and public service; and (2) responsiveness to public priorities and needs." (2008, p. 4). In this regard, SHEEOs have the high-level responsibility of articulating and advancing a public agenda for higher education for the overall good of the state (McGuinness, 2016; National Center for Public Policy and Higher Education, 2005).

Given the diversity of governance arrangements and SHEEOs' authority and specific responsibilities, it is important to set some common assumptions about how we will engage with the scope of this position, which may be more or less accurate in any given state but allows us to proceed from a point of shared understanding. In that regard, let us assume that when we refer to SHEEOs, we are referring to executive officers who oversee a number of institutions in their states and who maintain a dual obligation both to their states' citizens and lawmakers and to the institutions themselves. Further, these individuals have the responsibility for developing and articulating a broad public agenda for higher education in their states. In that sense, they are charged with advancing the public good through higher education.

WHY IS THE SHEEO IMPORTANT?

Operating under the assumption that a central responsibility of SHEEOs is to tend to the public good and to advance a public agenda for higher education, the forces operating against them are legion. Over the last 20 years,

U.S. News, Barron's, Peterson's, Fiske, and *Princeton Review* have dominated conversations surrounding institutional prestige so much so that institutions' actions in direct response to these rankings have impacted the racial composition of incoming cohorts, student acceptance rates, the share of accepted low-income students, the average SAT scores of incoming students, and institutional spending patterns, among other factors (e.g., Clarke, 2007; Ehrenberg, 2003, 2005; Espinosa, Crandall, & Tukibayeva, 2014; Farrell & Van Der Werf, 2007; Machung, 1995; McDonough, Lising, Walpole, & Perez, 1998; Meredith, 2004; Monks & Ehrenberg, 1999; O'Meara, 2007; Sharkey & Bromley, 2015; Shin, Toutkoushian, & Teichler, 2011). Higher education in the United States remains plagued by continued de facto wealth and racial segregation in both the types of institutions students enroll in and graduate from, and the likelihood experiencing either of those life markers at all (Bailey & Dynarski, 2011; Bischoff & Reardon, 2014; Chetty, Friedman, Saez, Turner, & Yagan, 2017; Gross, Torres, & Zerquera, 2012; Harper, Patton, & Wooden, 2009; Rodriguez, 2008; Ryan & Bauman, 2016). Key drivers of these persistent disparities have been attributed to tuition exceling beyond inflation (Flores & Shepherd, 2014; Long & Riley, 2007), need-based aid deteriorating in comparison to tuition prices (Castleman & Long, 2013; Lowry & Fryar, 2012), and state subsidies becoming scarce relative to tuition (State Higher Education Executive Officers Association, 2017) or based on inequitable performance measures (Jones et al., 2017). This has led to a divide in access points, with lower-income and racial/ethnic minorities overrepresented in lower prestige and lower resourced institutions (Chetty et al., 2017). Although societal inequities continue to dictate disparate private returns of a postsecondary degree by race and gender, the returns of earning any type of credential are exponential to both the individual and society (Baum et al., 2012; Chetty et al., 2017; Perna, 2005). These persistent issues represent a direct challenge to the public good, which falls squarely on the shoulders of SHEEOs.

Our country needs SHEEOs who are capable of leading diverse groups to develop and implement thoughtful, targeted, and effective public policy solutions. Only creative and inspiring leadership will be adequate to address the significant challenges facing our postsecondary systems and society as a whole. We therefore assert that greater attention needs to be paid to SHEEOs, the very individuals charged with implementing and sustaining policy solutions meant to increase educational attainment, close equity gaps, and effectively advance the public good generally.

Lingenfelter (2016) argued that the United States needs to finance and engage in the professional capacity building (research and training) of our educational leaders in order for our country to experience real improvement in educational outcomes. This is especially true when it comes to SHEEOs. These officials and the agencies they lead, when operating properly, are uniquely positioned to provide an informed, professional perspective on higher education policy development and implementation and to properly navigate and work within both the higher education and political environments. However, to date, little has been written about SHEEOs.

PURPOSE OF THE BOOK

This edited volume provides some of the only descriptive, theoretical, and empirical investigations and discussions of the SHEEO. We hope that both sitting and aspiring SHEEOs will find information they can apply to do their jobs better and that researchers will find tools and information they can use to further investigate this unique position. Chapters in this volume present original research, practical and theoretical considerations, historical discussions, and case studies, with the goal of providing a compelling argument for why the SHEEO is a critical policy actor worthy of practical, empirical, and theoretical consideration. In attempting to accomplish these goals, the volume specifically addresses:

- why the SHEEO is such an important state actor, especially in the current higher education policy context,
- how the SHEEO might be strengthened and better operate within this ever-changing context, and
- what a research agenda focused on the SHEEO might look like moving forward.

This volume is neither a how-to guide to the daily work of the SHEEO (although it provides some discussion on those duties) nor a completely scholarly engagement with the idea of this position (although academic research is explored). Instead, we hope that everyone who might be interested in state policy making generally and the SHEEO position specifically will find something useful and intriguing in this volume. In that regard, we have collected authors who are former SHEEOs and state higher education agency staff, renowned scholars, and individuals who have worked or are currently working at state higher education policy organizations to provide their thinking on important topics related to the SHEEO. Like Janus, the volume looks to the past, present, and future.

In looking forward, to achieve equity in higher education and to stand with our institutions and states to truly serve a public good, more diverse voices must be sought out and supported as necessary contributors to the state higher education leadership and policy conversation. The critique of limited voices is not lost on the editors of this volume and is discussed more fully in the Conclusion. We also hope the research agenda and practical applications within this book spark a critical conversation of where we have been, where we are, and where we are going. We advocate for greater diversity in the study of SHEEOs and among SHEEOs and for broader and more intentionally designed approaches to ensuring inclusion of these voices and perspectives.

CHAPTER SUMMARIES

This book is organized in three parts. Returning to the Janus metaphor, the contributions assembled here ask readers to look in multiple directions at once. The first part looks back at the creation of the SHEEO position and its subsequent evolution, placing the position in broader state and national policy contexts. The second part provides a deeper understanding of the SHEEO as a contemporary policy actor in states. The third part looks forward to how the role of the SHEEO may be conceptualized and measured in the future.

Part I: SHEEOs in Context: Developing a Base of Understanding

In Chapter 1, SHEEO President Emeritus Paul E. Lingenfelter shares the history and evolution of SHEEOs. From Thomas Jefferson to John Dale Russell to the current day, this chapter details how the "systemness" of higher education is deeply rooted in the history of our nation and our states. While the concept of higher education coordination was seen as early as Jefferson's *Notes on the State of Virginia*, Lingenfelter's analysis expands along with the changes to higher education in the mid-20th century and in the process established the foundational beliefs and intentions that have guided the development of the role of the SHEEO and state higher education governance in the United States. Weaving knowledge from historical documents, authors, and public records along with its author's experience as a higher education leader, the chapter provides the context needed for the rest of the volume.

SHEEOs are held to develop, advocate for, and implement a public agenda. But what does this really mean? In Chapter 2, higher education policy researcher and practitioner Neal Holly explores the "public" benefits and costs of higher education along with a thorough discussion of the roots of what is espoused as a "public good." Holly questions whether higher education remains a true public good as the traditional economic definition would dictate or whether SHEEOs occupy a space that may transform the unique nature of higher education.

Chapter 3 offers a reflection and analysis from long-time Tennessee SHEEO Richard G. Rhoda and University of Georgia doctoral student Kristen C. Linthicum. Tennessee has been a leader and innovator in higher education policy with the adoption of the nation's first performance funding model, attainment agenda, and most recently, free community college.

The chapter details changes in the political environment that led to the evolution of the state's higher education coordinating agency, Tennessee Higher Education Commission (THEC). Rhoda and Linthicum employ the Complete College Tennessee Act as a case study of state-level coordination to explore the role of an influential and long-serving SHEEO and to consider how the lessons learned from the experience can help SHEEOs, other state policymakers, and researchers.

A letter to a new SHEEO was penned by Thomas D. Layzell—a widely respected former SHEEO and system head in Illinois, Louisiana, Mississippi, and Kentucky—for Chapter 4. Layzell's practical advice not only reinforces important points from the previous three chapters but sets the stage for the forthcoming contemporary environment of the SHEEO. While written to a new SHEEO, current state higher education leaders, policymakers, researchers, and students will undoubtedly glean insight into what it takes to take on a role of such importance.

Part II: Where We Are: Contemporary Structures, Policies, and Politics

Policy scholars Alicia Kinne-Clawson and William M. Zumeta analyze recent finance and policy decisions in two governing board states (Wisconsin and Georgia) and two coordinating board states (Ohio and Maryland) in Chapter 5. The authors seek to contextualize the SHEEO with political actors focused on workforce development, college completion, and calls for greater accountability and with institutional leaders focused on maximizing the benefits to their institutions, within an economic recession and subsequent recovery. Kinne-Clawson and Zumeta rightfully note that while lawmakers view higher education funding as discretionary, the involvement of the governor—and perhaps more importantly the relationship (or lack thereof) between the governor and the SHEEO—can play a critical role in shaping the support the SHEEO receives and the type of attention higher education receives in the state capital and beyond.

The role of the SHEEO garners different amounts of power depending of the governance structure of each state. In Chapter 6, former chancellor of the Florida College System Randall W. Hanna and Florida State University doctoral candidate Jason P. Guilbeau explore changes to higher education governance structures in Florida, Tennessee, and Alabama. Through interviews and archival data analysis, the authors find policy windows occurred in each of these states when problems, politics, and policy aligned, which allowed powerful governors to make changes. This chapter portrays a picture of differing roles of the SHEEO when a governor or other statewide legislative leaders promote governance changes.

The role of intermediary organizations has amassed recent attention both in the literature and in policy circles. In Chapter 7, higher education researchers Erik C. Ness, James C. Hearn, and Paul G. Rubin provide insight into how these organizations can complement and compete with the work of SHEEOs and their agencies. The researchers propose four types of intermediary organizations that can be classified along a "two communities" continuum: researcher-based, researcher-leaning, policymaker-leaning, and policymaker-based. They next provide four case examples from Georgia, North Carolina, Tennessee, and Texas where SHEEOs sought support from an intermediary organization, where state political actors influenced SHEEOs to engage with intermediary organizations, or where intermediary organizations have inserted themselves into the policy discussion.

The focus of the boundary-spanning role of the SHEEO has so far focused on the state policy and political contexts. While these relationships and contexts are important, so too are the perceptions of campus leaders. In Chapter 8, political scientists Tracey Bark and Alisa Hicklin Fryar use data from a 2012 survey of 140 campus leaders to examine how SHEEOs are viewed at the campus level, how SHEEO structures influence and potentially mitigate the SHEEO–president relationship, and how variations among SHEEOs can influence relationships between campus leaders and state elected officials. The authors dive into the dual role of the SHEEO as an advocate and overseer.

Part III: What's Next: New Ways of Thinking About the SHEEO

Regardless of the structure of state higher education governance, states must do more to achieve postsecondary attainment goals in a continually changing society and economy. In Chapter 9, Brian A. Sponsler and Mary Fulton of Education Commission of the States argue that antiquated governance structures prevent needed innovation and essential responsibilities of today's higher education environment. The authors propose not a new structure—although nearly every state's arrangement would require adjustment—but instead a list of essential functions each state's governance system must accomplish to be viable moving forward.

SHEEOs have a complex and difficult job. In fact, in Chapter 10, David A. Tandberg and Jacob T. Fowles explain that the challenges facing SHEEOs are "wicked problems" deserving of serious theoretical consideration. They explain how the application of theory can help researchers study the SHEEO—and help SHEEOs operate more efficiently and effectively. The authors then discuss four such theories (the garbage can model of decision making, multiple streams, principal agent, and boundary spanning theory), applying them to the role and context of the SHEEO in order to illustrate the potential utility of such efforts in not only informing future research but also to aid current and future SHEEOs in understanding and contextualizing their own work.

The study of the SHEEO has largely employed qualitative methods, including within this volume. Moving forward, however, T. Austin Lacy and Tandberg argue that aspects of the position are not only possible to measure quantitatively but propose a framework, measures, methods, and data for doing so in order to advance our understanding of this critical position.

CONCLUSION

The authors and the editors have made every effort to produce a volume worthy of the reader's time and consideration. In doing so, we have attempted to avoid errors and aimed for the utmost quality. We wish to thank those we work for and with, and most importantly, we wish to thank those closest to us (you know who you are). Without their collective support, this volume would not have been possible. Despite our best efforts, where errors exist, they are the responsibility of the editors and the associated authors. Further, the opinions expressed in this volume do not necessarily represent the opinions of our employers and may only be attributed to the individual chapter authors.

We hope that this volume will expand the field's understanding of the SHEEO and that moving forward others will engage the topic of state higher education leadership. It is a topic worthy of further consideration.

REFERENCES

Bailey, M. J., & Dynarski, S. M. (2011). *Gains and gaps: Changing inequality in U.S. college entry and completion* (No. w17633). Washington, DC: National Bureau of Economic Research.

Baum, S., Breneman, D. W., Chingos, M. M., Ehrenberg, R. G., Fowler, P., . . . Whitehurst, G. (2012). *Beyond need and merit: Strength state grant programs.* Washington, DC: The Brookings Institute.

Bischoff, K., & Reardon, S. F. (2014). *Residential segregation by income, 1970–2009.* New York: Russell Sage Foundation.

Castleman, B. L., & Long, B. T. (2013). Looking beyond enrollment: The causal effect of need-based grants on college access, persistence, and graduation. *Journal of Labor Economics, 34*(4), 1023–1073.

Chetty, R., Friedman, J. N., Saez, E., Turner, N., & Yagan, D. (2017). *Mobility report cards: The role of colleges in intergenerational mobility.* Washington, DC: Internal Revenue Service.

Clarke, M. (2007). The impact of higher education rankings on student access, choice, and opportunity. *Higher Education in Europe, 32*(1), 59–70.

Ehrenberg, R. G. (2003). Reaching for the brass ring: the U.S. News & World Report ranking and competition. *Change, 26*(2), 145–162.

Ehrenberg, R. G. (2005). Method or madness? Inside the U.S. News & World Report college rankings. *Journal of College Admission, 189*, 29–35.

Espinosa, L. L., Crandall, J. R., & Tukibayeva, M. (2014). *Rankings, institutional behavior, and college and university choice: Framing the national dialogue on Obama's ratings plan.* Washington, DC: American Council on Education.

Farrell, E. F., & Van Der Werf, M. (2007). Playing the rankings game. *The Chronicle of Higher Education, 53*(38), A11.

Flores, S. M., & Shepherd, J. C. (2014). Pricing out the disadvantaged? The effect of tuition deregulation in Texas public four-year institutions. *The Annals of the American Academy of Political and Social Science, 655*(1), 99–122.

Glenny, L. A. (1959). *Autonomy of public colleges: The challenge of coordination.* New York: McGraw-Hill.

Gross, J. P. K., Torres, V., & Zerquera, D. (2012). Financial aid and attainment among students in a state with changing demographics. *Research in Higher Education, 54*(4), 383–406.

Harper, S. R., Patton, L. D., & Wooden, O. S. (2009). Access and equity for African American students in higher education: A critical race historical analysis of policy efforts. *The Journal of Higher Education, 80*(4), 389–414.

Jones, T., Jones, S. M., Elliott, K. C., Owens, L. R., Assalone, A. E., & Gándara, D. (2017). *Outcomes based funding and race in higher education: Can equity be bought?* New York: Springer.

Lingenfelter, P. E. (2012). *State policy leadership for higher education: A brief summary of the origins and continuing evolution of a profession.* Boulder, CO: State Higher Education Executive Officers Association.

Lingenfelter, P. E. (2016). Rebuilding confidence in educational leaders through evidence-based practice and policy. *Change: The magazine of higher learning, 48*(2), 48–53.

Lingenfelter, P. E., Novak, R. J., & Legon, R. (2008). *Excellence at scale: What is required of public leadership and governance in higher education?* Charlottesville, VA: Association of Governing Boards.

Long, B. T., & Riley, E. (2007). Financial aid: A broken bridge to college access? *Harvard Educational Review, 77*(1), 39–63.

Lowry, R. C., & Fryar, A. H. (2012). The politics of higher education. In V. Gray & R. L. Hanson (Eds.), *Politics in the American states* (10th ed.). Washington, DC: Congressional Quarterly Press.

Machung, A. (1995, May). *Changes in college rankings: How real are they?* Presented at the annual meeting of the Association for Institutional Research, Boston, MA.

McDonough, P., Lising, A., Walpole, M., & Perez, L. (1998). College rankings: Democratized college knowledge for whom? *Research in Higher Education, 45*(5), 513–537.

McGuinness, A. C. (2003). *Models of postsecondary education and governance in the states.* Denver, CO: Education Commission of the States.

McGuinness, A. C. (2016). *State policy leadership for the future: History of state coordination and governance and alternatives for the future.* Denver, CO: Education Commission of the States.

McGuinness, A. C., Epper, R. M., & Arredondo, S. (1997). *State postsecondary education structures sourcebook: 1997.* Denver, CO: Education Commission of the States.

McGuinness, A. C., & Fulton, M. (2007). *50-state comparison: State-level coordination and/or governing agency*. Denver, CO: Education Commission of the States. Retrieved from ecs.force.com/mbdata/mbquestRTL?Rep=PSG01

Meredith, M. (2004). Why do universities compete in the ratings game? An empirical analysis of the effects of the U.S. News & World Report college rankings. *Research in Higher Education, 45*(5), 443–461.

Monks, J., & Ehrenberg, R. G. (1999). The impact of the U.S. News & World Report college rankings on admission outcomes and pricing policies at selective private institutions. NBER Working Paper No. 7227. Cambridge, MA: National Bureau of Economic Research.

National Center for Public Policy and Higher Education. (2005). *State capacity for higher education policy*. San Jose, CA: Author.

O'Meara, K. (2007). Striving for what? Exploring the pursuit of prestige. In J. C. Smart (Ed.), *Higher education: Handbook of theory and research* (pp. 121–179). Dordrecht, The Netherlands: Springer.

Perna, L. W. (2005). The benefits of higher education: Sex, racial/ethnic, and socioeconomic group differences. *The Review of Higher Education, 29*(1), 23–52.

Rodriguez, C. G. (2008). Education and Hispanic philanthropy: Family, sacrifice, and community. In A. Walton & M. Gasman (Eds.), *Philanthropy, volunteerism, and fundraising in higher education* (pp. 796–803). Boston, MA: Pearson Custom.

Ryan, C. L., & Bauman, K. (2016). *Educational attainment in the United States: 2015*. Washington, DC: U.S. Census Bureau.

Sharkey, A. J., & Bromley, P. (2015). Can ratings have indirect effects? Evidence from organizational response to peer environmental ratings. *American Sociological Review, 80*(1), 63–91.

Shin, J. C., Toutkoushian, R. K., & Teichler, U. (2011). *University rankings: Theoretical basis, methodology and impacts on global higher education*. Dordrecht, The Netherlands: Springer.

State Higher Education Executive Officers Association. (2017). *State higher education finance (SHEF)*. Boulder, CO: Author.

State Higher Education Executive Officers Association. (n.d.). *About SHEEO*. Retrieved from sheeo.org/about

Tandberg, D. A., Fowles, J. T., & McLendon, M. K. (2017). The governor and the state higher education executive officer: How the relationship shapes state financial support for higher education. *The Journal of Higher Education, 88*(1), 110–134.

Part I

SHEEOs IN CONTEXT: DEVELOPING A BASE OF UNDERSTANDING

The Origins and Evolving Roles of State Higher Education Executives in American Higher Education

Paul E. Lingenfelter

At the end of the 20th century the system of postsecondary education in the United States was widely, perhaps universally, acknowledged as the best in the world. From time to time some higher education leaders, apparently seeking to minimize governmental steering and involvement, have opined that the source of higher education's greatness in the United States is that "it is *not* a system!"

Despite aversions to "systemness," to suggest there is no system of higher education in the United States is to deny the reality and the impact of intentional and massively consequential governmental actions to create higher education institutions and policies to meet state and national needs. Institutional diversity and support for both public and independent institutions have been integral to the system's design, establishing broad parameters and employing various mechanisms to achieve responsiveness to public needs. This chapter presents a brief history of those public actions and the particular role of state higher education executives in creating and nurturing the nation's system of higher education.

The role of state higher education executives was most prominent in the latter half of the 20th century when the U.S. system of higher education achieved unprecedented growth in size and in the depth and breadth of its contributions. State higher education leaders played a significant role in establishing the parameters and goals of this national expansion. In many states, they were leaders in developing the specific policies and actions that shaped it. To understand why and how the expansion of the late 20th century happened, it is useful to review what preceded it.

THE ORIGINS OF THE PROFESSION

Government and U.S. Higher Education Before the Mid-20th Century

Thomas Jefferson planted a seed for the idea of a state education executive when he published *Notes on the State of Virginia* in 1785 (Jefferson, 1832). Jefferson advocated a comprehensive system of public education providing universal (at least for White males) education for 3 years, followed by 1 or 2 more years of free education in one of 20 grammar schools for the "boy of best genius" in each local school. The "best genius" in these grammar schools (20 boys) would be given 6 more years of free education. Through the plan, Jefferson wrote, "twenty of the best geniuses will be raked from the rubbish annually" (p. 167). True to his meritocratic convictions, Jefferson then proposed that after 6 years, the best 10 of these 20 students should be given a 3-year scholarship to William and Mary, the oldest public university, founded in 1693.

As the first planner for the Virginia system of education, Jefferson advanced the idea of universal opportunity (within the constricted definition of his era), a system of schools with diversified missions and financial assistance to enable low-income students to pay for higher education. Implicitly this system would run parallel with the existing system of privately provided education (up to and including the university level) for those who could afford it. His plan for the University of Virginia came later.

Other seeds were planted in Georgia (1785), North Carolina (1789), Vermont (1791), and Tennessee (1794), which founded state-chartered and state-supported institutions before 1800 (Rudolph, 1962). During the colonial era and the early days of the republic, colonial governments and states also provided significant support for "private" colleges. They sometimes intervened or attempted to intervene in internal college affairs, temporarily taking over Columbia and the University of Pennsylvania, and placing members on the boards of Harvard, Yale, and William and Mary. According to Frederick Rudolph, "public hostility to denominational education" was a factor in state involvement in higher education, moderating excessive liberalism at Harvard and excessive conservatism at Yale.

A struggle for power between Dartmouth College President John Wheelock (the son of Dartmouth's founder Eleazar Wheelock) and his Board of Trustees led to a landmark Supreme Court decision that established the inviolability of contracts and incidentally erected a boundary between public and private institutions of higher education (Rudolph, 1962). The legislature of New Hampshire, at the instigation of the college president, transferred to the state the ownership of the charter previously granted to the Dartmouth board of trustees. The trustees' appeal of this action to the U.S. Supreme Court, famously argued by Daniel Webster, was successful. The court decision established the principle that a charter granted by the state is an irrevocable contract, which cannot be withdrawn by subsequent state action. The implications of this decision for contracts of all kinds extended far beyond its application to higher education, but it clearly facilitated the establishment of independent colleges by churches and communities throughout the young nation.

During the entire 19th century, higher education in the United States was delivered predominately by private colleges (Rudolph, 1962). These were frequently labeled "rich man's" colleges, and vigorous opposition by the affluent to the creation of public colleges sometimes justified the claim. In 1873, arguing against the establishment of a tax-supported national university, President Eliot of Harvard said, "Our ancestors well understood the principle that to make a people free and self-reliant, it is necessary to let them take care of themselves" (Rudolph, 1962, p. 185). Frederick Rudolph (1962) wryly notes that Harvard received more than 100 appropriations from the General Court of Massachusetts before 1789. If our ancestors had left Harvard to take care of itself, the university may not have been there for Eliot to lead.

In the 19th century the idea of public purposes for higher education was frequently overshadowed by aversion to expanding the role of government and the celebration of rugged individualism, a philosophy identified with Jefferson (depending on the issue) and more emphatically with Andrew Jackson. Despite such views, the seeds of public higher education were being planted by "Hamiltonian" public leaders who had a broader view of the role of government. Many other states soon created public universities, including South Carolina (1801), Ohio (1802), Virginia (1816), Indiana (1820), Michigan (chartered in 1817, opened in 1845), Wisconsin (1848), and Minnesota (1851) (Rudolph, 1962). The first "normal school" to train public school teachers was created in Massachusetts in 1839. In 1857 another normal school, later Illinois State University, became the state's first public institution of higher education.

In 1862, President Lincoln and his Republican Congress passed the Morrill Act, which granted federal lands to the states for the purpose of establishing land grant universities (Rudolph, 1962). This law established higher education as a national priority. It deliberately expanded the scope of higher education "to promote the liberal and practical education of the industrial classes in the several pursuits and professions of life"(Morrill Act of 1862, 2009). The Homestead Act and the Pacific Railroad Act of 1862 complemented the Morrill Act. All three initiatives were designed to enhance opportunity and the lives of ordinary people by expanding access to education and land (capital) and by public investments in infrastructure (McPherson, 1988).[1]

College enrollments and the roles of the states and the federal government in higher education grew throughout the 19th century, but the growth was gradual and relatively slow. In 1869–1870, there were 563 institutions of higher education in the nation with a total enrollment of 52,000, only 0.14% of the U.S. population (Lingenfelter, 2008). Most of the institutions were private, and although there were exceptions, both public and private institutions tended to have an elitist aura. But attitudes were changing. In *The Emergence of the American University*, Laurence Veysey writes, "The claims of democracy reinforced those of patriotic and institutional pride. By 1910, practically no one was left who would turn away the rising surge of ordinary youth which sought degrees" (1965, p. 439). By 1920, enrollments had grown to more than 600,000, representing 0.57% of the national population (Lingenfelter, 2008). Still, higher education remained essentially an elite enterprise, and enrollments in private institutions continued to exceed those in public institutions.

The move toward more widespread higher education gained momentum around the turn of the century and especially after World War I. William Rainey Harper (University of Chicago) and David Starr Jordan (Stanford University) advocated the creation of junior colleges, and Harper collaborated in the creation of Joliet Junior College in 1901. Although the motives for advocating junior colleges may have been partly or largely to enable universities to focus more rigorously on "higher learning" (Erdman & Ogden, 2000; Gray, 1915; Ratcliff, 1986), the effect was to provide better and more affordable pathways to higher education, as well as expanded opportunities in postsecondary education. In the 1920s, education scholars (notably among them John Dale Russell, a young professor at the University of Chicago) began writing and speaking about the need for universal opportunity in higher education and strategies for increasing educational attainment.[2]

By 1939, the United States had 1,708 institutions, enrolling 1.5 million students, slightly more than 1% of the population (Lingenfelter, 2008). Most of the institutions were still private, but for the first time in U.S. history, public institutions accounted for more than 50% of higher education enrollments.

Although fundamental changes in American society resulted from the hard-fought political battles of Franklin D. Roosevelt's first two terms, neither a working political consensus nor full economic recovery had been achieved by 1940. World War II advanced both, although the political "consensus" proved temporary. The war galvanized the country, created a sense of common purpose unusual in the history of the republic, and resulted in an industrial mobilization that eventually proved decisive in the conflict (Kennedy, 1999). The public debate about the role of government in higher education was not transformed by war, but the war directly and indirectly led to public investments that dramatically changed the scope and function of higher education in America.

The GI Bill and the Truman Commission: The Emergence of Mass Higher Education in the Mid-20th Century

The most direct, and perhaps the most consequential, effect of World War II on higher education was the passage of the Serviceman's Readjustment Act of 1944, commonly called the GI Bill. It received bipartisan support, partially because the treatment of World War I veterans had been a contentious, difficult political issue (Mettler, 2005). Educational benefits (funds for tuition and living expenses) were just one part of a package that included low-interest housing and business loans, unemployment insurance cash payments, and numerous other benefits (Social Security Administration, 1944). The educational benefits offered to 11 million veterans proved most consequential. They changed the face of higher education and eventually the face of the nation.

The GI Bill made higher education financially accessible to millions of young people who otherwise would not likely have enrolled. In effect, it substantially increased the participation rate in higher education and the capabilities of the American workforce.[3] It also increased the next generation's motivation and aspirations for higher education.

Although foreign policy and war occupied much of his time, President Truman was determined to advance and extend Roosevelt's active government policies to address social problems and expand opportunity through his "Fair Deal." The "Truman Commission," appointed by the president in 1946, generated a six-volume report that analyzed national needs for higher education and recommended a course of action to meet them. In many respects, the release of the report in 1947 and 1948 was a victory for those who advocated for more expansive educational opportunity over the previous century. Its published summary states:

> The report proposes sweeping changes in higher education. Specific recommendations include the abandonment of European concepts of education and the development of a curriculum attuned to the needs of a democracy; the doubling of college attendance by 1960; the integration of vocational and liberal education; the extension of free public education through the first 2 years of college for all youth who can profit from such education; the elimination of racial and religious discrimination; revision of the goals of graduate and professional school education to make them effective in training well-rounded persons as well as research specialists and technicians; and the expansion of Federal support for higher education through scholarships, fellowships, and general aid.
>
> In conclusion the report urges establishment of community colleges; the expansion of adult education programs; and the distribution of Federal aid to education in such a manner that the poorer States can bring their educational systems closer to the quality of the wealthier States. (Truman, 1947, para. 6–7)

John Dale Russell, who had left his professorship at the University of Chicago to become Director of the Division of Higher Education in the U.S. Office of Education, became the chief spokesperson for the Truman administration, advocating the implementation of the report's recommendations. In the April 1949 issue of the *Journal of Educational Sociology*, he published his argument supporting its recommendations (Russell, 1949a).

Excerpts from the Commission report cited by Russell included:

> American colleges and universities . . . can no longer consider themselves
> merely the instrument for producing intellectual elite; they must become the
> means by which every citizen, youth, and adult is enabled and encouraged to
> carry his education, formal and informal, as far as his native capacities permit.
> (President's Commission on Higher Education, 1947, p. 101)

> If the position is taken that the national economy is fixed and that expenditures
> for higher education are expenditures for consumption purposes only, then the
> view that America cannot afford the cost of the proposed program might appear
> justified. But such a position cannot be justified. Higher education is an invest-
> ment, not a cost. It is an investment in free men. It is an investment in social
> welfare, better living standards, better health, and less crime. It is an investment
> in higher production, increased income, and greater efficiency in agriculture,
> industry, and government. It is an investment in a bulwark against garbled
> information, half-truths, and untruths; against ignorance and intolerance. It is
> an investment in human talent, better human relationships, democracy, and
> peace. (President's Commission on Higher Education, 1947, pp. 26–28)

Russell concluded his case for the Commission with this statement:

> The President's Commission on Higher Education undertook the most far reach-
> ing evaluation of American higher education that has ever been attempted. Its
> conclusions have been startling to a great many people. Too often its recommen-
> dations have been reviewed outside the context of the arguments from which
> they arise. Stated thus baldly, the recommendations have seemed to many people
> to be idealistic and impossible of attainment. Read in the context of the report
> itself, the recommendations appear to be almost invariably the conclusions of
> a thoroughly rational analysis. To put these recommendations into effect will
> challenge the best efforts of American educators and statesmen. (1949a, p. 508)

Russell's passionate advocacy was not entirely persuasive. Companion
articles written by private college presidents Paul Swain Havens of Wilson
College and Allan P. Farrell of the University of Detroit in the April 1949
issue of the journal vigorously questioned both the practical and philosophical merits of the Commission's report. They doubted the nation needed or
could afford so much higher education. And they warned of governmental control and the loss of intellectual freedom. Although it garnered some
favorable reviews, the report of the Truman Commission was clearly ahead
of its time.[4]

But its time was coming. A surge in the post-war birth rate from 1946
to 1964, compounded by the greater visibility given higher education

opportunity by the GI Bill, created irresistible demand for the expansion of higher education.

State Higher Education Executives in the 1950s: The Founding of SHEEO

A handful of states had statewide governing or coordinating boards in 1950. Their powers, practices, and influence varied, and it was difficult to identify a common mission. The national agenda envisioned by the Truman Commission, however, required state action, and Russell began working to nurture the state leadership needed to realize that agenda.

In May 1949, Russell published an article in *State Government: The Magazine of State Affairs* entitled "The States in Higher Education" (Russell, 1949b). He outlined the various roles states have played in higher education and concluded by arguing that states should provide "equalization of opportunity for education for young people in accordance with their capabilities." He added that this role is

> perhaps not yet fully accepted. It is closely related to the needs of the democratic state for a supply of well educated persons and for a supply of well trained workers in all occupations [generally accepted state roles], but it approaches the problem, not from the point of view of the needs of society, but from that of the obligations of society to the individuals composing it. (Russell, 1949b)

On December 11, 1951, Russell gave a talk on "Patterns of Coordinated State Control Over Higher Education" (Russell, 1951). In this talk he outlined purposes and functions of state coordination, which anticipated virtually every purpose and approach for state coordination and governance that has been proposed or attempted in the United States since 1951. He concluded with two overarching observations:

1. The agency charged with responsibility for coordination should represent the interests of the state as a whole, rather than those of the individual institutions.
2. The arrangement should leave the maximum of autonomy to the individual institutions in managing their day-to-day operations.

In 1952, after leaving the Truman administration, Russell become Chancellor and Executive Secretary of the State Board of Educational Finance for New Mexico. In 1954, he invited state executives from Florida, Georgia, Iowa, Kansas, Mississippi, New York, North Dakota, Oklahoma, and Oregon to Santa Fe to a "Conference of Executive Officers of State-wide Boards of Higher Education" (Russell, 1949a, 1949b, 1954). Only the leader from New York declined the invitation, due to European travel plans.

The formal and informal responsibilities and powers of the state leaders invited to New Mexico varied, but they clearly were concerned with a common set of issues (Lingenfelter & Mingle, 2014). The main discussion topics on the agenda for the meeting included:

1. Coordination of instructional programs
2. Coordination of capital outlay programs
3. Coordination of other phases of institutional operation (personnel policies, admissions, tuition fees, board and room costs, state scholarships, purchasing, educational TV, etc.)
4. Administrative relationships (among institutions, the central board, state-level executives, state agencies, and the legislature)
5. Budgetary procedures

Within these broad categories, the educational executives discussed issues such as the allocation of programs to institutions (working to distinguish between appropriate and unnecessary duplication), the challenges of planning for enrollment expansion and allocating resources for capital facilities, approaches for achieving voluntary coordination and collaboration, equity in funding institutions, unit cost accounting, and "locating of responsibility for obtaining adequate support for the State's program of higher education."

The discussion, extending over 2 days, was captured in 75 pages of "Unofficial Proceedings," prepared by Russell and his assistant James Doi. At the conclusion of the meeting, the members agreed to continue annual summer meetings, rotating responsibility for planning future meetings among the members (Lingenfelter & Mingle, 2014). The members of the association of State Higher Education Executive Officers (SHEEO) have met annually without interruption from 1954 to the present.

Public Policy Thought Leaders in the Mid-20th Century

Russell did not work in isolation; he was member of a community of thought leaders pursuing public policies for higher education that would expand opportunity and attainment. A full account of all those making important contributions is far beyond the scope of this chapter, but a few notable examples may suggest the breadth of the national conversation.

T. R. McConnell, then a dean at the University of Minnesota, joined Russell in writing a supportive review of the Truman Commission in the previously cited 1949 issue of the *Journal of Educational Sociology*. While Chancellor of the University of Buffalo in 1953, McConnell was charged with leading a "re-study" of the Strayer Report, a postwar planning study seeking to mitigate and manage competition between the University of California and California State Colleges (Douglass, 2000). Later in 1956,

McConnell became the founding director of the Center for the Study of Higher Education at the University of California-Berkeley (Berkeley Center for Studies in Higher Education, n.d.). Clark Kerr, then chancellor of the Berkeley campus, was involved in the decision, and John Gardner, then president of the Carnegie Corporation, provided support and encouragement for the center. At the time, Carnegie also supported the founding of two other Centers for the Study of Higher Education, one at the University of Michigan led by Algo Henderson and one at Columbia headed by Earl McGrath (Cain, 2007). Henderson had been president of Antioch College and had served on the Truman Commission and on a New York Commission on the Need for a State University. McGrath, like Russell a University of Chicago professor, had been Commissioner of Education in the Truman Administration and an important figure in the report of the Truman Commission. While each of the centers took somewhat different directions, state policy became an important part of the work at both Berkeley and Michigan, led by James L. "Jerry" Miller, Jr., at Michigan and Lyman Glenny at Berkeley.

McConnell had recruited Glenny, a political science/government faculty member at Sacramento State University, to be a researcher in his center. Glenny conducted a 12-state study of statewide boards of higher education, both governing boards and coordinating boards. He had clear ideas of what state planning *should* be; in his oral history, Glenny commented that "the coordinating boards were really doing fairly superficial jobs—mostly budgeting kind of work. Very little planning for the development of new institutions, which were being created almost ad hoc without planning . . . [based on the power of particular legislators who would site new institutions] in their own districts" (Rabineau, 1990, p. 26).

Glenny's book *Autonomy of Public Colleges: The Challenge of Coordination* was the first significant study of state planning and coordination (Douglass & Cummins, 2001). For 3 years during his long career, he served as executive director of the Illinois Board of Higher Education and led the development of its first master plan, which shaped the governance and coordination of higher education for 30 years from 1965 to the mid-1990s. The plan included the development of a statewide community college system, the creation of upper-division universities to expand transfer opportunities for community college students, need-based financial assistance for students attending public and private institutions, and the expansion of all existing 4-year institutions to serve growing enrollments (Scott, 2008).

John D. Millett, a highly regarded professor of public administration at Columbia University, served as executive director of the Commission on the Financing of Higher Education, organized in 1949 by the Association of American Universities and financed by the Carnegie Corporation and the Rockefeller Foundation. His book *Financing Higher Education in the United States* (Millett, 1952) considered virtually every aspect of higher education and influenced the field for decades. In the concluding pages of this massive volume, Millett argued for rational planning and effective choices, while urging decisionmakers "to cultivate and promote competing centers of power, to avoid any centralized or single power, and to learn how to live successfully amid the complexities of diversity" (p. 481). Millett's counsel may have influenced Glenny's design of the "system of systems" (four multi-campus university governing boards and a community college coordinating board) for the coordination of higher education in Illinois.

Millett served as president of Miami University in Ohio from 1953 to 1964 and then served as the first chancellor of the Ohio Board of Regents from 1964 to 1972. As chancellor, he led the creation or expansion of public universities in every urban region of Ohio and the creation of the state's community college system. He continued his scholarship in higher education, writing *The Liberating Arts* (1957), *The Academic Community: An Essay on Organization* (1962), and *Politics and Higher Education* (1974).

Clark Kerr, chancellor of the University of California-Berkeley from 1952 to 1958 and president of the University of California system from 1958 to 1967, was widely credited as the "author" of the California Master Plan, passed by the legislature in 1960 (Douglass, 2000).[5] Kerr's priorities and political skills certainly played a central role in the design and final adoption of the California Master Plan, but the plan itself emerged from a long history of expansive educational aspirations and intense, political competition among sectors of higher education in the state of California. The well-known plan sought to provide universal, low- or no-cost opportunity through three systems—community colleges, 4-year state colleges, and research universities—with progressively selective admission requirements, sharply defined missions, and the assurance that academically successful students initially admitted to community colleges could transfer to 4-year institutions.

The sharp boundaries between the missions of the California systems appeared to minimize the need for active, continuous state-level coordination and planning that Russell and Glenny envisioned. Kerr's own assessment of the plan was that it "met the tests of that time and that place" (Callan, 2012, p. 82). A half-century later, Patrick Callan, a Kerr admirer, concluded that "[the plan's] rigidities in the face of changes in the state context over 50-plus years have resulted in a growing mismatch between institutional priorities and the needs of the state. . . . [The Master Plan] is not the plan for California in the twenty-first century" (p. 82).

Because he later chaired the Carnegie Commission on Higher Education and became an influential voice in federal policy deliberations, Kerr's leadership extended well beyond the California Master Plan (Douglass, 2005). The full range of his contributions is conveyed in Sheldon Rothblatt's edited volume, *Clark Kerr's World of Higher Education Reaches the 21st Century* (2012). The California Master Plan's strategies for dealing with access and mission differentiation, however widely known, were not implemented in other states. Instead, each state found its own pathway for expanding higher education opportunities, shaped by its own political culture and the influence of higher education institutions (Breneman & Lingenfelter, 2012).

From 1954 to 1970 the profession of state policy leadership became reasonably well established, with 26 state coordinating boards, 19 governing/coordinating boards, and only five states with neither (Lingenfelter & Mingle, 2014). Robert O. Berdahl's 1970 book *Statewide Coordination of Higher Education* exhaustively analyzed the issues, debates, and practices in this relatively new field, reflected the thinking of its leaders, and guided those beginning careers in state policy for higher education.

THE EVOLUTION OF THE PROFESSION: 1954 TO 2016

A changing array of higher education public policy issues and changing political dynamics in the states have shaped the profession of state policy leadership from the founding of the SHEEO Association in 1954 to the early 21st century. Before turning to the history of changing policy objectives and dynamics, it will be useful to consider what has been constant—contentious debates over who should lead state policy leadership for higher education.

State Policy Leadership for Higher Education: Contested Territory

The oldest claim for authority in higher education is that of the faculty. The idea of institutional autonomy based on scholarly expertise was born in 1088 when scholars organized themselves to deliver instruction in Bologna, Italy. It has persisted to this day: Academic expertise is naturally a legitimate claim for authority. But the legitimacy of expertise is not absolute. In Bologna, the faculty depended on the market, the willingness of students to pay for instruction. Also, the university in Bologna needed the approbation of the state's political authority in order to function. As higher education evolved over time, in virtually every nation the state has also become an important source of financial support to higher education.

Burton Clark's 1983 book on international higher governance identified these three sources of authority that compete and interact with each other. Figure 1.1, created to illustrate Clark's concept, depicts the independent standing of each source of authority and their interactions and interdependence.

State higher education executives work in the government/managerial space defined by three somewhat independent, yet interdependent actors: institutional leaders, legislators, and governors. The motivations, dispositions, and political resources of each of these actors shape what forms the policy agenda, what can be done, and how it can be done. State policy leadership is the art of working with and sometimes in opposition to these influential actors to achieve public purposes.

Figure 1.1. Clark's (1983) Three Interacting and Interdependent Sources of Influence in the Governance of Higher Education

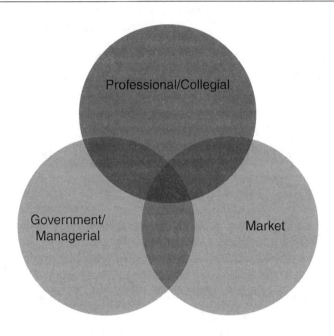

Institutional leaders. In important respects, campus presidents are politicians with constituents, political resources, ambitions, and political needs. Without exception, they need to be perceived on their campus as effective in acquiring resources and promoting the stature and reputation of the institution. They naturally form alliances with local legislators, and they seek the favor of legislative leaders and governors. Institutions naturally compete with other institutions for resources, students, and influence. When times are tough or new opportunities for gaining (or losing) relative advantage appear, competitive instincts grow stronger.

"Flagship" universities typically cultivate strong, direct relationships with political leaders and view the creation of statewide coordinating or governing boards as a loss of power, flexibility, and prestige. At times, some universities and community colleges have seen statewide coordination and governance as an ally in gaining resources, but eventually any entity standing between individual institutions and political leaders is likely to become or be perceived to be an impediment to the ability of each institution to freely pursue its own status and success. Competition among institutions is unavoidable and, to some extent, beneficial. Accommodating and somehow managing competition is an intrinsic part of the work of statewide policy leadership, but the role may not be appreciated. One campus president advised his state executive, New Jersey's Ted Hollander, to look in the mirror each morning and say, "I am an unnecessary evil." Hollander agreed to say, "I am a necessary evil" while shaving.

An effective state higher education executive will be both an advocate for higher education and an advocate for the public interest in higher education, recognizing that these roles may be in tension. To succeed, higher education policy leaders need to balance advocacy for higher education with responsiveness to public priorities and those of elected officials. Rarely is either constituency fully satisfied.

The legislature. While it must contend with the powers of the executive branch, the legislature has ultimate authority over state policy. Legislative power and influence are strongest when lawmakers are able to agree and when leadership is stable.

Individual legislators manage a dual loyalty—to the particular interests of the communities and constituents they represent and to their convictions about what serves the broader public interest. Legislators whose districts include one or more colleges and universities of substantial size naturally tend to support both higher education and the institutions in their districts.

State higher education executives need to establish positive relationships with individual legislators to promote general support for higher education and to manage those situations when a statewide perspective collides with local interests. It is especially important for them to gain the trust and support of legislative leaders.

Governors. Dick Wagner, a long-serving SHEEO, humorously attributed his successful tenure to the fact that "I chose my governors wisely!" The joke emphasizes the point that in most states the governor is by far the most influential actor in determining the shape of public policy. Legislatures can keep governors from achieving their agenda, but without the support of the governor not much can happen.

A state higher education executive who does not have a good working relationship with the governor will find it difficult to be a consequential leader on either significant policies or routine matters. Governors have frequently played a visible role in enacting significant higher education policy initiatives, and it is difficult to find examples of important actions that have occurred in spite of the opposition of a governor.

Although a strong working relationship with the governor is crucial to the effectiveness and influence of a state higher education executive, the influence of a SHEEO and his or her usefulness to a governor are diminished when the SHEEO is appointed by and serves at the pleasure of the governor (Lingenfelter, Novak, & Legon, 2008). Under these circumstances, the SHEEO is essentially considered another member of the governor's staff. Turnover tends to be more frequent, and it becomes more difficult for the SHEEO to build trusting relationships as an honest broker with legislators and institutions.

Each of these actors—institutional leaders, legislators, and governors—has a political base of support, constituents to serve, and political resources. State higher education executives (especially those heading coordinating boards) stand in the middle, without an independent base of political resources. Their effectiveness depends on their ability to establish working relationships with all those who have political resources. Because institutional leaders, legislators, and governors have both conflicting and common interests, a considerable amount of skill is required to do this work well.

The Catalyst for State Leadership: Enrollment Demand in the 1960s

The profession of state higher education policy leadership emerged in response to unprecedented enrollment demand in the 1960s. The launching of the Russian satellite Sputnik in 1957 intensified the salience of higher education. Within a year the National Defense Education Act was passed, providing federal funding to education at every level, including financial assistance to students through loans.

Even in the mid-1940s, bills began to be introduced in state legislatures around the country to create new institutions to meet the impending demand. In every state some variation of these elements appeared:

- Established public institutions sought to expand, and they opposed the creation of new institutions.
- If one public university was predominant in the state, it frequently sought to create branch campuses in geographical regions likely to call for more convenient access to higher education.
- If two or more public universities existed, they competed for additional resources and branch campuses through their legislative patrons.
- Public universities with limited missions in research and graduate/professional education sought to acquire and expand such programs.
- If no community colleges existed, the public universities sought to prevent their creation, sometimes by creating 2-year instructional centers in various locations.
- If community colleges existed, their missions and their expansion in numbers and size were contentiously debated.
- Private institutions worried that the growing availability of lower-cost public higher education would lead to their demise. They lobbied to limit the growth of the public sector and sought public financial support through scholarships and more direct means.

Competition within higher education for public support is as old as the republic, but in the mid-20th century the prospect of substantially greater resources and enrollments added unprecedented intensity. States handled these issues in different ways. As shown in Figure 1.2, 15 states with more than one state university had established a statewide coordinating or governing entity with a chief executive before 1960 (Lingenfelter & Mingle, 2014). Most of these states had governing boards, and it is reasonable to assume that these boards, acting in tandem with the governor and legislature, were engaged in discussions about managing growth. The remaining states invented their own ways of coping.

In California, the extensive negotiations that led to the 1960 master plan produced a "solution" for managing competition among sectors that initially established no continuing role for state policy leadership.

Fifteen states created coordinating boards for higher education between 1960 and 1970 (Lingenfelter & Mingle, 2014). The stories behind the creation of three of these boards illustrate the politics in play. In Illinois, legislative patrons of the University of Illinois and Southern Illinois University dominated the politics of higher education. Eventually a commission recommended the creation of the Illinois Board of Higher Education to give the governor and legislature advice on planning and budgeting for higher education. The board was created in 1961.

In 1963 the Ohio Board of Regents was created, with the legislation guided somewhat by the Illinois statute. In the case of Ohio, conflicts between Ohio State University and Ohio University over new programs were a catalyst.

Figure 1.2. Statewide Coordinating and Governing Boards with a Chief Executive

State governing or coordinating (*) boards established before 1960

Alaska, Arizona, Florida, Georgia, Hawaii, Kansas, Mississippi, New Mexico*, New York, North Carolina, North Dakota, Oklahoma*, Oregon, South Dakota, University of Vermont, Virginia*, University of Wyoming

State governing or coordinating (*) boards established 1960 to 1970

Alabama*, Arkansas*, Colorado*, Connecticut*, Idaho, Illinois*, Iowa, Kentucky*, Louisiana*, Maine, Minnesota*, Nevada, New Jersey*, Ohio*, South Carolina*, Tennessee*, Texas*, Utah, Vermont State Colleges, Washington*, West Virginia*

State governing or coordinating (*) boards established after 1970

Alaska*, California*, Delaware*, Indiana*, Maryland*, Massachusetts*, Missouri*, Montana, Nebraska, New Hampshire, Puerto Rico*, Rhode Island, Wisconsin, Wyoming Community Colleges*

*Coordinating Board; *Note:* Adapted from Lingenfelter and Mingle (2014). It is often difficult to identify precisely the date various state boards (or their predecessors) were established. This figure summarizes their initiation based on the history of past chief executives provided by current state agencies to SHEEO.

In 1965, the Coordinating Board for the Texas College and University System was created. Governor John Connally's charge to the board captured the essential thinking behind the creation of these boards:

> The greatest risk you face is an institutionalized system, with each college or university grasping for its own ends without regard to the needs of the people of the whole state, and perhaps without being aware of those needs. I don't say this critically of any college president or any institution, but this is human nature. There is nothing wrong with being competitive. . . .
>
> I assure you that you were not appointed to represent any institution; you were named to represent the State of Texas in the coordination of all higher education under state authority.
>
> Neither were you appointed to represent the geographical area where you were born, attended college, or where you now live. Texas, the entire state, the youth of this state, is your constituency, and to that constituency you owe your loyalty and allegiance.
>
> It is your responsibility to determine educational questions according to educational measures and standards. You should leave politics to the politicians and administration to the administrators. . . .
>
> You have been given the power to add planning, imagination, and coordination to supplement the taxpayers' dollars in higher education. I trust you will use them wisely. (Connally, 1965, para. 14–44)

Connally's charge did not presume state coordination would eliminate politics in higher education. Instead, he expected the board to *add* an independent voice to the political process focused on public needs and the public's interest in higher education. This requirement typically led the boards created during this period to seek chief executives who had credibility as educational leaders plus the ability to take a broad statewide perspective, working effectively with political leaders. The early SHEEOs were rarely appointed by the governor, but it was understood that they needed to be able to work with the governor, with legislators, and with institutional leaders to be successful. Their responsibility as state higher education policy leaders was to identify, articulate, and advocate the public interest in higher education; to persuade institutions, legislators, and governors to pursue it; and to help them create the means of realizing it.

The Contributions of Coordination and Planning: 1954 to 1975

The missions of instruction, research, the application of knowledge, and public service are all facets of the public interest in higher education. A large part of the challenge of planning is to identify and achieve a proper balance among these aspects. From 1960 until the end of the century, public investment permitted every facet of the mission to prosper. Research universities grew in enrollment; in the breadth of their instructional programs; in the production of undergraduate, graduate, and professional degrees; and in the depth and breadth of their research. Federal direct support for researchers, research assistants, and equipment was buttressed by state support for core faculty and facilities. Virtually all 4-year universities grew, and when justified by capability and need, many states universities were able to create graduate and professional programs with the blessing of their state coordinating or governing boards. Perhaps most significantly, systems of community colleges were established in nearly every state, providing access at lower expense to many previously unserved students. Despite the fears of independent colleges and universities, the expansion of the public sector did not result in the contraction of the independent sector. Private colleges also participated in the growth, in many cases benefiting from both federal and state student assistance programs.

Naturally, states differed in what they did and how they did it during this period, but all of them were driven by the same core objective: expanding access to a growing population and increasing the participation rate in higher education while enhancing graduate/professional education and research. In California, the master plan established the radical principle of low-cost, universal access to instruction. This was accompanied by negotiated, sharply bounded institutional missions established to control costs and pursue excellence in research and graduate education. No other state precisely emulated the means employed in California, but eventually nearly every state established community colleges and found a way to differentiate missions in order to meet the full range of these objectives (Breneman & Lingenfelter, 2012).

In many states new coordinating boards and their staffs played a key role in this process. They developed studies of operating costs and space requirements to plan for the creation of new institutions. They created budget formulas or other analytical approaches for achieving equity in funding among institutions with different instructional programs. They developed need-based financial assistance programs, often including strategies for providing support for students who chose private institutions. And they developed "master plans" for meeting emerging public needs. The "planning imperative" and these policy innovations and tools spread to every state, regardless of the structure employed or even the absence of such a structure. Russell, for example, had significant consulting assignments in 14 states, including extensive work on a plan to expand higher education with the creation of community colleges adopted by the Michigan legislature, a state that to this day has no statewide coordinating or governing board.

In states with a coordinating or governing board leader who worked effectively with the governor and legislature, plans seemed to be implemented more quickly, and the tools for analysis, planning, and budgeting became more sophisticated. But every state made significant changes in the delivery of higher education from 1950 to 1975. Among the leaders of that era were Millett in Ohio; Glenny in Illinois; John Folger in Tennessee; Jim Furman in Ohio, Washington, and later Illinois; Jack K. Williams and Bevington Reed in Texas; and Frank Abbott in Colorado. These higher education executives laid the philosophical and analytical foundation for the profession, planned the creation of new and expansion of established institutions, and created the capacity that enabled higher education enrollments to grow from 3.6 million in 1959–1960 to 8 million a decade later.

The rapid growth of higher education enrollments continued, although at a slightly reduced pace, during the 1970s, reaching 11.6 million by 1979–1980 (Lingenfelter, 2008). The success of planned growth in the 1960s likely inspired 1972 amendments to Higher Education Act of 1965, which provided incentives for states to establish "1202 commissions" to consider state needs in planning and coordinating postsecondary education. In some respects, the 1202 commissions broadened the responsibilities of state facilities planning agencies required in order to receive federal grants authorized by the Higher Education Facilities Act of 1963 (McGuinness, McKinney, & Millard, 1975). It was not, however, a new federal mandate as much as a recognition and potential reinforcement of the state level planning and coordinating efforts that had already occurred.

As shown previously on Figure 1.2, 38 state coordinating or governing boards were established before 1970, and 14 were established after 1970 (McGuinness, McKinney, & Millard, 1975). A few of these 14 were newly created 1202 commissions in states with no statewide agency. Most states, however, assigned 1202 responsibilities to existing agencies or commissions, augmented an existing body, or created a new commission alongside an existing state level board to handle regulatory matters for nonpublic institutions.

While it did not materially increase state coordination and planning, the creation of 1202 commissions did, however, shape the process of state planning. The act promoted an expanded purview of planning to include community colleges and vocational education, as well as the concerns of nonprofit and proprietary independent institutions. It implicitly recognized the inevitability of competition among sectors and sought to cultivate common purposes and reduce unproductive conflict. And in a parallel action, it created through section 1203 a mechanism for the federal government to provide financial support for state planning efforts.

The federal debate creating the 1202 commissions and the subsequent history of federal actions around state planning and coordination for postsecondary education illustrate the enduring tensions around educational "turf" in the states and the nation as a whole. Federal support for state planning and coordination was opposed by institutional interests in the 1970s, in the 1990s, and 20 years later in 2009. The overlapping responsibilities for vocational/occupational education between elementary/secondary education and postsecondary community colleges and vocational schools continue to be an issue today just as they were in the 1970s.

Stability After Growth: Improving System Effectiveness 1975 to 2000

By 1975, planning for extraordinary growth was no longer an urgent priority. Enrollments were still growing and new buildings were still required, but the pace of growth was slower. Inflation, energy shortages, and recessions constrained state governments. The work of program review, program approval, and budgeting became more salient than planning. The staffs of state higher education governing and coordinating boards began to refine the tools that emerged in the previous decades—tools for space allocation, maintenance, and planning; tools for cost analysis and program review; and budget formulas and data systems to guide public policy.

When planning for massive growth was no longer the highest priority, attention turned to policy issues that shape system effectiveness. What should tuition policy be? How much student assistance is needed, and on what basis should it be provided? Are state appropriations equitably and appropriately distributed among institutions and purposes? What kinds of data systems are needed to guide public policy? Can institutions become more efficient and effective by reallocating resources from lower to higher priorities? Who, using what kind of process, should identify lower and higher campus priorities? To what extent should performance indicators be the basis for state budget allocations? How and where should new programs be created, and how should existing programs be evaluated, improved, or eliminated if no longer justified by need or student demand?

From 1975 to 2000, a number of state leaders distinguished themselves by both their contributions and the duration of their service. In one or sometimes in two states the following leaders served more than 10 (in several cases more than 20) years as a SHEEO. In descending length of service they are: R. Wayne Richie (Iowa), William Friday (North Carolina), James McCormick (Pennsylvania and Minnesota), Gordon Davies (Virginia and Kentucky), Ken Ashworth (Texas), Edward Hollander (New York and New Jersey), Clyde Ingle (Minnesota and Indiana), Stanley Koplik (Kansas and Massachusetts), Richard Wagner (Illinois), Hans Brisch (Oklahoma), William Arceneaux (Louisiana), Patrick Callan (Washington and California), Henry Hector (Alabama), Wayne Brown (Tennessee), Norma Glasgow (Connecticut), Arliss Roaden (Tennessee), and David Longanecker (Minnesota and Colorado).

Although it is not possible to list the individual contributions of these leaders without serious omissions, in various states their long tenures enabled them to play critical roles in:

- establishing need-based student financial assistance programs to increase both access and choice;
- improving access to professional education for disadvantaged populations;

- developing novel approaches to budgeting and resource reallocation to more effectively address public and institutional priorities;
- assessing and improving student learning;
- improving preparation for college in K–12 education;
- increasing educational opportunities for returning adults;
- developing data and management systems to enhance the capabilities of both policymakers and institutional leaders; and
- sustaining (much of the time, at least) positive relationships between higher education and state policymakers and achieving the funding required to serve growing enrollments.

In the closing years of the century, however, the momentum supporting state policy leadership slowed in many states. From 1990 to 2000 public higher education enrollments grew at an annual rate of only 0.8%, compared with an annual growth rate of 2.4% between 1970 and 1990 (Lingenfelter, 2008). A strong economy combined with stable enrollments permitted relatively generous support for higher education and perhaps contributed to complacency about the need for policy leadership.

Then in 1992, an abortive federal initiative, the State Postsecondary Review Entity, sought to solve problems of fraud and abuse of federal student aid programs by turning to state higher education agencies to provide accountability oversight over all public and private institutions. The initiative was widely considered an intrusive, regulatory overreach and was eventually repealed by Congress after the Department of Education suspended its implementation. Perhaps in combination with good economic times and planning fatigue, it had a negative impact on the idea that state policy leadership is needed in higher education.

In the mid-1990s two states, New Jersey and Minnesota, which previously had strong coordinating agencies, significantly reduced the role and responsibilities of these agencies. In a third state, Illinois, two multicampus governing boards, the Board of Regents and the Board of Governors, were eliminated in favor of giving six universities their own individual boards. "Decentralization" in higher education gained traction. In 2001–2002, the association for the Study of Higher Education awarded its dissertation of the year award to Michael K. McLendon for a study entitled "Setting the Agenda for State Decentralization of Higher Education." Two years later, Dr. Toni Larson received the award for a massive study entitled "Decentralization in U.S. Public Higher Education: A Comparative Study of New Jersey, Illinois, and Arkansas." In the minds of many, the advantages of institutional autonomy trumped the need for state policy leadership. Although some have always doubted its importance, by the turn of the 21st century, growing numbers seemed to believe state policy leadership had outlived its usefulness.

STATE POLICY LEADERSHIP IN THE EARLY 21ST CENTURY:
AN EMERGING CRISIS

From Jefferson to Russell and those who followed them, the primary purpose of state policy leadership in higher education has been to achieve public purposes, not to constrain or regulate institutions. *Empowering* institutions to address public needs and *empowering* students to become educated have been and remain the principal objectives of higher education public policy.[6] But the sum of self-perceived institutional interests does not equal the public interest. Moreover, it is not possible to empower institutions to address public needs without articulating those needs and considering what policy actions and institutional practices might meet them. Although some will argue that the marketplace can naturally meet society's need for higher education, in the past two centuries, no nation has successfully met its educational needs without intervening in the market. The only debatable questions are: What should governments do? How should they do it?

At the beginning of the 21st century, it became increasingly evident that the standard of educational success achieved by the United States in the late 20th century was no longer good enough in the emerging global economy. While the rate of postsecondary educational attainment in the United States in the first decade of the century remained relatively stable at about 40% of the adult population, more than a dozen other countries exceeded the 40% rate of attainment for adults in the 25- to 34-year-old age group (Organisation for Economic Co-operation and Development, n.d.). Also in response to changing economic conditions, the U.S. employment market has shifted strongly in favor of those holding some postsecondary credential. By 2008 only 41% of the jobs in the United States were held by people with a high school diploma or less; in 1964 high school graduates or nongraduates held more than 80% of U.S. jobs. Adults without postsecondary education earn less and suffer higher unemployment rates (Carnevale, Smith, & Strohl, 2010).

No doubt because students read the signals in the labor market, postsecondary enrollment demand in the United States suddenly increased. From 2000 to 2010, public FTE enrollment grew from 8.6 million to 11.6 million, an average annual increase of 3%, faster than the average from 1970 to 1990 (State Higher Education Executive Officers, 2010).

Concerned about policy complacency in view of these trends, Pat Callan, former SHEEO in California, obtained foundation support to create the National Center for Public Policy and Higher Education. The Center developed the *Measuring Up* project, which graded states every 2 years from 2000 to 2008 on five dimensions relevant to higher education: preparation, participation, affordability, completion, and benefits. The center also articulated issues and highlighted notable state achievements through its publication, *Crosstalk*; in addition, it developed a strong position paper entitled "The Need for State Policy Leadership" (National Center for Public Policy and Higher Education, 2005) and awarded promising young leaders a year-long fellowship of professional development through its Associates program.

As they approached and entered the 21st century, a few states, which have lagged behind the national average in postsecondary attainment, launched reforms with the active engagement of their governors and SHEEOs. Indiana and Kentucky, which had not yet established viable community college systems, did so. Kentucky's Postsecondary Improvement Act of 1997 strengthened its Council on Postsecondary Education and, under the leadership of Gordon Davies, launched strategies for improvement based on goals for the state that have now been sustained for nearly 20 years (Kentucky Council on Postsecondary Education, 2016). Louisiana created a generous student assistance program, worked to improve teacher preparation, increased state support, and focused on strengthening the quality of every dimension of higher education in the state.

But the timing for a new burst of state policy leadership in higher education was inauspicious. The terrorist attacks of September 11, 2001, and a recession that same year distracted most national and state policymakers from focusing on higher education. States such as California, Illinois, Minnesota, New Jersey, and Ohio, which had produced higher education success stories in the 1970s, 1980s, and 1990s, failed to sustain their achievements in affordability, participation, and completion. Virtually every state struggled to maintain the support necessary for strong systems of higher education, and several severely reduced support for public higher education.

For 3 years, 2002–2004, state and local support for higher education was stable at $69 billion, while enrollments grew by 11.8% and inflation by 10.3%. State and local support recovered to increase to $89 billion by 2008, but then the Great Recession of 2008 produced a decline in state and local funding that, even with temporary federal assistance, persisted for 7 years (State Higher Education Executive Officers, 2003, 2004, 2005, 2006, 2007, 2008, 2009, 2010, 2011, 2012, 2013, 2014, 2015). Only in 2015 did state and local funding again reach $89 billion. FTE enrollment stabilized around 11 million after 2013, still substantially (13%) higher than in 2005. The net effect of these trends has been to shift the burden of paying for public higher education from the state to students and their families. Constant dollar total educational expenditures per FTE student has been $12,000 plus or minus $900 for the past 25 years, but students have paid a constantly growing share of the cost; in 2015 students paid 46.5% of that cost, compared to 25% in 1990. In constant 2015 dollars, net tuition was $2,896 in 1990, compared to $6,006 in 2015.

The growing financial burden on the states from pensions and health care is partly responsible for the failure of the states to keep pace with enrollment growth and inflation in higher education, but it is likely not the only factor at play. Some question whether higher levels of educational attainment are required for a large fraction of the population or argue that broad, "liberal" education is not needed by most people. And in an era of increasingly polarized politics, higher education as a social institution is increasingly identified with the left side of the polarity, even though its graduates fully populate the leadership of both sides.

The obvious erosion of financial support for higher education has been accompanied by a more subtle erosion of confidence in the leadership of higher education and of education generally (Lingenfelter, 2016). The loss of confidence is evident in the decisions governors and boards have made about state policy and institutional leaders and in growing turnover in leadership positions. Higher rates of turnover are especially evident in state level K–12 executives (where the median tenure of chief state school officers was 14 months in November 2015), but increasingly short tenure in office is also occurring among SHEEO ranks.

WOULD A RENEWAL OF STATE POLICY LEADERSHIP HELP? WHAT WOULD IT LOOK LIKE?

The substantive and political challenges facing American higher education in the 21st century are not the same as they were in the last half of the 20th century. In many respects, they are more difficult. These circumstances are likely to require state policy leaders to focus on different priorities, cultivate different skills, and establish a new basis for their relationships with governors, legislatures, and institutional leaders.

Different practices and priorities in policy leadership will be to no avail, however, without a supportive political climate and the willingness of governors and legislatures to employ professional leadership in meeting the policy challenges of higher education. The following briefly summarizes and comments on the challenges facing the field.

Mission Creep vs. Mission Expansion

Maintaining mission differentiation to control costs was a principal focus of state policy leadership from 1950 to 2000. "Mission creep" is still a concern, but it is not the main problem. The principal need in the 21st century is to expand the mission of postsecondary education to serve a larger fraction of the population, especially the people left behind for reasons of poverty, discrimination, and inadequate preparation. This is consistent with the goals motivating state policy leaders in the mid-20th century, but it will require more than simply the expansion of places in institutions offering traditional instruction.

Historically, sorting and selecting those students most likely to succeed has been the focus of institutional admission practices and a driver of mission creep, along with ambitions for offering professional and graduate education. In the 21st century, the public does not need better ways to sort and select. Instead it needs postsecondary institutions to improve instruction and student supports so a higher percentage of potential students enroll and complete valuable credentials and develop the knowledge and skill required for responsible citizenship and a fulfilling life. And it needs K–12 education to improve the percentage of students prepared for college and careers, which requires better approaches for educating teachers and school leaders. These objectives must become high priorities for state policy leaders.

To some, mission "expansion" in postsecondary education seems to mean broadening the scope of postsecondary degrees and certificates to include fields and competencies that have not traditionally been considered "higher" education and de-emphasizing less "practical" fields traditionally included in the liberal arts. The experience of the Morrill Act suggests that broadening the scope of postsecondary education is likely to be salutary, but not if it occurs at the expense of cultivating the critical thinking, communications, and problem-solving abilities associated with higher education. It will not serve students or the public well if the objective of more widespread attainment is met by substituting pedestrian outcomes for authentic, 21st-century knowledge and skill.

Funding Equity, Funding Adequacy, Funding Effectiveness

At the dawn of the profession, Glenny criticized coordinating boards for focusing on "superficial jobs, mostly budgeting kind of work" (Rabineau, 1990, p. 26). He wanted them to focus on planning—what kinds of institutions, in what places, and governed by what means—would meet public needs? Despite Glenny's critique, budgeting has always been and will always be a central and essential policy tool for meeting the public's need for higher education. But the focus of budgeting has often been on peripheral matters—equity among institutions within the state and parity with institutional competitors.

In an effort to make budgeting less peripheral to core objectives, policy leaders have periodically experimented with "performance budgeting," basing components of funding formulas on the achievement of public priorities such as higher rates of graduation. Although budget formulas should avoid perverse incentives for institutions to enroll students they are ill-prepared to serve, providing incentives for better performance is inadequate if institutions lack the know-how and resources to meet public goals.

Performance funding relies on the ability of budgetary incentives to improve institutional performance, but it works on the margins of budgetary allocations that are inherently biased against the success of economically and educationally disadvantaged students. The institutions enrolling students most likely to succeed tend to have resources well above other institutions, limited incentives to control costs, and incentives to increase tuition and recruit out-of-state and international students as a means of offsetting decreases in public support.

The institutions that enroll students most in need of better instruction and support typically have fewer resources and fewer options for increasing their resources through private giving or recruiting out-of-state students. In addition, their students often enroll part time due to inadequate financial assistance, a practice highly correlated with failure to complete. It is important to have incentives aligned with student success, but incentives without adequate resources are not enough. The United States cannot achieve widespread educational attainment without designing, financing, and implementing the policies and systems necessary to achieve the goal.

Budgeting among and especially within institutions must become more sophisticated to achieve higher educational attainment. Some aspects of budgeting (such as measuring workloads, need for financial aid, and financing price and salary increases) are unavoidably formulaic, but the most important budgetary questions demand deeper thought. Well-informed analysis and sound professional and policy judgments are required to identify high priorities, to distinguish them from lower priorities, and to support them adequately. What objectives are most important? What capabilities must be developed, what resources must be supplied, what obstacles must be overcome, and what behaviors must change in order to reach those objectives?

State and national policy leaders need to ask these questions and make sound judgments when allocating resources in the public policy domain, but policy should focus on broad-scale investments rather than fine-grained, prescriptive decisions about objectives, priorities, and strategies. Neither an economy nor a system of higher education can thrive under highly prescriptive top-down regulation. Excessive regulation risks creating perverse incentives and cultivates a compliance mentality rather than a performance mentality. Public policy should focus on the big picture.

Fine-grained decisions about objectives, priorities, and strategies are more successfully taken at the institutional level. After an extensive study of the implementation of state-level performance budgeting in the 1990s, Joseph C. Burke (2005) concluded that performance funding should occur at the institutional level, with the performance results reported to policymakers to inform broad-scale policies at intervals of 5 years. As an example, the Priorities, Quality, and Productivity (P*Q*P) initiative of the Illinois Board of Higher Education in the early 1990s resulted in $241.7 million in reallocations from lower to higher priorities aligned with shared state and institutional goals. The Board of Higher Education established the broad parameters of the program, but institutions retained decisionmaking authority. And the state, in response, increased its support (Wallhaus, 1996).

Polarized, Political Turmoil vs. a Working Consensus on Educational Goals

It has never been easy to obtain agreement on higher education policy, but at times it has been possible. Prime examples are the Morrill Act, the GI Bill, the National Defense in Education Act, the Higher Education Act of 1965, and initiatives through which governors and state legislatures expanded access to higher education in the past century. At those times, educational attainment and the prosperity and quality of life in American communities advanced.

Over the past quarter century, while improving education became a more urgent public priority, the ability of political leaders to agree on policy has degenerated. Rather than a working consensus emerging from debate, competing initiatives have been advanced, sometimes implemented, and then abandoned when failure becomes obvious or when a new administration takes office. Corrosive rhetoric and hardened ideological positions on a range of policy issues have made collaboration and compromise to achieve shared objectives too rare.

In some respects, institutional practices have contributed to the difficulty of developing a working consensus on higher education public policy. The natural tendency for institutions to compete with each other for standing, whether in academics or athletics, often seems to take priority over public purposes, especially when considering tuition and fee increases or recruiting out-of-state students. Also in polarized times, college and university communities sometimes find it difficult to avoid entanglement in ideological and partisan disputes, directly or indirectly. Both visible commitments to public priorities and efforts to assure and demonstrate nonpartisanship help build public support.

THE ROLES OF SHEEOs AND INSTITUTIONAL LEADERS
IN THE 21ST CENTURY

Supportive public policies are an essential foundation for a successful system of postsecondary education. The complex challenges described in this chapter call for SHEEOs who relentlessly maintain their focus on the goals of advancing educational attainment and the expansion of knowledge and who creatively inspire institutional and political leaders to play their respective roles in achieving educational progress. Positive change requires vision, initiative, and collaboration. Citing a few examples, effective state policy leaders in the 21st century have worked:

- to improve the effectiveness of teaching and learning in K–12 education, in order to advance preparation for postsecondary education;
- to assess learning and use the results to improve instruction in postsecondary education;

- to mobilize broad-based public support for increasing attainment;
- to develop creative, competency-based pathways for adults who have dropped out of college to complete degrees and credentials;
- to strengthen access to financial assistance for academically motivated low-income students;
- to improve remedial/developmental education;
- to increase state support and reduce the need for increases in tuition and fees;
- to help students avoid accumulating unnecessary credits and reduce the amount of time required to complete degrees and credentials; and
- to reduce regulatory barriers to educational innovation while working to improve quality and quality assurance.

More information on these and other current examples of state policy leadership can be found at the SHEEO website (www.sheeo.org/resources?type=state_policy_leadership&tid=All).

Although supportive state policies are essential for improving educational attainment, they can only complement, not substitute for, effective educational practices, institutional initiative, and engagement. Faculty members in every classroom and every institution of postsecondary education, from vocational schools to flagship universities, have essential roles to play in advancing educational attainment. Postsecondary education cannot thrive if individual institutional interests outweigh the common interests shared by institutions and the public alike.

CONCLUSION

For nearly 250 years, educational leaders in collaboration with state and national policymakers have created the U.S. system of postsecondary education. In the last half of the 20th century, state higher education executives, policy leaders with educational expertise and credibility, played especially influential roles in expanding the scope of the system and improving its quality.

At the beginning of the 21st century, both the roles of the states and of state policy leaders in higher education show signs of deteriorating. To say the least, this is poor timing when the world economy in increasingly based on the utilization of knowledge and skill.

Frequently educators have been blamed for failing to respond quickly and effectively to the higher expectations of the 21st century, with little recognition that fundamental and time-consuming changes in policy and practice are necessary to achieve significantly higher levels of educational attainment. Whether justified or not, the loss of confidence in educators has led to revolving doors in policy leadership positions and efforts to "fix" education by recruiting leaders from business, the military, or government. Some exceptional leaders have come from nontraditional sources, but on the whole policy instability has been more evident than educational progress.

It is pointless to criticize political leaders for losing confidence in educators: Confidence is not a right; it must be earned. But the slow pace of educational progress and growing financial problems in higher education have caused both educators and political leaders to lose public confidence. Educational outcomes will not get better without changes in policy and practice. A new vision of public priorities for higher education and of state policy leadership is needed. And a renewed partnership between educators and policymakers is needed to achieve educational progress.[7]

The partnership between educators and policymakers will be strengthened by better use of evidence to improve policy and practice. Research cannot and will not discover "silver bullets" (such as appointing a brilliant SHEEO, implementing a particular strategy of governance, or adopting a "killer app") that will improve higher education. But research and analysis can help guide the decisions of policymakers and practitioners as they work to improve performance and solve complex educational problems. Faculty members and institutional leaders need to know whether students are gaining the knowledge and skill life requires, and they need to use that knowledge continuously to improve teaching and learning. Policymakers need to monitor key indicators related to educational attainment (preparation, participation, affordability, and completion), and then they need to focus their attention on providing the policy tools and the financial and educational resources necessary to make progress.

Greater wealth and educational endowments give some states advantages over others. The characteristics and approaches of state policy and educational leaders vary, and states have employed different strategies for governing and coordinating higher education. Despite natural variation in endowments and approach, policy and practice in every state can become more effective and more efficient through the wise use of evidence.

Strong, visionary professional state policy leadership in higher education is required to meet the challenges of the 21st century. Although the necessary leadership approach will differ in important respects from that of the 20th century, it will be fundamentally the same—not based on dictatorial powers, but rather on professional expertise and the ability to work effectively and collaboratively with governors, legislators, and institutional leaders. Such leadership depends on mutual trust and respect: The SHEEO must be able to cultivate reciprocal trust and respect, and the governor, legislators, and institutional leaders must be willing to grant it, because they recognize it is in their collective best interests.

Finally, although I have suggested the profession generally has lost some of the influence it held in the 20th century, in some states strong SHEEOs have established the credibility necessary to bridge gubernatorial terms of office, and they are working productively on the issues most relevant to our time. If their examples inspire other states to strengthen state policy leadership, the national system of higher education and the nation will benefit.

NOTES

1. A second Morrill Act in 1890 required states to create separate land grant universities for people of color if the original land grant universities restricted admissions to Whites.

2. Despite primitive tools, Russell and one of his students performed a labor-intensive and stunningly sophisticated analysis of trends in private and public, in-state and out-of-state, tuition and fees from 1860 to 1932 (Russell, 1933). The study controlled for inflation both in prices and in salaries. Russell also was involved in studies documenting the academic success of junior college students who later enrolled at Stanford and the University of Chicago. He credited their success in part to the close alignment of their high school preparation with the junior college curriculum.

3. In 1939–1940, before World War II began, 1,708 institutions enrolled 1.5 million students, a participation rate of 1.1% of the U.S. population (Lingenfelter, 2008). In 1959–1960, before the baby boom generation graduated from high school, 2,004 institutions enrolled 3.6 million students, for a participation rate of 2.0%. By the end of the subsequent decade, 1969–1970, the baby boom generation and growing participation doubled enrollments to 8 million, and the national participation rate to 3.9% of the population.

4. More information on Russell and his role can be found in Lingenfelter (2013) and Lingenfelter and Mingle (2014).

5. *Time Magazine* put Kerr on the cover on October 17, 1960, in an article describing the California strategy for achieving widespread access to higher education while preserving the primacy of its research universities in research and graduate education.

6. Assuring quality and protecting against fraud and abuse are corollary purposes.

7. A more extensive treatment of this issue can be found in Lingenfelter's 2016 book *"Proof," Policy, and Practice: Understanding the Role of Evidence in Improving Education*; Sterling, VA: Stylus.

REFERENCES

Berdahl, R. O. (1970). *Statewide coordination of higher education.* Washington, DC: American Council on Education.

Berkeley Center for Studies in Higher Education. (n.d.). *History of CHSE.* Retrieved from cshe.berkeley.edu/about/history-cshe

Breneman, D. W., & Lingenfelter, P. E. (2012). The California Master Plan: Influential beyond state borders? In S. Rothblatt (Ed.), *Clark Kerr's world of higher education reaches the 21st century* (pp. 85–106). New York: Springer.

Burke, J. C. (2005). Reinventing accountability: From bureaucratic rules to performance results. In J. C. Burke (Ed.), *Achieving accountability in higher education: Balancing public, academic, and market demands* (pp. 216–245). San Francisco, CA: Jossey-Bass.

Cain, T. R. (2007). *Advancing the field: Fifty years of the Center for the Study of Higher and Postsecondary Education at the University of Michigan.* Ann Arbor: University of Michigan Center for the Study of Higher and Postsecondary Education.

Callan, P. M. (2012). The perils of success: Clark Kerr and the Master Plan for Higher Education. In S. Rothblatt (Ed.), *Clark Kerr's world of higher education reaches the 21st century* (pp. 61–84). New York: Springer.

Carnevale, A. P., Smith, N., & Strohl, J. (2010). *Help wanted: Projections of jobs and education requirements through 2018.* Retrieved from cew.georgetown .edu/wp-content/uploads/2014/12/fullreport.pdf

Clark, B. (1983). *The higher education system: Academic organizations in cross-national perspective.* Berkeley: University of California Press.

Connally, J. (1965). Charge to the Coordinating Board Texas College and University System. Austin: Texas Higher Education Coordinating Board. Retrieved from www.thecb.state.tx.us/reports/Docfetch.cfm?Docid=0002&Format=DOC

Douglass, J. A. (2000). *The California Idea and American Higher Education: 1850 to the Master Plan.* Stanford, CA: Stanford University Press.

Douglass, J. A. (2005). *The Carnegie Commission and Council on Higher Education: A retrospective.* Berkeley, CA: Center for Studies in Higher Education.

Douglass, J. A., & Cummins, J. (2001). In memoriam, Lyman Glenny, Professor of Higher Education Emeritus. Oakland: University of California Academic Senate. Retrieved from senate.universityofcalifornia.edu/inmemoriam/LymanGlenny.htm

Erdman, H., & Ogden, W. R. (2000). Reconsidering William Rainey Harper as "father of the junior college." *College Student Journal, 34*(3), 434.

Gray, A. A. (1915). The junior college in California. *The School Review, 23*(7), 465–473.

Jefferson, T. (1832). *Notes on the state of Virginia.* Boston, MA: Lilly and Wait. [Online Text] Retrieved from www.thefederalistpapers.org/wp-content/ uploads/2012/12/Thomas-Jefferson-Notes-On-The-State-Of-Virginia.pdf

Kennedy, D. M. (1999). *Freedom from fear: The American people in depression and war, 1929–1945.* New York: Oxford University Press.

Kentucky Council on Postsecondary Education. (2016). Stronger by degrees. Frankfort, KY: Author. Retrieved from cpe.ky.gov/ourwork/documents/ 201621strategicagenda.pdf

Lingenfelter, P. E. (2008). The financing of public colleges and universities in the United States. In H. F. Ladd & E. D. Fiske (Eds.), *Handbook of research in education finance and policy* (pp. 651–653). New York: Routledge.

Lingenfelter, P. E. (2013). State policy leadership for higher education: A summary of the origins and continuing evolution of a profession. *State Higher Education Executive Officers.* Retrieved from www.sheeo.org/sites/default/files/ publications/State_Policy_Leadership_History.pdf

Lingenfelter, P. E. (2016). Rebuilding confidence in educational leaders through evidence-based practice and policy. *Change: The Magazine of Higher Learning, 48*(3), 48–53.

Lingenfelter, P. E., & Mingle, J. R. (2014). *Public policy for higher education in the United States: A brief history of state leadership.* Boulder, CO: State Higher

Education Executive Officers. Retrieved from www.sheeo.org/sites/default/files/ History_Web.pdf

Lingenfelter, P. E., Novak, R. J., & Legon, R. (2008). *Excellence at scale–What is required of public leadership and governance in higher education?* Washington, DC: Association of Governing Boards.

McGuinness, A. C., McKinney, T. H., & Millard, R. M. (1975). *State postsecondary education commissions (1202): Their origin, development, and current status.* Denver, CO: Education Commission of the States.

McPherson, J. M. (1988). *Battle cry of freedom: The Civil War era.* New York: Ballantine Books.

Mettler, S. (2005). *Soldiers to citizens: The GI bill and the making of the greatest generation.* New York: Oxford University Press.

Millett, J. D. (1952). *Financing higher education in the United States.* New York: Columbia University Press.

Millett, J. D. (1957). *The liberating arts.* Cleveland, OH: H. Allen.

Millett, J. D. (1962). *The academic community: An essay on organization.* New York, NY: McGraw-Hill.

Millett, J. D. (1974). *Politics and higher education.* Tuscaloosa, AL: University of Alabama Press.

Morrill Act of 1862, 7 U.S.C. §§ 304 (2009).

National Center for Public Policy and Higher Education. (2005). *The need for state policy leadership.* San Jose, CA: Author. Retrieved from www.highereducation. org/crosstalk/ct0305/news0305-insert.pdf

Organisation for Economic Co-operation and Development. (n.d.). Population with tertiary education. Retrieved from data.oecd.org/eduatt/population-with-tertiary-education.htm

President's Commission on Higher Education. (1947). *Higher education for American democracy.* Washington, DC: U.S. Government Printing Office. Retrieved from babel.hathitrust.org/cgi/pt?id=mdp.39015046793876;view= 1up;seq=15

Rabineau, L. (1990). *Oral history of Dr. Lyman Glenny, Professor Emeritus, University of California, Berkeley.* Unpublished manuscript. Boulder, CO: State Higher Education Executive Officers.

Ratcliff, J. L. (1986). Should we forget William Rainey Harper? *Community College Review, 13*(4), 12–19.

Rothblatt, S. (Ed.). (2012). *Clark Kerr's world of higher education reaches the 21st century.* New York: Springer.

Rudolph, F. (1962). *The American college and university: A history.* New York: Vintage Books.

Russell, J. D. (1933). Student fees as a source of support. (Box 1). John D. Russell Papers, Harry S. Truman Library, Independence, MO.

Russell, J. D. (1949a). Basic conclusions and recommendations of the President's Commission on Higher Education. *Journal of Educational Sociology, 22*(8), 493–508.

Russell, J. D. (1949b). The states in higher education. *State Government: The Magazine of State Affairs, XXII*(5). (Box 14). John D. Russell Papers, Harry S. Truman Library, Independence, MO.

Russell, J. D. (1951). Patterns of coordinated state control over higher education. (Box 18). John D. Russell Papers, Harry S. Truman Library, Independence, MO.

Russell, J. D. (1954). Conference of executive officers of state-wide boards of higher education, Santa Fe, New Mexico. (Box 22). John D. Russell Papers, Harry S. Truman Library, Independence, MO.

Scott, D. W. (2008). The transformation of higher education in the 1960s: Master plans, community colleges, and emerging universities. *Journal of the Illinois State Historical Society, 101*(2), 177–192.

Social Security Administration. (1944). *Social Security Bulletin, 7*(7). Washington, DC: Office of Research, Evaluation, and Statistics. Retrieved from www.ssa .gov/policy/docs/ssb/v7n7/v7n7p3.pdf

State Higher Education Executive Officers. (2003). *State higher education finance.* Boulder, CO: Author.

State Higher Education Executive Officers. (2004). *State higher education finance.* Boulder, CO: Author.

State Higher Education Executive Officers. (2005). *State higher education finance.* Boulder, CO: Author.

State Higher Education Executive Officers. (2005). *State higher education finance.* Boulder, CO: Author.

State Higher Education Executive Officers. (2006). *State higher education finance.* Boulder, CO: Author.

State Higher Education Executive Officers. (2007). *State higher education finance.* Boulder, CO: Author.

State Higher Education Executive Officers. (2008). *State higher education finance.* Boulder, CO: Author.

State Higher Education Executive Officers. (2009). *State higher education finance.* Boulder, CO: Author.

State Higher Education Executive Officers. (2010). *State higher education finance.* Boulder, CO: Author.

State Higher Education Executive Officers. (2011). *State higher education finance.* Boulder, CO: Author.

State Higher Education Executive Officers. (2012). *State higher education finance.* Boulder, CO: Author.

State Higher Education Executive Officers. (2013). *State higher education finance.* Boulder, CO: Author.

State Higher Education Executive Officers. (2014). *State higher education finance.* Boulder, CO: Author.

State Higher Education Executive Officers. (2015). *State higher education finance.* Boulder, CO: Author.

Truman, H. (1947). Statement by the President making public a report of the Commission on Higher Education. Retrieved from www.presidency.ucsb.edu/ws/?pid=12802

Veysey, L. R. (1965). *The emergence of the American university.* Chicago, IL: University of Chicago Press.

Wallhaus, R. A. (1996). *Priorities, quality, and productivity in higher education: The Illinois P*Q*P Initiative.* Denver, CO: Education Commission of the States.

CHAPTER 2

The SHEEO and the Public Good

Neal Holly

The role and vitality of state higher education executive officer organizations has been questioned since their widespread inception in the 1960s. Often touted at the stewards of public dollars and resources focused on higher education, these organizations have grown and contracted in both scope and power over time. These changes have created a rich landscape of agencies with a range of responsibilities from approving new academic programs to administering state financial aid programs.

As this volume is being completed, another cycle of state-level gubernatorial and legislative review of SHEEO agencies appears to be underway. Chief administrators are often challenged to explain the functions of their agency and the reasoning behind certain powers the SHEEO has over institutions.

The line of questioning is often met with responses that can be summarized in three main points.

First, much of the work performed by SHEEO agencies has been developed by previous sessions of the legislature to address issues considered to be important at that time. Although the issues in question may have been resolved, the law states that the organization must continue to carry out the actions. It is often up to the SHEEO and staff to act as institutional memory for legislatures as members rotate off and on a chamber and its committees. This can be a difficult and frustrating task as SHEEOs are responsible for explaining decades of policies in a relatively short span of time from when new members take office to the point when they begin writing their own bills.

Second, SHEEOs articulate their roles as stewards of public resources. This is often the most controversial part of the case they are called to make, as the stewardship role is often in conflict with institutional ambitions. This area is also where legislators are more likely to question the duplication of some resources at both the state and institutional levels, as states have continued to give institutional boards greater authority. With decreasing state support for public institutions, this is an argument that institutions have been successfully winning, as legislators cede power in wake of fewer dollars.

The final point is usually focused on students and the need for someone independent of the institutions to serve in a consumer protection and educational advocate role. With variation in mission, SHEEOs are often responsible for postsecondary stakeholders to craft goals around enrollment, retention, and graduation to meet future workforce needs. This role can pit the SHEEOs against institutions whose ambitions are, at times, not aligned with state goals. It can also strain the relationships with institutions that are struggling to improve performance with limited resources and challenging student populations. The setting of tuition and fees, concerns over costs of living, transfer of earned credits, and performance of underrepresented students are other points that SHEEOs use to differentiate themselves from institutional leaderships and missions before legislators.

All three of these points intersect the concept of the public good in some fashion. Public agency leaders invoke the term *public good* when framing their mission, advocating a policy position, or, as mentioned earlier, defending their relevance to stakeholders. SHEEOs face the unique challenge of framing their organizations as agents of the public good in a unique educational marketplace where institutions, not the SHEEO organizations, have a high level of contact with the citizenry. Much of this dynamic deals with the location of the institution versus the SHEEO office, as students and families interact with academic, athletic, and/or cultural events at their local institution over the course of a lifetime. Politically, K–12 matters dominate the discourse and time in the legislature due to the nature of the enrollment and sheer amount of funding that is allocated toward the sector. Some would argue that not being in the legislature's crosshairs is not a bad thing, but for agencies that have little public attention, the loss of public presence and media coverage can be a detriment.

This chapter will explore additional challenges facing SHEEOs, framed in their relationship with the public good. But first, it is important that we have a functional understanding of what the public good means and how it has been applied toward higher education.

ALIGNING SHEEOs AND THE PUBLIC GOOD

Defining and contextualizing the public good within an educational context is important for several reasons. First, understanding the accepted definition of the public good gives one a common frame of reference, not just an assumption of the concept. Second, one must understand the tension between public goods and private goods in order to understand the current atmosphere around SHEEOs, institutions, and state legislators. Finally, there needs to be a logical connection built between the concept of the public good and the mission of SHEEO organizations.

In an article in *The Chronicle of Higher Education*, Carlson (2016) lamented the loss of college as a public good as access to public higher education increased for underrepresented minorities and low-income students, and investment in public higher education floundered. He contends that the bills' effects on the population were inequitable as African Americans were underrepresented in enrollment in both colleges and training programs. Enrollment for minorities increased during the 1960s and 1970s, but gains in enrollment began to decline as states cut higher education spending and tuition began to creep upward. Carlson goes on to discuss today's increasingly diverse demographic shift in the school-aged population and the anti-tax movement that began in the 1980s. Ultimately, he notes that reduced resources have led to the erosion of public institutions across all sectors at a time when the White population is moving from a racial majority to a minority, challenging notions about who has received the benefits of the revered education legislation. Carlson's piece invokes both a romanticized vision of the public good through those who directly benefited from the GI Bill and Higher Education Act and a challenge to its value through those who have been generationally separated from the intended impacts of the two efforts. To that end, what does the public good mean, and how do we leverage its use when describing public activities, institutions, and investments that may or may not benefit our society?

The term *public good* is based in the field of economics, where it generally relates to goods that are not private. Heilbroner and Thurow (1998) discussed three basic tenets of public goods:

- The consumption of one public good by any one individual does not interfere with its consumption by another.
- No one can be excluded from use of a public good.
- With normal goods, private consumption depends on individual decisions to spend or not spend one's income.

Public goods refer to "goods (or services) that can be enjoyed by everyone and that no one person's ability to have them is diminished by the number of people who enjoy them" (G. Williams, 2016, p. 136). This adheres to many definitions maintaining that a public good is "available to all," which implies universal affordability and raises a contentious issue of debate as to the reality of that notion. If public goods exist in such an environment like a medieval commons, it would stand that there lies a potential for a tragedy of the commons to occur where a "resource accessible to use by all" would need to be monitored (Marginson, 2011, p. 417).

Individuals cannot consume a good such as the National Weather Service in such a way that it provides an advantage. One may choose to ignore weather warnings, but they are still provided. Paying for public goods is inherently difficult, as economists expect individuals to act rationally in how goods are consumed. Rational people would set aside a portion of their income to help support the weather service as part of a cooperative. Yet, if given the choice between applying those funds to the weather service or a new item that benefits one personally, not everyone would choose the weather service. In a representative democracy, outside of direct ballot initiatives, individuals are rarely given that opportunity to choose how public funds should be allocated. Rather, elected representatives at every level make those decisions for the entire population.

The idea of public goods being entirely nonexcludable and nonrivalrous has been criticized as to the existence of such "pure" public goods, because certain elements that are considered public goods do not always adhere to such absolute guidelines (Hudson & Jones, 2005). Paul Samuelson, known for his contribution to public goods theories, realized that many items considered public goods did not fit the strict definition (Holtermann, 1972). Additionally, the degree of publicness varies across a spectrum and can be classified in multiple ways. Education, for example, is at times not seen as public in comparison to national defense because education involves "an investment in human capital," which does not necessarily benefit the public directly (Hudson & Jones, 2005, p. 277). Generally, then, a societal view on which goods and services are deemed more public serves to inform resource allocation. As applied to this discussion, this differentiation plays a role in how much more time state representatives spend on primary and secondary education than on higher education.

While directly applying the definition of public good toward higher education has some obstacles, Marginson's (2011) focus on "monitoring" provides an important link between the public resources dedicated to higher education and the role of the SHEEO. Here the SHEEO must function as a steward of public trust and ensure that the citizenry understands the value of higher education as a public enterprise. To do this, the SHEEO organization must continue to emphasize the shared values that provoke interest and support in higher education as public good. As costs to attend public institutions continue to rise and marginal gains are made in degree completion by underrepresented minorities and low-income students, having a dedicated resource to monitor or oversee institutions is more critical than ever (Perna, 2005; Ma, Pender, & Welch, 2016). Public higher education is not only an annual line item appropriation but a cumulative investment in dollars, buildings, and equipment. It only takes a few moments reviewing institutional data to see that public higher education is an enterprise worth billions of dollars in most states. Such investments should be monitored by a third party who is vested in the success of the entire enterprise and its constituents.

TENSIONS BETWEEN THE PUBLIC GOOD AND PRIVATIZATION OF PUBLIC ENTERPRISES

Many public services are facing similar pressures to shift to privatization in hopes of addressing issues of accessibility, availability, accountability, quality, and cost efficiency. Yet, this shift has implications for the values and mission of public services going forward and does not ensure that such a change will ameliorate the issues within the social systems. The idea of privatizing public services is often more controversial and widely known depending on the service and degree of exposure. For example, the debate and analysis regarding the privatization of public education is more commonly known than the similar central issues that the public health system faces when pressured to privatize (Gollust & Jacobson, 2006).

Trends in privatization across public service fields indicate that the reasoning for privatizing certain services stem from a lack of personnel and expertise, cost-efficiency, and flexibility (Chi, Arnold, & Perkins, 2003). The pervasive fear that privatization will replace state employees' positions and make them obsolete is a driving force of resistance against privatization initiatives. Many are equally divided in believing the likelihood that privatization of public services will increase or remain the same in the future. One example of a public service that is facing pressures to privatize certain aspects is public land management. Due to dwindling government budgets, land management agencies are forced to focus on strengthening partnerships that will increase their reliance on philanthropic funding, which at times introduces "inappropriate influence on policy related to the management" of public lands (Wade, 2005, p. 64). This demonstrates the potential influences of privatized entities on priorities of land managers who are already relying more heavily on alternate sources of funding. Another example of a public service that is veering toward privatizing components is water systems. Due to increased water standards from the Environmental Protection Agency, water systems have increasingly turned to the private sector to comply with the regulatory pressures since federal grants could not meet the need (Poole & Fixler, 1987). This led to a market opening for businesses such as engineering firms to develop and own public works projects, which alters the landscape of infrastructure practices. Public colleges and universities have increasingly turned to private developers to build and operate student housing close to campus. Doing so is often cheaper and more timely, as private developers do not have to comply with the same codes and regulations that buildings owned and operated by a state do.

HIGHER EDUCATION AND THE PUBLIC GOOD

The shift from considering knowledge as a public good to knowledge that contributes to society in various, often economic forms, marks a change in ideals. More recently, higher education as a public good relates to social justice and the ability of education to provide opportunities for social mobility as students can increase their earnings potential and overall employability (J. Williams, 2016). This demonstrates the idea that in terms of higher education as a public good, it has been reconceptualized to relate to the achievement of collective private gain. Higher education can be analogous to health or justice in that everyone should have access, yet it differs in that everyone does not always want to make use of this resource (G. Williams, 2016).

An argument for public education as a public good includes the creation of a common culture, yet this consideration negates many drivers of institutional diversity initiatives and raises the question as to who decides what the common culture is. A theme of a common culture could arguably be widespread institutional focus on equality and the goal that "higher education should contribute to the public good by promoting the reduction of inequality in its own activities and in society generally" (G. Williams, 2016, p. 136). The promotion of patriotism is another possible justification for higher education as a public service, yet many strive to adhere to postmodern beliefs in a way by resisting dominant narratives, so this reasoning could backfire.

It can also be argued that higher education is a public good due to the role of colleges as teaching institutions, which offer benefits of direct and indirect learning. Relatedly, the creation of knowledge through research produced by educators has the ability to contribute to the economic and social well-being of society (G. Williams, 2016). Therefore, this interplay of colleges' focus on teaching and research has the potential to lend credence to the argument of higher education as a public good. Ma, Pender, and Welch (2016) demonstrated that postsecondary graduates are more likely to have a positive impact on their local communities through increased volunteerism, participating in their children's education, and a lessened need for public assistance.

In a recent presentation, Weerts (2017) contended that there are three rival views of the public good in the context of higher education. The three views position the public good as the "good society," the "productive society," or the "equitable society." Weerts suggested that these views of the public good have evolved over the course of U.S. history, with changes responding to social and economic events of the day. For example, he noted the time period between 1910 and 1963 was dominated by the productive society, which had a stronger focus on human capital, economic freedom, and the perspective that student success resulted in success in the workforce. In the present day, Weerts suggested, these three views of the public good do not overlap but can contend with one another. With views of the public good intension with one another, it can be difficult to frame conversations around topics like student outcomes.

STATE GOVERNANCE AND THE PUBLIC GOOD

Longanecker (2005) contended that the current state of public higher education is part of an evolution, not just a black or white interpretation of higher education being a public or private good. Rather, higher education as a service field is shifting from providing a public good to finding a balance between its public and private purpose. This fits well with the funding-autonomy narrative that has transpired in the 12 years since Longanecker suggested such an evolution. He went on to state that the evolution can occur on three distinct paths. The first is the conjoining of public activities with private interests. This path is marked by institutions outsourcing services to private entities such as food service and printing facilities in an effort to reduce costs and increase efficiencies. Although this is a popular option for policymakers due to its practicality, these relationships can create operational tensions between public and private components of an institution. The second path is the courting of private gain to achieve the public good. This is especially applicable at career and technical colleges where developing specialized training for specific industries is commonplace. The same is true for large research universities that vie for federal and private research grants. The third path is the privatization of public institutions, where institutions are freed from the bureaucracy of the state to support themselves and thrive within the marketplace.

THE PUBLIC GOOD VERSUS THE PUBLIC SPHERE

The economic definition of the *public good* does not directly apply to public higher education. Inequities exist when it comes to how similar and dissimilar students access and complete higher education and fare in the marketplace after graduation. Yet, we continue to use the public good to focus attention on and attempt to correct those same inequities. Perhaps there is a way to avoid the term altogether via a substitute?

Pusser (2006) called attention to the *public sphere* as a new vehicle, apart but close to the popular idea of the public good and separate from the purely economic definitions of the private and public good. The public sphere is a space where public discourse can take place on the nature of where public and private interests begin and end. Pusser argues that for higher education to achieve the shared outcomes from the public sphere "demands for control will need to give way to contest, collaboration, and consensus" (p. 23).

While the public sphere avoids the economic trappings of the public good, it is difficult to escape such an encultured term. As Tierney (2006) remarked:

> Unfortunately, the phrase "public good" has gained a currency and cachet equivalent to other deceptively simple concepts that make it into the public domain stripped of all meaning other than what can be found in a sound bite. The public good also has the positive ring of authenticity. To betray the public good is bad; to speak on behalf of the public good is, well, good. The public good has become like motherhood and apple pie. (p. 2)

We are collectively trapped between the popular concept of the public good and the true economic meaning. However, the public good would not be the first time we have abandoned the true meaning or value of a definition or item for a substitute that is more palatable or publicly accepted. A quick search of the Internet of common misused definitions and phrases will produce a host of results that, over time, the public has co-opted to convey slightly different meaning from the original intent.

Moving forward, the reader should acknowledge the evolution of the economic definition of the public good but abandon it for the shared ideal that we have embraced and applied to public institutions, functions, and outcomes. Yet, our shared concept for the public good cannot be a default answer for discourse over public concerns that require complexity and nuance. Question: Why do we need so many colleges? Answer: They help support the public good. For some people that reply will suffice, but others want more detail as the shared idea of the public good is void for vagueness.

SHEEO organizations serve in a critical intermediary position between what the public desires from higher education and what is delivered. The following sections discuss the challenges SHEEOs face in delivering their mission and what they can do ensure they remain relevant to the public good in the future.

CHALLENGES TO THE SHEEO AND INFLUENCE OVER THE PUBLIC GOOD

Before SHEEO organizations can deliver services that support the public good, they must have the authority and organizational vitality to do so. Prior to discussing what would benefit agencies and their ability to serve the public good, it is important to recognize their current challenges. SHEEO organizations face a range of challenges that test their authority and, in some cases, their existence. These following four issues below are not siloed and should be considered concurring issues that SHEEO administrators must manage among multiple and competing stakeholders.

A New Austerity

The decline of support for public education can have an impact on how we perceive the value of those institutions moving forward. Our sense of the public good of K–12 and higher education institutions can change as we benefit from their services. State appropriations for public higher education dropped significantly during the Great Recession. While some states have begun to add additional dollars to current base appropriations, these funds have not returned appropriations to prerecession levels, on average (State Higher Education Executive Officers Association, 2017). The recession was delayed in agricultural and energy-producing states, where cuts continue consistent with declining prices among their dominant commodities. Institutions have been forced to make cuts and pass additional costs on to students through tuition increases. Institutional leaders have been creative in seeking out the types of private partnerships Longanecker (2005) mentioned in order to reduce costs. SHEEO organizations have also been affected by budget cuts that have resulted in reduced staffing and services for both institutions and students.

SHEEO organizations have been particularly vulnerable during this time, as lawmakers not only look for targets of opportunity for cuts but also seek targets that will have a minimal impact on their own constituents. A state representative may receive criticism over cuts that reach an institution in their district but will face less push back for reductions at the state agency level. Talks over agency reductions also invite conversations about the scope of the SHEEO's authority and mission. We have recently witnessed a range of changes to state higher education agencies, from closure of the California Postsecondary Education Commission in 2017 to the separation of the two largest public institutions from the West Virginia Higher Education Policy Commission in 2017.

Increased Institutional Autonomy

Legislators must make value judgments on how the public is best served by the resources that are currently available. Their perception of the public good and its relation to educational resources can change over time and be affected by the state's social and economic environment. As mentioned in the Introduction, SHEEO organizations face increasing scrutiny when state appropriations for higher education decrease from year to year. These decreases have led to institutions pressing lawmakers and other postsecondary stakeholders for additional autonomy from state-level oversight. The center of this argument is that if public institutions could operate under the same autonomy in the marketplace as not-for-profit and for-profit institutions do, then they could recoup the money lost from declining support. Additionally, institutions argue that increased administrative freedom from SHEEO organizations would relieve them from burdensome and costly policies and reporting requirements and that resources could be shifted to make up for reduced appropriations from the state. Over the last several decades, more states have ceded power away from SHEEO organizations and centralized state-level boards in favor of institutional-level boards with local control over institutions.

The local control argument has been successful, as legislators have found this to be the path of least resistance. Legislators balance a number of public goods and services with education funding. Health services, roads, and public safety are services that constituents use every day and thus receive more calls in support for funding. Citizen are more likely to drive through several potholes than to pay the costs of college tuition for themselves or family members. Thus, lawmakers are more likely to field constituent messages for support for services they use on a daily basis. This path also extends to state dollars for education, where, at any one time, more families are connected to K–12 utilization through their children or grandchildren than when those same children optionally enroll at a 2- or 4-year institution. When it comes to budget cuts, this makes higher education the logical target, and reducing state-level oversight of public institutions only softens the blow of additional appropriation cuts (Mitchell, Leachman, & Masterson, 2017).

Accumulated Responsibilities

In the past, SHEEOs have served a public good role for state-level policymakers as traditional bureaucracy tasked with delivering reports and acting on informational requests from higher education stakeholders. These actions meet a short- or long-term need within the public agenda. SHEEO organizations have a range of authorities that dictate their size in both staff and the resources they manage. Agencies can range from a staff of 10 to more than a 100. Most agencies fall somewhere in the middle, with staff handling academic program approval, institutional reauthorization, distribution of state financial aid programs, provision of college access and financial aid workshops, and audits of campus budgets. These are a mix of legislatively mandated and agency-selected activities, the breadth of which has grown over time with changing priorities from new legislative leaders and SHEEO leadership.

One of the challenges for SHEEO organizations is that responsibilities compound. One might argue that this is a good problem to have, as more output demonstrates a greater value proposition to stakeholders. However, budget cuts have exposed the realities of maintaining all these operations as SHEEOs have been forced to cut staff or faced the inability to grow or shift current organizational capacity to meet immediate postsecondary needs. It also means that it is difficult for the organizations to be nimble and respond to issues in a coordinated way in real time. Rather, issues are triaged and new ideas for responding to state-specific postsecondary policy issues are shelved. These actions come at the costs of institutional or state-level problems not being fully addressed, with the prospect of their return, and with the likelihood that added value is not realized. Over time, a detrimental impact on staff morale heightens creates challenges concerning staff recruitment and retention.

A Lack of Public Presence

For citizens to appreciate a public service or organization as public good, they first need to know that it exists and what functions it performs.

SHEEOs were designed to be quiet bureaucracies that stewarded public resources, not outward-focused organizations that compete for the public's attention. This is a critical problem during governance-restructuring discussions, as SHEEO organizations rarely have a lobby or constituent group in their corner. Institutions have far more support from current students, staff, and alumni, including alumni who are policymakers, to affect change on their behalf. Most citizens do not know what SHEEO organizations are or what they do. A student or parent may know of one aspect of an agency through attending a financial aid event or a receiving support through a GEAR-UP, but they do not know that it is part of an organization that provides additional services.

Today, the lack of public presence makes SHEEO organizations a target for both cuts and "reducing government" by eliminating or restructuring agencies. In turn, these changes put programs and resources the public receive at risk. While the governance role of SHEEO organizations continue to change, the agencies should not cling to what elements are left of their former selves. Rather they should measure their state's higher education needs and reinsert themselves into the policy process as an evolved entity. The SHEEO of the future must transition from a traditional state bureaucracy that quietly churns through its annual responsibilities to a more outward-focused organization that prioritizes postsecondary student success and the needs of the state.

A MASTER PLAN FOR THE SHEEO

What are the societal benefits of public agencies, beyond their perceived bureaucratic function? The public good can be served by stakeholders being able to access and understand the mission and goals of the agency. Most SHEEO organizations provide state postsecondary master planning, working with institutions and stakeholders to set state- and institutional-level goals focused on state priorities. Those plans are highly publicized and sometimes linked to the state's college attainment goals. Yet, it is not usually clear what role the SHEEO plays in supporting institutions to help meet their goals or whether agencies have an internal plan for meeting goals of their own.

An internal master plan for the SHEEO is a necessary document for several reasons. First, it gives the agency's staff a common understanding of what the organization's priorities are. Second, it gives the organization a vehicle to be intentional about articulating how each department or division contributes to each goal. Third, it provides a framework for communicating the SHEEO's progress and successes, the impact of which is amplified when linking agency efforts to that of institutions. Finally and most importantly, the plan can guide a process of eliminating projects that are not mission critical and can help the agency from creeping into missions that are not directly linked to priorities and goals.

Plans need to be living documents as the pace of change within and outside of higher education continues to accelerate. Technology, state revenue forecasts, new institutions, and changes to federal financial aid are just a few examples of areas that can dramatically change within a 3- to 5-year plan. Plans need to be flexible enough that SHEEO administrators can pivot strategies or change goals to enable the agency to engage a given issue. The plan needs to become part of the culture of the organization and a point of day-to-day reference. It can also be used to engage external constituents such as legislators and leadership in other state agencies to explain agency efforts and return on investment.

Self-Advocacy and Control of the Narrative

Outreach to the public has not been a priority role for the SHEEO. Even if obstacles are in place, SHEEOs need to take steps to be part of the public discourse and demonstrate their value to stakeholders. Regardless to whether an internal plan is in place, SHEEOs need a communication strategy that effectively tells the story of what the organization does to serve students and taxpayers. Traditionally, SHEEOs have focused their messaging and services to meet the needs of their primary audience, governors and state legislators. Yet, if the agency is marginalized by one or both, its ability to support policy development is greatly reduced. Then, as the old saying goes, if you're not at the table, you're usually what's for dinner.

SHEEO organizations need to be aggressive on social media and be physically available throughout the state. When agency employees provide a financial aid awareness event, agency branding should always be prominent, and there should be an elevator speech preceding the main content that explains the mission and roles of the SHEEO. Every engagement should be an opportunity to highlight other services the organization delivers and recent successes that directly affect students and families. Like any other business or nonprofit, SHEEOs should maintain good contact information of attendees and keep them informed of relevant news and future events through social media.

Self-advocacy does not come easy to SHEEOs, as this is not a legacy role. However, in today's climate of hostility toward big government, SHEEOs need friends—not just friends who receive monthly emails but a network of friends and supporters who can articulate the value of the SHEEO organization in their state. If the SHEEO reports to a board, this could be an excellent vehicle for developing additional relationships. Building this type of support is a long-game strategy that cannot be easily accomplished amid scrutiny.

SHEEOs also need to control the narrative about higher education in their states. In this endeavor, SHEEOs may be in competition with the state flagship institutions that have large communication staffs who are constantly pushing out information, sometimes even co-opting SHEEO services as their own. To match the media output of flagships, agencies can cross-train staff to help deliver messaging as part of their daily routine. SHEEOs can also establish stronger communications networks with regional 4-year and 2-year institutions that often require the support of SHEEO services and that compete for state allocations with flagships.

SHEEO administrators also need to leverage staff and supporters to actively lobby governor's office staff, legislators, and other critical stakeholders. SHEEO organizations were not designed to lobby, but the agencies compete with paid staff and hired third-party professional lobbyists representing the institutions for time and attention from state leaders. Again, these are relationships that need to be cultivated over time, not when a bill to eliminate the agency is introduced. Elections and legislative turnover means that SHEEO staff can develop these relationships faster than the network of supporters described previously. SHEEOs have a "home court advantage" in this arena as most of the offices are located near the state capital. This also means that SHEEO staff need to be intentional about planning events in more isolated districts and inviting legislators and legislative staff to participate.

Transition from Institutional to Student Advocate

For many, higher education transitions from a public good to individual burden when students drop out of college with debt and no degree to show for it. Greater scrutiny of college completion rates have placed increased pressure on the higher education community to develop new practices to help students complete their degrees in a timely manner. The rise of better unit record level data systems, new philanthropic dollars, and targeted research has changed the dynamic in the way both SHEEOs and institutions approach student success. As the student success movement has grown over the last decade, SHEEO organizations have played an important part in encouraging, and in some instance requiring, institutions to adopt strategies promoted by national philanthropies and third-party advocacy organizations such as Complete College America, the Bill and Melinda Gates Foundation, and the Lumina Foundation. SHEEOs act as a central point of delivery for these reforms at the campus level, and agency staff can help connect advocacy groups with state leadership and other stakeholders that can help promote adoption of the success initiatives.

Because of these student success initiatives, state agencies have become stronger advocates for students and, at times, have become less aligned with the internal goals of individual institutions. The institutional relationship has been further strained by campuses pushing for greater autonomy. In turn, state agencies have concentrated on adding resources on student success efforts through master plans, offering centralized support services through vendors, and advocating for legislation that codifies initiatives. Promoting student success and degree attainment has been a step forward for SHEEO agencies and a challenge for institutions that cannot dispute poor outcomes. Even in circumstances where the promoted initiatives were not as impactful as they may have been at other locations, the state has benefited from additional resources when there are fewer new dollars flowing to public higher education.

In addition to student success initiatives, SHEEOs' advocacy for students has moved into other areas such as affordability, financial aid, transfer, degree mapping and course availability, and campus safety. These efforts are not just driven by philanthropic dollars but by issues and ideas introduced by students, parents, lawmakers, and concerned citizens. Taking on these student-related issues is a positive for agencies, although it comes at a price. These efforts are compiling against already recurring annual requirements. The scope of work and limited resources can impact how well SHEEOs can advocate for and scale efforts that both serve students well and highlight agency value to the public.

Another emerging area of student advocacy is campus closures. The recent and sudden closure of ITT Technical Institute left thousands of students in a fragile academic and financial situation. SHEEO organizations often played a key role in helping students find new institutions to complete their degrees. Unfortunately, the trend of campus consolidation and closures will likely continue (Berman, 2017; Seltzer, 2017). Here again, SHEEOs serve a public asset to help provide continuity of educational services when institutional viability comes into question.

Parting from Academic Quality and Refocus on Equity and Outcomes

Although some may disagree with this point of view, one of the key moves SHEEOs can make is putting the burden of academic quality on the shoulders of accreditors. This should not be confused with program approval or institutional authorization, but distancing themselves from what goes on in the classroom. Rather, SHEEOs should be more concerned about the holistic experience of students and their ability to navigate institutions. One could argue that the current developmental education reform movement is not a reflection of quality instruction but a product of identifying a systemic institutionalized practice that served as a roadblock for a large number of students.

Developmental education reform is not only a student success issue but one of equity, as a majority of remedial courses are occupied by low-income and underrepresented minority students (Center for the Analysis of Postsecondary Readiness, 2017). Yet, the way developmental instruction has been traditionally delivered, despite the numbers of repeating and failing students, was not an issue for accreditors. It took third-party policy organizations (like Complete College America) and SHEEOs to drive changes across institutions that needed to occur to allow developmental reforms to happen (Edgecombe, Cormier, Bickerstaff, & Barragan, 2013; Hu, Park, Woods, Richard, Tandberg, & Jones, 2016).

Program approval and institutional authorization decisions need to be driven by available data, while it can be difficult for SHEEO agencies to accurately assess the quality of instruction. However, most SHEEO organizations have data systems capable of monitoring both program utilization and student progress at public institutions. Then, and most importantly, SHEEOs need to act on the data. Program approval can be achieved by demonstrating return on investment and graduate outcomes, recommending sunsetting, and highlighting programs that are helping to retain and graduate students. This focus is critical to student equity conversations, as we need a greater understanding of not only how many students are completing certain programs but who those students are.

The same could be said about institutional reauthorization. Rather than dealing with issues around institutional quality, SHEEOs need to focus processes on student outcomes. Time to completion, student debt, demographic profile of enrollment, reported crimes, and instructor-to-staff ratios are variables that are easily obtained for institutions at the aggregate level for all institutions operating in each state. SHEEOs need to leverage these data to identify institutions of concern and refer them to the accreditor and make public comparisons of all institutions easily available to students and families so they can make informed educational and financial choices. The SHEEO should also proactively share these data elements with the institutions, as institutions may not be monitoring the same measures or do not have the staff capacity to do so themselves. State agencies also need to highlight good actors and best practices across sectors. SHEEO organizations should be known for public stewardship of state educational resources and for a commitment to advance education, not just as another punitive bureaucracy.

A STEWARD OF GOODS

Although they may not signal it in the willingness to provide additional tax support, citizens want value from their public institutions, and they want current and previous investments in public resources to be maintained. Stewardship of these resources is a public good, and there can be dramatic consequences when disruptions in service occur. Since major cuts to public higher education began in the 1980s, the funding narrative has focused on year-to-year spending concerning legislative appropriations toward operations for the next calendar year. Rarely does one hear a narrative based on total investment in public higher education in a state over time. Yearly appropriations, land, bonds for buildings, equipment, savings through state purchasing contacts and insurance, in-kind services from other state agencies, and state financial aid programs are sources of revenue and resources cumulatively contributed to infrastructure and financial well-being of institutions.

Just the investment in real estate alone should concern legislators, as states consider closure or consolidation of public institutions. College and university buildings are not easily repurposed, and simply shuttering a building does not mean that it foregoes maintenance costs. There needs to be a third party with the resolve and resources to monitor these investments and make recommendations to the legislature concerning new buildings, long-term impact of bonds, and feasibility of institutional growth actually improving revenue. SHEEOs need to ensure that students are being served where they are, while ensuring that institutions are not financially or programmatically overcommitted. Public investments should favor students, not the vitality of an institution within its current physical footprint and business model.

SHEEO organizations should support institutions in right sizing, not passively partnering in growth. State agencies should publicly critique campus planning through a lens of student success. Institutions need to demonstrate how new investments in staff, programs, and infrastructure will deliver improved students outcomes. As Bowen (2012) argued, there has been significant investment in higher education, yet student outcomes have not improved at a rate that would call for the return of significant public support. Rather, investments continue to favor certain students and programs over others. This plays directly into the debate as to whether higher education is a public or private good. SHEEO organizations are uniquely situated to monitor such investments and investigate the impact they are having on student success. SHEEOs should also question the totality of public investment in institutions and programs and ask tough questions regarding short- and long-term student outcomes. If a new facility built 10 years ago did not impact retention and graduation rates, will another new facility planned for next year be any different?

CONCLUSION

SHEEOs have the opportunity to drive the conversation in their state about a common understanding of what the public good means in relation to higher education and the state's goals. SHEEOs have or can create the opportunity to engage their constituents in new ways to demonstrate the value of the public investment in higher education. Whether it is a governor, legislator, policy advisor, student, or neighbor, each of these parties will invoke the term *public good* but will hold a slightly different perspective on its meaning. Uniting constituents behind a common definition could prove to be a powerful resource for the SHEEO organization.

To serve the public good, SHEEO organizations must reinvent themselves as nimble, student-focused agencies. The public must know what SHEEOs are and what services they provide. To accomplish these goals, agencies will have to develop internal strategies that set clear goals for the organization, develop stronger communication strategies, and create organizational capacity to take on issue areas around student outcomes and equity. This will come at the cost of long-held operations and practices that must be minimized or purged from the organization. Despite size, governance style, or external challenges, SHEEO organizations have the capability to support the public good in working to ensure students receive a quality education at an affordable cost and ensuring that public assets are being used effectively.

Acknowledgments. The author would like to acknowledge the contributions of Briana Colon for her help in providing research and support for this piece. Briana is currently a graduate student in both the Higher Education and Public Policy Masters programs at the College of William and Mary. I appreciated her professionalism and diligence in supporting this work.

REFERENCES

Berman, J. (2017, June 17). Why so many small private colleges are in danger of closing. *MarketWatch*. Retrieved from www.marketwatch.com/story/why-so-many-small-private-colleges-are-in-danger-of-closing-2017-06-13

Bowen, W. G. (2012). The "cost disease" in higher education: Is technology the answer? The Tanner Lectures, Stanford University. Retrieved from www.ithaka.org/sites/default/files/files/ITHAKA-TheCostDiseaseinHigherEducation.pdf

Center for the Analysis of Postsecondary Readiness. (2017). Developmental education FAQs: Facts and stats in commonly asked questions. Retrieved from postsecondaryreadiness.org/developmental-education-faqs/

Carlson, S. (2016, November 27). When college was public good. *The Chronicle of Higher Education, 63*(15). Retrieved from www.chronicle.com/article/When-College-Was-a-Public-Good/238501

Chi, K. S., Arnold, K. A., & Perkins, H. M. (2003). Trends in state government management: Budget reduction, restructuring, privatization and performance budgeting. *The Book of the States, 35*, 419–427.

Edgecombe, N., Cormier, M., Bickerstaff, S., & Barragan, M. (2013). *Strengthening developmental education evidence on implementation efforts from the scaling innovation project* (CCRC Working Paper No. 61). New York: Columbia University, Teachers College, Community College Research Center.

Gollust, S. E., & Jacobson, P. D. (2006). Privatization of public services: Organizational reform efforts in public education and public health. *American Journal of Public Health*, 96(10), 1733–1739.

Heilbroner, R., & Thurow, L. (1998). *Economics explained*. New York: Touchstone.

Holtermann, S. E. (1972). Externalities and public goods. *Economica*, 39(153), 78–87.

Hu, S., Park, T., Woods, C., Richard, K., Tandberg, D. A., & Jones, T. B. (2016). Probabilities of success: Evaluation of Florida's developmental education redesign based on cohorts of first-time-in-college students from 2009–10 to 2014–2015. Retrieved from centerforpostsecondarysuccess.org/wpcontent/uploads/2016/07/StudentDataReport2016-1.pdf

Hudson, J., & Jones, P. (2005). "Public goods": An exercise in calibration. *Public Choice*, 124(3), 267–282.

Longanecker, D. (2005). State governance and the public good. In A. J. Kezar, T. C. Chambers, & J. C. Burkhardt (Eds.), *Higher education for the public good: Emerging voices from a national movement* (pp. 57–70). San Francisco, CA: Jossey-Bass.

Ma, J., Pender, M., & Welch, M. (2016). *Education pays 2016: The benefits of higher education for individuals and society*. New York: College Board.

Marginson, S. (2011). Higher education and public good. *Higher Education Quarterly*, 65(4), 411–433.

Mitchell, M., Leachman, M., & Masterson, K. (2017). A lost decade in higher education funding: State cuts have driven up tuition and reduced quality. Retrieved from www.cbpp.org/research/state-budget-and-tax/a-lost-decade-in-higher-education-funding

Perna, L. W. (2005). The benefits of higher education: Sex, racial/ethnic, and socioeconomic group differences. *Review of Higher Education, 29*, 23–52.

Poole, R. W., & Fixler, P. E. (1987). Privatization of public-sector services in practice: Experience and potential. *Journal of Policy Analysis and Management, 6*(4), 612–625.

Pusser, B. (2006). Reconsidering higher education and the public good. In W. G. Tierney (Ed.), *Governance and the public good* (pp. 11–28). Albany, NY: SUNY Press.

Seltzer, R. (2017, November 13). Days of reckoning. *Inside Higher Ed*. Retrieved from www.insidehighered.com/news/2017/11/13/spate-recent-college-closures-has-some-seeing-long-predicted-consolidation-taking

State Higher Education Executive Officers Association. (2017). *State higher education finance FY2016*. Boulder, CO: Author.

Tierney, W. G. (2006). Introduction. In W. G. Tierney (Ed.), *Governance and the public good* (pp. 2–10). Albany, NY: SUNY Press.

Wade, B. (2005). A new tragedy for the commons: The threat of privatization to national parks (and other public lands). *The George Wright Forum, 22*(2), 61–67.

Weerts, D. J. (2017). *Student success and rival views of higher education as a public good*. Presented at the annual SHEEO Higher Education Policy Conference, Minneapolis, MN.

Williams, G. (2016). Higher education: Public good or private commodity? *London Review of Education, 14*(1), 131–142.

Williams, J. (2016). A critical exploration of changing definitions of public good in relation to higher education. *Studies in Higher Education, 41*(4), 619–630.

CHAPTER 3

State Leadership for Student Success
The Role of the SHEEO

Richard G. Rhoda and Kristen C. Linthicum

Since the late 1970s, Tennessee's approach to higher education positioned the state as a leader in evidence-based policymaking. In 1979, Tennessee implemented the first and most consistent performance funding program in higher education (Banta, Rudolph, Van Dyke, & Fisher, 1996). This policy was established through thoughtful discussion among many political and campus actors, including the governor, the state's coordinating board, legislators, and campus leaders (Banta et al., 1996; Bogue & Johnson, 2010; Burke & Modarresi, 2000; Dougherty, Natow, Bork, Jones, & Vega, 2013; Dougherty et al., 2014). Many scholars have noted that Tennessee's performance funding policy was adopted and persisted because of policymakers' decisions to include clear metrics, focus on goal achievement and postsecondary quality, and maintain consistent funding in times of budget change (Burke & Modarresi, 2000). In addition, the policy's longevity is attributed to policymakers' decisions to allow sufficient time for policy implementation, incorporate campus input, and evaluate the policy's effectiveness every 5 years (Dougherty et al., 2014). Because of these decisions, the performance funding policy in Tennessee has maintained widespread political support and has persisted over time.

In 1979, the Tennessee Higher Education Commission (THEC) introduced the notion of performance funding to its funding formula for postsecondary institutions to incentivize institutions to improve outcomes. The policy innovation enabled institutions to initially earn a 2% increase in annual funding; this amount increased over time to 5.45%. Despite the modest increase allowed, the program was widely considered to have effectively incentivized institutions to improve quality and actively engage in performance funding deliberations. From the beginning, performance funding was embedded in an institution's total funding recommendation; it was not a set aside or bonus.

Following the introduction of performance funding, Tennessee assumed a leadership role in developing higher education policies based on research and intended to promote positive outcomes. Though Tennessee—and particularly THEC—spearheaded many innovations, several key policies that serve as examples of THEC's leadership include the 2002 Tennessee Education Lottery Scholarship program and the 2005 GEAR UP grant. For the design of the lottery scholarship program, the lead author, Richard G. Rhoda, chaired a legislative task force, and THEC staff provided the research and analysis. Guided by the expertise, leadership, and public support of higher education officials, Tennessee was able to adopt the lottery to implement the scholarship program (Ness & Mistretta, 2009). Following THEC's support and guidance, Tennessee introduced a program as a policy tool to improve student access and completion as well as economic development. With the 2005 federal GEAR UP grant, THEC pursued external funding to support the commission's ability to drive and support statewide initiatives. THEC obtained the 6-year, $26 million grant, which enabled the commission to engage directly with students, parents, and school officials throughout the state in an effort to coordinate P–16 initiatives. The success of this program allowed THEC to promote college access, success, and completion initiatives, and it transformed THEC into a state policy leader.

More recently, in 2010, Tennessee enacted the Complete College Tennessee Act (CCTA), a law designed to transform institutions through academic, fiscal, and administrative policies with the ultimate goal of providing greater numbers of Tennessee residents with postsecondary degrees. The CCTA is recognized as landmark higher education reform legislation in Tennessee, and it has served as the foundation for subsequent statewide reforms for the purpose of furthering the state's educational attainment and strengthening the link between education and economic development.

This chapter considers Tennessee's state policy context as a whole as well as the CCTA as a specific case through which to discuss the important role a state higher education executive officer can play in developing and implementing effective higher education policy. Using Rhoda's experience as the Tennessee SHEEO (executive director of THEC) from 1997 to 2014, the chapter will discuss the ways in which Tennessee's higher education policy context changed with a particular emphasis on the transformation that allowed THEC and the SHEEO to function as policy leaders in the state. Ultimately this chapter will demonstrate how, under the right circumstances, a SHEEO can provide an informed and professional perspective on higher education policy development and implementation. Further, a SHEEO with proper authority and political support can be a policy actor who navigates and works within both the higher education and political environments.

TENNESSEE POLICY CONTEXT

Tennessee Higher Education Governance

Tennessee's ability to innovate in the higher education policy arena was enabled by the state's policy context, which includes THEC and Rhoda, a long-serving SHEEO. The state context also included the University of Tennessee System and the Tennessee Board of Regents System, as well as the state's governor and General Assembly. In this section, we will discuss the state context, the changes to THEC during Rhoda's 17-year tenure, and the ways in which THEC worked with state policymakers to promote effective postsecondary policies. The section that follows will demonstrate the ways in which the policy context allowed for the enactment of a critical piece of legislation, the CCTA.

When the CCTA was enacted in 2010, the long-standing governance structure of Tennessee higher education consisted of the University of Tennessee System (UT), governed by the University of Tennessee Board of Trustees; the Tennessee Board of Regents System, governed by the Tennessee Board of Regents (TBR); and THEC, the statewide higher education coordinating board. THEC, established in 1967, served as a coordinating board for the two systems.[1]

The governor held the appointing authority for the membership of the three lay boards and served as a voting member and chair of the UT board and TBR. However, the governor was not a member of THEC. All lay members of the boards were appointed to serve six-year terms, and many were reappointed for subsequent terms. The chief executives of the UT system, TBR system, and THEC were appointed by and served at the pleasure of their respective boards.

The UT system included four universities, two institutes, and agricultural research and extension locations across the state. The TBR system comprised six comprehensive universities, 13 community colleges, and 27 colleges of applied technology. Total student enrollment among the UT and TBR systems in fall 2010 was 256,703 (THEC, 2016). Among all of these public institutions, the student population was 56% female and 44% male. About 71% of students identified as Caucasian, 19% as African-American, 2.2% as Hispanic, and 7.8% as another race or ethnicity. More than 90% of students were Tennessee residents (THEC, 2016). In 2010, Tennessee's universities in the UT and TBR systems had an average 83.9% retention rate, and the Tennessee community colleges (in the TBR system) retained students at an average 59.4%. In terms of college completion, the universities had an average 61% graduation rate, and the community colleges had an average 46.5% graduation rate.

When it was established in 1967, the statutory responsibilities of THEC were consistent with those of consolidated coordinating boards in other states at that time. Core responsibilities included developing the state master plan for higher education; reviewing and approving new academic programs; developing funding formulae and recommending the operating and capital budgets for public higher education; providing data and information to the public, institutions, legislature, and state government; and authorizing private postsecondary institutions operating within the state. The commission's scope of responsibilities broadened over time, with increasing emphasis on policy research and analysis, strategic planning, programmatic initiatives, and partnerships for increasing student access and success. By statute, the SHEEO is an ex-officio member of the UT board, the TBR, the State Board of Education, and the board of directors of the Tennessee Student Assistance Corporation. These memberships served to ensure direct communication among the boards and their staffs. Also, by statute, the three constitutional officers of the state—the Secretary of State, the Comptroller of the Treasury, and the State Treasurer—serve as voting members of THEC to directly inform and advise the commission on legislative matters. In Tennessee, the constitutional officers are elected by the General Assembly.

Changing THEC's Role in the Policy Process

During Rhoda's 17-year tenure as SHEEO, the role of the commission changed to become a more stable and research-based agency. Into the 1990s, THEC was largely regarded as the referee in UT and TBR conflicts, primarily concerning operating appropriations recommendations, capital project priorities, new academic programs, and off-campus locations. THEC in large part reacted to issues initiated by the two systems and often found itself marginalized in the process. It was not uncommon for legislation to be threatened, to eliminate or lessen the responsibilities of THEC as an expression of disapproval of actions by the commission or the SHEEO. Various forms of legislation also were proposed over the years to reorganize the higher education governance structure as a means to solving immediate management or budgetary problems at some or all institutions or to admonish THEC.

A change in the executive director of THEC in 1996 was forced by the sitting governor and may be seen as a turning point in the dynamics of that time. The SHEEO had strayed into political dispute with the state administration and legislature, which caused dysfunction and strained relationships within THEC and throughout the higher education community. The necessity and value added of THEC were openly questioned. Leadership of the commission recognized the immediate need for corrective action.

The enabling legislation for THEC speaks in general terms regarding qualifications of the executive director; in effect, provides that the director shall possess the experience and expertise the commission deems necessary in order to carry out the commission's work. In recruiting a new executive director, the THEC chair consulted with a number of sitting and retired higher education executives in the state. Based on those discussions, the commission selected Rhoda as the new SHEEO, initially on an interim basis. Prior to Rhoda assuming the role of SHEEO in 1997, he served for 20 years in the TBR system. His tenure there included senior staff positions and interim appointments as president at both Nashville State Community College and Austin Peay State University, as well as acting chancellor of TBR. Rhoda also was a member of the faculty at Vanderbilt University.

Upon Rhoda's appointment, his initial charge from the commission was straightforward. He was asked to return order in the work and condition of THEC staff and restore credibility of the commission with the state administration, legislature, and higher education community. Therefore, upon Rhoda's hiring, he began making decisions and concerted efforts to professionalize the staff, reaffirm the commission's role as an advocate for the institutions and boards, and concentrate on fulfilling the THEC's statutory responsibilities. Staff focused on drafting well-informed responses to legislative inquiries, scheduling regular briefings with the constitutional officers and key legislative staff, and maintaining a more structured approach to communication with THEC members, UT and TBR, and campus leaders.

To enhance the commission's staff, whenever there was an opening, Rhoda recruited talented young people who pursued ambitious research agendas. Rhoda developed collegial relationships among staff, in which they built trust and worked in a collaborative manner.

Rhoda also took steps to develop strong relationships with state policymakers and institution leaders to increase THEC's credibility. As policy decisions were being made, Rhoda and THEC staff engaged campus and system personnel to provide deliberate and meaningful feedback throughout the decision-making process.

The strategy of leveraging extensive personal relationships and the engagement of many stakeholders allowed THEC to earn and maintain a substantial role in the state policy process. By building relationships with lawmakers, THEC was increasingly viewed as a reliable resource for policy research and analysis.

THEC also was able to transition into a position to provide infrastructure for multiple statewide collaborations. It assumed leadership for the state P–16 council, which was composed of representatives from public and private higher education and public K–12. In lieu of creating new entities for ad hoc studies or statutory reporting, the P–16 council emerged as an umbrella for collaboration. Council representatives became accustomed to working together on myriad projects.

As a longer-term goal, Rhoda aimed to strengthen the policy research capacity of THEC staff and to pursue external support that would increase the institutions' and commission's capacity to carry out statewide initiatives. An example of this work is THEC's recommendation to use state lottery revenues to significantly increase its data system sophistication and analytic capacity. Although by statute the program was first and foremost a lottery imperative, THEC justified the collateral benefits of enhancing the commission's data and policy analysis work.

Throughout this process, Rhoda and commission members considered it critical that THEC was regarded as an objective third party that could provide high-quality policy research. In addition, the goal was for THEC to drive new and large-scale policy ideas. Change was gradual and not without false starts and distractions, but with consistent commission encouragement, there was momentum for THEC to function as an evidence-based organization that could operate effectively in the state policy context.

One additional factor that influenced and enabled THEC's transition was the coordinated approach to lobbying for higher education in the state. Both the UT and TBR systems encouraged their institutional heads to maintain sound relationships with their legislative delegations. Campuses were restricted, however, from lobbying for legislation or funding that were outside recommendations and priorities adopted at the system and THEC levels. Hiring of professional lobbyists by the institutions was off-limits. During annual legislative sessions, the government relations staff of THEC, UT, TBR, the Tennessee Student Assistance Corporation, and the Tennessee Independent College and University Association met regularly to coordinate a nonpartisan legislative agenda, promote unity on matters whenever possible, discuss lobbying strategies, and share information for the common good.

Results of THEC's Evolution

As a product of these and other developments leading to 2010, THEC matured as a coordinating board. It shifted from the reactive role of refereeing issues between UT and TBR to initiating policy research and analysis and engaging directly in the organization and implementation of statewide initiatives. THEC transformed from a state government agency overseeing higher education to an organization composed of engaged private citizens and the state's constitutional officers serving as the board, with a staff of higher education professionals. In turn, the types of conversations within higher education changed. Instead of discussions about what individual institutions wanted from the state, THEC—with the encouragement of Governor Phil Bredesen—led conversations about what the state needed from the institutions. The state was able to identify opportunities to produce increased numbers of graduates with credentials as well as skills that were demanded by the workforce, due in large part to Bredesen's emphasis on linking higher education to economic and community development. These efforts were precursors to development of the state's longitudinal data system. In addition, the commission and its staff were increasingly exercising leadership in the completion agenda as it was unfolding.

Over time, the relationship between the commission, the SHEEO, and staff solidified, and the commission delegated substantial formal and informal authority to the SHEEO to speak and act on its behalf. One example of this high level of trust is the legislative decision to charge THEC and Rhoda with leading the state lottery scholarship development effort—a decision the state would not have made prior to THEC's evolution. The commission also broadened the scope of Rhoda's authority to take interim action for the commission when it was not in session.

As Tennessee began focusing on issues related to college completion and increasing attainment levels in the state, the established practice of consensus building between THEC, UT, and TBR extended to policy considerations related to the completion agenda, including the establishment of a universal general education core and common transfer and articulation provisions. Standing committees and task forces, which included campus and system staff, were broadened to engage legislative and state administration representatives.

In addition, as the governor and General Assembly gained confidence in the work of the commission and staff, Rhoda never was subjected to undue interference to compromise his position or to preempt the commission's judgment. With ongoing support from the commission, he was allowed to manage staffing decisions, and as an agency at arm's length from the state administration, THEC was not bound to state government's bureaucracy in the hiring or promotion of staff. Consequently, with attrition of staff over time, it was possible to recruit professional staff with credible higher education experience and specific expertise. The culture of the staff and commission was collegial and empathetic to campus and board issues, and THEC staff attempted to function as an extension of the institutions. In that regard, THEC staff aimed to engage with all statewide higher education associations. Particular emphasis was placed on direct involvement with the Tennessee Association of Institutional Research (TENNAIR). THEC staff participated in all TENNAIR meetings, which fostered strong collegial relationships between THEC and campus institutional researchers.

In addition, THEC and Rhoda sought to build meaningful connections with research universities, principally Vanderbilt University, to enhance the commission's research orientation. University faculty were consulted on policy issues ranging from financial aid to governance. Faculty also were provided with access to THEC data and analysis to further their research interests. In addition to consulting with faculty members on THEC projects, members of the THEC staff taught graduate courses at Vanderbilt as adjunct faculty and participated in Vanderbilt students' dissertation committees. This led to an informal program of talent development in the form of graduate student internships and assistantships at THEC. Further, a number of students studying higher education administration and public policy joined THEC as full-time staff members on completion of their degrees.

Another significant dimension of THEC's development as a coordinating board was the role played by commission members. As noted previously, the state's three constitutional officers provided the commission and staff with an informed sense of legislative issues and concerns with higher education matters. Lay commission members, as a group, were consistent over time in their understanding of coordinating board prerogatives and responsibilities versus those of governing boards. Missteps occurred occasionally, however, when individual commission members breached accepted practices, such as engaging in campus management issues or speaking publicly on behalf of the commission without authorization. A positive organizational behavior that developed with time was open communication between commission members and staff. Rhoda and his senior staff briefed the commission and committee chairs in advance of all THEC meetings. Although it was understood that Rhoda was the link between staff and commission members, staff gave presentations and led discussion at THEC meetings and were encouraged to build working relationships with individual commission members. Staff also produced an informal weekly e-newsletter highlighting major events and staff activities of the week. Originally addressed only to commission members, the newsletter attracted readership throughout the extended statewide higher education community.

Summary

Although the state faced contentious fiscal issues and setbacks, THEC's relationships with key policy actors ensured that none of the challenges was severe or posed lasting problems with respect to the work or standing of THEC. The state constitutional officers' close involvement with THEC went a long way in maintaining sound relationships with the legislature. These relationships helped Tennessee to chart a path leading to implementing a college completion agenda in the state. Because THEC as well as UT and TBR had broadened their bases of expertise and capacity, they were able to collaborate in the development and implementation of a comprehensive state-level completion policy. In addition, the state forged important partnerships with major funders and intermediary organizations, such as the Lumina Foundation, the Southern Regional Education Board (SREB), the National Center for Higher Education Management Systems (NCHEMS), and Complete College America. Equally important, fellow SHEEOs from other states provided Rhoda and his staff candid feedback and encouragement. The intermediary organizations facilitated key conversations that focused on links between higher education, K–12, and increasing educational attainment across the state.

CCTA AS A CASE STUDY

In advance of CCTA's 2010 passage, the broader environment in Tennessee higher education was experiencing a challenging period related to the national recession as well as higher education leadership changes in Tennessee. The recession caused the state to address a plunge in state revenues. As a result, state cuts in funding for higher education were significant. Leading up to the recession, the state had not been able to fund new capital projects for a number of years, and in response to reductions in operating appropriations, student tuition and fees increased considerably. Frustrations internal and external to higher education were profound. The UT and TBR systems were experiencing difficult leadership and management challenges. The UT board encountered a rapid succession of three failed system presidents. The TBR system chancellor position was in transition. These system-level problems had a direct impact on the institutions' ability to manage difficult situations, serious budget and personnel reductions chief among them.

Despite these challenges, the state policy environment was correctly aligned for the introduction of completion-related legislation. As SHEEO, Rhoda had developed a sound working relationship with Governor Bredesen and key members of the governor's staff. The governor had demonstrated an interest in higher education and was willing to develop policies to promote increased postsecondary outcomes in the state. In the years leading up to 2010, Rhoda and Bredesen engaged in candid conversations on various subjects, including ways in which a completion policy could work. Bredesen's interests and THEC's continuing research on outcomes-based funding policies were in sync. Going beyond a simple outcomes-based funding policy, Bredesen and THEC developed the framework for the CCTA. Their efforts were aided by the fact that the leadership—vice chairs and other lay members—of the UT board and TBR were directly involved in discussions. This policy context, with fewer policy levers and fewer actors, allowed for an opportunity to focus statewide efforts on college completion.

In January 2010, the Tennessee General Assembly enacted the CCTA, a comprehensive reform agenda to transform public higher education through changes in academic, fiscal, and administrative policies at the state and institutional levels. The legislation was introduced by Bredesen, who engaged legislative leadership and forged bipartisan consensus around the issue. Drawing on its reservoir of confidence among policymakers, THEC presented nuanced ideas about college completion policy to legislators in a clear format. At the center of the reforms was the state's expressed need for more Tennesseans to be better educated and trained, while also acknowledging the state's limited fiscal capacity to support higher education.

CCTA's primary policy levers for addressing the state's educational needs were a new funding formula predicated on outcomes instead of enrollments; a revised performance funding program that focuses on quality assurance; and the establishment of institutional mission profiles that emphasize institutional distinctiveness, which promotes institutional efficiencies, guards against program duplication, and best serves Tennessee's workforce needs. The outcomes-based funding formula constructs an institution's entire annual allocation of state operating appropriations on the basis of outcomes, including but not limited to degree production; research funding and graduation rates at universities; and student remediation, job placements, and student transfer and associates degrees at community colleges. Each of these outcomes is uniquely weighted at each institution to reinforce mission and Carnegie classification and to reflect the priority given to each outcome.

In addition to incentivizing institutions to enhance statewide attainment levels, the CCTA directed THEC to develop a new master plan for higher education, the Public Agenda, which established the direct link between the state's economic development and its educational system. The overarching goal of the Public Agenda was for Tennessee to meet the projected national average in educational attainment by 2025. Also, the CCTA directed the development and implementation of a number of initiatives aimed at improving student success and easing students' transitions between institutions. These initiatives include requiring a universal general education core, requiring the development of transfer pathways from community colleges to universities, requiring dual admissions policies between community colleges and universities, and directing TBR to unify the organization and operations of the community colleges.

PROVIDING LESSONS FOR SHEEOs

Many lessons may be learned from the impact of the SHEEO in the policy decisions in Tennessee that have been recognized as reshaping the face of higher education in the state.

1. Demonstrating effective leadership as a SHEEO: It is critical that the SHEEO's leadership does not overemphasize the individual who assumes the role. Instead, it is important for the SHEEO to focus on promoting the success of the institutions and on advancing higher education in the state. To advance the interests of higher education, it was important for Rhoda to partner with other stakeholders in Tennessee. As Rhoda assumed the SHEEO position in Tennessee, he began to convene thought leaders. With the ultimate goal of supporting the state's postsecondary system, Rhoda interacted with business, governmental, and professional education groups in order to build coalitions and gain insight into the policy process.

2. Developing an effective coordinating board staff: To advance legislation that promotes higher education, it is important for a coordinating board's staff to be considered a useful source of research for state policymakers. In Tennessee, it was essential for THEC staff to be knowledgeable about research and able to communicate the information to critical stakeholders. THEC's staff was accomplished, recognized, professional, and collaborative when working with campuses and boards. In addition, it was important for the staff to be a cohesive unit that could advocate on behalf of higher education in Tennessee. Because there were not competing institutional boards in the state, THEC was able to consistently promote the state's entire higher education system. THEC's staff were viewed as engaged proponents of the campuses, and they were seen as acting in the institutions' best interests.

3. Developing strong relationships with state policymakers: The enactment of CCTA demonstrated that it is critical for a SHEEO and the coordinating board's staff to engage in the legislative process as a part of a constructive partnership. Rhoda and his staff participated in drafting the CCTA legislation, and they were called on to implement the act. Throughout the legislative process, Rhoda and the staff believed it was important to collaborate with state policymakers, and they picked their battles among certain issues to reduce confusion or competition. For instance, they believed it important for THEC to approve institutional mission profiles, not mission statements, to avoid clashes with institutional prerogatives and accreditation. Ultimately, throughout the CCTA process, it was clear that THEC's relationships with key state policymakers— principally the governor—allowed THEC to partner with the state to implement meaningful legislation.

4. Leveraging the governance structure: To enact CCTA, Tennessee's governance structure mattered. At the time, Tennessee's higher education system was composed solely of statewide boards, making statewide initiatives more feasible. Further, the dynamics within the higher education context played a significant role in how CCTA was developed. THEC was ready and capable of leading a change. Because of their policy expertise and nonpartisan credibility, Rhoda and the THEC staff were trusted with policy leadership. THEC was a stable organization with a consistent staff and no consequential issues of distraction, and it was able to lead the policy innovations. Ultimately, THEC could assume the role it did because of the commission's reputation and skills and the substantial support of state leadership.

5. Leveraging timing: In Tennessee, the planets were aligned for major reform. The policy context for CCTA included the support of the

governor, legislative leaders, and THEC/SHEEO. This degree of alignment was unprecedented. With the governor's leadership, higher education became part of the state's overall public policy agenda. The governor connected higher education with K–12 education and economic development and linked higher education reform to K–12 reform (the state's bid for a Race to the Top grant), which was critical to the passage of the CCTA. Further, it was essential to introduce the CCTA in a special session of the state's General Assembly. Although the completion agenda and an outcomes-based funding formula were a long time in the making, their accelerated consideration in a 1-week special session made them happen. In addition, as the 2008 recession had caused serious fiscal issues for higher education, a tipping point in the reform discussion was when there was consensus that it served no purpose to continue using the enrollment-based funding formula. It had not been fully funded in many years, and its incentives did not promote student completion. Therefore, it was important to position the outcomes-based funding formula as a policy tool for implementing the CCTA. In this context, policymakers supported the notion of funding outcomes, not student census and square footage.

6. Reorganizing governance structures may not address priorities. Although some policymakers suggested governance reorganization as a solution to higher education problems, Bredesen worked with the existing governance structure to enact CCTA and to achieve goals related to increasing college completion. He firmly believed that reorganization would disrupt the system, delay reform, and potentially undermine the implementation of completion policies. Instead of reorganizing the governance structure, Bredesen advocated for enhanced policy alignment and strengthening THEC's coordination responsibilities. Accountability for implementation of the CCTA, which was embedded in the legislation, affirmed the coordinating role of THEC, the governance prerogatives of the UT board and TBR, and the expectation of collaboration throughout the implementation process.

PROVIDING LESSONS TO RESEARCHERS

Both the passage of CCTA as well as Rhoda's long-standing tenure offer several opportunities for researchers to consider future studies.

1. Incentivizing collaboration: THEC's effectiveness in the Tennessee policy environment was due in part to the statewide perception that the staff and its SHEEO were working to advance higher

education in the state. However, in states with competing boards, it is important to consider the ways in which states can incentivize institutions to collaborate in order to advance state-level postsecondary priorities.

2. Increasing attainment: In light of completion efforts, it is important to identify the ways in which states can increase attainment. Researchers can identify strategies to improve a state's higher education capacity as well as strategies to promote collaboration among institutions.

CONCLUSION

Throughout Rhoda's experience as Tennessee's SHEEO, several management strategies were essential: partnering with state policymakers, developing an effective staff at THEC, and focusing on Tennessee's most pressing needs related to higher education. By leveraging the lessons that Rhoda learned throughout his career at THEC, individuals serving as SHEEOs can enhance their staffs' talent and experience and further serve the needs of their states' higher education systems.

NOTE

1. The FOCUS Act of 2016 removed the six TBR universities from the TBR system and established independent boards for each of the universities.

REFERENCES

Banta, T. W., Rudolph, L. B., Van Dyke, J., & Fisher, H. S. (1996). Performance funding comes of age in Tennessee. *The Journal of Higher Education, 67*(1), 23–45.

Bogue, E. G., & Johnson, B. D. (2010). Performance incentives and public college accountability in the United States: A quarter century policy audit. Higher Education Management and Policy. *Higher Education Management and Policy, 22*(2), 9–30.

Burke, J. C., & Modarresi, S. (2000). To keep or not to keep performance funding: Signals from stakeholders. *The Journal of Higher Education, 71*(4), 432–453.

Dougherty, K. J., Natow, R. S., Bork, R. H., Jones, S. M., & Vega, B. E. (2013). Accounting for higher education accountability: Political origins of state performance funding for higher education. *Teachers College Record, 115*, 1–50.

Dougherty, K. J., Natow, R. S., Jones, S. M., Lahr, H., Pheatt, L., & Reddy, V. (2014). *The political origins of performance funding 2.0 in Indiana, Ohio, and Tennessee: Theoretical perspectives and comparisons with performance funding 1.0.*

(Working Paper No. 68). New York, NY: Community College Research Center, Teachers College, Columbia University.

Ness, E. C., & Mistretta, M. A. (2009). Policy adoption in North Carolina and Tennessee: A comparative case study of lottery beneficiaries. *The Review of Higher Education, 32*(4), 489–514.

Tennessee Higher Education Commission. (2016). Tennessee higher education fact book. Retrieved from www.tn.gov/assets/entities/thec/attachments/2016-17 _Fact_Book_Suppressed_Final_2.pdf

CHAPTER 4

Letter to a New SHEEO

Thomas D. Layzell

Dear New SHEEO:

I offer this letter in the hope that you will find it useful as you undertake your new responsibilities. You have one of the most challenging and important tasks in American higher education. You sit at the intersection of public priorities and institutional capacities and are charged with aligning them to improve your state's quality of life and standard of living through development of an accessible, affordable, and excellent postsecondary education system. Your role in achieving these goals will not be exclusive, nor will it always be visible (or unchallenged), but it will be essential to the success of the effort. I spent 24 years as a SHEEO or multicampus system head serving in four states in either permanent or interim positions. I found the work always interesting and challenging. I hope you will, too.

THE EMPHASIS OF THIS LETTER

States have conducted many experiments with the composition and responsibilities of statewide boards over the years in their quests to develop an accessible, affordable, and excellent postsecondary education system. Some have created statewide governing boards, some have created policymaking boards, and some have created statewide coordinating boards. One has chosen to create a council of presidents to coordinate the operations of its public colleges and universities.

The SHEEO website lists 61 individuals serving the states, the District of Columbia, and the territories of Puerto Rico and the Northern Mariana Islands. Every state has at least one SHEEO. Eight states have two. Even this description is incomplete in that it doesn't reflect different treatments by states of community and technical colleges, private nonprofit and proprietary institutions, financial aid agencies, coordination with elementary and secondary education, or coordination with state agencies on workforce and economic development issues.

Suffice it to say, you are entering a complicated environment, both structurally and operationally. My emphasis in this letter will be on actions and issues that will affect your ability to successfully navigate the rocks and shoals of that environment.

SOME FUNDAMENTALS

As athletic coaches often stress, a review of fundamentals is always in order. The following paragraphs offer three for your consideration.

As you begin to execute your responsibilities, make sure you understand the expectations associated with your new position. In your investigation of the position, you no doubt discussed the expectations of the board, the presidents, and political leaders regarding your performance. You should periodically recheck your understandings, especially when changes have occurred. New leaders bring new ideas, and as soon as possible you want to know the potential changes that may flow from those new ideas. Listen more than you talk in these meetings.

A closely related fundamental to understanding what is expected of you is understanding the essence of your role. Your role will be both explicitly and implicitly defined by the language of the laws and policies that govern the exercise of your duties and responsibilities, by the historic understandings and interpretations of those laws and policies, and by your own actions in implementing your responsibilities. You will be called on to play many roles: an initiator of recommendations; an interpreter of the actions of your board to policymakers, the public, and the institutions and vice versa; a negotiator and mediator; a declarer of the public interest; an envoy to other governmental agencies; a strategic scapegoat; and a manager of the governance process. In all of these roles, your primary objective must be to identify and pursue the public interest however faint its glow.

A third fundamental is described in a statement attributed to Henry Kissinger by the historian Barbara Tuchman: "Public life is a struggle to rescue an element of choice from the pressure of circumstance" (1982, p. 219). You will battle the pressure of circumstance every day. The art lies in winning more of those battles than you lose.

ESSENTIAL PERSONAL CHARACTERISTICS

Your success or failure will to a great extent depend on the perceptions of your performance by others, especially those of your board, the institutional leaders you are expected to govern or coordinate, and political leaders. Like it or not, you are almost always on stage, and you must act accordingly, always bearing in mind that observance of the proprieties and the common courtesies are essential to your success.

In 2000, I participated in a study of system leadership with a particular focus on the role of the system head. The study was later published by the Association of Governing Boards of Universities and Colleges (AGB) and authored by a former institutional and system leader. Participants were asked to identify the qualities of a good system head. A former governor who became a system head listed five major desirable attributes:

- The ability to see the big picture.
- The willingness to empower as well as to roll heads (and to know when to do which).
- The habit of listening selectively, coupled with the right amount of disciplined impatience.
- The ability to adjust to but not to succumb to political pressure.
- The personal style that makes networking possible (and even enjoyable). (Fretwell, 2000, p. 11)

The governor's comments were particularly interesting given that he had been both actor and audience.

My own experience and reading lead me to add a few other attributes to the governor's list: a willingness to share credit and take responsibility, a talent for conflict resolution, patience and persistence, objectivity, honesty, and a sense of what is doable at any given point in time.

No one possesses a full measure of all these attributes, but most, if not all, can be learned and developed.

THE IMPORTANCE OF RELATIONSHIPS

As you assume your new SHEEO position, you will quickly discover that your ability to develop and sustain strong, positive relationships is central to your success. On any given day, you will have numerous opportunities to establish or strengthen relationships. The impact of those efforts may not be immediate, but done properly and sincerely, they will ultimately bear fruit. In real estate, the mantra is location, location, location. In your case, it is relationships, relationships, relationships.

The stronger the relationships you develop and sustain with your board, institutional and political leaders, and the myriad other actors you will encounter, the more credible and effective you will be.

Relationship building places a premium on the arts of persuasion and negotiation, especially those related to listening and the ability to see an issue from another's perspective. (The Harvard Negotiation Project is an excellent resource in this regard.)

The process of relationship building is never-ending and often frustrating, but as a SHEEO friend of mine often says, "We don't have time for mad!" Her point is well taken. Focusing on your frustrations diverts your attention from the challenges facing you. Keep your focus on issues and interests instead of people and positions.

The SHEEO's world is inhabited by people with large egos and strong personalities who expect their views and actions to be treated with respect and deference. This is all well and good, but always remember that respect and deference are two-way streets. Give them where due but also expect them where due.

This latter point is illustrated by an example from my experience as a junior staff member at the Illinois Board of Higher Education.

The board was conducting budget hearings. Staff had presented their budget recommendations to the board when one of the presidents sought to bypass the normal discussion of the staff recommendations and be allowed to make a de novo appeal to the board at another time. The board chair calmly noted that the board had set aside two days for public hearings, and that if the president had something to say, he should "say it now."

The chair's response illustrates two important points. First, seize a "teachable moment," and second, if it becomes necessary to draw a line, do it clearly, do it firmly, and do it without rancor.

Another important point about relationship building is that it exposes you to the challenges faced by other actors and offers opportunities for collaborative solutions.

An example from my time as president of the Kentucky Council on Postsecondary Education helps make the point. We shared a common problem with the Kentucky Department of Education in not having the resources necessary to create a shared longitudinal data system. We worked with the commissioner of education to develop a task force to study the issue. We ultimately came up with the idea of submitting a joint or parallel budget request for the two systems. Simple as it sounds, the coordinated approach had never been tried before. To our great surprise, we received funding for the request. The collaboration between the two agencies was an important factor in having the request funded.

THE BOARD, THE PRESIDENTS, AND POLITICAL LEADERS

Relationships need constant attention, especially those with your board, the presidents you are expected to govern or coordinate, and the political leaders who determine your fiscal, operational, and programmatic fates. Numerous other relationships come into play over time, but these three groups are essential to your success.

"No surprises" is a cardinal rule in organizational relationships. It is a rule that is often honored more in the breach than in the observance. It is simply stated but not always easily applied. It means different things to different people, and you will often find others holding you to a more rigorous standard than they apply to themselves. There is no cookbook on when to invoke the rule but err on the side of invoking it. Carefully consider whom to inform, when to inform them, and what to inform them about. What you consider minor or inconsequential may loom larger in others' eyes than it does in yours. The best response when someone accuses you of violating the rule is to apologize and move on. There is no point in trying to convince someone that they were not surprised.

The Board

The SHEEO organization indicates 33 SHEEOs represent coordinating or policymaking boards, and 28 represent statewide governing boards. While they have some different responsibilities, the two boards share a common responsibility for coordination of programmatic and financial initiatives. Coordination is one of your most essential, difficult, and politically risky responsibilities. It almost always eliminates something or thwarts plans to expand. Most institutions and most political leaders are for coordination in the abstract. Opposition develops when you get specific. It calls to mind the remark about tax reform attributed to former Louisiana Senator Russell B. Long, "Don't tax you, don't tax me, tax that man behind the tree."

Since the mid-1990s, most states have developed public agendas to guide their planning efforts. "Public agenda" is a generic term for a plan that addresses how a state's higher education system can help meet long-term state needs. The central components of a public agenda are goals (especially educational attainment), strategies, and performance metrics based on data analyses. A public agenda can support and facilitate coordination of programmatic and financial initiatives. If your state has one, make sure it is up to date. If it does not, begin the development process.

A former SHEEO was often cited for the remark that, "The board you have is the board you have, and it may not be the one that appointed you." This pithy statement is a reminder of the importance of the board to your effectiveness. You can do nothing without its implicit or explicit support. A political leader may ask your opinion on a potential board appointment, but in general, you will have little or no say about board appointments. You are not the board, even though you may be its public face. Forgetting this point can lead to a short tenure.

Another point to remember is that the board has a right to be wrong. One of my former board members told me this one day when I questioned his vote on a matter. As it turned out, he was right, and I was wrong.

Given their importance, you should know as much about your members as you can both personally and professionally. Who appointed them? What are their business, professional, political, and personal relationships? What are their relationships with the institutions? What are their relationships with your staff? How do they view their role and your role? How did they work with your predecessor? The more you know about your board members, the more effectively you can serve them.

It is essential that you help the board understand the institutions and vice versa. The better they understand each other, the more effectively the system will work. Board retreats, campus visits, and presentations at board meetings are all effective tools for enhancing understanding. In systems where individual institutional boards exist, an annual trusteeship conference has proven helpful to improved understanding of statewide and institutional roles and responsibilities.

Board members will generally defer to the chair's wishes on meeting plans. In conjunction with the chair, you must plan the meetings and agendas, educate the board on important policy issues, and help members to become the best board they can be. These responsibilities take a lot of time, but it will be time well spent. The better the board is in performing its duties, the better SHEEO you will be.

Today's challenges require a higher level of board engagement than ever before. Board engagement does not just happen. It requires continuous effort and attention by each member and a systematic process of board development that focuses both on "what" must be done and "how" to do it most effectively.

Most board members have a history of professional and personal accomplishment, and most are on the board to serve, but those things in themselves do not make them an effective board. Development of an effective board is a function of effective practices such as:

- A written set of expectations for board member participation and behavior
- A comprehensive orientation program for new board members, which includes a review of current and long-term strategic and operational issues and of board culture and values
- A board education plan that provides opportunities for board members to better understand their responsibilities
- An annual board work plan linked to the board's master plan or public agenda, with an annual report on results achieved
- An annual board retreat that focuses on strategic priorities and stronger board relationships
- A periodic assessment of board and executive performance using the services of an outside facilitator
- A consent agenda to make effective use of board members' time and to ensure major issues receive appropriate attention

- Periodic meetings between the board and major constituencies and public and private leaders
- Assessing risks and thinking about "what ifs?"
- Periodic reviews of board policies and statutory responsibilities
- A crisis communications plan (in advance of a crisis)
- A public agenda or master plan

You and your chair should ensure that each board member is invited to engage in the development and implementation of these practices. It will take time, but the more engaged the members are in development and implementation, the more effective they will be.

The Chair

The chair has the responsibility for leading the board, but you must help the chair fulfill that responsibility. Some chairs will need your help more than others. A set of guidelines for chairing the board is a useful tool for both experienced and inexperienced chairs and may help the SHEEO help the chair. Jim Mullen (2009), a former chair of the University of Maine System, developed a set of guidelines for chairing a public board, *Public Board Chairing for Dummies (Twelve Easy Steps to Success)*. The guidelines are constructed in two parts, a statement of principle in bold face type, followed by an elaboration of the principle.

- *Run the Board—Not the Institution.* As in the corporate world, the CEO is charged with running the entity, not the board chair. And don't let the institution run the board.
- *Maintain the Board's Focus and Direction.* It is very easy to get bogged down in either topical issues or institutional minutiae. Balance relevance and perspective.
- *Harness Board Members' Talents and Interests.* Don't assume the backgrounds necessarily match interests. Interested committee chairs always do a better job.
- *Never Underestimate Constituencies.* Hell hath no fury like legislators, alumni, faculty, students, and taxpayers who feel that they are out of the loop.
- *Understand the Importance of Collegial Governance.* The corporate template for decision making doesn't work in academia, and board members from the business world need to learn to accept that early on.
- *Use the "Bully Pulpit," but Use It Wisely.* Leading the board toward their conclusion is better than just giving them the chair's conclusion.
- *Always Be the Best Prepared Board Member.* The board chair should do his/her homework, and plan how he/she wants the board meeting to run. "Fail to Prepare—Prepare to Fail."

- *Understand How the Board Works.* The board chair should be the expert on board policies and procedures. Few other board members will.
- *Understand How a University Works.* The institution is so complex that board chairs will likely never understand it all. But the chair needs to know the basics.
- *Problem Trustees Are a Problem.* The chair should either deal with them directly or work around them but shouldn't let them become (or remain) an obstacle.
- *Know What You Want to Say to the Press.* The chair should always have two or three "must" airs that they want to convey.
- *Hire a Very Good CEO.* The chair's headaches will be inversely proportional to the breadth of capabilities of the CEO. This is the most important determinant of how well or how poorly your term as chair will go.

Mullen's guidelines are pragmatic and written in a style appealing to lay board members. I have shared them with a number of different board members, and without exception, they have found them useful.

The Institutional Presidents

Even in the best of situations there's an inherent tension in your relationship with institutional leaders. Presidents want (and need) substantial autonomy in the performance of their duties and responsibilities. Your duties and responsibilities are often developed (or perceived) as a check and balance on the president's autonomy. It is always subject to question whether you or a president has gone "too far" in a given situation.

You and the presidents are both responsible for meeting the public interest, and you both may define that interest differently. Successful reconciliation of those competing definitions is a delicate balancing act that relies heavily on the strength of your personal and political relationships.

Former SHEEOs (and former presidents) Steve Reno and Tom Meredith made a presentation at the 2011 SHEEO national meeting on the subject of SHEEO/president relationships. The title of their presentation was *Talking With, Not Talking Past: Working with the Aspirations, Needs, and Personalities of Institutional Presidents*. The centerpiece of the presentation was a statement of guiding principles for the SHEEO and presidents to working together, beginning with a commitment to abide by the Golden Rule. This commitment was followed by 27 statements of principle:

- To trust each other.
- To practice the highest level of integrity and honesty.
- To practice civility in all conversations while being candid.
- To respect each other.

- To listen carefully to each other, seeking first to understand and then to be understood.
- To keep confidential matters confidential.
- To commit to mutuality.
- To know our colleagues personally and to be empathetic.
- To commit to transparency in our professional relationships.
- To demonstrate good humor.
- To show up for meetings and to be prepared.
- To be inclusive and to embrace new colleagues.
- To act in a manner that evidences objectivity, fairness, and allegiance to the institution and the system.
- To make our institutions the very best and to fulfill our institution's role in the system.
- To promote teamwork.
- To practice altruistic leadership in the very best interest of the public good.
- To a continuing dialogue about our shared vision of our system and public higher education.
- To be open to change.
- To respect and support the final decisions of the President and our colleagues and to express any dissenting views in a positive and constructive manner.
- To commit to build and maintain stronger relationships with our colleagues and to seek the views of the President and our colleagues in forming our opinions.
- To seek and accept constructive comments from others.
- To commit to no surprises.
- To be mutually supportive of the President's office and the Chancellors.
- To give each other and the President the benefit of the doubt.
- To commit to no end runs.
- To continually ask "Would I think this was appropriate if I were the President/Chancellor?"
- To appreciate the enormous responsibility we have undertaken and to enjoy it.

The principles are a good catalogue of common stress points in the SHEEO/president relationship. However difficult they may be to apply in a given situation, their potential for strengthening the system makes them worth pursuing.

Political Leaders

I attended a national higher education meeting in Denver in the early 1990s where Colorado Governor Roy Roemer was the luncheon speaker. He began his remarks by reciting a litany of policy issues confronting him in transportation, public health, juvenile justice, K–12 education, welfare, and other important social services. He ended his remarks by telling the audience of higher education leaders, "And you people aren't helping me!" Dead silence greeted his remarks. He went on to explain he wanted the help and expertise of colleges and universities in dealing with the policy issues confronting him (and other governors). Indeed, he seemed to believe he was entitled to that help. In effect, without using the words, he was asking for a public agenda.

It took a few years, but the public agenda movement began to pick up steam in the mid-1990s, and postsecondary education began to talk more about its responsibilities to the state. Governors today might think higher education is not doing "enough" to help them with their problems, but it is doubtful that any would say categorically that "no help" is being given.

Governors and legislators are central to the success of higher education through their power to grant or withhold appropriations and to enact laws or policies that enhance or impede operational or programmatic issues. Thus, developing a positive relationship with governors and legislators is an extremely important objective for a SHEEO. It is also at times an ephemeral one. A lobbyist friend used to describe this aspect of the relationship by saying, "No deals for all day."

SHEEOs are responsible for the implementation and performance of a wide variety of powers and duties. The breadth and depth of those powers and duties are products of their state's history and politics, but they are always subject to interpretation by political leaders, or even to being ignored if current politics demand it. A broad statement of powers and duties means nothing if political leaders fail to support it. You must spend substantial time communicating with governors, legislators, and their staffs responding to their requests, making a case for their support, keeping them informed of both good and bad news, and interpreting their needs to the board and the presidents (who may have their own channels of communication with political leaders). Interactions with political leaders must be characterized by respect for their positions, responsibilities, and political challenges, and by strict adherence to the "no surprise" rule. Thank them for their support when you can and remain silent when you can't (don't burn bridges; there's always tomorrow).

Some SHEEOs are members of the governor's cabinet and are direct reports. This is a more sensitive relationship than a traditional SHEEO reporting to a board. If you have a direct reporting relationship, you must ensure that the governor understands that you are there to represent both their office and the higher education system and that it is in their best interests that you should be allowed to do so. A former board member who had been very close to a former governor once told me that he had never compromised his principles in his advice to the governor, but that he had done a lot of adjusting. It's a good point to remember.

From the institutional perspective, you are well placed to help the institutions understand the governor's challenges and intentions. Get as much time with the governor and legislative leaders as you can. Visit them in their offices, invite them to meet with the board and to speak at board-sponsored events. Every personal meeting is an opportunity to establish or strengthen the relationship. Where circumstances permit, invite board members and presidents to accompany you to meetings with legislators in their areas. At the very least, let them know you will be conducting such visits.

In a 2004 article, former SHEEO President Paul E. Lingenfelter described the work associated with articulating and pursuing a public agenda for higher education. Lingenfelter's list is a catalog of actions that strengthen relationships with political leaders:

- Collecting and providing public access to comprehensive, relevant data on higher education to help the state develop its vision and agenda for higher education.
- Analyzing and articulating policy issues such as workforce needs, PK–12 student preparation, student aspirations and demands, research needs and opportunities, the affordability of higher education to students and their parents, and the needs of different geographic regions.
- Understanding deeply the contributions, potential, and limitations of existing resources (institutional and otherwise) to meet these needs.
- Working with legislators to develop and implement strategies to meet state needs, and to increase higher education's quality, efficiency and productivity.
- Working with the governor and legislature to develop and gain support for an agenda for higher education that addresses their priorities and vision for the state.
- Helping the governor and legislature develop budget allocations that address state priorities, reflect the state's fiscal capacities, address the needs and utilize the resources of existing and new programs and enhance the cost effectiveness of higher education. (p. 54)

SHEEO AGENCIES (AND SHEEOs) OF THE FUTURE

In 2016, the Education Commission of the States (ECS) published a document authored by Aims McGuinness that traces the history of state coordination and governance. It also suggests some alternative forms of governance that might appear in the future. McGuinness built on a 2005 policy brief by the National Center for Public Policy and Higher Education (NCPPHE) that recommended each state have a broad-based independent, credible public entity with a clear charge to increase the state's educational attainment and workforce development. The brief contended that existing

SHEEO agencies were considered deficient in their capacity to deal with these issues.

In the ECS document titled *State Policy Leadership for the Future*, McGuinness (2016) asserted that the issues raised by the 2005 policy brief had become even more "complex and problematic." It identified six essential functions in state higher education policymaking and traced their development beginning in the 19th century and ending with the 2008 recession and the economic recovery that followed. In brief, the six essential functions were state-level planning, state financial policy, data collection and analysis, institutional and programmatic regulation, administration of state-level services such as financial aid, and system and institutional governance. Implicitly, McGuinness traced the rise and fall of SHEEO influence as states responded to changing views of the efficacy of centralization and decentralization.

My home state of Illinois is an example. For 30 years the higher education governance structure was a "system of systems," comprising four university system governing boards: the Illinois Community College Board, the Illinois Student Assistance Commission, the Federation of Independent Colleges and Universities, and the Illinois Board of Higher Education, which was responsible for statewide coordination. The system was restructured in 1995 to eliminate two of the system governing boards and replace them with seven institutional boards. The purpose of the restructuring, as one legislative leader said to me, was "to let presidents be presidents." The system of systems was distinguished by its checks and balances that promoted both institutional interests and the public interest. Over time the checks and balances have weakened, and it is an open question whether the restructuring has resulted in a gain or a loss for the state.

McGuinness (2016) reported that 31 states had a statewide entity that could assume the policy role envisioned by the NCPPHE policy brief, 21 had a statewide coordinating board, and 10 had a statewide governing board. He also concluded that the idea of a single entity responsible for all six state-level functions may no longer be feasible or desirable. McGuinness foresaw the SHEEO of the future as likely to be "represented by four distinct components located at different points in the overall state structure" (p. 2). The four components are described as statewide policy leadership, statewide coordination/implementation of cross-sector initiatives, statewide service agency administration, and system and institutional governance.

McGuinness's conclusion that the idea of a single entity responsible for all six state-level functions may no longer be feasible or desirable is debatable, but one you may well face in your career. It is a debate that can be influenced either way by your performance. The more you and your board are seen as adding value to the development of higher education policy, the more likely you will be able to resist major structural change.

Your capacity to add value is, of course, dependent on the strength and breadth of the relationships you have been able to establish, especially through partnering with other state agencies with missions that require the capacity only postsecondary education can supply. It is becoming more common for states to create coordinating mechanisms that engage SHEEOs with other pertinent agencies in addressing workforce and economic development issues. That seems a more likely evolution to me than the replacement of SHEEOs and their agencies with an as-yet unknown entity.

CAUTIONS AND REMINDERS

Over the years, I have kept a running list of thoughts, quotes, and observations that provided insights helpful to understanding my job as a SHEEO and helped me to avoid repeating mistakes. There are more examples than time or space permits, but the following are some you may find useful. There is no particular order to the listing.

- Remember that how and when you say something is often as important as what you say.
- Know what you are for as well as what you are against. You can't beat something with nothing.
- Be patient. Be persistent. Be attentive to process.
- Understand your legal authority and use it judiciously. Do not confuse legal authority and political power. Politics will almost always trump policy.
- Be wary of advice to be "bold," especially when given by those with no responsibility to act.
- Be wary of "issues of principle." They may be issues of ego in disguise.
- Stay out of board and partisan politics. Politics is addition not subtraction.
- Don't get too far ahead of your board. Know what's doable at any given point in time.
- Don't pick fights you cannot win.
- Focus on what you can do instead of what you can't. There are never enough time, data, or resources.
- Act with the knowledge that what goes around comes around.
- Never present a problem without also recommending a solution.
- Data is both a question and an answer. The best way to improve the quality of data is to use it.
- Be mindful of Eisenhower's (1957) observation that "plans are worthless, but planning is everything."

THE ART OF QUESTIONS

Governance is about making decisions, setting directions, and implementing strategies to enhance the public interest. It is also about asking the right questions at the right time. The following are examples of questions that foster broad engagement.

- What's our mission?
- Who do we serve and what do they need?
- What's the public interest?
- What's our duty?
- What are we trying to do?
- What results have we had?
- What will it take? Financially? Operationally? Programmatically?
- What is doable and in what time period?
- What can be done with existing resources and what cannot?
- What can go wrong?
- Do we have a Plan B? (Or even a Plan C and D?)
- So what?

These are not easy questions to ask or answer, but they, and questions like them, will lead to richer discussions of just where the public interest might lie in a given instance.

CONCLUSION

The pressures to significantly increase educational attainment and to better align postsecondary education capacities with workforce demands makes your leadership role in the development of state higher education policy even more important than it was in the past.

There has been some erosion in the capacities of SHEEOs to provide the leadership today's issues demand, but it is not beyond recovery. I hope my comments have been of some help, and I wish you well as you take up the challenge of your new position.

REFERENCES

Eisenhower, D. D. (1957). Remarks at National Defense Executive Reserve Conference. Washington, DC.

Fretwell, Jr., E. K. (2000). *System heads, boards, and state officials: More than management* (Occasional Paper). Washington, DC: Association of Governing Boards of Universities and Colleges.

Lingenfelter, P. E. (2004). The state and higher education: An essential partnership. *New Directions for Higher Education, 127*, 47–59.

McGuinness, A. C. (2016). *State policy leadership for the future*. Denver, CO: Education Commission of the States.

Mullen, J. (2009). *Public board chairing for dummies (Twelve easy steps to success)*. Preconference Workshop, Leadership Strategies for Board Chairs of Public Colleges, Universities, and Systems, Association of Governing Boards of Universities and Colleges, National Conference on Trusteeship, San Diego, CA.

National Center for Public Policy and Higher Education. (2005). *State capacity for higher education policy leadership*. San Jose, CA: Author.

Reno, S., & Meredith, T. (2011). *Talking with, not talking past: Working with the aspirations, needs, and personalities of institutional presidents*. Presentation at State Higher Education Executive Officers National Meeting, Denver, CO.

Tuchman, B. (1982). *Practicing history: Selected essays*. New York: Ballantine.

Part II

WHERE WE ARE: CONTEMPORARY STRUCTURES, POLICIES, AND POLITICS

The State Higher Education Executive Officer and Higher Education Finance and Policy

Structure, Policy Orientation, and Relationships Matter

Alicia Kinne-Clawson and William M. Zumeta

Over the past decade, researchers have paid close attention to the multitude of factors that are thought to have an impact on state higher education policy and especially on finance and accountability policy (McLendon, Hearn, & Mokher, 2009; McLendon, Tandberg, & Hillman, 2014; Tandberg, 2010; Tandberg, Fowles, & McLendon, 2017; Weerts & Ronca, 2012). Yet, as Tandberg and colleagues (2017) correctly point out, until recently little systematic attention has been given to certain political actors involved in higher education finance—especially state higher education executive officers.

In this chapter, we investigate the role of the SHEEO in higher education finance and related policymaking. We suggest that the SHEEO's influence is related to the relative structural and historical strength of the higher education coordinating or governing board in the state, which the SHEEO by definition directs. Further, we suggest that the SHEEO's relationship with the governor, both formal and informal, and the extent to which higher education is a gubernatorial priority, profoundly impact the ability of the SHEEO to influence higher education appropriations at any given time. Given commonly scarce resources in state government and sometimes conflicting policy goals, SHEEOs are often forced to navigate complex political environments among their agencies, state policymakers, and institutional leaders in support of what they see as the public interest in higher education (McGuinness, 2016). As McGuinness asserts, and as we show in this chapter, for better or worse SHEEOs and their agencies are not always even the central players. Within this complex context, SHEEOs certainly advocate for basic state support of the higher education enterprise. Yet, there are broader concerns about efficiency and accountability in public spending, achievement of policy goals and outcomes (such as degree production and close workforce linkages), affordability for students, and the state's economic and fiscal climate to be considered as well. This means that success for a SHEEO cannot simply be measured by how much state money flows to higher education, although this outcome is the focus of much of the recent quantitative literature.[1]

After providing some orienting context about state finance and policy trends, we briefly summarize the insights pertinent to our inquiry from the extant literature about SHEEOs, their agencies, and policy matters closely tied to state support for higher education. Then, using a multisite case study approach that draws primarily on published studies of particular states, we examine recent experiences in several states that are illustrative of—or occasionally raise questions about—the broader findings of the literature. We pay particular attention to the nature of the SHEEO's influence as it relates to policy areas that are closely linked to state higher education finance. From these brief case studies, we conclude by seeking to draw out some overarching insights and implications for future research.

THE CURRENT POLICY AND FISCAL CONTEXT

Prominent in current state policy discussions regarding higher education are several issues of particular relevance to our topic. First is the widespread push for higher numbers of college degree and credential completions, especially in fields thought to be closely tied to state workforce development needs. Second, the affordability of college for students and families in the face of recent tuition spikes and long-term real tuition growth has become an even more pressing issue than in the past. Finally, we would add the increasingly explicit accountability of colleges (and of policymakers) for achievement of these and other state policy goals. The first and last issues are tightly linked in an increasing number of states as policymakers seek to pointedly refocus institutions' attention via public performance goals, and often performance-based funding arrangements, on students' completion of degree and credential programs that link to perceived state workforce and economic development needs (Davies, 2014). As important is the increased recent attention of policymakers to college affordability issues as a result of constituents making clear to them that the long upward trend in tuition relative to incomes—and the most recent sharp spike in tuition following the Great Recession's budget cuts—is being painfully felt (The College Board, 2015).

It is in this policy context that SHEEOs and other state policy leaders think about finance issues today. On the one hand, it clearly takes resources to enroll and educate students and move them to the completion of meaningful degree and credential programs, and it may well require more resources to successfully educate the growing share of college students who come to college with educational disadvantages. There are also state resource implications to maintaining affordability for students since the primary components of public college budgets are tuition and state support, with state student aid funding playing a role as well. Another key part of the fiscal policy equation is that state policymakers are also under pressure from taxpayers to contain budgets and taxes (O'Leary, 2011), so they press higher education, along with other components of state spending, for efficiencies to an extent not seen in the early postwar decades. Indeed, the pressures on state budgets have been building since the era of Proposition 13, which was passed by voters in California in 1978 to contain the growth of taxes, and the diffusion of tax and expenditure limitations across the states that began shortly thereafter (Moore, 1998).[2]

The challenge facing those leading the higher education sector is all the greater because, structurally speaking, higher education occupies a weak position relative to other major state functions as a claimant for support, particularly when state funds are tight, as in recessionary periods. This weak position arises for two reasons. First, unlike Medicaid, K–12 education or corrections, higher education "caseloads" (enrollments) need not be funded by lawmakers in the way that constitutional or federal mandates require states to respond to growth in citizens eligible for Medicaid or corrections services, which tend to increase in recessions, or to numbers of pupils in the public schools. Rather, higher education funding is considered the major discretionary item in state general fund budgets, and it is all the easier to restrain or cut because its customers (students) can be charged more, unlike those served in the other functions.

Indeed, research has shown that higher education has long been the "balance wheel" for state budgets in economic downturns (Delaney & Doyle, 2007; Hovey, 1999). As McLendon and colleagues (2009) asserted, "higher education's needs tend to be less visibly pressing in the public arena as its base tends to be less secure, and its state funding is less likely to be formulaically tied to other sources of revenue" (p. 687). Okunade (2004) confirmed the balance wheel idea, finding that competing interests, such as corrections, K–12 education, health care, and welfare, tend to fare better than higher education when limited funding is available. Overlaying this pattern has also been a longer-term, more gradual decline in various measures of state support for higher education, with the Great Recession and its aftermath dramatically steepening this decline.

State support for public higher education has sustained unprecedented declines over the past decade and a half. Two close-together national recessions—the "dotcom" recession of 2000–2001 and most recently the Great Recession of 2007–2009 and its lingering aftermath—have resulted in weak state tax revenue and budget deficits that, as explained previously, disproportionately impact postsecondary education. Higher education appropriations suffered an average decline of 9% between 2000 and 2004, roughly the period of the dotcom recession and its aftermath, recovering to previous levels (in aggregate across the states) for 1 year in 2008 before declining an additional 7% as of 2011 (State Higher Education Executive Officers, 2012). In total, in 37 states higher education sustained cuts greater than 5% during the Great Recession time frame, with reductions up to 35% seen in some states. By 2013, state economies were recovering slowly with higher education seeing the first modest increase in aggregate state support since 2008. As of 2015, state support of higher education had made modest improvements since the Great Recession but inflation-adjusted spending per student remained over 15% below pre-recession levels (State Higher Education Executive Officers, 2016).

FACTORS INFLUENCING STATE SUPPORT OF HIGHER EDUCATION

Recent empirical studies have sought to understand the economic, demographic, higher education governance, and political variables associated with the rise and fall of state appropriations for higher education over the past several decades (Weerts & Ronca, 2012). As these authors put it, "per capita income, availability of state revenues, and tax capacity are key factors in determining the level at which the state will fund its public universities" (p. 157). It is within this context that SHEEOs and their agencies operate in the finance realm, so a discussion of the implications of this literature is pertinent here.

Of particular interest for our purposes, Tandberg (2013) finds— unexpectedly in light of prior theorizing—that the presence of a consolidated governing board for higher education was associated with significantly *lower* state higher education support (per $1,000 of state personal income), net of many other variables and including fixed effects for both state and year. These findings are derived from a panel regression study spanning the years 1976–2004. Earlier scholars had thought that a consolidated board would be able to make a stronger case to policymakers for higher education support than less centralized arrangements (mostly those involving nongoverning coordinating boards of varying strength). Instead, it appears that, according to Tandberg (2013), the more centralized governance setup may moderate the direct impact of institutional lobbying and the like and thus both reduce and "rationalize" state spending (see also Tandberg, 2010).

The role of political variables in relation to state higher education appropriations has certainly been brought to the fore by the empirical studies of

McLendon, Hearn, and Mokher (2009); McLendon, Tandberg, and Hillman (2017); Tandberg (2010); and Tandberg, Fowles, and McLendon (2016), which have also shown that the nature of the SHEEO agency (i.e., governing board versus coordinating or planning board) is a factor in how these variables operate. For example, Tandberg (2010, 2013) has shown that the density of higher education interest groups, as measured by the ratio of these interest groups (mostly public institutions) to all registered interest groups in the state, has a significant impact on state higher education support across the states. When the analysis is run using interaction terms for type of governance structure and run on the two governance types separately, it becomes apparent that the interest group effect is strongest in states lacking a state governing board arrangement for higher education (Tandberg, 2013). Also, recent research has demonstrated that gubernatorial advocacy on behalf of higher education can have a significant impact on state support and that this also interacts with the nature of the SHEEO agency, as is explained in the next section.

A similar result appears with respect to the effect of electoral competition: More electoral competitiveness seems to boost higher education spending significantly more in states with a less centralized higher education governance structure—that is, no governing board (Tandberg, 2013). Again, these results suggest that centralized governing boards may be effective in moderating the direct influence of institutional political influence in driving state spending. Interestingly, legislative professionalism, which is associated with higher state spending on higher education in general, has a stronger effect when a consolidated governing board is present, which might also be read as reinforcing the earlier point about such boards helping to "rationalize" state spending.

GOVERNORS, THE SHEEO, AND HIGHER EDUCATION FINANCE

Much attention has been paid in political science literature to the role of the governor in agenda setting and state fiscal policy. Until recently, however, higher education research has paid little attention to the role of the governor in relation to the SHEEO and the effect of the relationship between the governor and SHEEO on postsecondary policy and finance. Multiple studies have found that the most important role the governor plays in state budgets generally is to act as a check on spending (Barrilleaux & Berkman, 2003; Kousser & Philips, 2012). Political science literature examines the success of a governor through two sources of gubernatorial power. The first is the ability to successfully lead a political party, which is primarily a function of the governor's leadership and political skills. The second is the governor's formal institutional powers, which are rooted in how the chief executive's office is designed by the state constitution and statutes (Barrilleaux &

Berkman, 2003). These powers vary considerably across states. Informal leadership skills and the governor's formal institutional powers both appear to have important consequences in the higher education arena.

Tandberg's (2013) analysis finds that the strength of the governor's budgetary powers[3] works differently in terms of state higher education spending results under the different types of state governance regimes. In state-years where a consolidated governing board was present, more powerful governors were associated with lower higher education spending but in the less centralized state-year cases, the opposite was true. One explanation implying how the impact of the governing board set up works would be that, in governing board states, the governor and board work together successfully to pursue "rationalized" higher education policies that cost less overall. In the less centralized states on the other hand, where individual institutions have more direct influence, governors are either persuaded to support the schools' spending requests for policy or political reasons, or are unable to stop them effectively in spite of their powers. Also, all else held constant, Tandberg's analysis finds that Democratic governors are associated with greater spending for higher education, but the effect is only significant in the state-years where no governing board is in place. This would also be consistent with the idea that consolidated governing boards are a moderating, and perhaps rationalizing and depoliticizing, influence on spending.

While the ability to lead and coordinate the policy agenda for a state represent important and, in part, informal powers of the governor, the formal responsibility for appointing and dismissing agency leadership can also be important to directing the governor's leadership agenda. In the context of the SHEEO, Tandberg and colleagues (2017) find the governor's authority over the appointment and dismissal of this actor to be a little studied yet important gubernatorial role that works in somewhat surprising ways. In a multivariate panel data analysis with state and year fixed effects spanning the years 1985–2009, Tandberg and colleagues find that, in state-years where the governor appointed the SHEEO directly, there was a significant positive association with all of their state support measures.[4] Also, state support was significantly correlated with the percentage of the SHEEO agency board appointed by the governor. On the other hand, in cases where the SHEEO served at the pleasure of the governor (i.e., could be removed by the governor regardless of who appointed the SHEEO), state support was significantly lower and this negative association was more than twice as large as the positive one with governor's power to appoint the SHEEO.

The authors interpret these results in light of the broad finding in the state policy and politics literature that governors tend to play an expenditure-dampening role where they can. They

> theorize that being appointed by the governor alone may not be a sufficiently strong monitoring mechanism to orient the SHEEO to the governor's

preferences, which may allow the SHEEO to remain oriented to the needs and desires of the individual higher education institutions. At the same time being appointed by the governor may increase the SHEEO's effectiveness as an advocate for higher education. (Tandberg et al., 2017, p. 125)

On the other hand,

> when a SHEEO's ability to continue in their role is dependent on the governor, this may cause the SHEEO to orient herself more closely to the governor rather than the institutions and moderate his or her budget recommendations, as governors generally serve as a check on state spending and specifically on state spending for higher education. (p. 125)

Still, governors actually appoint and dismiss SHEEOs in a relatively small number of state-years in the data set (Tandberg et al., 2017). More commonly, governors seek to exercise their influence by appointing members of SHEEO agency boards (i.e., state boards of regents or higher education coordinating boards), as Tandberg and colleagues attempt to operationalize with their "percent of board appointed by the governor" variable.[5] Typically, the board in turn appoints the SHEEO but probably rarely without some level of input from the governor or his/her advisors. The nature of such indirect gubernatorial influence over SHEEOs remains to be systematically examined.[6] In any case, we think that the state-specific case analyses provided next can offer some useful qualitative insights into the interplay of SHEEOs and the agencies they lead with other policy actors in the context of contemporary finance-related policy issues.

The broad statistical association between centralized governing boards and lower state spending on higher education is not, by itself, necessarily desirable or undesirable from a public interest standpoint. Indeed, observers of state higher education policy developments over many years tend to see problems with the necessary focus of these boards on the interests and management of the public institutions to the detriment of other higher education players, especially private institutions (Zumeta, 1992, 1996), and broader state policy concerns (McGuinness, 2016). Indeed, McGuinness (2016) points out that, unlike in the immediate postwar decades, SHEEO agencies are no longer the only source of expertise on state higher education matters. They must now work in collaboration not only with institutions and the governor and their increasingly sophisticated staffs but also with a range of other actors, including legislators and their staffs who claim expertise and may have influence in higher education matters. Indeed, the SHEEO may not always be the lead player in some policy activities that touch on higher education finance (McGuinness, 2016).

In recent years, for example, many governors have recognized the role of higher education in economic development and encouraged investments in their state's colleges and universities. Using their agenda-setting powers, these chief executives have led their parties and legislatures to deliver new policies and investments that are often linked with science, technology, and engineering (STEM) degrees or workforce goals. In other cases, recent governors have led efforts to significantly reduce higher education spending in the name of greater efficiency and sometimes affordability for students as well. Such efforts often coincide with a push for greater accountability and may use some form of performance funding (Zumeta & Kinne-Clawson, 2011). What role SHEEOs and their agencies play in such initiatives and whether and how the structure and powers of these agencies matter are worthy questions for qualitative investigation. We seek to make a modest start along these lines in the four brief state case studies that follow, which draw on recently published studies. These case studies serve to highlight some of the benefits and drawbacks that the current, multipolar higher education policy environment typically presents.

CASE STUDY STATES AND RATIONALE

We examine relatively recent developments that help to illuminate the role of SHEEOs in finance-related policy activities in four prominent states that exhibit a range of state governance arrangements. These include Wisconsin and Georgia, which both have statewide governing boards responsible for large numbers of 2-year and 4-year institutions, and Ohio and Maryland which have coordinating boards for higher education.

Wisconsin is a midsize governing board state with 26 colleges and universities, including 2-year colleges, organized under the University of Wisconsin System and its Board of Regents. The state was one of the first to invest heavily in a public higher education system and Robert LaFollette's "Wisconsin Idea" has been a widely admired model embodying the state service mission of public higher education. Yet, Wisconsin has seen some of the deepest declines in state support for public colleges and universities in the last decade.

The University of Georgia System, also governed by a Board of Regents, is the fifth-largest system of higher education in the United States. It encompasses 29 colleges and universities, including 2-year schools (but not the technical institutes). Under the leadership of Chancellor (SHEEO) Hank Huckaby, it recently undertook the challenging task of consolidating eight of its constituent institutions into four.

Ohio is a large state with a history, until fairly recently, of extensive "local control" in higher education and other policy areas. Its 4-year universities are not part of multi-university systems, although several of the universities have regional campuses. Finally, Maryland is a smaller state with a multicampus system that includes the majority, but not all, of its 4-year

Table 5.1. Higher Education Governance Structures

Type of Board	Coordinating Boards/Agencies with Authority to Coordinate All of Higher Education or Multiple Governing Boards for Systems and Public Institutions	System Governing Board for All Public Institutions or Two or More System Governing Boards and Several Institutional Governing Boards
Statewide Planning Authority	Yes	Yes, state-level entity charged with authority for statewide planning/public agenda for all higher education or planning for individual systems or institutions
Budget Role	Consolidated or aggregated budget	Budget role for governing systems and public higher education institutions under each board's jurisdiction
Classification	Strong coordinating board	Governing board
State	Ohio, Maryland	Georgia, Wisconsin

Source: McGuinness (2016).

institutions and has a separate set of mostly locally governed community colleges. At the state level, both the Ohio and Maryland systems have coordinating boards rather than statewide governing boards.

In most cases the policy efforts that we examine have spanned several gubernatorial administrations and even governors from different political parties. Thus they provide some basis for enriching understanding about how the findings from statistical analyses of long-term, cross-state patterns in regard to the role of SHEEOs in state finance of higher education may play out on the ground. Table 5.1 draws on McGuinness (2016) to depict the key structural features of statewide higher education governance in these four states.

Wisconsin

Wisconsin has been the scene of significant direct gubernatorial involvement in higher education recently in ways probably unprecedented in the state and unusual in American higher education. The recent history in Wisconsin is consistent with Tandberg's (2013) finding that states with a consolidated governing board tend to spend less on higher education than is true in states where individual institutions have more direct influence. Yet, the link between the SHEEOs' and the governors' approaches during this period has been different from the typical pattern. In this case study, we seek to sort out the impact of the SHEEO on recent developments in state finance of Wisconsin's public institutions in the context of the initiatives of a strong, budget-slashing Republican governor and lean fiscal conditions in the state, as well as structural aspects of the governing board and gubernatorial appointment powers.

In 2010, Wisconsin voters elected Governor Scott Walker, a Republican, who came to Madison armed with an ambitious agenda to overhaul the state budget and, alongside that, specific plans to fundamentally reshape public higher education (Thomason, 2015). Prior to the Great Recession and Walker's tenure, the University of Wisconsin System had seen nearly 3 decades of remarkable growth and political stability. Dating back to its early history, Wisconsin was among the first states to provide robust public support to higher education and through this relationship the Wisconsin Idea was developed (McLendon, 2003; Thomason, 2015). Since the birth of the Wisconsin Idea, the ideals of public higher education and the public in the badger state have generally been congruent. Originally articulated by University of Wisconsin President Charles Van Hise in 1904, the Wisconsin Idea broadly symbolizes the university's commitment to public service and holds that the work of the university should be applied to solve the problems of the citizens of the state (University of Wisconsin-Madison, 2016). Over time, the university system and the legislature have combined to produce "such groundbreaking laws as the nation's first workers compensation legislation, tax reforms, and the public regulation of utilities" (University of Wisconsin-Madison, 2016). For decades, the Wisconsin Idea has represented the expressed mission of the University of Wisconsin-Madison but in recent years has been embraced by the system as a whole (University of Wisconsin-Madison, 2016, para. 1).

Prior to 1971, the University of Wisconsin-Madison had its own governing board, which was separate from the rest of public higher education in the state. Between 1971 and 1974, the legislature worked to establish The University of Wisconsin System by combining the two public university systems under a single governing board of regents (University of Wisconsin System, 2015). Today, the University of Wisconsin System consists of two doctoral campuses (with the University of Wisconsin-Madison serving as the historic flagship), 11 comprehensive universities, 13 two-year colleges, and the University of Wisconsin Extension. The system is governed by the Board of Regents with 18 members, 16 of which are appointed by the governor subject to confirmation by the Senate. The other two are student members. The board is responsible for establishing policies and rules governing the system, planning to meet future state needs for university education, setting admission standards and policies, reviewing and approving university budgets that allocate resources among the various institutions, and establishing the regulatory framework within which the individual units operate. The basic principle of the framework is to provide the widest degree of institutional autonomy possible under the controlling limits of systemwide policies and priorities established by the board. The board appoints the president of the university system (the state's SHEEO) and the chancellors of the 13 universities and of UW-Extension and the UW Colleges (2-year colleges). All of these executives serve at the pleasure of the board (University of Wisconsin System, 2015).

Since 1971 there have been seven presidents of the University of Wisconsin System. Under their leadership, and with generally positive relationships with the state capital, enrollment doubled and spending remained relatively generous compared to higher education appropriations nationally.

As of 2014, state and local higher education spending in Wisconsin was almost 10 percent above the national average as a share of state income. According to the 2014 State Higher Education Finance report (SHEEO, 2014), Wisconsin allocated seven percent of state and local tax revenue to higher education, the highest percentage in the Midwest. Viewed from another angle, Wisconsin's state and local spending per capita on higher education was $1,028 compared with a national level of $864. In 2014 that ranked 12th highest in the country. (Hefty, 2014, para. 14)

While many states have seen their revenues and budgets recover considerably since the aftermath of the Great Recession, Wisconsin continues to suffer economically. Nearly all economic indicators, including job and wage growth, have been below national averages since the recession. Walker successfully pursued 6 straight years of cuts to both the income and property tax rate levels (Meyers, 2016). As a result, in nearly every year that Walker has been in office, the state has faced a structural deficit with spending projected to outpace current state revenues. In order to meet this challenge, Wisconsin has made deep cuts to discretionary areas of the budget, including higher education. While (largely mandatory) Medicaid and corrections costs have gone up, spending on the University of Wisconsin System dropped 21% between 2005 and 2015 (Cornelius, 2015). As Figure 5.1 shows, the last decade has been marked by a steep and consistent real decline in state support per student (lower bars) in Wisconsin, while tuition (upper bars) has risen sharply to offset the lost state support.

Thus, for Wisconsin, the story of higher education funding over the last few years has been almost entirely driven by the agenda of an ambitious governor seeking to reduce spending rather than by leadership from the SHEEO and University of Wisconsin System. In many ways, the recent changes to higher education funding and policy have occurred despite an outcry from system and campus leaders. For Kevin Reilly, who served as President of the University of Wisconsin System from 2004 to 2013, the last few years of his term—those under Walker—were the most tumultuous.

Figure 5.1. Wisconsin Public FTE Enrollment and Educational Appropriations per FTE, FY 1991–2016

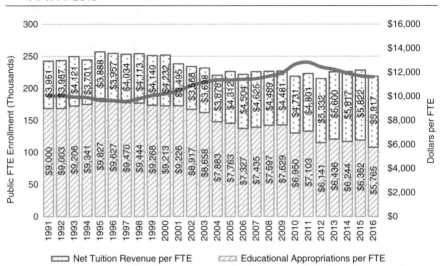

Net Tuition Revenue per FTE   Educational Appropriations per FTE

Data adjusted for inflation using the Higher Education Cost Adjustment (HECA). Full-time equivalent (FTE) enrollment equates student credit hours to full-time, academic year students but excludes medical students. Educational appropriations are a measure of state and local support available for public higher education operating expenses, including ARRA funds, and exclude appropriations for independent institutions, financial aid for students attending independent institutions, research, hospitals, and medical education. Net tuition revenue is calculated by taking the gross amount of tuition and fees, less state and institutional financial aid, tuition waivers or discounts, and medical student tuition and fees. Net tuition revenue used for capital debt service is included in the net tuition revenue figures.

Source: 2016 SHEF Report, State Higher Education Executive Officers

Immediately after Walker took office in early 2011, he and the chancellor of the University of Wisconsin-Madison secretly supported a plan to split the flagship campus from the system in an effort to help reduce state funding obligations in return for campus autonomy. Such autonomy would have permitted UW-Madison to pursue alternative revenues more freely. After the plan fell apart in the face of stiff opposition a few months later, the UW-Madison chancellor left for a new job at a small private college (Herzog, 2013). Since then, Walker has continued to push through a variety of higher education reforms designed in part to reduce state spending over time but also to impose his vision of the university. These changes have included additional autonomy for the system in exchange for budget cuts, removing faculty tenure protections from state law, and restrictions on faculty collective bargaining (Thomason, 2015).

In 2014, Ray Cross was appointed president of the University of Wisconsin System (i.e., the SHEEO) by vote of the regents and inherited an especially tense political relationship with the governor and Republican-controlled legislature. While the governor and legislature have no direct power over the president's appointment, several members of the legislature wrote letters of support for Cross's appointment to the regents' selection committee (Herzog, 2014). At the outset of Cross's term, the governor had proposed a $300 million cut in state appropriations to the UW system—and the new president threatened his resignation if such budget cuts were approved or if faculty tenure was destroyed by the legislature (Schmidt, 2016). After much negotiation, the state budget cuts were reduced to $250 million and, while tenure provisions for faculty were stricken from state law (an unusual place for them in any case compared to other states), the UW System Board of Regents and boards at each campus were given some discretion over tenure policies (Schmidt, 2016).

This example, like much out of Wisconsin recently, portrays a SHEEO who walks a fine line between a governor—and to a considerable extent, a legislature—with a higher education agenda that is substantially different from that of the University of Wisconsin's institutional leaders. Over the course of Walker's term, nearly all of the system's regents, who are gubernatorial appointees, have been replaced with regents who more closely share the governor's vision for a much leaner higher education system. The most recent decade of budget reductions in the University of Wisconsin System seem to illustrate vividly Tandberg's (2013) finding that the presence of a powerful governor and a consolidated governing board may work together on a low-spending higher education agenda, even if in this case the SHEEOs and board were, at best, reluctant partners.

The extent to which the SHEEO can influence postsecondary funding in Wisconsin seems to be moderated by the appointment and dismissal powers of the governor over the Board of Regents—providing an important link between the powers of the governor and their agenda. While Tandberg and colleagues (2017) found that a large share of the board members being gubernatorial appointees (as is the case in Wisconsin) generally had a positive effect on higher education spending, Wisconsin recently seems to defy this pattern in light of the governor's agenda. It appears that the ability of the SHEEO to affect higher education funding in Wisconsin under Walker has gone only so far as that the SHEEO has been part of a successful campaign to marshal regent support to persuade lawmakers to moderate the governor's proposed cuts to the institution.

The current era in Wisconsin state politics represents a significant departure from that of the days of the origins of the Wisconsin Idea and of a close and intertwined relationship between the university system and public policymakers. Then, and for many years afterward, this governing board, where the governor does not have appointment or removal authority over the SHEEO, was associated with a relatively high level of state budgetary support. Contemporary politics, polarization, and constrained resources have contributed to a SHEEO that at best serves to defend the university against the budget-cutting inclinations of the governor and his supporters and to act as a buffer between an increasingly distrustful faculty and the state capital. This type of buffering when necessary is, it should be noted, one of the original dimensions of the SHEEO role as it evolved in the post-war decades (Berdahl, 1971).

Yet, the SHEEO is also hired and subject to termination by the gubernatorially appointed regents—nearly all of whom had been appointed by Walker. It seems plausible, and even likely, that the appointment power of the governor over the regents weakens the buffering role of the SHEEO between the university system and the political institutions of the state and provides a determined, two-term governor considerable leverage over the system. Similar to Tandberg's (2013) findings related to the termination power of the governor over the SHEEO, it would appear that the governor's influence may well extend beyond direct authority over the SHEEO's incumbency when the state board of regents are all gubernatorial appointees. Eventually, the board could remove a SHEEO who was not to the governor's liking and thereby further weaken the SHEEO's traditional buffering role. On the other hand, SHEEOs may also be able to "educate" new regents to the full scope of their public interest responsibilities as trustees of a public higher education enterprise that carries on beyond the tenure of any governor.

Georgia

The Board of Regents of the University System of Georgia (USG) was created in 1931 to oversee the state's higher education system, a move that was part of a reorganization of Georgia's state government. Today, the USG consists of 29 colleges and universities and is governed by the gubernatorially appointed board of regents. The board of regents is composed of 19 members, 5 of whom are appointed from the state at large with the others chosen from each of the 14 congressional districts. The board in turn elects a chancellor who serves as its chief executive officer as well as the university system's CEO (i.e., the SHEEO), overseeing all matters pertaining to the funding, administration, and operation of public universities and colleges. The presidents of the institutions are appointed by the board on the recommendation of the chancellor. Among the important responsibilities of the board of regents are statewide planning and coordination, institutional budget review, and program review (Board of Regents of the University System of Georgia, 2016; Fincher, 2016; McGuinness & Fulton, 2007).

Since its origin, the USG has experienced continued growth despite some of the most challenging demographic and educational attainment patterns in the country. In 2012, the high school graduation rate in Georgia was just 62%, well below the national rate of 73% and among the worst in the South (Finney, Perna, & Callan, 2012). At the postsecondary level, Georgia's performance in preparation for college, participation in college, and college completion also continues to lag behind the national averages. In 1991, just before implementation of the now renowned Helping Outstanding Pupils Educationally (HOPE) scholarship program, the proportion of 18- to 24-year-olds enrolled in some type of postsecondary education was a mere 23% (Finney et al., 2012).

In part in response to this latter deficiency, the HOPE scholarship program was designed under the leadership of Democratic Governor Zell Miller, the idea having been a centerpiece of his campaign for office (Henry & Bulger, 2004). This lottery-funded program pays for tuition, fees, and books at any public college or university in the state for any Georgia student who graduates from high school with a B or better grade point average (Rubenstein, 2003). Prior to the establishment of the HOPE program, Georgia ranked near the bottom in publicly funded aid for higher education (Rubenstein, 2003). At its implementation, the HOPE scholarship was a means tested program—only providing aid to those students from families who earned less than $100,000 annually. Within a few years, the lottery revenues had grown to the point that it was deemed possible to expand eligibility to every student who met the academic requirements and was a Georgia resident, regardless of income (Rubenstein, 2003). As of 2013–2014, Georgia's total spending on student aid had soared from near the bottom among the states 2 decades earlier to being behind only California, New York, and Texas (National Association of State Student Grant Aid Programs, 2014). Yet, the state's support of need-based student aid has remained minimal, and the HOPE grants disproportionately served more affluent white students (Rubenstein, 2003).

The decade after passage of the HOPE scholarship proved to be the most prosperous in the university system's history. As Figure 5.2 shows, state spending per student nearly doubled while tuition remained flat in inflation-adjusted terms. This decade of growth for the system is a story of a strong economy and an inventive governor as well as of a symbiotic relationship between the governor, the SHEEO, the board of regents, and strong allies in the General Assembly (Fairchild-Pierce, 2008). Richardson, Reeves, Bracco, Callan, and Finney (1999) write that the governor's power over higher education arises from the appointment of board members and oversight of the state budget. Thus, it is no surprise that the USG regents selected a SHEEO whose vision was right in line with the governor's goals.[7]

Leading this period of unprecedented change for the University System of Georgia was Chancellor Stephen R. Portch. Portch was selected to lead the system just prior to the start of Miller's second term. Although Miller did not appoint Portch as SHEEO, the two quickly developed a

Figure 5.2. Georgia Public FTE Enrollment and Educational Appropriations per FTE, FY 1991–2016

FY	Net Tuition Revenue per FTE	Educational Appropriations per FTE
1991	$2,670	$9,168
1992	$2,745	$7,700
1993	$2,799	$7,823
1994	$2,891	$8,492
1995	$2,877	$9,108
1996	$2,922	$9,392
1997	$3,155	$10,418
1998	$3,230	$10,584
1999	$3,535	$11,334
2000	$2,629	$14,163
2001	$2,483	$11,850
2002	$2,008	$10,529
2003	$1,599	$9,477
2004	$1,591	$9,130
2005	$1,537	$9,127
2006	$2,043	$9,616
2007	$2,214	$9,587
2008	$2,354	$9,477
2009	$2,219	$8,481
2010	$2,676	$7,795
2011	$2,514	$7,389
2012	$3,671	$6,752
2013	$4,349	$6,822
2014	$4,454	$7,275
2015	$4,661	$7,524
2016	$4,831	$7,754

Left axis: Public FTE Enrollment (Thousands) — 0 to 450. Right axis: Dollars per FTE — $0 to $18,000.

Source: 2016 SHEF Report, State Higher Education Executive Officers

bond. Among their accomplishments over the next 4 years were a massive construction program across the system, investments in increased faculty salaries, and the creation of state business alliances (Cumming, 1998). Richardson and colleagues (1999) described Portch's effectiveness as in part a function of his effective communication style as well as his voluntary accountability initiative that directly linked budget requests with board goals and key legislative priorities. Both the governor and legislature considered the system to be very responsive to state needs (Fairchild-Pierce, 2008; Richardson et al., 1999).

Beyond his role with external political actors, Portch built a relationship with each of the campus presidents, rewarding their initiatives by securing special funds from the legislature beyond the regular budget and, alternately, holding presidents in check when needed to assert broader system needs. This is the essence of the higher education coordinating role, although in a typical governing board state like Georgia, it does not officially span across institutions and sectors outside the public college and university system. In recapping Portch's tenure in 1998, the *Atlanta Journal Constitution* described him as "the most powerful chancellor since Georgia created a university system in 1932" (Cumming, 1998, para. 24). It no doubt helped that he served during a period of ample state revenues that made it easier to forge agreements. Still, it is notable that, at least during this period, the governing board arrangement was associated with generous state spending on higher education, consistent with Tandberg's (2013) findings, even if the underlying factors supporting these outcomes were largely not due to anything the chancellor did or could have done.

Since the tenure of Chancellor Portch, there have been three SHEEOs in Georgia. For the most part, the terms of the most recent chancellors have largely mirrored the policy priorities of the governors in place, which seems to speak to the nature of the relationship between the two offices in this state. Although governors do not appoint or remove the SHEEO in Georgia, Chancellor Errol B. David shared, in 2011 when announcing his retirement at the conclusion of Governor Sonny Perdue's term, a notable comment: "The advent of a new governor does mean that the University System chancellor needs to establish a long-term working relationship in order to be effective. It is therefore appropriate that I step down at the end of my contract year and allow my successor to establish this necessary relationship" (Millsaps, 2010, para. 3). This is a telling statement about the way SHEEOs see their role in Georgia. We observe that it is functionally similar to the cases identified by Tandberg and colleagues (2017) where SHEEOs serve at the governor's pleasure, although that is not formally the case in Georgia.

The most recent USG chancellor, Hank Huckaby, was appointed in 2011 (University System of Georgia, 2016). Prior to becoming chancellor, he served in various roles, including as an administrator in the system, director of the governor's budget office, and later as a state legislator. Huckaby entered the SHEEO role at a time when costs were at the forefront of discussion regarding higher education across the country as states struggled with the aftermath of the Great Recession (Hayes, 2015). Unlike Portch, Huckaby took the helm of a system that was faced with the "new normal" of little to no new resources for higher education and "doing more with less." Huckaby was hired with the primary charge of "rightsizing the system" and consolidating of some of its campuses (Hayes, 2015), which was congruent with the governor's goals. Since he took office in 2011, Huckaby has overseen the consolidation of four institutions into two, with another four currently being consolidated. The chancellor has worked closely with the governor, ensuring his support of the mergers and his commitment that the mergers would not mean reduced state support (Hayes, 2015). In this period, the SHEEO's efforts were focused on cost control at the behest of the governor, rather than on growth as in the Miller–Portch era. The chancellor was an important player in both periods, but the results in terms of state spending were different because the times were different and, most importantly, because the governor's priorities were quite different.

Georgia's governance structure has been described as one of the "most simple" of higher education governance structures in the United States (Richardson et al., 1999). As Chancellor Huckaby recently described it in the context of the campus mergers, "Our governance structure has made this easier. The University System of Georgia has one board, and because of our legal standing—with the system set up by the constitution—we are not treated like a typical state agency. When the legislature appropriates funding to the system, in effect it works like a block grant for which the system's board and staff determine the appropriate allocations" (Hayes, 2015, para. 2). This resource flexibility enables system leaders to make difficult structural and financial decisions largely outside the politics of the legislature. Further, as evidenced by the leadership of both Portch and Huckaby, the informal involvement of the governor in the appointment process and the relative importance of higher education to the governor's agenda during these periods meant that the two offices generally worked together to advance shared higher education goals.

As other case studies illustrate and the literature supports, the extent to which the SHEEO in Georgia has been successful has been largely a function of the chancellor's relationship with the governor. Somewhat contrary to the case in Wisconsin but consistent with Tandberg and colleagues' (2017) general findings, the large portion of the USG's board that is appointed by the governor seems to have helped—or at least not harmed—funding for the system. As the mid-1990s in Georgia highlight, Portch was able to successfully leverage the leadership of a higher education oriented governor, coupled with a strong economy, into robust investments in the system. If measured by new state investment, Huckaby saw less success 15 years later. In many ways, though, Huckaby's tenure is more consistent with what we generally see in the literature. A governing board state where regents are appointed by the governor in an era where spending is largely restrained led to a campus consolidation effort that is as much about governing in the new era of reduced state support as it is a reflection of a fiscally conservative governor alone. If anything, Portch's tenure as SHEEO may be more an anomaly than the norm in terms of fiscal outcomes. His decade of leadership was marked by his strong governance skills but also by a rich fiscal context with unusual gubernatorial interest in driving state resources toward higher education. Looking ahead, such circumstances may not come together often again.

Ohio

The last decade or so of policy change in Ohio provides an intriguing example of the important interplay between the SHEEO and the governor as well as the importance of both the formal and informal powers of the state's chief executive in influencing and executing state higher education policy (see Figure 5.3 for recent fiscal and enrollment trends). Unlike in Wisconsin and Georgia, in Ohio the state higher education agency is a coordinating, not a governing, board. It has responsibility not only for the 4-year colleges and universities but also for community colleges and technical education centers that mostly serve working adults. For most of its history, the agency

Figure 5.3. Ohio Public FTE Enrollment and Educational Appropriations per FTE, FY 1991–2016

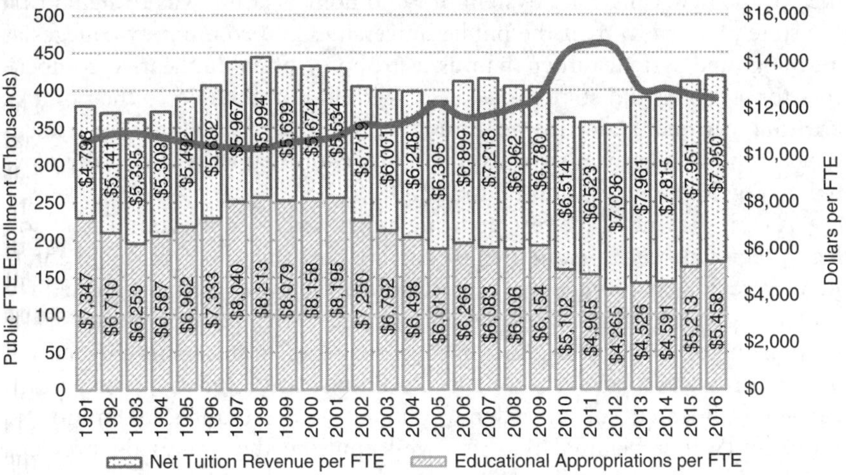

Source: 2016 SHEF Report, State Higher Education Executive Officers

was known simply as the Ohio Board of Regents (BOR), despite its lack of governing board powers. Recently, the BOR was subsumed within a new state Department of Higher Education and made a cabinet-level agency, which signals the importance placed on higher education policy by the past two governors, Democrat Ted Strickland and Republican John Kasich. The chancellor of higher education (the SHEEO) and members of the Board of Regents are appointed by the governor. In addition, the House and Senate education committee chairs, as well as the chancellor, serve as ex officio members of the regents. Ohio has long had another important player in its higher education deliberations as well, the Interuniversity Council, which is a membership organization of the public 4-year institutions with a small but influential staff located in the state capital. There is also a parallel Ohio Association of Community Colleges headquartered in Columbus.

Beginning early in the administration of Democratic Governor Ted Strickland (2007–2011), the until-then relatively decentralized higher education system was completely restructured under a 10-year system strategic plan, enacted in 2008. This plan centralized authority and gave the governor more direct influence by allowing the governor to appoint the SHEEO, who was at that point rechristened the Chancellor of the University System of Ohio. This new relationship between the SHEEO and the governor was intended to allow the governor to manage an ambitious higher education reform agenda without dealing directly in time-consuming negotiations with all of the stakeholders involved, which is the role of the SHEEO (Fischer, 2008). Moreover, by virtue of gubernatorial appointment, the chancellor's hand was considerably strengthened, in the vein noted by Tandberg and colleagues (2017). The idea of the new University System of Ohio nomenclature was to signal that the state planned to treat the public universities and community colleges as an integrated system rather than as a group of often-duplicative competitors for students and state funds, even if it did not quite go to the point of creating a formal statewide governing board. The regents and department have certainly become a strong version of a coordinating board in the sense defined by McGuinness and Fulton (2007).

A major theme of the restructuring effort was to utilize community colleges, regional branch campuses of universities, and adult training centers in a strategic way to make higher education widely accessible—termed the "30 mile promise" regarding proximity of access to a public college—while minimizing duplication and facilitating "seamless" transfers to universities. The reform effort also consolidated administrative functions, expanded capacity, allocated substantial new money—more than $500 million in Strickland's first biennial budget—while putting the brakes on previous rapid tuition increases. It also included the implementation of a much broader system of performance-based funding than had existed previously (Fingerhut, 2008a).

Strickland appointed former state senator and U.S. Congressman Eric Fingerhut to the chancellor's position early in his term and unofficially made him part of the governor's cabinet, a significant move in step with the approach of a governor who made "higher education a cornerstone of his four years in office" (Grasgreen, 2010, para. 14). Later, the SHEEO agency's cabinet status was made official. SHEEO Fingerhut (2008b) was the leading author of the blueprint for the reform program, the *Strategic Plan for Higher Education, 2008–2017*, so he clearly had a crucial role in fleshing out the governor's general vision for higher education. This governor viewed the state's colleges and universities as a critical economic development tool and actively supported investments in them before the state legislature as a way to grow the state's economy (Fischer, 2008). There was also a related push to keep college graduates in the state (many had been leaving previously) by connecting students to cooperative education and internship placements while in school (Grasgreen, 2010). About $250 million was appropriated over 5 years for this effort as part of the reform program. In addition, the "Third Frontier" program was reauthorized, which links universities aggressively with industrial research and development to "create new technology-based products, companies, industries and jobs" (Grasgreen, 2010). This effort was supported by a voter-approved bond issue initially enacted in 2002 and refunded in the same manner, for $700 million, in 2010.

Fingerhut played a key role in conceptualizing and executing this agenda under the overall leadership of a supportive governor who had appointed him. Indeed, it is clear that the SHEEO and governor in this period worked together extremely closely to devise and enact a reform strategy that involved additional expenditures but at the same time pursued economies as well. The strategic plan was built around the idea of reigning in the previous tendencies toward undisciplined spending, as well as tuition growth, that were thought to be the product of a too loosely coordinated system (Fingerhut, 2008a, 2008b).

It is notable that many of Strickland's reforms were enacted at a time when the opposite party, the Republicans, controlled both houses of the legislature, so the effort had to be bipartisan. This is likely why its essence largely survived both the budget stringencies of the Great Recession and aftermath and the gubernatorial turnover to Republican Kasich, who defeated Strickland in a hard-fought race in November 2010. Kasich had to make big cuts in state support initially that were not part of the strategic plan in order to cope with a large state budget deficit resulting from the recession. Significantly, though, there was not any wholesale shift away from the earlier plan, even though it had been initiated by a governor of the opposite party.

Notably, Kasich did not work as much through his SHEEOs as had Strickland.[8] (One source suggests that Kasich did not see eye to eye with the first SHEEO he appointed.) Instead, after a couple years, he called upon a large figure in Ohio higher education whom he had long known and trusted, Ohio State University President Gordon Gee, to exert leadership in the higher education policy space (Kiley, 2013). Gee deftly led two task forces during 2013 that helped work through key aspects of higher education policy plans for the governor in the areas of performance-funding formula reforms and allocation of capital funding, for which the system had been starved during the recession years. In effect, Gee's stature, credibility with other players, such as the institutions and their associations as well as the legislature, and relationship with the governor allowed him to serve in the sort of role that is often envisioned for SHEEOs but which they do not in all circumstances have the stature, relationships, and authority to pull off.[9]

Kasich's regime has emphasized—as had other recent Ohio governors—the connections of higher education to the need to modernize the state's economy, both to educate more people, including working adults, and to prepare more of them in STEM fields. There has long been an emphasis in Ohio on academic research tied to industrial needs, and this too continues. Kasich and his SHEEOs, plus prominently President Gee, have refined and fully implemented the performance-funding regime initiated by Strickland and Fingerhut,[10] which pays institutions for courses and degrees completed, not enrollments. Kasich and the SHEEO agency have also pushed hard for efficiencies in all areas of higher education, from administrative streamlining to better articulation across educational levels and campuses to an effort to expand competency-based certification in order to reduce the need for traditional enrollment (Kiley, 2013). These kinds of tasks, however, do not rise to the kind of strategic visioning and negotiations that were carried out by Fingerhut and then Gee.

The Kasich administration has also sustained Strickland's emphasis on affordability for students by restricting tuition increases, adding some funding to the state student aid program, and pursuing ideas like competency assessment and a 3-year degree, among a range of ideas propounded by Kasich's Affordability and Efficiency Commission (launched in 2015). Kasich is clearly an efficiency-oriented, businesslike Republican whose administration seeks to trim taxes wherever it can, so this mentality pervades state policy thinking about higher education. Broadly speaking, the legislature, although one of its houses has generally been controlled by Democrats, seems to be on board with this cost-conscious approach, at least in higher education. Again, the current policy regime had clear roots in the Strickland period and was enacted in a bipartisan mode with broad agreement that higher education was both important to the state's future and in need of being more efficiently managed. Thus, during the Kasich era, the SHEEO role, including what Gee did functionally, might be more closely associated with spending limitations than would be true during the Strickland years, reflecting the philosophies and emphases of the respective governors and the times they faced.

In the main, though, the point is that SHEEOs who are seen as effective will typically have close relationships with their governors and will reflect their priorities. If the SHEEO is not up to the task for whatever reason and the times call for it, a governor who is focused on higher education may well look for a surrogate who has the clout to be an effective policy leader. That Kasich depended later on a broadly based Accountability and Efficiency Commission, rather than the SHEEO agency alone, is also notable in this same vein. This could be due to Kasich's personal predilections, but it might also relate to the structural limitations of a SHEEO office that is seen as so closely tied to the governor; Kasich may have felt that he needed to broaden the base of support for certain policy directions. Additionally, the recent experience in Ohio suggests that a strong coordinating board arrangement can exert as tight control over higher education spending as a governing board might, if such is the governor's orientation.

Maryland

Maryland has 13 public 4-year colleges and universities and 16 community colleges, in addition to 22 private nonprofit colleges (Perna & Finney, 2014) (see Figure 5.4 for recent fiscal and enrollment trends). In 1988, 11 of the 13 public 4-year institutions were consolidated into the University System of Maryland (USM) in order to improve coordination, but two smaller schools— St. Mary's College and historically black Morgan State University—remain independent of the USM. Also, the community colleges, which enroll almost

Figure 5.4. Maryland Public FTE Enrollment and Educational Appropriations per FTE, FY 1991–2016

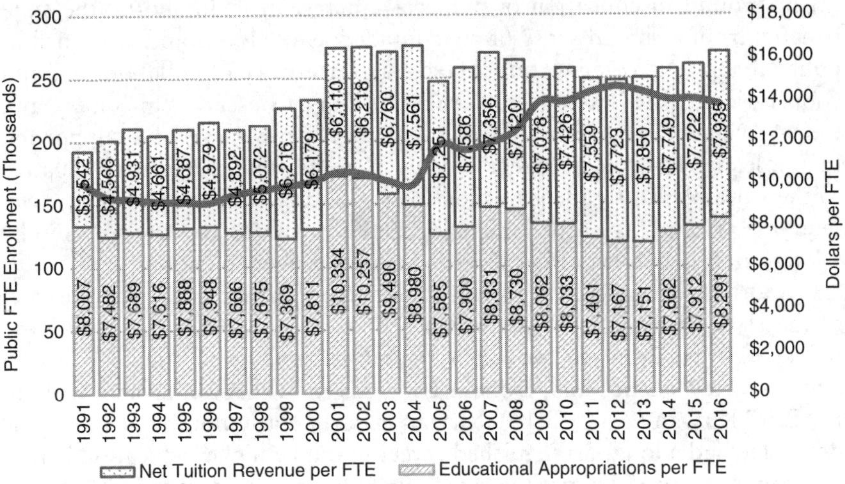

Source: 2016 SHEF Report, State Higher Education Executive Officers

as many students as the 4-year publics in total, are not part of USM and with one exception are locally based. The Maryland Higher Education Commission (MHEC), the SHEEO agency, is responsible for "the planning, supervision, and coordination" of the entire system (Perna & Finney, 2014, p. 115). MHEC's executive director, the state's SHEEO, serves as Secretary of Higher Education and is a member of the governor's Executive Council.

Also of note is that 17 of the state's private nonprofit colleges are eligible for direct state support according to a formula that ties the amount they receive per Maryland-resident undergraduate they enroll to the per-student funding of USM. This is a unique arrangement among the 50 states. The community colleges' state funding is also linked to that of the USM (Perna & Finney, 2014). These longstanding fiscal linkage arrangements help to minimize some of the usual inter-institutional rivalries over funding that arise in most states (although they, correspondingly, do not readily allow for shifts in emphasis when needs shift).

Indeed, Perna and Finney catalogue Maryland's relatively high recent performance in higher education and attribute this record to such attributes as "stable and respected political and higher education leadership; a record of collaboration across and within educational sectors . . . and strategic use of fiscal resources to achieve state goals and priorities" (p. 119). They suggest that the record of enlightened and collaborative leadership goes back a long way: The funding linkage arrangements date to the 1970s and the formation of the USM and the overarching coordinating commission to 1988. Maryland is a well-educated state, and these authors note how many of the governors and key legislators in recent decades have had either a background in education or a special interest in it. In short, "the state benefits from a shared sense of civic-mindedness, a longstanding record of political support for educational goals, and a history of collaboration and cooperation" (p. 118). Indeed, Perna and Finney observe, "In some ways, the Maryland Higher Education Commission plays more of a supporting than a leadership role in higher education in the state, particularly relative to the roles played by the governor, the legislature, and the University System of Maryland" (p. 120). Unlike in Ohio, this subsidiary role seems to be a longstanding pattern rather than a short-term phenomenon.

Another factor leading to this result may be that, since the creation of the USM in 1988, the system that represents most of the state's 4-year universities has been led for nearly the whole time by two highly capable and respected chancellors, Donald Langenberg (1989–2002) and William E. "Brit" Kirwan (2002–2014). Kirwan is particularly notable for our purposes. He had a long, distinguished career in public higher education before becoming the USM chancellor, which included a near decade-long stint as president of the system's flagship College Park campus (after a faculty career there), as well as a period as president of Ohio State University. When Kirwan was asked to return to Maryland in 2002 to succeed Langenberg as system chancellor, the state was suffering the effects of the "dotcom" recession, and higher education had sustained substantial cuts in state funding. Consequently, tuition had jumped by 40% and was well above peer averages. Enrollment was restricted, and there was pent-up demand for access (Kirwan, 2007).

Looking ahead, Kirwan felt that USM and the rest of the state's system needed to become more efficient in use of resources (partly to maintain affordability) and more effective in producing graduates. The governor who took office in January 2003, Republican Thomas Ehrlich, was faced with continuing revenue problems and was philosophically supportive of Kirwan's "Effectiveness and Efficiency Initiative." The effort included tightening articulation between the state's community colleges and University of Maryland University College, an institution that features online degree completion programs; offering more courses and programs on community college campuses and at regional centers where several institutions cooperated; paring back "unnecessary" (beyond 120) credits for bachelor's degrees; requiring 12 credits to be taken outside the college classroom (via Advanced Placement courses, study abroad, internships, etc.); requiring academic units to increase average full-time faculty teaching assignments by 10%; using facilities more intensively; and aiming to achieve administrative savings in energy use, purchasing, and various back-room operations. Savings were reported to be around 3.5% of USM's general fund appropriations, and tuition was frozen for a period as a result of the savings (Kirwan, 2007).

In addition to pleasing the governor, this "running a tight ship" approach helped Kirwan to cultivate legislative support, which is important in Maryland where the legislative body plays a particularly important role in higher education policymaking (Perna & Finney, 2014). The program included outreach to the community colleges; to the extent USM ultimately benefited in budgetary terms, so did they (as did the influential independent colleges). When state resources were available again, USM and the other sectors whose support was linked to the system were well treated. Thus, Kirwan's efforts and the cross-sector budgetary linkage formula in tandem played a coordinating role that may have given MHEC relatively little to do.

Democratic Governor Martin O'Malley, elected in November 2006, was also supportive of higher education and continued efforts to "buy down" tuition increases by offering for several years to substitute state funds for the revenue they would bring in (Perna & Finney, 2014). When the Great Recession reared its head, higher education was largely protected, to an extent that was unusual among the states. The state stuck to commitments to try to drive tuition down to national norms and to benchmark higher education funding to competitor states. Remarkably, O'Malley, Kirwan, and the state legislative leadership, working closely together, even pushed through a corporate tax increase to fund a Higher Education Investment Fund to cushion higher education support—and tuition—to a degree from inevitable economic volatility (Perna & Finney, 2014).

It seems likely that part of the impact of the efforts of Chancellor Kirwan and the other leaders may be to reduce the volatility of both higher education support and tuition; that is, the highs of both should be dampened and the lows softened. We note that the overall effect on state higher education support in Maryland of the increased trust and the investment fund might well be consistent with the general finding in the literature that coordinating board states tend to spend more on higher education, but probably not so here for the typical reasons. Indeed, by all accounts, the coordinating board played a secondary role in these developments.

The Maryland Higher Education Commission did play a role in some aspects of this policy reform effort but was evidently not a lead player overall (Perna & Finney, 2014). It appears that, during this crucial period, Kirwan largely played the kind of strategic and coordinating role originally envisioned by the early literature on SHEEOs. This seems to have come about by virtue not only of his personal authority and a vision that fit the times, but also with the help of the relatively strong structural position of the USM chancellor given his control over the large majority of the public 4-year campuses and the existence of longstanding funding linkages helping to bring the other sectors along. There are interesting similarities to what Ohio State President Gordon Gee did to enhance system coordination during the Kasich administration. Kirwan certainly had similar personal stature in Maryland and the benefits of a close relationship with the governor, especially O'Malley, but his effort took place over a much longer time period and from what appears to have been a stronger structural position as a system head. (Ohio has no comparable multicampus system to the University System of Maryland.)

The moral here is not that SHEEOs do not matter for finance outcomes in coordinating board states: The Strickland–Fingerhut period in Ohio suggests that a skilled SHEEO who is deeply trusted by a committed governor can have such an influence. But if the SHEEO does not fit the bill and since successful flagship (campus or system) presidents may be more likely to do so in some states and at particular times, then such a leader may at times serve in effect as the de facto statewide policy coordinator under a coordinating board setup.

At the same time, there are significant and notable risks to a flagship leader taking the helm of statewide leadership in absence of a strong SHEEO. As Callan (2011), Perna and Finney (2014), and McGuinness (2016), among others, have argued, the public interest in higher education is more than the sum of the interests of each of the institutions within a state. Indeed, the public interest does not always even align with institutional interests (Zumeta, 2007). Furthermore, there may be significant risks to the less prestigious and lower resourced community and technical colleges as well as to regional comprehensive institutions when major university leaders have outsized influence in statewide policymaking (Schneider & Deane, 2015). The interests of the university leaders, however well-intentioned and broadminded they are, may not align well with the values, missions, and needs of their less prestigious and prominent counterparts. In the absence of a postsecondary leader who can speak more broadly to the role and purpose of all of higher education within a state, important needs may remain unaddressed by the prevailing policy strategy and message. Ideally, it is this public interest role that SHEEOs and their agencies are designed to play.

CONCLUSION

This brief excursion into the recent history of state policy leadership in relation to finance and related issues in four states—two with governing boards and two with coordinating boards for higher education—suggests, in light of the more systematic but less textured quantitative empirical literature, that SHEEOs and the structures they work within can matter for outcomes. At the same time, the influence of SHEEOs may be tempered by a range of factors. We did not examine a state with truly weak coordination, except indirectly in learning about the prestructural reform conditions in Ohio and Maryland. In these cases, it appears that high levels of state support that might have been achieved in the past under such loose oversight simply did not seem to fit contemporary, straitened state budgetary circumstances.

In the period we studied, both Ohio and Maryland, the two coordinating board states, moved in the direction of tighter system coordination, but SHEEOs did not always play the most important role in this shift. In terms of finance, this direction seemed to be associated with both the moderation of drastic cuts during the recession and a renewed focus on efficiency and accountability, with carefully measured investments and broad ownership, as the fiscal picture improved. The efficiency and accountability emphasis does not necessarily mean low spending but rather disciplined spending. Thus, such moves seem likely to moderate spending going forward compared to a looser coordinating arrangement, with the additional potential to better connect higher education expenditures to state policy goals such as higher student completion rates and tighter links to workforce needs. In no small part, these changes have been at least influenced, if not driven, by an interest on the part of governors in policy goals of broader access and affordability. Also, to the extent that a solid partnership among key players—including, prominently, the SHEEO and the governor—can moderate higher education's notorious boom-and-bust cycles in state support and student tuition rates, which would seem a desirable result that could emerge if the recent reforms hold.

Yet, it is not clear that the apparent qualified successes forged in Ohio and Maryland over a period of some years can be sustained. In Ohio, Chancellor Fingerhut played an important role while Governor Strickland was in office. Yet, even with the enhanced powers of the SHEEO under Governor Kasich, the system evidently needed help from a unique figure in the state's higher education scene—former Ohio State University President Gordon Gee. Similarly, in the coordinating board state of Maryland, which has been blessed with strong educational leaders, the chancellor of the University System of Maryland has played a more prominent role in policy leadership in recent years than the SHEEO. In both these states during the period we examined, gubernatorial interest in higher education was also high. In sum, then, it is not clear that the coordinating structures alone in these two states can sustain successful finance and policy outcomes without similar conditions and leaders going forward. Moreover, in Maryland, the SHEEO has evidently for a long time played a secondary role relative to the USM chancellor in what might be thought of as systemic higher education coordination. There are notable concerns and risks to having a state's flagship university or system leader also serve as the de facto provider of higher education policy leadership on behalf of the state. For many states and periods, the SHEEO has played the important role of moderating the influence of those institutions with the most political capital and helping to ensure that the state's broader interests in higher education are articulated and protected.

Does having a statewide governing board provide more assurance of sustained successful outcomes? The two governing board states that we studied, Georgia and Wisconsin, both have longstanding, traditionally strong and respected statewide boards with expansive authority. Georgia's Board of Regents is appointed by the governor, and the board's chief executive (the SHEEO) is typically appointed by the board with strong but informal gubernatorial influence. This form was associated with the favorable treatment of higher education during the Zell Miller administration of the 1990s, when Stephen Portch was chancellor, and with the efforts at achieving efficiencies through campus consolidation and other measures of the last few years under the leadership of Chancellor Hank Huckaby. Huckaby's prior experience in the state legislature seems to have helped enable him to adeptly navigate the political challenges of consolidating campuses across the state—something prior chancellors had failed to do. Yet, substantial challenges remain in closing educational achievement gaps and addressing low college-going rates of low-income students and those of color.

Wisconsin's Board of Regents and SHEEO are structurally more insulated from gubernatorial and legislative priorities than is the case in Georgia, for better or worse. The "Wisconsin Idea" was born in an era where state political leadership was generally supportive of higher education and willing to grant it considerable autonomy. Investment in the state's higher education institutions was long a leading priority. There was much less urgency then around hardheaded strategic planning to "get the most for the least." Yet, the recent political leadership in the governor's seat and the legislature have been unprecedentedly critical of public higher education in Wisconsin and have pushed—though not without dissenting political voices—massive budget cuts and something of a privatization agenda. While the governor has made an effort to replace many of the university system's regents with his own political appointees, skepticism toward Walker's agenda has remained. The governor has maintained an ambitious higher education agenda, but unlike in Georgia, the regents and especially the chancellor (SHEEO) have not fully shared the governor's priorities.

Unfavorable economic conditions, coupled with a fiscally conservative governor skeptical about higher education, have contributed to a substantial decline in state support for the UW system over the last seven years. Yet, a SHEEO closely tied to the most recent gubernatorial administration, such as is the case in Georgia, would likely have fared even worse strictly in terms of state support. It is hard to tell what the future holds for higher education in Wisconsin given the direction of the state's policy leadership and its politics. The current SHEEO has had some recent success preserving the essential core of the system and laying the groundwork for a future time when a more integrated strategic policy approach to higher education may be possible. Yet, the SHEEO walks a delicate tightrope between managing the needs of the higher education system and navigating the politics of the state legislature, as well as pressure that is undoubtedly felt from regents appointed by the governor.

Finally, the importance of the relationship between the governor and the SHEEO is evident in all four case studies. As was the case in Georgia, a strong SHEEO who shares the goals of the governor can serve to amplify the higher education policy achievements of that administration. In addition, the gains made by higher education in Ohio under Governor Strickland's administration seem to be, at least in part, attributable to the start provided by the leadership of the governor and Chancellor Fingerhut, as well as their symbiotic relationship. The Kasich administration has built on this foundation but without utilizing the SHEEO to the same extent. In the absence of a strong SHEEO, a flagship university leader, as was the case with Gordon Gee in Ohio under Kasich and with William Kirwan in Maryland under two governors, may play this important role of bridging between the executive's office and higher education. Such an unbalanced arrangement may not be best for a state in the long run, however.

Finally, Wisconsin seems to serve as a reminder that SHEEOs and governors may not always share a similar agenda for higher education even if the governor has considerable influence over the SHEEO's appointment. It could be argued that even the limited insulation of the SHEEOs in recent years in Wisconsin has helped to moderate the impact of what some would call a destructive gubernatorial policy agenda.

Taken together, these case studies offer important insights into both the opportunities and challenges of the relationship between SHEEOs and governors. Clearly, this partnership is likely to be easier when the governor has an interest in investing strategically in higher education. Under these circumstances, a capable SHEEO trusted by the governor can play an important role in effectively guiding and channeling that momentum from the governor's office into productive public policies for higher education. Yet, when the governor's values and ambitions do not seem well aligned with the long-term interests of the state in higher education, a SHEEO with sufficient autonomy may only be able to moderate the potential damage to the system. Of course, if one feels that the governor more often knows best, then one might seek to reduce the structural insulation of the SHEEO from the influence of the state's highest elective office. We would argue, based on the findings of these case studies, that there are clearly risks in too close as well as too-distant relationships between SHEEOs and elected political leaders.

FUTURE RESEARCH

It seems to us that future research around state higher education governance and finance issues would benefit from a broader conceptualization of the key concerns in the present era. First, researchers should care about outcomes beyond just how much higher education receives from state budgets. The *stability* of funding over time is particularly important to consider given the problem of "higher education as balance wheel" in state budgeting. Closely related, particular attention should be paid to what happens to tuition and state financial aid support—that is, to affordability for students. Reasonable stability in these components is surely as important as what the totals are. Qualitative research might try to take an even broader look by seeking to focus on and better conceptualize sets of policy outcomes that are related to finance but hard to easily quantify for statistical studies (e.g., the quality of a state's higher education and its match to population needs, a better educated populace for its context, better workforce linkages).

On the explanatory variable side, our brief examination and the larger studies by scholars such as McGuinness (2016) and Perna and Finney (2014) illustrate the limitations of focusing strictly on SHEEOs or even their specific agencies. For better or worse, SHEEOs may or may not be critical players in effective state higher education policymaking at any specific point. As McGuinness (2016) argues, influence and expertise around higher education policy and its potential impacts are much more broadly distributed in the present day than when SHEEO agencies were created. Researchers should recognize this reality as they seek to understand what drives policy outcomes.

The policy coordination (or, perhaps more to the point, policy brokering and integration) role is crucial, even if this responsibility is not always most effectively carried out by the SHEEO. Indeed, as the case studies from Maryland and Ohio demonstrate, there may not need to be a single leader if there is broad enough ownership of the process of policymaking and state political leadership that is somewhat enlightened about higher education's broad potential and willing to sustain attention to it (Zumeta, 2007). Still, we think the SHEEO agency has a role to play in most circumstances, since it generally has the broadest perspective and greatest expertise. As is clear from the Wisconsin, Georgia, and Ohio cases, the role of governors and their relationships with SHEEOs warrant greater scrutiny in understanding more precisely how SHEEOs influence the policy and finance environment. There is an opportunity for SHEEOs to provide a stabilizing element among increasingly politically turbulent state legislatures and governorships, although this potential could be mitigated by the particularities of political appointment powers over SHEEOs and their boards. A better understanding of the dynamics of these interactions in different eras and contexts may be the most we can hope to achieve through research in this domain.

NOTES

1. Institutional advocates may, however, see the magnitude of state funding flows as a key performance indicator for the SHEEO, which creates a natural tension in the SHEEO role.

2. Other factors squeezing state governments have included the ongoing shift in the economy away from goods subject to sales taxes toward services that are much more lightly tapped by state tax systems. States have also been unable to fully respond to the impact of Internet sales that cut across state lines (Dadayan & Boyd, 2016).

3. The budgetary powers of the governor are based on, "a continuous scale from 0 to 7 and includes data from 1976 to 2004 across all 50 states. The items included are whether state agencies make requests directly to the governor or to the legislature; whether the executive budget document is the working copy for legislation or if the legislature can introduce budget bills of its own, or whether the legislature or the executive introduces another document later in the process; whether the governor can reorganize departments without legislative approval; whether revenue estimates are made by the governor, the legislature, or another agency, or if the process is shared; whether revenue revisions are made by the governor, the legislature, or another agency, or if the process is shared; whether the governor has the line item veto; and whether the legislature can override the line item veto by a simple majority. Each of these has a value of 0 to 1" (Tandberg, 2013, p. 519).

4. Note the different period covered as compared to Tandberg's earlier (2013) analysis, which also employed somewhat different measures of higher education spending. These differences make direct comparison of the results of these studies somewhat problematic.

5. In this study the authors utilize a "centralization index" created by Lacy (2011) rather than the usual dichotomous variable for the type of state governance board. In their preferred specification of the state-spending variable, the centralization index is significantly related to spending, but this is not the case for two alternative specifications of this dependent variable.

6. It seems most promising to consider both types of influence over SHEEOs simultaneously to decipher whether the precise arrangements matter or not and whether this depends on the nature of the SHEEO agency (governing or coordinating/planning board).

7. Such congruence seems to be the general pattern even if the appointment of President Cross in Wisconsin in 2014 does not fit it so well.

8. Fingerhut submitted his resignation upon Strickland's electoral defeat.

9. There are down sides to this role substitution, of course, about which we have more to say later.

10. One can actually trace the roots of both the technology-based economic development and performance-based budgeting emphases in Ohio back to the 1990s or earlier.

REFERENCES

Barrilleaux, C., & Berkman, M. (2003). Do governors matter? Budgeting rules and the politics of state policymaking. *Political Research Quarterly*, *56*(4), 409–417.

Berdahl, R. O. (1971). *Statewide coordination of higher education*. Washington, DC: American Council on Education.

Board of Regents of the University System of Georgia. (2016). *Overseeing the public colleges and universities that comprise the University System of Georgia.* Retrieved from www.usg.edu/regents/

Callan, P. M. (2011). Reframing access and opportunity: Public policy dimensions. In D. Heller (Ed.), *The states and public higher education policy,* 2nd ed. (pp. 87–105). Baltimore, MD: Johns Hopkins University Press.

College Board, The (2015). *Trends in college prices.* Princeton, NJ: Author.

Cornelius, T. (2015, November 19). *Wisconsin spending more on corrections, less on schools and universities.* Retrieved from www.wisconsinbudgetproject.org/wisconsin-spending-more-on-corrections-less-on-schools-and-universities

Cumming, D. (1998, Fall). Georgia's momentum: The magic of a popular lottery-funded college scholarship program. *National Crosstalk.* Retrieved from www.highereducation.org/crosstalk/ct1098/news1098-georgia.shtml

Dadayan, L., & Boyd, D. (2016). *Softening third-quarter growth in state taxes, weak forecasts for fiscal 2016 and 2017.* Rockefeller Institute. Albany, NY: SUNY.

Davies, L. (2014). *State 'shared responsibility'.* Washington, DC: HCM Strategists. Retrieved from hcmstrategists.com/wp-content/uploads/2014/04/HCM-State-Shared-Responsibility-RADD-2.0.pdf

Delaney, J., & Doyle, W. R. (2007). The role of higher education in state budgets. In D. E. Heller, & K. M. Shaw (Eds.), *State postsecondary education research: New methods to inform policy and practice* (pp. 55–76). Sterling, VA: Stylus.

Fairchild-Pierce, J. E. (2008). *A historical analysis of the leadership and strategic plan of Chancellor Stephen R. Portch in the University System of Georgia.* Atlanta: Georgia State University. Retrieved from scholarworks.gsu.edu/cgi/viewcontent.cgi?article=1050&context=eps_diss

Fincher, C. (2016, April 6). *University System of Georgia.* Retrieved from www.georgiaencyclopedia.org/articles/education/university-system-georgia

Fingerhut, E. (2008a, November). Restoring Ohio's heritage in higher education. *University Business.*

Fingerhut, E. (2008b). *Strategic plan for higher education, 2008–2017.* Columbus: Ohio Board of Regents.

Finney, J. E., Perna, L. W., & Callan, P. M. (2012). *Perpetuating disparity: Performance and policy in Georgia higher education.* Philadelphia, PA: Institute for Research on Higher Education.

Fischer, K. (2008, November 14). Ohio's public colleges lure businesses with the promise of a skilled workforce. *The Chronicle of Higher Education.* Retrieved from chronicle.com/article/Ohios-Public-Colleges-Lure/19207

Grasgreen, A. (2010, October 27). High stakes in Ohio. *Inside Higher Ed.* Retrieved from www.insidehighered.com/news/2010/10/27/ohio

Hayes, C. R. (2015, August). Rightsizing a system. *Business Officer Magazine.* Retrieved from www.nacubo.org/Business_Officer_Magazine/Magazine_Archives/July_August_2015/Progressive_Planning/Rightsizing_a_System.html

Hefty, T. (2014). *Wisconsin has a spending problem.* Retrieved from www.wpri.org/WPRI/Commentary/Wisconsin-Has-a-Spending-Problem.htm

Henry, G. T., & Bulger, D. T. (2004, November). Is HOPE enough? Impacts of receiving and losing merit-based financial aid. *Educational Policy, 18,* 686–709.

Herzog, K. (2013, December 27). Kevin Reilly ending chapter as UW System president. *Milwaukee Journal Sentinel.* Retrieved from www.jsonline.com/news/education/kevin-reilly-ending-chapter-as-uw-system-president-b99170536z1-237593351.html

Herzog, K. (2014, January 9). Ray Cross chosen as University of Wisconsin System president. *Milwaukee Journal Sentinel.* Retrieved from archive.jsonline .com/news/education/ray-cross-is-chosen-as-next-university-of-wisconsin-system-president-b99180472z1-239495111.html

Hovey, H. A. (1999). *State spending for higher education in the next decade: The battle to sustain current support.* San Jose, CA: National Center for Public Policy and Higher Education. Retrieved from www.higheredinfo.org/analyses /State_Spending_Hovey.pdf

Kiley, K. (2013, July 23). Personalities and policies. *Inside Higher Ed.* Retrieved from www.insidehighered.com/news/2013/07/23/ohio-state-president-steered-state-policy-two-years-thanks-relationship-governor

Kirwan, W. E. (2007). Top to bottom reengineering: University System of Maryland enhances productivity, improves accountability, and maintains quality. *New Directions for Higher Education, 140,* 41–49.

Kousser, T., & Philips, J. H. (2012). *The power of American governors: Winning on budgets and losing on policy.* New York: Cambridge University Press.

Lacy, T. A. (2011). Measuring state postsecondary governance: Developing a new continuum of centralization (Unpublished doctoral dissertation). University of Georgia, Athens, Georgia.

McGuinness, A. C. (2016). *State policy leadership for the future: History of state coordination and governance and alternatives for the future.* Denver, CO: Education Commission of the States.

McGuinness, A. C., & Fulton, M. (2007). *Postsecondary governance structures: State profiles.* Washington, DC: Education Commission of the States. Retrieved from www.ecs.org/postsecondary-governance-structures-state-profiles/

McLendon, M. K. (2003). State governance reform of higher education: Patterns, trends, and theories of the public policy process. In J. Smart (Ed.), *Higher education: Handbook of theory and research* (Vol. 18, pp. 57–143). London: Kluwer.

McLendon, M. K., Hearn, J. C., & Mokher, C. G. (2009). Partisans, professionals, and power: The role of political factors in higher education funding. *Journal of Higher Education, 80*(6), 686–713.

McLendon, M. K., Tandberg, D. A., & Hillman, N. W. (2014). Financing college opportunity: Factors influencing state spending on student financial aid and campus appropriations, 1990–2010. *The Annals of The American Academy of Political and Social Science, 655*(1), 143–162.

Meyers, S. L. (2016, May 13). *Marquette University economist weighs in on Walker's economic optimism.* Retrieved from www.wpr.org/marquette-university-economist-weighs-walkers-economic-optimism

Millsaps, J. (2010, October 7). *Erroll B. Davis Jr. announces plans to retire as university system head.* Retrieved from www.usg.edu/news/release/erroll_b._davis _jr._announces_plans_to_retire_as_university_system_head

Moore, S. (1998). *Proposition 13 then, now, and forever.* Washington, DC: The Cato Institute. Retrieved from www.cato.org/publications/commentary/proposition-13 -then-now-forever

National Association of State Student Grant Aid Programs. (2014). *45th Annual survey report on state-sponsored student financial aid.* Washington, DC: National Association of State Student Grant Aid Programs.

Okunade, A. A. (2004). What factors influence state appropriations for public higher education in the United States? *Journal of Education Finance, 30*(2), 123–138.

O'Leary, J. (2011, February 15). Do budget cuts drive efficiency? *Governing Magazine.* Retrieved from www.governing.com/blogs/bfc/Do-Budget-Cuts-Drive -Efficiency.html

Perna, L. W., & Finney, J. E. (2014). *The attainment agenda: State policy leadership in higher education.* Baltimore, MD: Johns Hopkins University Press.

Richardson, R. C., Bracco, K. R., Callan, P. M., & Finney, J. E. (1999). Designing state higher education systems for a new century. *American Council on Education/ Oryx Press series on higher education.* Phoenix, AZ: Oryx Press.

Rubenstein, R. (2003). Helping outstanding pupils educationally: Public policy issues of the Georgia HOPE scholarship program and the lottery for education. Syracuse, NY: Center for Policy Research.

Schmidt, P. (2016, March 2). Heading a university system with nervous professors [Video recording]. *The Chronicle of Higher Education.* Retrieved from chronicle.com/article/Video-Heading-a-University/235555

Schneider, M., & Deane, K. C. (2015). *The university next door: What is a comprehensive university, who does it educate, and can it survive?* New York: Teachers College Press.

State Higher Education Executive Officers. (2012). *SHEF: FY 2011.* Boulder, CO: Author.

State Higher Education Executive Officers. (2014). *SHEF: FY 2013.* Boulder, CO: Author.

State Higher Education Executive Officers. (2016). *SHEF: FY 2015.* Boulder, CO: Author.

State Higher Education Executive Officers. (2017). *SHEF: FY 2016.* Boulder, CO: Author.

Tandberg, D. A. (2010). Interest groups and state funding of public higher education. *Research in Higher Education, 51*(5), 416–450.

Tandberg, D. A. (2013). The conditioning role of state governance structures. *Journal of Higher Education, 84*(4), 506–543.

Tandberg, D. A., Fowles, J. T., & McLendon, M. K. (2017). The governor and the state higher education executive officer: How the relationship shapes state financial support for higher education. *Journal of Higher Education, 88*(1), 110–134.

Thomason, A. (2015, July 13). A brief history of Scott Walker's war over higher education. *The Chronicle of Higher Education.* Retrieved from chronicle.com /blogs/ticker/a-brief-history-of-scott-walkers-war-over-higher-education/101819

University of Wisconsin System. (2015). *2014-15 UW System fact book.* Madison: University of Wisconsin System. Retrieved from www.wisconsin.edu/download /publications(2)/Fact-Book.pdf

University of Wisconsin-Madison. (2016). *The Wisconsin Idea.* Retrieved from www.wisc.edu/wisconsin-idea/

University System of Georgia. (2016). *Chancellor*. Retrieved from www.usg.edu /chancellor/

Weerts, D. J., & Ronca, J. M. (2012). Understanding differences in state support for higher education across states, sectors, and institutions: A longitudinal study. *Journal of Higher Education, 83*(2), 155–185.

Zumeta, W. M. (1992). State policies and private higher education: Policies, correlates and linkages. *Journal of Higher Education, 63*(4), 363–417.

Zumeta, W. M. (1996). Meeting the demand for higher education without breaking the bank: A framework for the design of state higher education policies for an era of increasing demand. *Journal of Higher Education 67*(4), 367–425.

Zumeta, W. M. (2007). The new accountability: The potential of performance compacts in higher education. *National CrossTalk, 15*(1), 12–13.

Zumeta, W. M., & Kinne-Clawson, A. (2011). The recession is not over for higher education. *The NEA 2011 Almanac of Higher Education* (pp. 29–41). Washington, DC: National Education Association.

CHAPTER 6

The Role of the SHEEO and the Board in Changes in Higher Education Governance

Randall W. Hanna and Jason P. Guilbeau

The organization and coordination of the nation's thousands of public colleges and universities form a history of political power contending with public policy. At the state level, goals of individual states and their political and nonpolitical policymakers have been hotly debated. The solutions these actors offer often contend with academic deference and freedom at the campus level, along with college and university leaders' desires to advance their individual campuses. This political and policy environment has been nested within myriad local, regional, state, and national educational, economic, political, and social issues. As such, in making a presentation to a committee of the most recent State of Florida Constitutional Revision Commission (a unique committee empaneled every 20 years to review and propose amendments to the state's constitution), State University System Chancellor Marshall Criser (2017), quoting a financial analyst involved in higher education, said, "If you have seen one system of higher education, you have seen one."

As such, McGuinness and Fulton (2007) described higher education systems on a continuum from coordinating to governing agencies, with each of the 50 states having unique features tied to its history and politics. While some states have a strong centralized board, others have no single statewide board but instead several focused on different sectors of higher education (universities, colleges, and technical institutions). The duties of these organizations vary just as widely as do their structures: hiring and firing institutional leaders, settling disputes among postsecondary institutions, prioritizing capital projects for legislative funding, developing innovative strategies to achieve a public agenda, and approving the creation of new degree programs, to name but a few. Regardless of function or structure, these agencies are normally governed by a lay board with members who are often appointed by the governor (many times with legislative approval) or the legislature but in some instances (e.g., Nevada) are elected. Because boards meet infrequently (in most cases), they empower an agency executive to carry out the duties of the organization, manage the day-to-day activities of staff, and keep the board up to date. While the power to hire and dismiss these leaders typically rests with the board itself, in states such as Tennessee, the governor now retains this power with respect to the Tennessee Higher Education Commission. Thus, just as the boards vary, so too do the responsibilities and powers of SHEEOs.

Although beholden to their board's decisions, SHEEOs can be powerful actors because of the role of their position (e.g., they may sit on the governor's cabinet) or because of experience or personal characteristics (e.g., a former legislator may wield tremendous connections in the state capital). Ultimately, the SHEEO sits at the nexus of higher education policy and political leadership. But unlike the 50 commissioners of education, the role and influence of a state's SHEEO (or SHEEOs) vary tremendously across state lines.

In recent years, changes to these governance arrangements and the role of the SHEEO have arrived on policy agendas based on the actions (or lack thereof) of state higher education executive officers and governing boards. In some cases, SHEEOs and their boards find their positions in conflict with legislative leadership, who typically control the budget for higher education institutions. In other instances, these agencies find institutional leaders under their control clamoring for more independence or even protections by the SHEEO and the board. In still other cases, frustration with SHEEOs has been brought about by actions by the individuals themselves. These circumstances can lead to disagreements between SHEEOs and policymakers regarding the appropriate course of action to take, especially in the area of governance. Regardless of the circumstance, the SHEEO must be aware of the most current political and policy trends and stay in close contact with legislators, the governor, board members, and institutional leaders, in addition to other policy entrepreneurs who are constantly pushing for changes in the landscape of higher education. The SHEEO sits at the nexus of problem solver, policy developer, and implementer and must navigate these roles in a highly political environment.

In an effort to better understand how agencies, boards, SHEEOs, governors, legislatures, and others work together (or in some cases do not), this chapter analyzes changes in governance of state higher education organizations that have occurred in three states over the past 15 years. These changes in Florida, Tennessee, and Alabama were initiated primarily by the governor. In Florida, governance changes reflected concerns about past actions of the SHEEO and the governing board. All three states were chosen because of the significant power of the governor to implement changes in governance regardless of the position of the SHEEO or the board. Changes in Florida and Alabama also reflected the desires of the changes in political party control in both the legislatures and the executive branches. In both Florida and Tennessee, institutional leaders had expressed a desire for more flexibility from the statewide board. These changes substantively changed higher education governance in each state and subsequently the job description of the SHEEO.

While other chapters in this volume showcase the ability of the SHEEO to implement policy and influence change, this chapter instead details the political environment in which these individuals must exist and how contentions between problems, politics, and policy can lead to significant changes in higher education governance separate and apart from the active involvement of the SHEEO and the governing board. This chapter seeks to understand how fundamental policy changes proposed by elected officials can impact the role and power of the SHEEO and ultimately the state's public agenda. Furthermore, this chapter analyzes how the existing governance structures can be disrupted when governors and legislative leaders propose major changes and how SHEEOs and governing boards can anticipate or influence those decisions. Finally, we attempt to stress the importance of the governor and the legislative branch in policy decisions, especially those regarding governance—remembering that in most cases, the existing governance structure was approved by prior legislators and governors. While some argue that the purpose of SHEEOs and governing boards is to insulate academia from political decisions, we attempt to point out the reality of politics being a critical part of the decisionmaking process at the state level.

METHODS

States Selected for the Study

The three states selected exhibit the political environment the SHEEO and board members may find themselves embedded in and the development of policy changes when problems are perceived.

In Florida, two constitutional amendments, a historical election of a Republican governor, and significant legislative action led to the abolishment of a centralized board of regents governing state universities, establishment of local boards of trustees, and the subsequent establishment of a less powerful Board of Governors. These changes occurred after the failure of the SHEEO and the governing board to approve several initiatives supported by the universities and the legislature. Although the role of the SHEEO agency, statewide coordination, and institutional governance were fundamentally changed, the views of the SHEEO at the time and the board were clearly not reflected in the ultimate decisions.

The case of changes in Tennessee centered on both state political actors and at least two universities vying for greater flexibility. Statutory changes proposed by the governor led to powers of the state's coordinating board, the Tennessee Higher Education Commission (THEC), being increased while the power of the Tennessee Board of Regents (TBR) to govern the regional comprehensive universities was transferred to newly created local boards appointed by the governor. While some argue the change was made to allow the University of Memphis to have greater flexibility, the governor, in proposing the action, spoke to greater flexibility for all regional universities while allowing the TBR to be singularly focused on workforce development through the community colleges and colleges of applied technology. The governor's proposal was made shortly after the retirement of the long-standing and well-respected THEC executive director.

Finally, corruption and high turnover in the SHEEO suite and other factors led to the removal of the governing responsibility of the state's community college system from the elected Alabama Board of Education (which also governed K–12 education) and placed it in the hands of a new State Board of Community Colleges. Although the change was touted to provide more focus on the community colleges, it followed a change in the state's political leadership and a significant change in the political power of an advocacy group that had previously attacked one of the previous chancellors of the system in his campaign for governor. The SHEEO was absent from much of the discussion, as he found himself reporting to an existing board that strongly opposed the move.

Analytical Method

Semi-structured interviews were conducted with current and former SHEEOs, policy leaders, and political leaders in the states of Florida, Tennessee, and Alabama. Additionally, the researchers used archival data from public records as well as press coverage of events during the time of inquiry. The narratives offered by the interviewees were analyzed to develop or match to an existing theory to best understand how these major changes came about. Kingdon's multiple streams theory explained the perceived problems touted by lawmakers or the governor, the solutions offered (namely by the governor, legislators, or other parties), and the ultimate policy implications for the state higher education environment (namely a fundamental change to higher education governance and additional power gained by the governor).

Kingdon's Streams

Nearly every state has developed a higher education coordinating or governance systembased on its unique history and politics. Much of this development began in the mid-20th century and states continue to change today. In the three cases detailed here, the achieved shifts in governance upheld the "Agendas, Alternatives, and Public Policies" notions of Kingdon (2011), who found public policy decisions could be analyzed through three different streams: the problem stream, the political stream, and the policy stream. In the problem stream, issues (or perceived issues) rise to greater attention, often triggered by a situation or actor. The political stream considers the ideology of actors in the arena. And the policy stream are the solutions that may address the problem.

Kingdon (2011) argued that when these three streams meet or converge, public policy changes can be made in what he called a *policy window*. Kingdon also noted that these three streams flow independently of each other and not necessarily in a set order, as will be evidenced in the case studies presented here. As such, a policy may search for a problem, or politics may lead to development of a policy where a problem does not exist. Within the three states, perceived and touted problems led to the formulation of an agenda through gaining political support and ultimately formulation of a policy change. However, whether the problem truly proceeded the policy was debated in two of the three cases, and all three cases are informed by politics.

As such—and in line with Kingdon (2011)—regardless of the structure, SHEEOs and board members must be astute not only in public policy matters (i.e., achieving the public agenda of higher education) but also in political matters. Tandberg and Fowles summarize in Chapter 10 of this volume the political and policy nature of Kingdon's theory and apply it to the position of the SHEEO:

> [SHEEOs not only] must work with colleges and university leaders but also be effective governmental and political actors. SHEEOs and their staffs work with governors and their staffs, legislators and their staffs, and other agency heads and their staffs. SHEEOs potentially may be involved with every aspect of the policy process with respect to higher education. While the roles vary from state to state based on laws, regulations, norms, and traditions, SHEEOs may propose new policies (legislation, rules, regulations, procedures, guidelines, etc.), play a role in advancing proposed policies, implement policies, and evaluate and revise policies. Understanding how government and the policy development process work may help SHEEOs carry out these tasks more effectively and efficiently

The following sections outline these issues, employing Kingdon's streams. In addition, the concept of direct democracy could potentially be attributed to Mazzoni's (1991) first area model. In the discussion of the constitutional amendment in Florida, we utilize previous research to analyze these actions under this theory.

FLORIDA: ONE SHEEO JOB ABOLISHED AND ANOTHER SIGNIFICANTLY CHANGED[1]

Confronting a growing population and expanded higher education enrollments, the Florida legislature established a centralized Board of Regents (BOR) effective as of 1965 with direct power to govern and lead higher education in the state through the State University System (SUS). While Florida State University and the University of Florida remained the two "preeminent" universities—a designation subsequently recognized by the legislature—other institutions grew at a rapid pace and played a critical role in the development of postsecondary education. As of 2016, there were 12 state universities serving more than 339,000 students, 28 colleges serving approximately 800,000 students (State University System of Florida, 2017), and 29 private nonprofit universities serving 130,000 students (Independent Colleges and Universities of Florida, 2017). In addition, there were more than 1,000 proprietary institutions in the state ranging from small cosmetology schools to large universities such as the University of Phoenix.

Context: Higher Education Governance

Due to its management and coordination of this growth during the latter half of the 20th century, by 2001 the BOR had become a powerful body. Board members were politically savvy and well-connected business leaders in the state who subsequently appointed competent leaders as the agency's chancellor. At the time, Florida had a bifurcated system with a chancellor of the SUS, an executive director of the state community college system, and the director of the state's Postsecondary Education Planning Commission (PEPC), the state's higher education policy and planning agency. Each of these officials was considered a SHEEO. The community colleges had individual boards of trustees, but all of the universities reported to the statewide BOR.

The longest serving chancellor of the SUS and generally recognized as the most powerful was Charlie Reed. Reed had previously served as an education advisor and then Chief of Staff to Florida's popular Democratic Governor Bob Graham. Although appointed chancellor during Graham's tenure in 1985, Reed continued to serve under governing boards appointed by both a Republican governor (Martinez) and a Democratic governor (Chiles) through 1998. Reed ran the Florida system with strong support of his board and Graham. While few students knew his name, policymakers in Florida and higher education leaders across the country equated Florida's system with Charlie Reed.

Reed's successor, Adam Herbert, a former president of the University of North Florida, took office with strong support from the BOR and university and state officials. However, just as Herbert took office, a decade of changes to Florida's higher education governance structure was beginning. The following sections provide an overview of how political and policy streams along with a successful effort of direct democracy continued to shift the postsecondary governance from a strong centralized governing board in the BOR to decentralized institutional governing boards combined with a statewide board.

Policy Stream: Shifting to a Red State

In 1998, Florida elected Jeb Bush, only its third Republican governor since Reconstruction. While Bush had lost in a close election in 1994 to incumbent Democratic Governor Lawton Chiles, the changing demographics of the state and his popularity led to his election and subsequent reelection in 2002. Fortunately for his conservative agenda, Bush was elected only 2 years after the beginning of what has been a long period of Republican control of both chambers of the Florida legislature. In 2000, both houses of the legislature were, for the first time since Reconstruction, controlled by the Republican Party. The Speaker of the Florida House of Representatives for the 1999–2000 term was John Thrasher, a graduate and strong supporter of Florida State University. In our interview with the former governor, Bush expressed his belief (which would be the mantra of the state's new Republican government) that the best decisions were made from the bottom up and not as a directive from state government: "In any policy area, you ought to have high expectations with clear accountability that's transparent and measurable, and that's a useful state function. And we shouldn't be telling people how to go about achieving whatever those objectives are."

Newly installed Chancellor Herbert was faced with a governor who wanted more entrepreneurial actions by Florida's universities and who disliked the top-down approach to higher education governance of the BOR and PEPC. Bush also wanted greater coordination among all sectors of the K–20 education system. While the BOR had the power to hire and fire university presidents, adopt rules, and approve new programs, budget authority remained in the hands of the Florida legislature. The rapid growth of the universities, the relationships between the individual institutions and members of the legislature, and the desire of the institutions to expand programs, especially in the professional graduate areas, ultimately led to tension between the BOR and the institutions.

Political Stream: Program Expansions

Early in Herbert's term, significant tensions arose as four schools sought to expand professional programs. To advance their efforts to gain a law school, Florida A&M corralled the predominately African-American Democratic legislative delegation, while Florida International University did the same with the predominately Hispanic Republican caucus. At the same time, Florida State University and University of Central Florida were both vying to create separate medical schools. The BOR and Herbert opposed the expansion of both the law and medical schools, citing the lack of need for more lawyers and duplication with the two existing public medical schools at the University of Florida and the University of South Florida and the publicly supported medical school at the University of Miami.

Although Herbert had significant political clout as he was a Republican, a strong supporter of Bush, and the leader of his gubernatorial transition team when Bush was first elected, he found himself in the crosshairs of a heavily lobbied legislature. While the legislature was strongly in support of the medical and law schools, Bush—in line with the BOR and Herbert—was initially concerned about the new medical schools. However, in the end, the governor ultimately supported creation of the medical and law schools. Acknowledging both the policy and political impacts in our interview, Bush remarked:

> You can make a compelling point, which I get, that medical schools are expensive, but . . . I was confident that you're [going to] provide access to people that otherwise wouldn't become a doctor, or even with the law [schools]. . . . You know I didn't embrace this to begin with. I spent a lot of time, so to speak, getting lobbied by both sides. I took the time to try to fully understand it before I took a position, and frankly, as you know so well, there's a lot of this. . . . I did this out of loyalty to the guy who was probably more loyal to me in the legislative process than anybody else, so it wasn't just good policy. It was also a recognition that John Thrasher made my initial start as governor successful. He and [Senate President] Toni Jennings both, but for them, I would have not gotten off to the start [as governor] that I got off to.

While Bush cited the need for more minority doctors, his decision was also in part because of the strong support of then House Speaker and now Florida State University President John Thrasher as well as the Senate President who represented the city of Orlando, home of the University of Central Florida. The legislature ultimately approved the four professional schools, and in later years a medical school was established at Florida Atlantic University.

Political Stream: A More Conservative Government and the Bush-Thrasher Dinner

While universities were advocating for law and medical schools, a wave of change was coming from both the governor's office and the legislature. Bush envisioned a different type of government, one that was more diverse and conservative:

> I don't want to overstate it, but the Blue Key,[2] center-left, White male politician that . . . had been running the state for the last 50 years. I felt it was time to change that and reflect the new Florida, and the new Florida, in my mind, I was very comfortable with looking different. More women, more African Americans, more Hispanics, and certainly, more conservatives.

Bush, a strong proponent of enhancing education standards (especially at the K–12 level), envisioned a system of better cooperation between the K–12, community college, and university systems. In our interview, he remarked:

> My belief was that there was too much top down telling people what line to get into, but not enough entrepreneurial activity. . . . The Board of Regents was highly centralized and I just heard over and over again the frustration that university presidents had and people in the community that their universities really weren't theirs, and that might have been partially the result of a strong head of the Board of Regents that existed prior to my arrival.

Bush was referring to the consolidated power held by the BOR and especially that of widely respected and long-serving Chancellor Reed. The contention between the campuses, the legislature, and the BOR was an example of Bush's idea of local innovation being stymied by a centralized bureaucracy.

While the decentralization of university governance was ultimately implemented through legislative actions in two sessions and through two task forces, significant attention was given in the press to the fact that the overall structure for education was drawn by Bush and Thrasher on a napkin after dinner approximately a year and a half before the passage of the final legislation (Trombley, 2001). Bush, in our interview, acknowledged mapping out the plan on a napkin after dinner at a restaurant in Orlando and specifically noted those initial plans show the interaction between policy and politics:

> What I remember . . . was that I pulled out a napkin with a Sharpie and gave it to [Thrasher] after I did my little diagram. Had a little food stain on it. . . . Effectively, it was to shift power to the universities and have them be held to account directly, and that's kind of where we ended up.

The plan, which was ultimately implemented through legislation, was to abolish the BOR and PEPC and create local governing boards for each university as well as a K–20 planning agency.

Higher education leaders were skeptical of the proposed changes. In our interview with Tom Healy (a longtime colleague of Herbert's and vice chancellor for government affairs during his entire term as chancellor), he shared the concern that removing the power to hire and fire presidents from the BOR and transferring that power to local boards would lead to institutions becoming less accountable. Herbert also said that it would ultimately lead to less coordinating and evolve into a "turf war" (Oppel, 2000).

Not only would the governance of higher education be fundamentally restructured, so too would the state's planning, policy, and data agency,

PEPC. Bush, in our interview, acknowledged the benefit of having PEPC but thought it was inconsistent with his views of higher education governance. Bush specifically acknowledged the good work that had been done by PEPC but felt the functions should be part of the state university system.

> [PEPC] seemed to me to be disconnected from the governance of higher education, which was top down. . . . It didn't make sense to me. . . . I thought that the intellectual capital there was potentially important. It was useful. You know a data-driven policy needs data to be analyzed, and I had . . . a series of meetings to discuss policy with members of PEPC, and . . . I found it all useful. . . . I just think in terms of governance, having this thing be separate and apart from the university system didn't make any sense to me.

While many see the actions by Bush and the legislature to abolish the BOR as actions taken because of its failure to support the new professional schools, others, because of past opposition to the BOR, saw it as a case where they "took an opportunity in Florida's political environment to solve what appeared to be a problematic structure" (Borman & Dorn, 2007, p. 8).

Direct Democracy: The Graham Amendment

While there was strong support for the new governance system in the legislature and ultimately from the presidents of the universities, opposition from former governor and then U.S. Senator Bob Graham and his supporters formed almost immediately. Graham was familiar with legislative dissatisfaction with the BOR. In the early 1980s, Graham vetoed a bill approved by a democratically controlled legislature that would have abolished the Board of Regents and merged four separate universities into two. In his veto message, Graham wrote that a strong university system should have, in part, "an independent board serving as an intermediary between the academic community and political institutions" (Johnson & Borman, 2007, p. 192).

In an effort to retain the strong governing board structure, Graham enlisted the support of a loyal group of former political appointees and senior members of his administration, including his former Chancellor Charlie Reed, who was now serving as a SHEEO in California as the chancellor of the California State University System. Graham remained popular in the state, which helped counter the opposition from Bush supporters as well as from Bush's appointees to the new boards of trustees. Rather than go through the legislative process (an effort that would have been fruitless in the Republican-controlled houses), Graham elected to go directly to the voters to re-establish a statewide governing board for the state universities. Through initial polling, Graham and his team realized that the local boards of trustees were popular with voters so they decided to propose a Board of Governors (BOG), which would work with the local boards of trustees (Rayfield, 2004).

The effort collected enough signatures to be placed on the statewide ballot. Although the amendment passed by with 60% of the vote and the effort raised more money than that of opponents to the measure, there was minimal statewide interest in the issue. Bush and his supporters were focused on his reelection campaign, and several other constitutional amendments were of higher interest. Most credited Graham's popularity for the success of the initiative.

Summary

After the significant legislative and constitutional changes led by two of the most popular governors in Florida history, those two governors appear to believe the current system works well. However, their philosophical and political differences are apparent when they talk about the role of the BOG.

Bush, in our interview, acknowledged that he wished some of the local trustees would have taken their accountability role more seriously and today recognizes the importance of the BOG combined with the local boards of trustees:

> The principle mission was for [trustees] to really hold the administrations to account and to support the universities in a businesslike way, not just being cheerleaders. And to be honest with you . . . you know I don't know if they achieved that. . . . I'm not sure that they took the accountability. I think [some boards] got into being supportive of the university without saying, "Hey, we've got to have outcomes that we want to measure."

Bush also reflected on the Board of Governors created by the Graham Amendment and appears to believe the right balance has been found:

> Yeah. I think [the members of the Board of Governors] are less hands on in the day-to-day activities of the universities and more policy focused. At least talking to members of the Board of Governors . . . I think they found the proper balance. . . . The Board of Governors does have, now, constitutional powers that superseded whatever the Board of Regents had. . . . If [the Board of Governors] wanted to exert that power and test it, you could have a lot of friction and chaos. But . . . they've . . . managed to find the proper positioning.

In our interview, Graham agreed with Bush that the current system works well, noting that the university system had grown significantly since the Board of Control (the predecessor to the Board of Regents) was founded in 1905. Graham noted that the old system was primarily a unitary decision with all actions, no matter how small, having to go through the BOR. However, while stating that there is a need for local boards to work with local issues and a state board to deal with state issues, Graham believes the BOG could go further to reduce the impact of politics in higher education:

> I think the [Graham Amendment] put a suture on what would have been a hemorrhage of decisions based on politics rather than sound academic policy. There are areas where the amendment has not been fully implemented which would further the positives it could accomplish. It would take a governor and possible a cooperative legislature who are prepared to push politics off the stage of higher education policymaking in Florida.

The reasons for the demise of the BOR to individual boards and a state-wide board overseeing K–20 education fit nicely into at least two streams of Kingdon's theory. From a policy standpoint, Bush wanted a more bottom-up approach, which he believed would lead to more innovation. Politically, the heavily lobbied legislature (in a newly "red" state) was upset with the BOR for its failure to approve the new medical and law schools. However, frustration with the BOR was not a new to the state, with a legislature having passed similar legislation in the early 1980s. While the changes were vetoed by Graham, the streams aligned for Bush in his first term to allow for the fundamental change to higher education governance.

The enactment of the constitutional amendment by acquiring the requisite number of signatures and having adequate votes to overturn a legislative action could be attributed to Mazzoni's (1991) first arena model, whereby policy changes were made in response to changes required by the general public. This process represents a shift from representative democracy to direct democracy. Rayfield (2004) revised Mazzoni's model and found a number of other factors led to the enactment of the Graham amendment, including the timing of the amendment in conjunction with the governor's reelection campaign and the political climate of the state. In both cases the popularity of the primary supporter of the change was a significant factor in the adoption of the legislation (Bush) and the enactment of the constitutional amendment establishing the Board of Governors (Graham).

Implications for the SHEEO

It is impossible to determine whether a different approach to the events outlined here would have made a difference in the ultimate role of the SHEEO and the demise of the BOR and PEPC. Still, it is important to realize that in a short period the responsibilities of two SHEEOs in the state were significantly changed because of a combination of political and policy issues.

The authors of this chapter have discussed on numerous occasions how Chancellor Reed would have responded to the "perfect storm" of events that led to the creation of individual boards and the demise of the BOR.[3] Some have surmised that Reed had greater political instincts than Herbert, who was a traditional academician. Some think Reed would have found a way to meet the desires of the institutions and the legislature to create the professional schools as well as achieve Bush's goal of decentralization, which would have dampened the anger of the legislature. We are less certain that Reed would have been willing to work in any decentralized system, so it is unclear whether he would have worked with Bush and Thrasher to find a solution that met their needs. Graham, in our interview, said Reed would have made sure that all possible alternatives to meet the goals of the legislature in regard to the professional schools had been fully presented to the decisionmakers.

Herbert found himself in a tough position before he even took office. While he had significant experience as a university president and a lobbyist for his university and had close relations with Bush, he was seemingly unable to influence the final decision in one of the most challenging confluences of political and policy issues in American public higher education at the time. It is unclear whether the actions by Herbert and the BOR led to the abolishment of the BOR or whether this was just another in a long line of legislative frustrations with the BOR that led to the ultimate changes. Herbert was politically aligned with the governor, but had strong beliefs about the ultimate policy decisions. In addition, he found himself and his board in the crosshairs of a legislature that was upset about the lack of support for the new professional schools. Shortly after the adoption of the legislation abolishing the BOR, Herbert, the first and thus far only African-American chancellor of the SUS, resigned and returned to the University of North Florida. Herbert ultimately became the president of Indiana University.

In our interview, Healy (Herbert's close colleague and then vice chancellor) argued that Herbert understood the political ramifications of his decisions. He also said that decisions Herbert and the BOR made regarding the expansion of new programs were data-based, not political. Healy stressed that Herbert understood the need for more doctors in the state but felt the three existing state-supported programs should have been expanded as opposed to creating new more expensive programs.

The cost of underestimating the impact of the political process and the strong influence of institutional leaders had a significant impact on governance of Florida state universities, which is still being felt today. For a period of time, the newly created BOG failed to exercise significant authority. In 2013, the BOG (although it eventually withdrew) and backers of Graham sued the Florida legislature to determine who had authority to set tuition for the universities. The court decided in favor of the legislature, which historically retained this power (Graham, 2013). In recent years the BOG and its chancellor have exercised more of its constitutional authority, including working with the legislature on the implementation of a performance funding system and with Governor Rick Scott for no tuition increases. The BOG has also adopted uniform rules regarding the selection process for institutional presidents, placed BOG members on local presidential selection committees, and on one occasion, weighed in on specific presidential compensation. While local boards of trustees continue to hire and fire presidents, hiring and renewal decisions must be approved by the BOG.

Since the enactment of the Graham Amendment, Florida has had four permanent chancellors of the State University System appointed by the BOG, including Bush's former Lieutenant Governor Frank Brogan. Moving from a strong governing system with a strong chancellor to one that works with both a board of governors and 12 individual boards of trustees has significantly changed the role of the SUS chancellor. Today, while the BOG has significant constitutional powers, the Florida chancellor spends a lot of time building consensus, including within and between individual institutions and members of the legislature. Presidents in the system will attest that Bush's desire to have more decisions made at the institutional level has been accomplished; however, the BOG is beginning to exercise more of its constitutional authority.

TENNESSEE: INNOVATION AND POLITICS

Tennessee is a state that has been recognized for taking innovative steps in higher education reform. The first sustainable performance-based funding system in the United States started in Tennessee under the leadership of the Tennessee Higher Education Commission. The state's Colleges of Applied Technology (a system of technical institutes that provide workforce training and certificates) was one of the first adopters in the nation of block scheduling. And all of the institutions in the Tennessee Board of Regents (TBR) were early adopters of methods to improve completion rates through the adoption of the Complete College Tennessee Act. Most recently, under the leadership of Republican Governor Bill Haslam, the state adopted the first free community college program in the nation, Tennessee Promise.

Like Florida, Tennessee has several different systems of higher education, with approximately 43,000 students enrolled the University of Tennessee system, 87,000 in regional universities, 86,000 in community colleges, 20,000 in colleges of applied technology, 81,000 in not-for-profit colleges and universities, and 13,000 in proprietary schools (Tennessee Higher Education Commission, 2017).

Context: Higher Education Governance

Public higher education governance in the state had remained fairly stable with three separate boards governing two systems of higher education. First, the University of Tennessee system (UT System) has been the governing board for the University of Tennessee Knoxville, Chattanooga, Martin, Health Science Center, and Institute of Agriculture. As a land grant institution, the University of Tennessee is located in every county in the state and has significant political support.

Secondly, the Tennessee Board of Regents (TBR) originally governed a system of 46 institutions of higher education, comprising six comprehensive universities (including the University of Memphis, a Carnegie-classified research/doctoral university), 13 community colleges, and 27 colleges of applied technology. Like the UT System, the TBR board also appoints a leader, the chancellor of the TBR. The chancellor and the TBR appointed all of the presidents of the regional universities and the community colleges and the directors of the applied institutions. John Morgan, a deputy to former Governor Phil Bredesen, was appointed chancellor of the TBR in 2010. While he had primarily served in Democratic administrations, he was well received by Haslam and his appointees to the TBR, including receiving positive reviews from board members. He was especially recognized across the state and the country for his work on college completion initiatives, including serving as a board member of Complete College America.

Finally, the Tennessee Higher Education Commission (THEC) has served as the statewide coordinating board and has been given significant credit for working with the two other boards as well as campuses to implement performance funding and the Complete College Tennessee Act. While the executive director of THEC has traditionally been appointed by the board, legislation was adopted in 2012 to allow the governor to appoint and remove the director. In November 2014, long-serving THEC Executive Director Rich Rhoda retired, and Haslam appointed Russ Deaton, a long-time executive at THEC, as the interim executive director.

For purposes of this chapter, the president of the UT System, the chancellor of TBR, and the executive director of THEC would all be considered SHEEOs. Because the three SHEEOs and their three boards had traditionally worked well together, allowing the state to be at the forefront of higher education changes, many in the state were surprised when Haslam announced proposed legislation to reorganize the state's postsecondary governance system. The following sections will provide an overview of the perceived problems of the existing system, the reorganization proposal by Haslam, and the politics of a powerful governor coupled with a legislature that had traditionally been supportive of postsecondary policies proposed by the executive branch.

Policy Stream: The FOCUS Act

In the fall of 2015, Haslam proposed new legislation, the Focus on College and University Success Act (FOCUS Act). The legislation sought to create a new governance structure by removing universities from the control of the TBR and creating individual boards of trustees at the state's six universities: Austin Peay State University, East Tennessee State University, Middle Tennessee State University, Tennessee Technological University, and the University of Memphis. This change would ultimately reduce the number of students and perhaps influence and power of the TBR and its chancellor.

At the same time, Haslam proposed increasing the powers of the THEC and its executive director. Our interviews showed that Haslam had been working on a reorganization plan at least for several months before announcing his plans. In fact, state officials interviewed indicated that Haslam met with Morgan and Vice Chair Emily Reynolds roughly 2 months prior to the public announcement to discuss his ideas. In announcing the initiative, Haslam created a transition task force composed of a steering committee for high-level implementation guidance and a working group for technical assistance.

Problem Stream: Achieving the Drive to 55

In speaking before the TBR shortly after announcing the proposed legislation to be considered by the 2016 General Assembly, Haslam made it clear that his support for the change was not because of his unhappiness with the direction of the TBR or its chancellor, John Morgan. Haslam told the board that his support for the change was due in part to its tremendous success and its emphasis on Drive to 55, a statewide completion initiative adopted in 2013 to encourage 55% of Tennessee's adult population to earn a postsecondary certificate or degree. The effort was touted as two parts: to allow for greater coordination of the state's community and technical colleges through the TBR while granting universities autonomy at the local level. In our interview with Mike Krause, an aide to Haslam, the purpose of the FOCUS Act was developed in consideration of institutional missions. Krause highlighted the BOR had been charged with managing "everything from technical colleges that offer short-term 4-month certificates to Research 1, medical school, law school, university activities." He continued:

> The reality is our community colleges really had to adopt a much more systematic approach, and that's hard to do when you have 200,000 students. And, that is exactly the posture the former Board of Regents structure was . . . [a] more critical focus on community and technical college success, while also recognizing that the six universities—while they had a lot in common, probably, in 1972 when the Board of Regents was formed—have less and less in common now.

For the state's community and technical colleges, enrollments would soon be exploding as the new Tennessee Promise granted free community college and free classes. For the universities, Haslam (2015) stressed these potential enrollment shifts was reason to give them more flexibility and agility, noting that it is hard to "compete with free."

Political Stream: Limited Opposition to Change and the General Assembly

Opposition to the FOCUS Act immediately arose from two separate areas. Morgan expressed his opposition to the proposal and resigned as chancellor with relatively short notice in order to actively work against it. While members of the TBR personally discussed issues and some concerns regarding the FOCUS Act with Haslam and members of his staff, publicly the board members stressed the importance of implementing the governor's vision regarding degree completion and the Drive to 55 initiative and the importance of the community colleges and the applied technical colleges in achieving those goals. This left Morgan as one of the few public higher education officials willing to oppose the governor. Unlike Herbert who opposed Bush's reorganization plan in Florida while remaining as chancellor (although with the support of the BOR), Morgan clearly felt that he could not publicly oppose the governor's position while remaining as chancellor. In an interview, one TBR board member noted that once the legislation was filed and the proposal gained momentum, the board began to focus on implementation issues in order to ensure a smooth transition.

Morgan, who originally planned to resign in January 2017, left a year early and stated in his resignation letter:

> Throughout my long career in public service, I have observed that ambiguity is the ally of ineffectiveness and inefficiency. Intentionally, clear accountability was designed as the heart of the Complete College Tennessee Act of 2010, with responsibility and authority co-located. As outlined, the FOCUS proposal will not lead us closer to the State's goals. Instead, it disperses authority and responsibility so that the institutions, the System or THEC can always implicate one or the other if goals are not achieved. (Morgan, 2016, para. 5)

TBR immediately appointed David Gregory, a long-time state employee, aide to former Democratic Governor Ned Ray McWherter, and the lobbyist for the system, as the interim chancellor.

The other opposition to the FOCUS Act came from supporters of the historically Black institution Tennessee State University, who expressed concern that the university would not have the same protections and support for its mission as under the TBR. At one hearing, approximately 200 supporters of TSU went to the state capitol to oppose the legislation. The argument was that TSU would have to compete with more politically connected institutions in the TBR and the UT System for funding and capital projects (Stockard, 2016). TSU President Glenda Glover said, "There's no way that could be considered fair by any shape, form or fashion to have an academic monopoly on one hand [with the UT system which would remain consolidated under one board] and on the other hand you have six institutions to compete with that political power" (Tamburin, 2015, para. 13). Bill Freeman, a successful Nashville businessman and a member of the TSU Foundation board, echoed Glover's comments:

> I smell an unfair advantage. . . . I'm all for climbing the ladder to success. Increasing enrollment, endowments and high-caliber alumni are smart goals for colleges and universities. But kicking people in the teeth to get them down the ladder isn't the same as climbing up that ladder. (Freeman, 2016)

However, outside of Morgan and TSU advocates, there was little opposition. The other five presidents of the universities remained neutral or actively supported the legislation, and the president of the UT System stood with Haslam as he announced the FOCUS Act. The legislation rapidly moved through the General Assembly with almost unanimous support.

Some credit the tremendous support from the General Assembly for the FOCUS Act to the historical deference the legislative branch has given to the governor in higher education areas. However, both Rhoda and Krause noted in our interviews that the General Assembly was actively involved in reviewing the FOCUS Act and continues to become even more involved in higher education matters. This increased interest may have been evident in the 2018 legislative session where House Bill 1198 returned the power to appoint and remove the THEC executive director from the governor back to the commission itself.

Political Stream: The University of Memphis

Another factor also played a major role in the adoption of the legislation. The University of Memphis had long pushed for a local board of trustees to govern the large institution of more than 20,000 students. Officials from the University of Memphis had lobbied former Governors Sundquist and Bredesen in addition to Haslam (Corbert, 2016).

On the day Haslam announced the FOCUS Act, University of Memphis President M. David Rudd said, "The U of M is unique among public institutions across the state, and this change would enable us to better serve our students and our community, and compete more effectively on the national stage. We are excited about what independent governance means for the future of our university and city" (Tamburin, 2016, para. 16). While supporters of other regional universities had not previously publicly endorsed the idea of local boards of trustees, our interviews show that at least one of the other five university presidents had been privately supportive of the idea.

Krause, in our interview, specifically addressed the issue of whether the change was made to appease supporters of the University of Memphis:

This [was] a longstanding request from the University of Memphis that I think reflected their shift to a research-intensive university, centered within a major metropolitan area. And, University of Memphis' advocacy for our local board was certainly important for the legislation being passed, but it was not the predicate for the policy.

The lobbying efforts from Memphis were no secret, as Senate Majority Leader Mark Norris commented during Haslam's press conference: "I know that they're dancing in the streets at home at the University of Memphis thinking about what may come to pass with this level of autonomy" (Tamburin, 2016, para. 9). Regardless of whether the desires of supporters of the University of Memphis were a primary factor in the proposal by Haslam, a desire for greater independence from at least two universities in the TBR were clearly factors in the ultimate support from the General Assembly.

With Morgan's departure from the chancellor's position, interim leaders were in charge at THEC and TBR. Members of the General Assembly did not hear opposition from many within Tennessee government and primarily heard support from their local university leaders.

Political Stream: Haslam and His Staff

Working behind the scenes and with legislators, Haslam aide Krause and other members of the governor's staff played a major role in the adoption of the legislation. Krause—an Army veteran, Austin Peay graduate, and former employee of THEC—had significant respect among legislators. With interim leaders at the helm at THEC and TBR, many of the policy decisions regarding higher education reorganization were coming directly from the governor's office. However, even if there had been permanent leaders in the two SHEEO positions, the ability to oppose the governor may have been limited. Shortly after the passage of the FOCUS Act, Haslam named Krause as the new executive director of THEC with the responsibility of implementing the new enhanced duties. THEC's expanded duties included setting tuition and fee policies for all state public institutions, determining capital investment needs and priorities, and orienting and convening leaders of institutions, boards, and systems as necessary to coordinate the state's attainment goal (Tennessee Board of Regents, 2016).

Summary

Unlike Florida, there did not seem to be a conflict between the executive and legislative branches and the state higher education organizations. It does appear that there was some dissatisfaction with the current organizational structure from at least two of the universities. While some solely credit the strong support from the supporters of the University of Memphis for the change, Krause strongly denied that influence in our interview. He did, however, acknowledge the importance of that support in the enactment of the legislation. At the end of the legislative process and the appointment of the new trustees, even the president of TSU softened her opposition to the FOCUS Act. She worked with Haslam and his staff to make sure that TSU would not be at a competitive disadvantage to the UT system and the other five institutions previously under control of the TBR.

Like Bush in Florida who implemented a similar change, Haslam used task forces to further develop the FOCUS Act during the legislative process and to implement the legislation when adopted. At the heart of adoption of the FOCUS Act was Haslam's power and support in the General Assembly. Haslam also dealt with opposition to the legislation by increasing the power of THEC and its SHEEO to provide a level playing field. Regardless of its primary impetus, the adoption of the FOCUS Act clearly encompassed the policy and political streams of Kingdon's theories with a touted problem of achieving the Drive to 55. Within the six months from announcement to adoption, the powers of the TBR had been dramatically modified, one SHEEO had resigned (from TBR), and the powers of another SHEEO (of THEC) had been enhanced.

Implications for the SHEEOs

Like Florida, this analysis of the changes in governance in Tennessee show the significant impact a popular governor with strong legislative support can have on higher education matters and the importance of SHEEOs being aligned with the executive and legislative branches. Unlike the BOR in Florida, members of the TBR did not publicly oppose the governor's proposal (nor were they asked to do so). Morgan and the TBR could potentially have been more aware of the concerns expressed by the University of Memphis and proposed in earlier years a proactive solution like the North Carolina structure (which Morgan advocated for in his resignation letter). However, it is unclear whether any such proposed structure would have been acceptable to Haslam, who wanted greater focus on the Drive to 55 initiative.

While the FOCUS Act significantly diminished the scope of the power of the chancellor of TBR, it also increased the power of THEC and its executive director to solve disputes between institutions and decide funding for capital projects. Krause and Haslam clearly understood the argument that creating local boards could lead to a fight for resources between institutions in the UT system, the TBR, and the now independent universities.

Like Herbert in Florida, Morgan found himself on the opposite side of a popular governor with strong views regarding higher education reorganization. In Tennessee, Haslam and past governors had taken innovative steps in higher education, especially in college completion. While Morgan was an astute political and policy participant, including his service as a deputy to Governor Bredesen, in the face of strong gubernatorial support his ability to effectively impact the final decision was limited.

ALABAMA: LEADERS AND SCANDALS

Former Alabama Governor George C. Wallace had a national reputation for his strident support of segregation and state rights, unsuccessful runs for the presidency as both an independent and Democrat, and the attempt by Arthur Bremer to take his life in a parking lot in Maryland. However, across Alabama, Wallace was known for his sometime populist political stands and the creation of a large community college system. Known as the "Father of Alabama's Two-Year Colleges" (Katsinas, 1994), Wallace— through a series of shrewd political moves that solidified his support across the state—created a robust system of community colleges and technical centers. Katsinas noted that at one time two colleges were named for Wallace, one for his wife Lurleen (who also served a 15-month stint as governor), and one for his late father. In visits to 41 institutions in Alabama, Katsinas noted "at least thirty George C. Wallace buildings and ten Lurleen B. Wallace buildings or halls" (p. 447).

Today, the Alabama Community College System is composed of 25 comprehensive community and technical colleges and one 2-year military college (Alabama Community College System, 2016). Collectively, the colleges serve approximately 185,000 students.

Context: Higher Education Governance

In terms of postsecondary governance, Alabama has had a bifurcated system of higher education. The Alabama Commission on Higher Education, with members appointed by the governor, makes budget recommendations for all higher education institutions in the state and approves new programs. Each university is governed by a local board of trustees who are also appointed by the governor. Community colleges, however, were historically governed (along with the state's K–12 institutions) by the elected Alabama State Board of Education. The board appointed a chancellor of the community college system. Presidents of the institutions were hired by the chancellor with approval by the board. On the surface, governance of community colleges in Alabama was similar to Florida, where the Florida Board of Education is responsible for both K–12 and the Florida College System. Unlike Florida,

Alabama does not have individual boards governing the community colleges, and the State Board of Education had significantly more power over the colleges.

Until about 2010, the Alabama Education Association (AEA) arguably was the most important political organization in the state. Under the leadership of Paul Hubbert and Joe Reed starting in 1969 and generous political contributions, the organization had a disproportionate impact on Alabama politics, including the State Board of Education. "Hubbert was known for sitting in the gallery overlooking the Legislature and giving hand signals indicating which way he wanted lawmakers to vote on whatever bill was being considered" (Sims, 2016, para. 5).

The Alabama Community College System also had significant influence over the legislature. Another state official said while the legislators working for or affiliated with the community college system might not have been able to bring the legislature to a halt, they certainly could have bogged things down. At one time, numerous members of the Alabama legislature worked in the Alabama Community College System, including a few institutional presidents.

Problem Stream: A Revolving Door and Corruption

Roy Johnson was appointed chancellor of the community college system in May 2002, replacing long-serving Fred Gainous, who had been named president of Florida A&M University. Johnson, a former community college president and Tuscaloosa county legislator, was viewed as a strong leader for the system. One former leader of a college in the system said Johnson was a great chancellor but "turned out to be a crook." By 2006, a federal investigation had opened into the operation of the community college system, the hiring of Johnson's relatives at the Alabama Fire College at Shelton State College, and numerous reports of bribes and fraud. In all, 16 people—including the chancellor, one state senator, two state representatives, one community college president, the wife of another community college president, and various contractors and business owners—either pled guilty or were found guilty in federal district court (Faulk, 2016).

Some have commented the corruption overshadowed the good Johnson did for the system. In an interview, one state official noted Johnson's strengths but emphasized the damage of the corruption:

> Roy Johnson probably understood what needed to be done . . . better than only other Chancellor. . . . He just absolutely did things other than that which were not acceptable. . . . It was just crooked business, but [he] understood what needed to be done and was not a bad chancellor if you considered that only. But the other things were the downfall of him and the damage to the system.

The Alabama Board of Education fired Johnson as chancellor before he pled guilty. For the following 6 years, the role would become a revolving door of leadership.

Political Stream: The Governor and the AEA

Following two interim chancellors who lasted a total of 9 months, the board appointed Republican State Senator Bradley Byrne (who had his eyes on a run for governor) as chancellor. Byrne had strong support from Governor Bob Riley as well as from his former colleagues in the legislature. His appointment, however, was immediately met with a lawsuit filed by the AEA regarding the hiring process. While the lawsuit was ultimately unsuccessful, it was representative of the tensions between Byrne and the AEA. Byrne took over in the middle of the federal investigation of Johnson and immediately took steps to clean up the leftover corruption, including the adoption of a policy that prohibited legislators from serving as community college employees.

Byrne left the post after only 2 years to run as the favorite for the Republican nomination for governor. In what some credit in part to the diminished power of the AEA, the union organization spent millions in negative television ads against Byrne. Hubbert said the organization only got involved in the governor's race because of Byrne's position on tenure and legislators working at the community colleges and specifically because Byrne threatened "to burn [the AEA's] house down" (Lowry, 2010). Byrne ultimately lost the nomination to Robert Bentley, who was subsequently elected. Steve Flowers, an author and political observer, said, "You might say that was the beginning of the downfall for the AEA" (Sharp, 2017, para. 17).

Byrne was replaced by Freida Hill, a Georgia Technical College System administrator who lasted less than 3 years after receiving mixed reviews from her board. In the fall of 2012, the board selected Mark Heinrich, who was serving as president at Shelton State Community College, as the new chancellor. Although Heinrich became the seventh interim or permanent chancellor in 6 years, his hiring was seen as the beginning of stability in the community college system.

Policy Stream: A Separate Community College Board

Despite that seeming stability, our interviews showed that leaders of institutions had complained for years about the inability of the State Board of Education to provide adequate attention to both community colleges and the K–12 system. Signals that potential changes were coming to the system coincided with Heinrich's appointment, as Byrne noted, "The community college system in Alabama is widely considered to be the most corrupt part of state government . . . but I don't see corruption in the system anymore"

(Tilsley, 2012, para. 13). Byrne publicly stated what many in the state had talked about for years, the creation of a board separated from the K–12 system to govern the community colleges: "It's such a big job that I think it's very difficult, if not impossible, for a board to oversee both effectively. K–12 gets more of the attention, and it needs it, but there needs to be a board to give equal attention to postsecondary" (para. 19).

A little more than 2 years after Heinrich's appointment, legislation was filed with the strong support of the governor and legislative leadership to create a separate state board of community colleges. Seth Hammett—chief of staff to Bentley, a former president of Lurleen B. Wallace Community College, and a former speaker of the Alabama House of Representatives— strongly pushed the legislation on behalf of the governor, stressing the politics of the Alabama Board of Education as one of the primary factors for a separate board:

> The members of the board were elected by districts, and they thought of the colleges in their district as being theirs. They were less interested in statewide policy for the system, and we needed a greater focus on technical education.

Hammett also stressed a desire on behalf of the governor for additional consolidation of the colleges in the system as a reason behind the legislation. Members of the Alabama Board of Education adopted a resolution opposing the legislation. However, with Bentley's support, the Republican-controlled legislature easily adopted the legislation, citing a need for a greater focus on workforce development.

According to several political observers, this was the first time Bentley, who had been strongly supported by the AEA over Byrne, had supported a separate state board of community colleges. In swearing in the newly appointed members of the board, the governor said, "This may go down in history as one of the greatest things we've done for this state in a long time, so what we've done today is important" (Associated Press, 2015, para. 3).

Unfortunately, shortly after the appointment of the new board, Heinrich developed serious medical issues, asked the newly appointed board for a leave of absence, and subsequently resigned. Jimmy Baker, an astute Alabama participant and observer and the former finance director for the state had been named as chief of staff to Heinrich and was appointed as the new chancellor when Heinrich went on medical leave.

Summary

A convergence of factors led to the creation of the State Board of Community Colleges in Alabama: a period of corruption resulting in 16 federal guilty findings or pleas, rapid and considerable turnover in the leadership of the community college system, a concern that the state board of education could not adequately focus on both K–12 and postsecondary education, a desire for a greater focus on workforce education, the demise of the AEA, the support of a governor who had been supported by the previously powerful AEA, and a change in the Alabama legislature to Republican control. All of Kingdon's streams—problems, policy, and politics—led to the governance of the college system being moved from an elected to an appointed board.

While all of these factors led to the creation of the separate state board for the community college system, two factors appear to be primary. The Alabama community college system had to fight for time and attention from the Alabama Board of Education, which also had responsibility for K–12 education in the state. Only two other states (Florida and Nevada) had similar systems where community colleges and K–12 are combined.

SHEEOs operating in this environment must fight for attention within their own agencies and governing boards while trying to provide for both accountability and advocacy for the colleges and students. It is difficult to operate effectively within such an inherently political governance structure, with elected board members and the AEA's outsized influence. Exacerbating this problem was the corruption scandal that rocked the system and the rapid turnover of leadership. While not one of these particular issues may have led to the adoption of the legislation, the combination of all of these factors resulted in its easy passage.

Implications for the SHEEO

Of particular interest for any higher education governance system is stability in the position of SHEEO. The Alabama community college system had seven interim or permanent chancellors in 6 years. Shortly after the legislature approved the change in governance, the sitting chancellor took a leave of absence and subsequently resigned for medical reasons. The ability of a SHEEO or a system to achieve long-term goals and implement initiatives is severely hampered with such rapid turnover. The other primary factor was a desire of legislative leaders and the governor to focus on workforce issues. Similar to the argument Haslam made in Tennessee, Bentley and supporters of the legislation stressed the need to enhance workforce education in the state.

Other than Byrne, who was "at war" with the AEA, in the words of one observer, during his term as chancellor and his gubernatorial run, no other chancellor of the system appears to have publicly supported the idea of a separate board (though perhaps, they were not in office long enough to even consider it). This is not surprising since the State Board of Education hires and fires the chancellor and actively opposed the move, calling it a "power grab" (Associated Press, 2015).

A SHEEO in this situation is in a tough position, reporting to a board that opposed legislation that, based on the variety of issues that had surrounded the Alabama Community College System, was clearly going to pass. Opposing legislative leaders who would determine funding levels in the future and the governor who would appoint the members of the new board would be a move that could have significant negative consequences. Baker confirmed in an interview with one of the authors of this chapter that Heinrich took no position and was not involved in the drafting of the legislation.

FUTURE RESEARCH

These three case studies present unique situations faced by the SHEEOs in each state. While the authors have presented several conclusions, further research should be conducted to understand how SHEEOs can most effectively operate in an environment where higher education issues have become part of the constant political discussion. In particular, we suggest a review of the success of SHEEOs with past political experience as opposed to those without such experience. Such analysis should include those who have served in elected, appointed, and staff positions. Additional research should also analyze success of SHEEOs after a change in the governor of the state. This research should also analyze the true or implied power of the governor to replace the SHEEO even if the higher education executive is appointed by a board.

Further, quantitative studies could be conducted to determine whether potential achievements proposed by the proponents of governance changes have occurred since the changes, especially in the areas of student success, graduation rates, and enhanced workforce education. For example, a quantitative evaluation of the benefits of Tennessee's FOCUS Act on community colleges and technical centers could be conducted since the act was implemented (controlling, of course, for the variety of other policy innovations in recent years). Additional research could also be done in the area of evaluating the performance of local and state boards and the time they spend on student success and accountability measures, including the performance of the president or system head, as applicable, and on long-term strategic planning. For example, do the local boards in Florida and Tennessee consistently or accurately evaluate the performance of campus leaders?

CONCLUSION

We must return to a point made at the outset: While other chapters in this volume have highlighted how SHEEOs can be at the nexus of the state's higher education agenda and activities, this chapter sheds light on what happens when governors or other powerful leaders propose changes to governance that are opposed by the SHEEO or in the absence of a permanent SHEEO.

In Florida, changes in governance coincided with the end of an era of Reed's strong leadership. In all three states, leadership in the governor's office heralded or strongly supported the change. And in all three states, power was moved from the SHEEO and the SHEEO agency to the governor. Each of these states exhibited the streams of Kingdon's theory, albeit in different and important ways. The implications for the SHEEO are vast.

The problem stream and the problems within it could be contested as real or perceived, but nonetheless created a window of opportunity for these three governors. In Alabama, the true problems of corruption and a revolving door of SHEEOs led to inconsistent leadership. This state exhibited the clearest path of problems and politics interacting and leading to policy changes. It is less clear whether all three streams were present in Florida and Tennessee, a concept Kingdon considered as well.

In Tennessee, where leadership in higher education innovation has been a mainstay, the success of the Drive to 55 initiative was seen as being enhanced by allowing the TBR to be focused just on community colleges and applied technical centers. However, lobbying by the University of Memphis called opponents to question whether the policy was a solution to a problem or a policy in search of a problem. In Florida, rifts between lawmakers and the BOR as well as calls for decentralization led to an overhaul of postsecondary governance.

Of particular importance in all three states was the political stream, especially that of the governor's office. These governors (more notably Bush and Haslam) favored decentralization to local boards while working to maintain accountability. In Alabama, decentralization was not from state to local, but from a broader state board to a focused state board.

It is important to consider how Kingdon's identified streams are managed and who manages them. While SHEEOs are touted as policy actors in the state, often charged with implementing the edicts of their boards, so too are they political actors, as these three cases demonstrate. The SHEEOs must also remember that by their nature, public colleges and universities are political in nature. Political bodies created these entities and, subject to regional and specialized accreditation standards, have the power to significantly adjust the duties given to state and institutional leaders. In all three states, the governor or supporters initiated or supported changes in line with their political paradigm as well as a way, arguably, to coalesce power within their office. In Florida, the governor now appoints all members of the Board of Governors (with the exception of a student and faculty member) but appoints only half of the members of university and college governing boards. However, the other half of the local boards are appointed by the Board of Governors, who are appointed by the governor. In Tennessee, the governor now appoints the THEC executive director, members of the THEC board, and all members of local governing boards. And in Alabama, the governing power of the state's community colleges was removed from the elected Board of Education to a statewide board now appointed by the governor.

SHEEOs must be attuned to the interactions of problems, policy, and politics in their states, the history of their governance structure, and the limits of their influence. They must also be aware that their role is to manage and balance these streams. Otherwise, their power, functions, and most importantly, their ability to provide for a coordinated statewide public agenda will be threatened.

Some may argue that this chapter describes SHEEOs who did not have political expertise to deal with the situations they faced. The authors strongly disagree. When faced with decisions proposed by popular governors (who appoint SHEEO boards) or legislative leadership (who control higher education budgets), SHEEOs are in a difficult position. As higher education issues take on more visibility and attention by both the public and policymakers, the direct involvement by governors and legislators will become more prevalent. It will be a rare case when a SHEEO can successfully oppose major policy initiatives proposed by a popular governor with strong legislative allies.

SHEEOs must, however, work with governors and legislative leadership to understand their priorities and remain attuned to signals that institutional leaders are delivering to policymakers. Failure to do so can lead to clashes, as evidenced in both Florida and Tennessee. It is unclear whether or what type of higher education governance reform Bush would have proposed if the BOR had not been at such significant odds with the legislature over the funding of the professional schools.

In his resignation letter, Morgan proposed a governance system similar to North Carolina's. One must question how such a proposal would have been received in earlier years if it had been proposed by Morgan and the TBR or THEC under the leadership of Rhoda, especially knowing that supporters of the University of Memphis had been lobbying for years for a local board.

The situation in Alabama had been filled with political ramifications for years. The complex political relationship between the AEA, the State Board of Education, Byrne, legislators who worked for colleges in the community college system, and Republican legislators who had less allegiance to the AEA were all factors in the background as the change in governance was enacted. While Heinrich did not take a position and did not review the legislation before it was proposed, one can surmise that he supported the change, as did most in the community college system. However, with his current employer, the State Board of Education, opposing the change, he had to publicly remain on the sidelines.

While these studies dealt with the one issue that may by its nature present the most inherent conflict—higher education governance—it can be expected that other high-profile policy issues will garner the attention of governors and legislative leaders. Keeping tuition low and enhancing college completion rates are just two of several issues that have been pushed by policy entrepreneurs and governors.

Some may argue that the ability to foresee future proposed changes will require SHEEOs to be fortune tellers. While such skills would be beneficial, it is more likely that SHEEOs will be required to spend considerable time working both with institutional leaders and policymakers and maintaining a clear understanding of where both are going in the future. In a perfect world, policymakers should first learn of new ideas in higher education from the SHEEO.

While this chapter may present conclusions that are more daunting than optimistic, the role of the SHEEO is imperative even within limits, and those limits may, in some cases, be erased or at least impacted with closer attention paid to potential actions by executive and legislative branch leaders.

NOTES

1. Hanna, one of the authors of this chapter, has been involved in higher education in the state of Florida since 1991. While his relationships with Graham, Bush, and Thrasher and other participants in the Florida higher education arena have aided in providing significant insight for this section, we caution the reader of potential for researcher bias.

2. Florida Blue Key is a student honorary organization at the University of Florida of which many state leaders were members.

3. Reed was hospitalized the weekend before our scheduled interview for this chapter and died before we were able to discuss this issue with him in a formal context.

REFERENCES

Alabama Community College System. (2016). *Annual report*. Retrieved from www .accs.cc/default/assets/File/DPE_Stat/annualreport_2015.pdf

Associated Press. (2015, May 27). Alabama's new 2-year college board holds first meeting. *The Birmingham News*. Retrieved from www.al.com/news/index .ssf/2015/05/alabamas_new_2-year_college_bo.html

Borman, K. M., & Dorn, S. (2007). Introduction: Issues in Florida education reform. In K. M. Borman & S. Dorn (Eds.), *Reform in Florida: Diversity and equity in public policy* (pp. 1–18). Albany: State University of New York Press.

Corbert, M. (2016, November 24). University of Memphis, by Memphis. *Memphis Business Journal*. Retrieved from www.bizjournals.com/memphis/news/2016 /11/24/university-of-memphis-governing-board-takes-shape.html

Criser, M. (2017, October 5). Comment made during public meeting of the Florida Constitutional Review Commission, Tallahassee, FL.

Faulk, K. (2016, September 20). Where are the defendants convicted in Alabama's two-year college scandal? *The Birmingham News*. Retrieved from www.al.com/ news/birmingham/index.ssf/2016/09/where_are_they_now_defendants.html

Freeman, B. (2016, March 24). FOCUS Act could bring imbalance to TN's schools. *Tennessean*. Retrieved from www.tennessean.com/story/opinion/contributors/2016/03/24/focus-act-could-bring-imbalance-tns-schools/82139998/

Graham v. Haridopolos, 108 So. 3d 597 (Fla 2013).

Haslam, W. E. (2015). Comment made during public meeting of the Tennessee Board of Regents, Nashville.

Independent Colleges and Universities of Florida. (2017). *Institutions*. Retrieved from www.icuf.org/institutions/

Johnson, L., & Borman, K. M. (2007). Competing agendas for university governance: Placing the conflict between Jeb Bush and Bob Graham in context. In K. M. Borman & S. Dorn (Eds.), *Reform in Florida: Diversity and equity in public policy* (pp. 185–210). Albany: State University of New York Press.

Katsinas, S. G. (1994). George C. Wallace and the founding of Alabama's public two-year colleges. *Journal of Higher Education, 65*(4), 447–472.

Kingdon, J. W. (2011). *Agendas, alternatives, and public policies* (4th ed.). London: HarperCollins.

Lowry, B. (2010, July 14). AEA Executive Secretary Paul Hubbert: Bradley Byrne 'threatened to burn our house down.' *The Huntsville Times*. Retrieved from blog.al.com/breaking/2010/07/hubbert_byrne_threatened_to_bu.html.

Mazzoni, T. L. (1991). Analyzing state school policymaking: An arena model. *Educational Evaluation and Policy Analysis, 13*, 115–138.

McGuiness, A. C., & Fulton, M. (2007). *50-state comparison: State-level coordination and/or governing agency*. Boulder, CO: Education Commission of the States. Retrieved from ecs.force.com/mbdata/mbquestRTL? Rep=PSG01

Morgan, J. C. (2016). *Letter of resignation*. Retrieved from www.insidehighered.com/sites/default/server_files/files/JohnMorganLetterToGovHaslam.pdf

Oppel, S. (2000, June 20). Bush signs law abolishing board of regents. *St. Petersburg Times*.

Rayfield, S. E. (2004). Higher education policy making, from representative democracy to direct democracy: A case study (Unpublished doctoral dissertation). Vanderbilt University, Nashville, TN.

Sharp, J. (2017, August 31). Why Bradley Byrne isn't seeking to avenge 2010 gubernatorial loss. *The Birmingham News*. Retrieved from www.al.com/news/mobile/index.ssf/2017/08/why_bradley_byrne_isnt_seeking.html

Sims, C. (2016, January 21). Collapse of Alabama teachers union complete as AEA officially halts political donations. *Yellow Hammer*. Retrieved from yellowhammernews.com/politics-2/collapse-of-alabama-teachers-union-complete-as-aea-officially-halts-political-donations/

State University System of Florida. (2017). *Fact book* [Data file]. Retrieved from www.flbog.edu/resources/factbooks/

Stockard, S. (2016, October 28). Haslam's board picks lauded by schools. *The Ledger*. Retrieved from www.tnledger.com/editorial/Article.aspx?id=92609

Tamburin, A. (2015, December 1). Major overhaul planned for Tennessee colleges. *Tennessean*. Retrieved from www.tennessean.com/story/news/education/2015/12/01/gov-haslam-make-significant-college-announcement/76581840/

Tamburin, A. (2016, March 1). TSU students protest Haslam's college restructuring plan. *Tennessean*. Retrieved from www.tennessean.com/story/news/education/2016/03/01/tsu-students-protest-haslams-college-plan/81157002/

Tennessee Board of Regents. (2016). Legislation impacting the Tennessee Board of Regents and member institutions. Retrieved from www.tbr.edu/sites/tbr.edu/files/media/2016/07/2016%20Legislative%20Compilation.pdf

Tennessee Higher Education Commission. (2017). *2016–2017 Tennessee higher education fact book*. Nashville, TN: Author.

Tilsley, A. (2012, September 17). A stable job? *Inside Higher Ed*. Retrieved from www.insidehighered.com/news/2012/09/17/alabama-names-seventh-new-community-college-chancellor-six-years

Trombley, W. (2001, Spring). Florida's new "K-20" model: An intensely political battle is waged over controversial kindergarten-through graduate-school governance structure. *National Crosstalk*. Retrieved from www.highereducation.org/crosstalk/ct0401/news0401-florida.shtml

University of Tennessee. (n.d.). *UT Board of Trustees*. Retrieved from trustees.tennessee.edu/

CHAPTER 7

The SHEEO and Intermediary Organizations

Erik C. Ness, James C. Hearn, and Paul G. Rubin

Many factors affect SHEEOs' work in leading states' public higher education sectors. Other chapters in this volume highlight the longstanding influence of board members, governance structures, and campus leaders. In recent years, observers have begun to realize the increasingly active roles of other regional or national organizations in state higher education policy arenas (Hall & Thomas, 2012; Hillman, Tandberg, & Sponsler, 2015; Ness, 2010; Ness & Gándara, 2014). As a prime example, *The Chronicle of Higher Education* published a special report, "The Gates Effect," in 2013 outlining the role of the Bill and Melinda Gates Foundation in funding more than $472 million on higher education (Parry, Field, & Supiano, 2013). The report's accompanying interactive beneficiaries database reported dozens of nongovernmental organizations (e.g., Complete College America, Jobs for the Future, National Center for Higher Education Management Systems) seeking to influence state and federal higher education policy. Researchers often refer to these organizations as *intermediaries*, or intermediary organizations, due to their role in connecting governmental and private actors with higher education campuses or systems. Although intermediaries vary in how they influence the policymaking process, they nearly always serve as boundary-spanning organizations that connect state elected officials with higher education leaders or national experts with elected officials, state higher education agencies, or campus leaders. Unfortunately, despite this rising visibility and influence of intermediary organizations, little attention has been paid to arguably the key actor most prominently involved with these organizations: the SHEEO.

To understand relationships between SHEEOs and intermediary organizations, it is first necessary to understand the state context within which SHEEOs operate and the various types of intermediary organizations. The first section of this chapter discusses the context within which SHEEOs and intermediaries exist. We outline four sources of influence upon SHEEOs and include examples of how these affect SHEEOs in various states. This discussion of the state-level environmental context also serves as a reminder of how these factors may moderate SHEEOs' engagement with intermediary organizations.

In the subsequent sections, we draw on our broader research effort examining of the role that intermediary organizations play in fostering research use in state-level college completion policy activities in four states: Georgia, North Carolina, Tennessee, and Texas. These states are members of the Southern Regional Education Board (SREB), which provides some regional consistency across cases. However, the states also vary in some key aspects: Notably, Georgia and North Carolina have consolidated state governing boards, and Tennessee and Texas have statewide coordinating boards. Table 7.1 reports additional key characteristics.

The data for this project came from three main sources: (1) interviews with 99 policy actors, including elected officials and their aides, state higher education leaders, campus officials, and intermediary organization leaders; (2) observations of many meetings, hearings, and convened sessions; and (3) documents and archival materials. Ultimately, the analysis revealed dozens of intermediaries that state-level policy actors identified as playing significant roles in the ultimate college completion policies adopted by the state. The primary focus for the broader project was on the role that information played in supporting these college completion efforts, including how intermediary organizations framed their policy preferences and how state-level political and organizational characteristics affected intermediary activities.

For this chapter, the focus is on the specific role of the SHEEO and the SHEEO agency in their interactions with intermediary organizations. The chapter draws heavily on our interviews with six former or current SHEEOs in these four states. This study also highlights the intermediary organizations that these SHEEOs, as opposed to other key actors, identified influencing college completion efforts in their states. We classify these intermediary organizations into four categories based on their primary audiences and activities. Next, the chapter includes a vignette from each of the four states that illustrates how the SHEEO interacted with a distinct type of intermediary. From this classification and the vignettes, the chapter concludes with a discussion of important policy implications for state higher education leaders and future research activities that would increase the descriptive and conceptual understanding of the SHEEO–intermediary connections in all states.

FOUR DISTINCT STATE-LEVEL SOURCES OF INFLUENCE

State higher education executive officers operate in a complex environment at the intersection of multiple actors, conditions, laws, and interests, some extending beyond their home states. Four reasonably distinct sources of influence facing SHEEOs may be identified in each state: (1) socioeconomic context, (2) organizational and policy context, (3) politico-institutional context, and (4) external context. We discuss each of these contexts and report key characteristics across theses contexts for the four states in this study in Table 7.1.

State Socioeconomic Context

A state's socioeconomic context provides resources for higher education but also can produce constraints and problems for the work of SHEEOs and their agencies. For example, research across varied policy arenas suggested that more populous states may require more complex, technically sophisticated programs and policies (Berry & Berry, 1990). In higher education, there was evidence that more populous states tend to require integrated, across-level student unit-record systems to support analysis and policymaking on such issues as student achievement and degree attainment (Hearn, McLendon, & Mokher, 2008). In recent years, however, the profusion of these systems across a majority of states (see Education Commission of the States, 2017) may dilute the power of this earlier finding.

Beyond raw population size, the work of SHEEOs is also influenced by states' population distributions. The youthfulness or, alternatively, the agedness of a state's population can determine the extent to which leaders must attend to postsecondary education issues (Doyle, 2006; Tandberg & Ness, 2011), and such population characteristics as growth, density, diversity, urbanicity, and educational attainment levels may also be influential. Regarding educational attainment levels, in particular, one can envision both "supply" and "demand" factors influencing SHEEOs' work. On the demand side, states with low levels of educational attainment may require relatively greater investment in financial aid and other forms of state support to improve affordability and information regarding college enrollment and thus stimulate attainment. State merit-scholarship programs, for example, may help deepen a state's supply of human capital (e.g., Doyle, 2006; Heller, 2002). On the supply side, there was some evidence that high levels of educational attainment in a state can be associated with greater knowledge and openness to new state policy approaches (Berry & Berry, 2014), making the climate potentially more receptive for novel higher-education policy initiatives.

Purely economic characteristics, such as state wealth, employment, and gross product, can also be associated with state policy development and support of higher education and thus influence the work of SHEEOs. As with educational attainment, this connection can work both ways. Wealthier states will tend to be more highly educated and to devote more money to higher education support, including new initiatives, but some higher

Table 7.1. Key State Characteristics

	GEORGIA	NORTH CAROLINA	TENNESSEE	TEXAS
Socioeconomic Context				
Population Rank[a]	8	9	16	2
Postsecondary Degree Attainment (Ranking Nationally)[b]	39.11% (31)	40.94% (26)	34.73% (41)	36.44% (39)
State Unemployment Rate (Ranking Nationally)[c]	4.9% (40)	4.5% (32)	4.0% (21)	4.8% (39)
State Postsecondary Organizational and Policy Context				
SHEEO Agency	University System of Georgia	University of North Carolina	Tennessee Higher Education Commission	Texas Higher Education Coordinating Board
Governance Structure	Consolidated Governing Board	Consolidated Governing Board	Coordinating Board	Coordinating Board
Agency Board Voting Membership	19	32	9	9
State Politico-Institutional Context				
Political Partisanship	Republican (Governor) Republican (Legislative)	Republican/ Democratic (Governor) Republican (Legislative)	Republican (Governor) Republican (Legislative)	Republican (Governor) Republican (Legislative)
Legislative Professionalism[d]	38	21	37	14
Gubernatorial Power[e]	3.0	2.5	2.75	2.8

SHEEO Appointment	Agency Board Appointed	Agency Board Appointed	Governor Appointed	Agency Board Appointed
Agency Board Appointment	Governor Appointed and GA Senate Confirmed (19)	Elected by NC Senate and NC House of Representatives (32); 1 Student representative (nonvoting)	Governor Appointed (9); 3 Constitutional Officers (Comptroller, State Treasurer, and Secretary of State; ex officio); 2 Student members (ex officio); Executive Director of the State Board of Education (ex officio)	Governor Appointed (9); 1 Student representative (nonvoting)
Out-of-State Context				
CCA Alliance	Yes	No	Yes	Yes
Regional Compact	SREB	SREB	SREB	SREB

a. Population rank was drawn from the U.S. Census estimates for 2016.

b. Degree attainment rate is adapted from the 2015 U.S. Census Bureau, American Community Survey. This figure considered percentage of adults (25 to 64) with an associate's degree or higher.

c. Unemployment rate figures came from the U.S. Department of Labor's Bureau of Labor Statistics.

d. Squire (2012) ranked the legislative professionalism of the 50 states in 2009 based on the number of months in session, the number of permanent staff, and monetary compensation provided to general assemblypersons. The higher ranking represents a more professionalized legislature.

e. Ferguson (2013) constructed an "institutional powers" measurement for governors based on the powers provided by the state constitution, state statutes, and the voting public. For purposes of comparison, she measured the national average across the 50 states to be 3.3.

education policy adoption studies have suggested that economic disadvantage is associated with policy experimentation in such areas as merit scholarship programs, state-funded eminent scholars policies, and research and development tax credits (Hearn, McLendon, & Linthicum, 2017).[1] In general, ample fiscal resources may increase the likelihood of states considering and implementing expensive policies and programs to be administered by SHEEO agencies, but economic disadvantage may prompt consideration and implementation of new, often revenue-neutral, policies aimed at improving a state's economic and infrastructural capacity. For example, enlisting private corporate and university support for recruitment of elite research faculty may be cost-effective for states with less- robust coffers (Hearn, McLendon, & Lacy, 2013).

State Postsecondary Organizational and Policy Context

Each state has a distinctive organizational and policy context for postsecondary education. Consider the wide variation in the number and the proportional distribution of institutions and students within a state, both by control (public or private) and by level (2-year or 4-year); such factors make the job of a SHEEO in Arizona or Florida notably different from the job of a SHEEO in Massachusetts. Similarly, consider students' migration patterns: Some states choose to accommodate large numbers of out-of-state students in their public institutions, capitalizing on revenues from higher tuition rates (e.g., Virginia), while some lose high proportions of students to institutions in other states (e.g., New Jersey). And, from both a supply and demand side, SHEEOs must work with their states' university research capacity (i.e., the number and strength of research institutions in the state). These "ecological" patterns produce different kinds of pressures, problems, and opportunities for SHEEOs (Hossler, Lund, Ramin, Westfall, & Irish, 1997; McLendon & Mokher, 2009; Zumeta, 1992, 1996).

Of course, states also vary in the nature of their higher education governance arrangements, their independent policymaking authority (e.g., Lacy, 2011), and their capacity for policy research, analysis, and evaluation. Some agencies feature a consolidated central governing board under which SHEEOs and their boards have authority over presidential hires, mission differentiation, and tuition setting, but other states defer power to institutions and political authorities (as will be discussed later in this chapter). Similarly, some SHEEO offices, such as the Tennessee Higher Education Commission, have ample human and technical resources to provide information, data, and research for policymakers, covering such topics as cost-effectiveness evaluations and longitudinal analyses of student access and success, while other SHEEO offices, including the South Carolina Commission on Higher Education, are lean and almost entirely focused on the mechanics of program delivery. These variations in governance are central to the nature of SHEEO work and are discussed at length later in this chapter.

Also critical in the state policy contexts facing SHEEOs are postsecondary appropriations, tuition levels, and enrollments. States vary significantly in their funding levels and funding effort (relative to the states' educational and economic development), and these variations in policy postures may shape the attention of policymakers to newer ideas or proposals. For example, the "high-tuition high-aid" approach historically pursued in such states as Pennsylvania and New York might seem inconceivable in states like Arizona or Mississippi, which operate very different funding traditions. Similarly, major surges in demand for postsecondary education, as those seen in Sunbelt states since the 1980s, can push SHEEOs and policymakers toward efforts to expand postsecondary educational capacity. Conversely, tuition rises on public campuses can prompt state efforts not only to devise innovative ways to help citizens pay for college but also to tighten institutional oversight (McLendon & Hearn, 2013; Mumper, 2001).

State Politico-Institutional Context

As Tandberg and Griffith (2013) have suggested, state attitudes and actions in higher education are rooted in far more than their socioeconomic and policy environments. SHEEOs work within distinct political conditions and institutionalized arrangements. A state's politico-institutional context influences its state higher education offices' approach to policy identification, policy implementation, and policy analysis.

For example, a state's *political ideology* plays a role in determining which issues are raised, when those issues are raised, what solutions are on the table, and how policies and programs are evaluated (Doyle, 2006; Hearn et al., 2017; Louis, Febey, & Gordon 2015; Nicholson-Crotty & Meier, 2003; Tandberg, 2010a, 2010b, 2013). More traditionally conservative states, for example, may wish to tie higher education resource allocations directly to performance incentives or tie students' financial aid awards to academic performance through merit-aid awards, as seen by the merit-based HOPE Scholarship in Georgia or long-standing tradition of performance-based funding in Tennessee (e.g., Li, 2017).

In addition, the level of *legislative professionalism* in states (i.e., lengthy legislative sessions, ample resources for committee and personal staff, and high pay for members) may be associated with more generous allocations to higher education and more attention to higher education as a policy issue (Lacy & Tandberg, 2014; Ness & Tandberg, 2013; Nicholson-Crotty & Meier, 2003; Squire, 2012; Tandberg, 2013; Toutkoushian & Hollis, 1998). Highly professionalized legislatures may facilitate more robust and enduring relationships between SHEEOs and legislators, as well as between SHEEOs and legislative committee staff and political staff. Clearly, SHEEO offices must be responsive to the knowledge levels and sensitivities of legislators and their staff and be willing to provide additional research support in states with lower legislative research capabilities.

A politico-institutional factor often ignored in research studies—but never neglected in policy debates and never far from the minds of most SHEEOs—is the nature of *partisanship* in the states (McLendon, 2003). Several studies, for example, have found associations between Republican or Democratic control of legislatures and governorships and the nature of policy debates and actions regarding higher education (Archibald & Feldman, 2006; Dougherty, Natow, Bork, Jones, & Vega, 2013; Fryar & Meier, 2008; Lowry, 2007). Similarly, *electoral factors* also shape SHEEO work. The level of competitiveness, timing of elections, and other such state characteristics cannot be ignored by any actors in a state's policy environment, and certainly not by SHEEOs (Hearn et al., 2017). Clearly, SHEEOs must remain closely attentive to political winds as they do their jobs.

Relatedly, *gubernatorial strength and tenure* can play a strong role in the interplay of interests around policy issues in a state. Constitutionally "strong" governors can determine what is prominent on the policy agenda and can use their influence to shape policy adoptions and support (e.g., Dougherty et al., 2014; Ferguson, 2013; Hearn et al., 2013; Hearn et al., 2014; Lowry, 2001; Mokher, 2010; Mokher & McLendon, 2009; Ness & Tandberg, 2013; Tandberg, 2010a, 2010b, 2013). Strong governors can also provide critical political support or opposition for SHEEOs, agencies, and institutional leaders (e.g., Marcus, 1997; McGuinness, 2016; McLendon, 2003). Regarding tenure in office, veteran governors can be empowered or constrained in ways that are distinct from leaders new to their office.

Governors can be key figures in the careers of SHEEOs in another way, of course: In many states, governors appoint the SHEEO. In others, the SHEEO's selection lies with the legislature or the governing or coordinating board itself. According to work by Tandberg, Fowles, and McLendon (2017), *SHEEO appointment characteristics* involve a fundamental power that can critically influence what is done and not done, and emphasized and not emphasized, in the office. The individual, group, or office that controls formal appointment power plays a substantial role in the decisions and priorities of SHEEOs. For instance, in this examination of four states, we found distinctive appointment arrangements to be associated with distinctive policymaking approaches. In Georgia and Texas, the boards appoint the SHEEO; in Tennessee, the governor appoints the SHEEO; and in North Carolina, the legislature appoints the SHEEO.

Our final politico-institutional factor involving SHEEOs is the state's *interest-group climate*. States vary in the density, concentration, and strength of the interest groups focusing on higher education issues—that is, in the degree to which higher education is an active concern in lobbying work in the state (Hearn et al., 2017; Ness & Tandberg, 2013; Ness, Tandberg, & McLendon, 2015; Tandberg, 2010a, 2010b, 2013; Tandberg & Ness, 2011). For example, there was evidence that the relative size of the higher education lobby positively affected the level of state higher-education spending (Tandberg, 2013), and there can be little question the nature of the work of SHEEOs was affected as well.

Beyond external interest groups, it is important to consider how higher education governance arrangements organize and channel interests around postsecondary initiatives. SHEEO offices are not purely organizational features in a state; they are also key features of a state's interest networks, deeply embedded in policy processes involving governors, legislators, interest groups, institutions, media, and students. This involvement can span the range from the generation of postsecondary policy ideas to analysis, debate, and implementation of those ideas.

To illustrate, consider the difference in interest channels and lobbying between systems with a single governing board for all public institutions, as in our focal states of North Carolina and Georgia, and systems with weaker coordinating arrangements and boards attached to distinctive postsecondary sectors, as in our focal states of Tennessee and Texas.[2] In consolidated settings, singular boards become foci of attention by governors, legislators, and interest groups, and the centralized board, led by the SHEEO, becomes a key agent speaking for higher education interests as a whole. In contrast, attention is more atomized in coordinating arrangements, empowering the constituent institutions. Initially designed as buffering bodies with dual obligations to campuses and the state, coordinating boards work to balance different, often competing, interests. Lacking the institutions as a core power base/constituency, these boards can be more directly influenced by elected officials. Most notably, governors often choose the members of coordinating boards and can thus shape the policy priorities and oversight practices of those bodies. At the far extreme, consider how interests play out in Michigan, a state with neither a coordinating board nor a consolidated governing board. That state's constitution grants the boards of the largest and oldest schools authority over their own academic and fiscal affairs, making the state's central higher education planning agency rather powerless relative to the universities. Influence efforts largely involve the individual institutions, bypassing the planning agency (which is left mainly to collect data and manage financial aid allocations).

A substantial and growing body of research confirms that governing arrangements be considered both an organizational and political feature in the contexts facing SHEEOs and that these state-to-state variations are important (McLendon, Deaton, & Hearn, 2007; McLendon, Hearn, & Deaton, 2006; Tandberg, 2013). A SHEEO accustomed to leadership under a consolidated arrangement may initially feel disoriented in the seemingly anarchic world of a coordinating board. Hearn and Ness (in press) reviewed the substantial research evidence for the importance of governing arrangements in shaping not only the work of SHEEOs but also the nature of state policy choices and outcomes.

External Context

The fourth contextual factor shaping SHEEO work looks beyond intrastate influences to the larger national context. Outside of their home states lie several forms of potential influences on SHEEOs' attention and actions. Most obviously, neighboring states' higher education policies can raise alarms or spur mimicry. Georgia's introduction of merit scholarships for talented in-state students in the early 1990s sparked realization that such programs can "capture" students who might otherwise head across state borders for college. In Tennessee, Florida, and other close-by states, it was not long before similar programs were launched, effectively helping "seal the borders" by lessening the interstate flow of students in that region. While Georgia's SHEEO was not the originator of the state's HOPE Scholarship idea, he became a key figure in its implementation and evolution. And, in each state following Georgia's lead, SHEEOs played key roles in new merit scholarship programs.[3] States can also influence each other through the transmission of novel postsecondary policy ideas outside of undergraduate education. Georgia launched one of the nation's earliest "eminent scholars" programs to recruit talented research faculty for major public and private universities, and soon similar efforts emerged nationwide (Hearn et al., 2013).

SHEEOs can and do play a major role in the interstate migration of policy ideas. They can engage in a variety of multistate networks, such as the State Higher Education Executive Officers Association (SHEEO), American Association of State Colleges and Universities (AASCU), and Association of Public and Land Grant Universities (APLU) at the national level and the Southern Regional Education Board (SREB) and the Western Interstate Commission on Higher Education (WICHE) at the regional level. By doing so, SHEEOs learn what has been working or not working in other settings and can bring the best ideas and lessons home (Lacy & Tandberg, 2014; Li, 2017).

SHEEOs also work in an environment defined more broadly than state lines. Vendors selling database management tools and enterprise systems influence the work of SHEEOs and their institutions: The expansion and migration of tools like PeopleSoft may foster a common language and common set of assumptions, at the expense of other framings of data and issues.

What is more, the attention of SHEEOs (as well as governors and legislators) is shaped by across-state policy champions or entrepreneurs. In three of our four focal states, it was rare to meet with state officials or campus leaders without their mentioning Complete College America, the Lumina Foundation, or the Gates Foundation. Increasingly, these intermediary organizations are playing a role in determining what topics are being considered and studied, and what ideas are implemented and how across the states. For that reason, these organizations merit extended treatment here.

INTERMEDIARY ORGANIZATIONS

This study of college completion initiatives found that intermediary organizations, such as foundations, associations, think tanks, and policy organizations, have become increasingly influential in state higher education policy decisions. In large part this impact is due to the engagement of these organizations between what many have referred to as "two communities" (Snow, 1961), which is reflected in the title of Birnbaum's (2000) widely cited article, "Policy Scholars Are From Venus, Policy Makers Are From Mars." This longstanding divide between research and policy communities has been attributed to the distinct objectives, norms, and even language of each community. For example, researcher communities tend to value systematic, rigorous analysis with an aim to inform decisions rather than promote specific policies. Policymaker communities, on the other hand, tend to value direct positions that are practical, timely, and cognizant of political realities. Intermediary organizations represent the entities that work within this divide, often with an express interest in connecting these communities through boundary-spanning (Guston, 2000) or knowledge-brokering (Daly et al., 2014; Lomas, 2007) activities, such as sharing and filtering information, translating key findings to policymakers, advocating for certain policy solutions, and serving as a trusted and credible organization by both researchers and policymakers.

The examination of college completion policy activity in four states revealed dozens of intermediary organizations that acted in various ways to influence state college completion. Based on a review of these organizations' materials and on interviews with state policymakers, it was found that intermediary organizations can be classified by using the two communities perspective (Ness, Hearn, & Rubin, 2017). That is, the activities and services of intermediary organizations seemed highly related to whether the organization was more closely connected to researcher or policymaker communities. Thus, we suggest that four types of intermediary organizations can be classified along a two communities continuum: researcher-based, researcher-leaning, policymaker-leaning, and policymaker-based.

Before introducing each category, we must mention a few caveats. First, this classification is meant to provide conceptual clarity about the distinctions among intermediary organizations rather than a strict descriptive inventory of organizations by category. We recognize that many organizations do not fit neatly into only one category, and some organizations have characteristics that might reasonably place them in multiple categories.

Our primary intent was to identify key distinguishing elements of intermediaries that would help researchers and policymakers better understand their role and influence in the policymaking process.

Researcher-Based Intermediaries

These organizations serve the traditional role of producing and disseminating empirical research evidence. With few exceptions, these intermediaries are led by academics and housed within centers or other units of universities, such as the Community College Research Center (CCRC) at Teachers College, Columbia University; Georgetown University's Center on Education and the Workforce (CEW); the Charles Dana Center at University of Texas, Austin; and the RAND Corporation. The research capacity of these intermediaries is robust due to their orientation within more traditional academic communities that emphasize sound arguments, rigorous research designs, and measured, precise discussion of key findings and their implications.

Researcher-Leaning Intermediaries

These organizations retain many of the characteristics of the researcher-based intermediaries, most notably their emphasis on producing and disseminating information. Yet, these organizations are not housed within universities; rather they exist as independent nonprofit organizations, such as the Education Commission of the States (ECS), National Center for Higher Education Management Systems (NCHEMS), Southern Region Educational Board (SREB), State Higher Education Executive Officers (SHEEO), and Western Interstate Commission on Higher Education (WICHE). Although many of these organizations have elected officials that serve on their boards, their senior staff members have significant experience in state higher education systems and academic training. While we contend that they lean toward research communities, these organizations are less directly connected to academic norms and conventions, instead emphasizing how data can inform current policy issues and directions. Many of these organizations also work to build and facilitate networks of researchers and policymakers across states. Yet, because many of these intermediaries are member-organizations with multiple states paying dues for services, these organizations often refrain from advocating for specific policy solutions that might divide policymakers along partisan or ideological lines.

Policymaker-Leaning Intermediaries

These organizations connect more closely with policymaker communities and are more likely to advocate for specific policy solutions. While these organizations often disseminate research evidence and other information, they are less likely to produce the research and instead serve as a filter to promote certain policy objectives or solutions to policymakers. This type of intermediary organizations is the most independent from researcher and policymaker communities, with funding coming directly from donors or benefactors such as states' chambers of commerce or business roundtables. Other policymaker-leaning intermediaries include the Gates, Kresge, and Lumina foundations and many organizations funded primarily by these foundations, such as Achieving the Dream, Complete College America (CCA), and Jobs for the Future. Although the organizational missions may differ, as a group these intermediaries tend to focus more on advancing specific policy solutions rather than broadly informing policymakers of the key considerations. These organizations are also often able to provide resources, namely grant funding, in support of the policies for which they advocate.

Policymaker-Based Intermediaries

These organizations directly serve the policymaker communities by providing policy-relevant information, networks with other policymakers, and often tools to promote certain policies. These intermediaries are essentially the professional associations for individual elected officials, governors, and legislators and include both nonpartisan organizations, such as the National Conference of State Legislators (NCSL) and National Governors Association (NGA), and more partisan organizations, such as the Democratic and Republican Governors Associations and the American Legislative Exchange Council (ALEC). Whereas NCSL and NGA most often serve as information providers and are less likely to advocate for specific policies due to the range of policy preferences among all governors or legislators, respondents in our study indicated that ALEC and RGA played more advocacy roles, including the distribution of model bills by ALEC and the sharing of policy emphases and strategies to gain support among a network of education advisors to governors facilitated by RCA.

These four categories of intermediary organizations represent varying approaches to serving as an external influence on the policymaking process. We do not view these categories as entirely discrete or impermeable and expect that some organizations could shift categories, especially between the researcher-leaning and policymaker-leaning types, over time or even depending on the policy issue. That said, our analysis of college completion activity in four states suggests that, at least on that specific policy issue, this continuum of intermediaries reflects the distinct roles that organizations play related to the production, dissemination, and use of empirical research and other policy-relevant information. The next section provides examples of how a few of these organizations have been active with the SHEEOs in four states. We follow the same order beginning with researcher-based organizations in North Carolina, then researcher-leaning intermediaries in Tennessee, and ending with two examples of policymaking-leaning organizations in Georgia and Texas. We do not include an example of policymaker-based organizations, in large part because these organizations were not seen as significant players as were intermediaries of the other three types in these four states. We also found the policymaker-leaning organizations to exhibit the most variation within category, so these two state examples serve to illustrate these varying roles.

CASE NARRATIVES

North Carolina: Georgetown University Center on Education and the Workforce and The Community College Research Center at Teachers College, Columbia University

North Carolina, which operates under a consolidated governing board structure, maintains the University of North Carolina System (UNC) as its primary SHEEO agency, overseeing 16 university campuses and the North Carolina School of Science and Mathematics. The creation of UNC was mandated by Sections 8 and 9 of the North Carolina Constitution, which outlined the primary functions and oversight responsibilities of the governing agency. Likewise, although not a part of the official SHEEO agency of the state, the community college sector is overseen by the North Carolina Community College System (NCCCS), which has similar responsibilities as UNC and serves as a coordinating agency for the 58 public 2-year institutions. While UNC and NCCCS serve different institutional sectors, interviews with representatives from both agencies highlighted the involvement of each organization's respective leader in connecting with external researcher-based intermediaries, specifically the Georgetown University Center on Education and the Workforce and the Community College Research Center at Teachers College, Columbia University.

The Georgetown University Center on Education and the Workforce (CEW), led by Professor Anthony Carnevale, has been viewed as a leading nonpartisan organization providing data and empirical work investigating the alignment between the education sector and labor market demand. Affiliated with Georgetown's McCourt School of Public Policy, CEW is staffed primarily by economists and other researchers, with the aim of informing and impacting the policymaking process at the federal, state, and local level. In particular, CEW has long emphasized the lack of adults holding postsecondary credentials to meet the workforce needs of the United States (e.g., Carnevale & Rose, 2011; Carnevale, Smith, & Strohl, 2013), contributing early to the attention focused on increasing college completion rates nationally.

Respondents from UNC noted their use of CEW data helped individuals understand the need for improving attainment rates across North Carolina. For example, the state's former SHEEO, President Tom Ross, noted a "willingness by [UNC Board members] to challenge workforce data . . . [including] the work done at Georgetown, that it just couldn't possibly be right . . . but [after presenting CEW findings] I think they also became convinced that we needed to increase educational attainment." Although other UNC officials noted that they presented CEW data along with other statistics, specifically studies suggesting degree completion was currently sufficient, Ross emphasized that the "Georgetown workforce study was based on . . . what [the] data . . . really meant," which may have contributed to it being influential among decisionmakers.

Similar to CEW, the Community College Research Center (CCRC) at Teachers College is an independent organization affiliated with a postsecondary institution that is staffed primarily by academics and researchers. Aimed at informing research, policy, and practice around America's two-year public colleges, CCRC is led by Professor Thomas Bailey and has become a leading voice and data source regarding student success within the community college sector. Respondents from NCCCS discussed an even more robust partnership with this research organization compared to other intermediaries, with some officials referencing the "unique relationship" NCCCS has with CCRC.

As explained by then-President Scott Ralls, NCCCS's relationship with CCRC "started early on . . . [and] they became involved with us from the very beginning in terms of helping examine issues." In particular, Ralls noted, "things like how we developed our performance funding [and] certainly developmental education has been heavily influenced by CCRC research over time." Further, NCCCS "worked out a relationship where [CCRC] has a large volume of [their] student data records" to conduct research (e.g., Belfield & Crosta, 2012; Kalamkarian, Raufman, & Edgecombe, 2015) that can be used, in turn, to influence policy decisions across North Carolina's 2-year sector. Indeed, the partnership between NCCCS and CCRC reached far beyond simply a source of information and research, with one community college official noting Bailey's involvement in "state board meetings . . . to talk to the board about different topics"; in addition, "the head researcher of [a CCRC project] . . . spoke to the [NCCCS] system conference in 2012."

Ultimately, although the level of involvement varied, the relationships between UNC and CEW and between NCCCS and CCRC illustrate the SHEEO's intentional decisions to associate with researcher-based organizations. Each agency leader sought data and research capacity from independent organizations to inform and provide an unbiased perspective to decisionmakers in charge of system-level and statewide policies. Notably, based on remarks from the agency leaders, the decision to partner with these intermediaries was made entirely within UNC and NCCCS, although external forces, such as the emergence of strong political partisanship in North Carolina in recent years, may have served as a catalyst for these associations. Whatever the impetus, the partnerships between NCCCS and CCRC and between UNC and CEW highlight the potential range of opportunity that research-based intermediary organizations can provide to SHEEOs and their agencies.

Tennessee: National Center for Higher Education Management Systems (NCHEMS)

The Tennessee Higher Education Commission (THEC) operates as the state's coordinating board, overseeing Tennessee's two systems of higher education—the University of Tennessee, which is overseen by the University of Tennessee Board of Trustees, and the 13 community colleges and 27 technology centers governed by the Tennessee Board of Regents—and the six independent public university boards created under the 2016 Focus on College and University Success (FOCUS) Act (Tamburin, 2016). Established in 1967 by the state's General Assembly, THEC has recently been championed as a central cog in the establishment and updates to the performance-based funding (PBF) formula that has become synonymous with Tennessee's postsecondary sector (e.g., Bogue, 2002; Dougherty & Natow, 2015; Johnson & Yanagiura, 2016). Consequently, Tennessee's association with intermediary organizations has focused primarily on data and information support to further the existing PBF model and other college completion initiatives, which has led to a strong partnership between THEC and a researcher-leaning intermediary, the National Center for Higher Education Management Systems (NCHEMS).

Established in 1969, NCHEMS aims to bridge the "gap between research and practice by placing the latest concepts and tools in the hands of higher education policy makers and administrators" (NCHEMS, 2016). To this end, NCHEMS has provided extensive research and data, as well as technical assistance, through partnerships with institutions, policy organizations, and state higher education agencies, around various postsecondary topics, including state governance structures, assessment and accountability, the K–16 pipeline, and, most recently, assistance in improving postsecondary completion rates. However, the center's partnership with THEC transcends any specific policy issue and stands as a more institutionalized relationship.

For example, when discussing sources of information and research evidence around decisions, multiple THEC officials noted the importance of "personal communications" and "informal relationships" with various organizations and postsecondary policy experts, including Dennis Jones, president emeritus at NCHEMS, and Aims McGuinness, senior fellow at NCHEMS. Further, Richard G. Rhoda, former executive director of THEC, suggested these personal relationships at times supplant the use of other sources of information, due to the professional expertise and knowledge individuals associated with NCHEMS bring. As one THEC official noted, "we will email [NCHEMS], we'll call them . . . it's more in the idea development stage, and . . . in the informal evaluation stage. 'Just asking, are these things worth thinking about? Have other states thought of something similar? What did they run into? What worked there?' So, with NCHEMS and those folks, it's . . . a function of the relationship we have." When following up about the beginnings of the association between THEC and NCHEMS, though, a more complex relationship was outlined.

One official explained that THEC was awarded a "learning year grant" and

> contracted with [NCHEMS] to do a policy audit . . . as well as a brief memo to Dr. Rhoda, which I asked them to create saying . . . "Here are the findings of where the major misalignments are that need to be addressed." Then, I asked Dennis [Jones] to write a memo to [THEC] saying if [he] was the SHEEO in Tennessee, these are the first five things I would do, and that . . . became our base of operation from that point forward in what finally culminated in the CCTA, Complete College Tennessee Act.

Other respondents, including Rhoda and THEC Interim Executive Director Russ Deaton, emphasized that it was the involvement of Dennis Jones and NCHEMS during this policy audit that cemented the longstanding partnership between the two organizations. NCHEMS's work has supported much of Tennessee's college completion policy initiatives and has continued to be a source of support and advice.

From the perspective of the SHEEO, the affiliation between THEC and NCHEMS emphasizes the importance of satisfying the agency and state's needs and recognizes the value of personal networks. The partnership between the two organizations began through THEC's desire to better understand the state's policy needs. While this immediate goal was accomplished, it had additional effects on the policy direction of Tennessee. Further, because of the central role of NCHEMS and reputation of its staff—especially Jones and McGuinness—multiple THEC officials suggested their perspectives served as a point of "external validation," which helped ease their minds and convince state policymakers to support their initiatives. THEC continues to turn to Jones and NCHEMS for policy requests and more informal information gathering, reiterating the importance and success that the original collaboration generated.

Georgia: Complete College America

Georgia maintains a consolidated governing board structure, with the University System of Georgia (USG) leading the 28 public colleges and universities. The USG Chancellor serves as the state's official SHEEO. A key difference between USG and other state higher education agencies centers on the fact that it was established by the constitution of the state of Georgia rather than by an action of the General Assembly, granting greater autonomy from the state in guiding state postsecondary education policy. As a result, the legislature has less oversight and authority related to higher education, which one respondent claimed led to "negative perceptions and feelings towards public higher education" across the General Assembly. The governor, however, remains closely involved with USG, appointing all 19 members of the Board of Regents, which suggests an avenue for greater influence in decisionmaking and policy direction. To this end, it is unsurprising that Complete College America (CCA), a policymaker-leaning organization that prioritizes and targets the governor's office in recruiting member states to its "Alliance of States" (Complete College America, 2014), has played a significant role in the development and implementation of college completion policy in Georgia.

CCA serves as one of the largest single-issue intermediary organizations currently involved in postsecondary education, specifically focused on improving college completion nationally. Established in 2009, CCA membership currently includes 35 U.S. states and additional institutional consortia in its Alliance of States. Underlying its work, CCA has outlined and advocated for five original "game changers" to increase college completion (Complete College America, 2013): (1) a shift to performance funding of public institutions;[4] (2) transformation of remedial education to provide a parallel curriculum; (3) incentives for full-time students to enroll in 15 credits per semester; (4) structured schedules of class offerings to provide working students the ability to predict class availability; and (5) guided pathways to completion, whereby students can be tracked into disciplines and know when required courses should be taken. CCA seeks pledges from governors, in partnership with their states' colleges and universities, to make completion a statewide priority. Accordingly, in August 2011, Georgia joined CCA (State of Georgia, Office of the Governor, 2011) and has since become a model for its policies (e.g., Complete College America, 2016).

In interviews with our research team, the chancellor of USG and other agency officials made clear the importance of this partnership for Georgia's postsecondary initiatives. In fact, former Chancellor Hank Huckaby noted, "I don't think there's any doubt that the CCA effort . . . has been critical in Georgia opting in to achieve the goal of greater college [completion]," suggesting CCA was overall central in making increasing postsecondary attainment rates a central policy concern. Specifically, the chancellor emphasized that CCA provided an established idea that legislators could understand, with a "goal [and] purpose [that] resonated extremely well," which was imperative given the historical disconnect between legislators and USG. Ultimately, CCA's legitimizing role underscored Georgia's significant interest in joining.

Another USG official agreed, arguing that the state's policy direction had "focused largely on Complete College America [initiatives] and turned that into Complete College Georgia, trying to make sure that those that are in the [postsecondary] pipeline reach conclusion of credential." In particular, efforts to reform remedial education, improve advising and the use of predictive analytics, and consider the implementation of performance-based funding have been key initiatives for Complete College Georgia that draw heavily on research and best practices highlighted by CCA. Therefore, beyond validating and legitimizing postsecondary completion as a policy concern, CCA also played a significant role in providing information and advocating for specific policy initiatives that ultimately shaped Georgia's higher education policy agenda.

Interestingly, the strength of the partnership between CCA and USG may be waning. As one USG official noted, after several years of being a part of the Alliance of States, Georgia's higher education sector was "not the same entity at all anymore. So we're . . . definitely on the same page with CCA, but we have formulated our own goals at this point, so they're a little different." Another official emphasized that CCA "[does not] have the monopoly" on college completion policy and information; in other words, USG does not depend on this organization solely to further goals and already established initiatives. Consequently, while CCA recently highlighted Georgia as a model for corequisite remediation (Complete College America, 2016), the longevity of a CCA–USG partnership is unclear as USG seems unlikely to continue to rely solely on CCA to support Georgia's completion efforts.

That said, there are strong structural connections between CCA and USG. Based on CCA's strategy of recruiting member states through their governors, which in Georgia holds complete appointment power over USG, the close relationship between the SHEEO agency and CCA should be of little surprise. However, the means by which USG has maximized this partnership highlights the SHEEO's adept understanding of the needs of the state's postsecondary sector. In particular, the higher education executive was able to utilize CCA's platform to draw support for policy initiatives from legislators, who normally had a more tenuous relationship with USG. Further, by connecting themselves with a national organization, USG officials noted additional benefits of the partnership, including maximizing an understanding of best practices nationally. Although respondents indicated USG had been relying less on CCA for information and policy solutions, leadership changes within the agency may reshape this partnership once again.

Texas: The Texas Association of Business

In the structurally complex state of Texas, the Texas Higher Education Coordinating Board (THECB) serves as the primary agency overseeing the state's higher education sector. That sector includes 10 public universities systems, 46 public universities, 50 community college districts, and 4 technical colleges, represented by the Texas State Technical College System. While Texas is home to more postsecondary institutions than any other state nationally, there has been consistent resistance to outside influence across all sectors. Indeed, the interaction of THECB and its SHEEO, Commissioner Raymund Paredes, with intermediary organizations seems to be greatly influenced by characteristics that foster an insular state culture. As noted by Jillson (2012), "independence, autonomy, and personal responsibility . . . [are] central to the Anglo Texan sense of self" (p. 11), which leads to opposition and suspicion of intervention and involvement of external parties in the policymaking process (Malandra, 2012; Meinig, 1969).

Regarding the development and implementation of the state's college completion agenda, one intermediary organization often mentioned by members of THECB, and whom Paredes described in an interview as a "very powerful organization in Texas," was the policymaking-leaning intermediary Texas Association of Business (TAB). Led by CEO Bill Hammond, TAB's work centers on its mission: "To Make the Texas Business Climate the Best in the World." Since its inception in 1922, TAB has served as the primary voice for the Texas business community and has become a central player in any policy deemed influential on the status of the workforce. Consequently, higher education has been a longstanding area of interest for TAB, with the goal of improving Texas postsecondary institutions to ensure the development of a qualified workforce and the future of the business community statewide.

TAB has been involved extensively through multiple statewide presentations on the current status of Texas postsecondary education and has influenced the policymaking process via connections to more than 200 chambers of commerce across the state. However, its most newsworthy effort was a pair of billboards in 2011, including one that appeared near Austin Community College (ACC) bearing the message: "4% of ACC Students Graduate in 3 Years. Is that a Good Use of Tax $? TX Association of Business." In an interview, Hammond noted, "[TAB] spent $300 bucks on it . . . that was the best money we ever spent . . . because it permeated the cranium . . . [and] became a discussion point." In fact, Paredes agreed with the significance of TAB's billboards, suggesting it "changed everything" regarding how Texas institutions and policymakers perceived postsecondary completion and led to immediate action by institutional actors that quickened statewide policy action.[5]

TAB and other Texas-based intermediaries, including the Texas Business Leadership Council and Texas Public Policy Foundation, focus at the state level, in contrast to previously discussed intermediary organizations with a national scope, which presents unique implications for THECB. For instance, TAB has the ability to endorse and maintain close ties to legislators and other state policymakers, which Paredes emphasized, underlies the need to cooperate with these groups given their influence in the political environment. In fact, THECB respondents noted that when producing the board's Texas Higher Education Almanac, a compendium of state and institutional data compiled annually, they were sure to "send it to leaders of the business community," along with more traditional recipients, such as the governor's office, legislators, and institutional leaders. One THECB official even suggested that the prominence of TAB led to the "data-centric culture" and necessitated THECB's production of the almanac.

While the influence of TAB in the Texas postsecondary policy process seems clear, it is less clear whether this partnership was based on a strategic choice made by the SHEEO and the agency or if it was necessitated by the position of the greater business community within state-level decisionmaking. Indeed, among the policymaker-leaning intermediaries, TAB seems to be closest to the policymaker end of the continuum. In fact, Paredes emphasized the broad support of the business mindset by suggesting the inevitability of the adoption of outcomes-based funding models for 4-year institutions,[6] arguing that it will provide an avenue to gauge improvement more easily. Consequently, though there existed a working relationship between TAB and THECB, the SHEEO did not appear to have been central in the creation of this partnership, which seems to be a function of a policymaker-leaning organization and the underlying statewide environment necessitating a higher education–business connection.

CONCLUSION

These case narratives highlight three ways SHEEOs may encounter the actors and actions of intermediary organizations in their work. First, of course, SHEEOs may invite intermediary organizations to consult on policy and practice issues, collect data, or become engaged in presentations and deliberations with policy players in their state context. In North Carolina, the involvement of the Community College Research Center and the Center on Education and the Workforce was solicited through the actions of higher education leaders and was influential in sustaining and advancing higher education in the state. A similar process emerged in Tennessee, where state agency leaders involved the National Center for Higher Education Management Systems over a number of years, to the point that their engagement in central policy issues became almost institutionalized over several years and two governorships.

Second, outside actors or internal state actors such as governors, foundations, or legislators may directly influence SHEEOs to become engaged with an intermediary organization focused on the state's policies and practices. In Georgia the close relationships forged between the governor and Complete College America helped ensure that the state's postsecondary systems would attend to that organization's priorities. Although the University System of Georgia maintains substantial constitutional authority within the state, developing the system's connections to and collaborations with the CCA grew increasingly necessary as its primacy for the governor and his allies became clearer.

Third, SHEEOs may learn indirectly of activity by intermediary organizations within the state and find themselves debating alternative levels and approaches for engagement with these organizations and their agendas. In Texas, the state business association injected itself into postsecondary policy concerns regarding the community college system, emerging as a significant player when its startlingly accusatory billboards made it necessary for SHEEOs to shift their internal and external strategies in response (Gándara & Hearn, in press).

These three distinctive modes of intermediary involvement each call for political astuteness by SHEEOs, who need to cultivate organizational and political skills that can be drawn upon selectively for such challenges. Four, in particular, seem critical:

1. *Mapping:* It is imperative for SHEEOs to begin mapping the political terrain from the day of their appointment onward. Knowing and understanding the state's key political players and their interests, backgrounds, and personalities will facilitate making astute choices to deal effectively with outside organizations with comparable or even superior political power. In addition to the political terrain, SHEEOs must also map the demographic and economic landscapes of their states. This may lead to opportunities to partner with intermediaries that support populations underrepresented in higher education.

2. *Seeding:* Effective SHEEOs will not only understand the existing players in their states' political contexts but also players who might become engaged in the future. Both potential allies and potential enemies merit attention. As an example, in many states, the activities of ALEC in higher education in recent years have been largely unanticipated, placing SHEEOs in catch-up mode in responding.

3. *Validating:* As legislators and other political leaders in the states continue their attention to prospective policy changes in such

arenas as performance funding and "campus carry," SHEEOs may be wise to anticipate the need to affirm the quality of existing practices and policies against initiatives unsupported by data. Some intermediary organizations can provide resources in support of such defensive operations. For example, efforts to raise teaching loads, cut liberal arts classes, or freeze faculty salaries might be countered by reference to regional or national data provided by such organizations as SHEEO or SREB regarding practices in other states and institutions (and especially states and institutions deemed competitors by policy advocates). Of course, the reverse is true as well: Intermediary organizations may provide support for initiatives being pushed by SHEEOs and their allies.

4. *Staffing:* Debates around policy and practice issues in higher education often devolve into a dialogue of conflicting data claims. SHEEO offices must be prepared to compete in the world of, if not "alternative facts," at least alternative interpretations of data. Winning in such debates depends on being well equipped to probe and understand "big data" and to present findings from those data in effective ways to outside parties widely varying in their understanding and training. Although all SHEEO offices have staff savvy in the use of state data and Integrated Postsecondary Education Data Sets (IPEDS), not all of them have staff sufficiently trained to engage in larger political debates. Some of those debates will call for offensive data use, and some will call for defensive data use, but all will benefit from sophistication in statistics and communication. Such skills are necessary for SHEEO office staffing.

We conclude with a discussion of future research activities that would increase the descriptive and conceptual understanding of the SHEEO–intermediary connections in all states. First, researchers might examine the associations between state context and intermediary organization activity. The extent to which policymakers might be influenced by intermediary organizations seems likely to relate in some way to various state characteristics. For example, how robust is the research capacity of the state legislature, governor's office, and SHEEO agency? The effects of this capacity are woefully underexamined, so it is unclear whether states with greater research capacity are more likely to rely on intermediary organizations because they have the research expertise to acquire and interpret this information. Alternatively, these states could use their research capacity to build in-state data systems and analysis. Also, to what extent does political party or ideology influence the preferred information sources? In some states, governors may be tightly connected to the Republican or Democratic Governors Association, or legislators may be inclined to rely on the ALEC. These stronger connections could restrict SHEEO agency engagement with other intermediary organizations that elected officials could view as counter to their political positions.

Second, further analysis into the personal networks that SHEEOs bring to their agencies would increase the understanding of the SHEEO–intermediary connection. As other chapters in this volume reflect, SHEEOs often have longstanding connections to many intermediary organizations that stand to influence. The strong connection of NCHEMS with the Tennessee SHEEO (and surely with other SHEEOs) may also lead to additional intermediary connections. Social network analysis could be particularly fruitful to identify the density of ties among and between individual SHEEOs and a broad range of intermediary organizations. This network analysis could also examine the role of individual characteristics (i.e., gender, race, education, experience) of SHEEOs and intermediary leaders among whom White males are overrepresented. Such an analysis would be an excellent empirical start to understanding these networks and could lead to additional examination as to the effect of the networks on various postsecondary education policy decisions.

Third, researchers might examine the role of regional, national, and ad hoc networks or convenings in shaping state-level policy decisions. This strand of research could begin with the social network analysis of SHEEOs, or it could begin by identifying and analyzing the networks created by various intermediary organizations. The regional compacts, for example, each have regular meetings of their members and various policymakers to share information related to policy issues facing their regions. Similarly, the Gates and Lumina foundations often host convenings with campus, state, and national higher education policy leaders and researchers to discuss policy trends and seek innovative policy decisions. This activity seems to have increased in recent years, yet there has been little scholarly attention to its effects.

A state's SHEEO plays a pivotal role in how other policy organizations influence higher education policy. Our chapter suggests that SHEEO and intermediary activity in the states is fundamentally influenced by the state's various social, organizational, and political contexts. Just as these state contexts vary, so too do the types of intermediary organizations active in state higher education policy. By placing these organizations on the researcher–policymaker continuum, we contend that SHEEOs might be better able to identify their strengths, emphases, and possible connections to the higher education policy decisions in their states.

Acknowledgments. Work on this chapter, including gathering and interpreting the state-level evidence presented here, was supported by a William T. Grant Foundation research grant for our larger project titled "The Distinct Role of Intermediary Organizations in Fostering Research Utilization for State College Completion Policy." In addition to the authors' grateful acknowledgement of this generous support, we also acknowledge and appreciate the data collection and analysis contributions of Denisa Gándara, Lori Prince Hagood, Lindsey Hammond, Kristen C. Linthicum, Jennifer Rippner, and Tiffanie Spencer. Finally, we note with appreciation the insightful comments and suggestions of the editors of this volume.

NOTES

1. Hearn, McLendon, and Linthicum (2017) and Hearn and Ness (in press) provided more detailed reviews of research on this and other contextual factors influencing higher education policy adoption and scope.

2. Our focal state of Tennessee has provided a solid example of this duality, as it went through a controversial, politically sensitive reorganization of its governing arrangements in the direction of institution-specific boards (Sandoval, 2016).

3. Interestingly, the merit scholarship idea caught on quickly in states well beyond Georgia's home region, making this a case of national rather than purely regional policy diffusion. Presumably states across the country were making preemptive strikes to lessen student outflows and improve in-state educational quality (Doyle, 2006; Heller, 2002; Ness, 2008).

4. CCA revamped its list of "game changers" in 2016 and replaced performance funding with a goal of reforming "math pathways" at institutions. This new focus aims to change academic curricula to align math requirements more closely to a student's chosen program of study rather than uniformly selecting a default gateway math course.

5. Gándara and Hearn (in press) provided more detailed analysis of the influence of TAB and other organizations active in Texas completion efforts.

6. Texas adopted performance-based funding for 2-year colleges (community colleges and technical colleges) in 2013.

REFERENCES

Archibald, R. B., & Feldman, D. H. (2006). State higher education spending and the tax revolt. *Journal of Higher Education, 77*(4), 618–644.

Belfield, C., & Crosta, P. M. (2012). *Predicting success in college: The importance of placement tests and high school transcripts* (CCRC Working Paper No. 42). New York: Community College Research Center, Teachers College, Columbia University.

Berry, F. S., & Berry, W. D. (1990). State lottery adoptions as policy innovations: An event history analysis. *American Political Science Review, 84*(2), 295–416.

Berry, F. S., & Berry, W. D. (2014). Innovation and diffusion models in policy research. In P. A. Sabatier & C. Weible (Eds.), *Theories of the policy process* (pp. 307–338). Boulder, CO: Westview Press.

Birnbaum, R. (2000). Policy scholars are from Venus; Policy makers are from Mars. *The Review of Higher Education, 23*(2), 119–132.

Bogue, E. G. (2002). Twenty years of performance funding in Tennessee: A case study of policy intent and effectiveness. In J. C. Burke (Ed.), *Funding public colleges and universities for performance: Popularity, problems, and prospects* (pp. 85–105). Albany, NY: Rockefeller Institute Press.

Carnevale, A. P., & Rose, S. J. (2011). *The undereducated American.* Washington, DC: Georgetown University Center on Education and the Workforce.

Carnevale, A. P., Smith, N., & Strohl, J. (2013). *Recovery: Job growth and education requirements through 2020.* Washington, DC: Georgetown University Center on Education and the Workforce.

Complete College America. (2013). *The game changers: Are states implementing the best reforms to get more college graduates?* Indianapolis, IN: Author.

Complete College America. (2014). Alliance of states: Leading the college completion movement. Retrieved from completecollege.org/the-alliance-of-states/

Complete College America. (2016). *Corequisite remediation: Spanning the completion divide.* Retrieved from completecollege.org/spanningthedivide/#home

Daly, A. J., Finnigan, K. S., Moolenaar, N. M., & Che, J. (2014). The critical role of brokers in the access and use of evidence at the school and district level. In K. S. Finnigan & A. J. Daly (Eds.), *Using research evidence in education: From the schoolhouse door to Capitol Hill* (pp. 13–31). New York, NY: Springer.

Dougherty, K. J., & Natow, R. S. (2015). *The politics of performance funding for higher education: Origins, discontinuations, and transformations.* Baltimore, MD: Johns Hopkins University Press.

Dougherty, K. J., Natow, R. S., Bork, R. H., Jones, S. M., & Vega, B. E. (2013). Accounting for higher education accountability: Political origins of state performance funding for higher education. *Teachers College Record, 115,* 1–50.

Dougherty, K. J., Natow, R. S., Jones, S. M., Lahr, H., Pheatt, L., & Reddy, V. (2014). The political origins of performance funding 2.0 in Indiana, Ohio, and Tennessee: Theoretical perspectives and comparisons with performance funding 1.0 (Working Paper No. 68). New York: Community College Research Center, Teachers College, Columbia University.

Doyle, W. R. (2006). Adoption of merit-based student grant programs: An event history analysis. *Educational Evaluation and Policy Analysis, 28*(3), 259–285.

Education Commission of the States. (2017). *50-state comparison: Statewide longitudinal data systems.* Retrieved from www.ecs.org/state-longitudinal-data-systems

Ferguson, M. (2013). Governors and the executive branch. In V. Gray, R. L. Hanson, & T. Kousser (Eds.), *Politics in the American states: A comparative analysis* (10th ed., pp. 208–250). Thousand Oaks, CA: Sage.

Fryar, A. H., & Meier, K. J. (2008). Race, structure, and state governments: The politics of higher education diversity. *Journal of Politics, 70*(3), 851–860.

Gándara, D., & Hearn, J. C. (in press). College completion, the Texas way: An examination of the development of college completion policy in a distinctive political culture. *Teachers College Record.*

Guston, D. H. (2000). *Between politics and science: Credibility on the line.* New York: Cambridge University Press.

Hall, C. E., & Thomas, S. L. (2012). "Advocacy philanthropy" and the public policy agenda: The role of modern foundations in American higher education.

Paper presented at the American Educational Research Association, Vancouver, Canada.

Hearn, J. C., Lacy, T. A., & Warshaw, J. B. (2014). State research and development tax credits: The historical emergence of a distinctive economic policy instrument. *Economic Development Quarterly, 28*(2), 166–181.

Hearn, J. C., McLendon, M. K., & Lacy, T. A. (2013). State-funded "eminent scholars" programs: University faculty recruitment as an emerging policy instrument. *Journal of Higher Education, 84*(5), 601–641.

Hearn, J. C., McLendon, M. K., & Linthicum, K. C. (2017). Conceptualizing state policy adoption and diffusion. In M. P. Paulsen (Ed.), *Higher education: Handbook of theory and research* (Vol. 32, pp. 309–354). New York, NY: Springer.

Hearn, J. C., McLendon, M. K., & Mokher, C. G. (2008). Accounting for student success: An empirical analysis of the origins and spread of state student unit-record systems. *Research in Higher Education, 50*(1), 665–683.

Hearn, J. C., & Ness, E. C. (in press). The ecology of state higher-education policymaking in the U.S. In D. Palfreyman, T. Tapper, & S. Thomas (Eds.), *The funding of higher education: Higher education as a public or private good?* Oxfordshire, England: Routledge.

Heller, D. E. (2002). State merit scholarship programs: An overview. In D. E. Heller & P. Marin (Eds.), *State merit scholarship programs and racial inequality* (pp. 13–22). Cambridge, MA: The Civil Rights Project at Harvard University.

Hillman, N. W., Tandberg, D. A., & Sponsler, B. A. (2015). Public policy and higher education strategies for framing a research agenda. *ASHE Higher Education Report, 41*(2).

Hossler, D., Lund, J. P., Ramin, J., Westfall, S., & Irish, S. (1997). State funding for higher education: The Sisyphean task. *Journal of Higher Education. 68*(2), 160–188.

Jillson, C. C. (2012). *Lone star tarnished: A critical look at Texas politics and public policy*. New York, NY: Routledge.

Johnson, N., & Yanagiura, T. (2016). *Early results of outcomes-based funding in Tennessee* (Lumina Issue Papers). Indianapolis, IN: Lumina Foundation.

Kalamkarian, H. S., Raufman, J., & Edgecombe, N. (2015). *Statewide developmental education reform: Early implementation in Virginia and North Carolina.* New York: Community College Research Center, Teachers College, Columbia University.

Lacy, T. A. (2011). *Measuring governance: State postsecondary structures and a continuum of centralization* (Unpublished doctoral dissertation). Athens: University of Georgia.

Lacy, T. A., & Tandberg, D. A. (2014). Rethinking policy diffusion: The interstate spread of "finance innovations." *Research in Higher Education, 55*(7), 627–649.

Li, A. Y. (2017). Covet thy neighbor or "reverse policy diffusion"? State adoption of performance funding 2.0. *Research in Higher Education, 58,* 746–771.

Lomas, J. (2007). The in-between world of knowledge brokering. *British Medical Journal, 334,* 129–132.

Louis, K. S., Febey, K., & Gordon, M. F. (2015). Political cultures in education: Emerging perspectives. In B. S. Cooper, J. G. Cibulka, & L. D. Fusarelli (Eds.), *Handbook of education politics and policy* (pp. 118–147). New York: Routledge.

Lowry, R. C. (2001). The effects of state political interests and campus outputs on public university revenues. *Economics of Education Review, 20*, 105–119.

Lowry, R. C. (2007). The political economy of public universities in the United States. *State Politics and Policy Quarterly, 7*(3), 303–324.

Malandra, G. H. (2012). Efforts to improve productivity: The impact of higher education reform in Texas. In A. P. Kelly & M. Schneider (Eds.), *Getting to graduation: The completion agenda in higher education* (pp. 246–268). Baltimore, MD: Johns Hopkins University Press.

Marcus, L. R. (1997). Restructuring state higher education governance patterns. *Review of Higher Education, 20*(4), 399–418.

McGuinness, A. C. (2016). *State policy leadership for the future: History of state coordination and governance and alternatives for the future.* Denver, CO: Education Commission of the States.

McLendon, M. K. (2003). Setting the governmental agenda for state decentralization of higher education. *Journal of Higher Education, 74*(5), 479–515.

McLendon, M. K., Deaton, R., & Hearn, J.C. (2007). The enactment of reforms in state governance of higher education: Testing the political-instability hypothesis. *Journal of Higher Education, 78*(6), 645–675.

McLendon, M. K., & Hearn, J. C. (2013). The resurgent interest in performance-based funding for higher education. *Academe, 99*(6), 25–30.

McLendon, M. K., Hearn, J. C., & Deaton, R. (2006). Called to account: Analyzing the origins and spread of state performance-accountability policies for higher education. *Educational Evaluation and Policy Analysis, 28*(1), 1–24.

McLendon, M. K., & Mokher, C. G. (2009). The origins and growth of state policies that privatize public higher education. In C. Morphew & P. Eckel (Eds.), *Privatizing the public university: Perspectives from across the academy* (pp. 7–32). Baltimore, MD: Johns Hopkins University Press.

Meinig, D. W. (1969). *Imperial Texas: An interpretive essay in cultural geography.* Austin: University of Texas Press.

Mokher, C. G. (2010). Do "education governors" matter? The case of statewide P–16 councils. *Educational Evaluation and Policy Analysis, 32*(4), 476–497.

Mokher, C. G., & McLendon, M. K. (2009). Uniting secondary and postsecondary education: An event history analysis of state adoption of dual enrollment policies. *American Journal of Education, 115*, 249–277.

Mumper, M. (2001). The paradox of college prices: Five stories with no clear lesson. In D. Heller (Ed.), *The states and public higher education policy: Affordability, access, and accountability* (pp. 39–63). Baltimore, MD: Johns Hopkins University Press.

National Center for Higher Education Management Systems. (2016). *About NCHEMS.* Retrieved from www.nchems.org/about/index.php

Ness, E. C. (2008). *Merit aid and the politics of education.* New York: Routledge.

Ness, E. C. (2010). The role of information in the policy process: Implications for the examination of research utilization in higher education policy. In J. C. Smart (Ed.), *Higher education: Handbook of theory and research* (Vol. 25, pp. 1–49). New York, NY: Springer.

Ness, E. C., & Gándara, D. (2014). Ideological think tanks in the states: An inventory of their prevalence, networks, and higher education policy activity. *Educational Policy, 28*(2), 258–280.

Ness, E. C, Hearn, J. C., & Rubin, P. G. (2017, May). Intermediaries in higher education: A typology of organizations influence the college completion efforts. Paper presented at the annual meeting of the American Educational Research Association, San Antonio, TX.

Ness, E. C., & Tandberg, D. A. (2013). The determinants of state spending on higher education: How capital project funding differs from general fund appropriations. *Journal of Higher Education, 84*(3), 329–357.

Ness, E.C., Tandberg, D. A., & McLendon, M. K. (2015). Interest groups and state policy for higher education: New conceptual understandings and future research directions. In M. B. Paulsen (Ed.), *Higher education: Handbook of theory and research* (Vol. 30, pp. 151–186). Dordrecht, The Netherlands: Springer.

Nicholson-Crotty, J., & Meier, K. J. (2003). Politics, structure, and public policy: The case of higher education. *Educational Policy, 17*(1), 80–97.

Parry, M., Field, K., & Supiano, B. (2013, July 14). The Gates effect. *The Chronicle of Higher Education.* Retrieved from www.chronicle.com/article/The-Gates-Effect/140323

Sandoval, G. (2016, June 9). Tennessee governor signs plan to create new university boards. *Chronicle of Higher Education.* Retrieved from www.chronicle.com/blogs/ticker/tennessee-governor-signs-plan-to-create-new-university-boards/112049

Snow, C. P. (1961). *Science and government.* Cambridge, MA: Harvard University Press.

Squire, P. (2012). *The evolution of American legislatures.* Ann Arbor, MI: University of Michigan Press.

State of Georgia, Office of the Governor. (2011). Deal announces $1 million grant, Complete College Georgia initiative. Retrieved from gov.georgia.gov/press-releases/2011-08-04/deal-announces-1-million-grant-complete-college-georgia-initiative

Tamburin, A. (2016, June 8). Gov. Bill Haslam signs transformative college overhaul. *The Tennessean.* Retrieved from www.tennessean.com/story/news/education/2016/06/08/gov-bill-haslam-signs-transformative-college-overhaul/85604390/

Tandberg, D. A. (2010a). Politics, interest groups and state funding of public higher education. *Research in Higher Education, 51*(5), 416–450.

Tandberg, D. A. (2010b). Interest groups and governmental institutions: The politics of state funding of public higher education. *Educational Policy, 24*(5), 735–778.

Tandberg, D. A. (2013). The conditioning role of state higher education governance structures. *Journal of Higher Education, 84*(4), 506–543.

Tandberg, D. A, Fowles, J. T., & McLendon, M. K. (2017). The governor and the state higher education executive officer: How the relationship shapes state financial support for higher education. *Journal of Higher Education, 18*(1), 1–25.

Tandberg, D. A., & Griffith, C. (2013). State support of higher education: Data, measures, findings, and directions for future research. In M. B. Paulsen (Ed.), *Higher education: Handbook of theory and research* (Vol. 28, pp. 613–685). New York: Springer.

Tandberg, D. A., & Ness, E. C. (2011). State capital expenditures for higher education: "Where the politics really happens." *Journal of Education Finance, 36*(4), 394–423.

Toutkoushian, R. K., & Hollis, P. (1998). Using panel data to examine legislative demand for higher education. *Education Economics, 6*(2), 141–158.

Zumeta, W. M. (1992). State policies and private higher education: Policies, correlates, and linkages. *Journal of Higher Education, 63*(4), 363–417.

Zumeta, W. M. (1996). Meeting the demand for higher education without breaking the bank: A framework for the design of state higher education policies for an era of increasing demand. *Journal of Higher Education, 67*(4), 367–425.

CHAPTER 8

Politics and Presidents

The Relationship Between SHEEOs
and Campus Leaders

Tracey Bark and Alisa Hicklin Fryar

SHEEOs, the individuals who lead state higher education boards, are often portrayed as the man or woman in the middle. Their core functions are to work on behalf of state elected officials in efforts to hold institutions accountable and, at the same time, serve as the leading representative of the institutions of higher education in the state (Bracco, Richardson, Callan, & Finney, 1999). Having to serve as both overseer and advocate inevitably leads to conflict, uncertainty, and a leadership role that can vary tremendously across states and over time (Tierney, 2006). Given the centrality, diversity, and significance of this role, it is remarkable to see so little scholarship on the role of the SHEEO and the SHEEO's organization in higher education governance. Emerging research, like the work found in this volume, is sorely needed.

In discussing the creation of the SHEEO organizations, Hearn and Griswold traced their origins to a need for state elected officials to find a better way to deal with the "increased political infighting for resources and increased lobbying by institutions" (1994, p. 161). Similarly, Ness argued that these organizations were created "with the primary function to buffer state governments *from* postsecondary institutions" [emphasis added] (2010, p. 40). Although Hillman, Tandberg, and Sponsler noted the importance of the SHEEO's "responsibility to colleges and universities in the SHEEO's state," (2015, pp. 29–30) we have little evidence that speaks to how SHEEOs balance these commitments or whether campus leaders recognize this dual role of the SHEEO.

This chapter relies on theories of accountability, oversight, and management to inform an analysis of the dual role of SHEEOs and their organizations, with greater attention devoted to the relationships between SHEEOs and campus leaders. The data was drawn from an original survey of university presidents to offer a look at how presidents view the SHEEOs' organizations in their states; whether variations in political dynamics, state governance structures, and individual characteristics influence both direct roles of SHEEOs; and how variations among SHEEOs can influence relationships between campus leaders and state elected officials.

LITERATURE REVIEW

Higher Education Governance

Much of the early scholarship related to statewide higher education agencies and the executives who run them concentrated on structural issues. Many scholars focused on the organization of and authority granted to governance boards in each state (Hines, 1988; Hughes & Mills, 1975). Due to the variation that exists across states, several of these scholars created typologies to categorize such boards in order to make them amenable to study. The primary division of these classifications has been between those boards with coordinating authority and those with broader governing authority over public institutions (Berdahl, 1971; McGuinness, 2003; Millett, 1984).

Beginning in the late 1980s, the literature moved toward assessing governance boards as accountability structures, a perspective that borrowed heavily from the public administration study of bureaucratic control and the earlier work in economics on principal-agent theory. According to this literature, bureaucratic agencies are intended to be largely under the control of political principals (Waterman, Rouse, & Wright, 1998). When creating a new bureaucratic agency, politicians must structure it in such a way as to incentivize it to do what the creators intended (Moe, 1995). The main focus of these works was the potential for different incentives between the two organizations, thereby inducing the problem of moral hazard, in which an information asymmetry is created when agents possess more experience and expertise in a given policy area than do their political principals (Miller, 2005). This situation may lead the bureaucratic agents to act in accordance with their own perspective, which does not necessarily align with the intentions of the principals. It was this concern that scholars addressed in studying statewide governance boards as accountability mechanisms. From this viewpoint, state agencies have usually been seen as an extension of the legislature in imposing regulations and oversight on the colleges and universities within a state (Heller, 2001).

Researchers focusing on higher education governance utilized this approach in the early work exploring relationships between state boards and campus leaders, seeking to determine whether governance structures play a significant role in promoting different incentive structures and managerial behaviors (Knott & Payne, 2004). In this top-down view, statewide governance boards have often been considered the agent of the state government and assessed in terms of their cooperation with state policy. The tension between state authority and institutional autonomy has been most apparent in three areas: financial and budgetary matters, personnel and appointive powers, and academic policy (Volkwein, 1986). Scholars have examined each of these areas in turn, although financial and budgetary matters have been subject to the most attention.

The findings of these studies have been somewhat mixed. Volkwein (1986) and Volkwein and Malik (1997) found little evidence that state regulation and control of public universities was related to campus quality, while Knott and Payne (2004) found that the structure of state boards influenced managerial choices of resource allocation. Others have shown a strong link between governance structures and institutional performance on affordability (Bowen et al., 1997) as well as between structure and the ability of political forces to influence higher education (Nicholson-Crotty & Meier, 2003). Centralization has also been found to play a role in these relationships, both in terms of a university system's response to statewide political priorities (Knott & Payne, 2004) and with respect to student outcomes (Manna, 2013). Despite the lack of consensus about the specific impacts of state authority on higher education institutions, this body of research was consistent in viewing statewide governance bodies primarily as bureaucratic agents of the political powers within state government.

Role and Relationships of the SHEEOs and Their Organizations

The prevalence of a top-down perspective in higher education governance literature on policy implementation seems to be rooted in researchers' assumptions that power flows from the state government downward through governance boards to the higher education institutions in a state. This has caused them to focus on the relationship between governance boards and other actors at the state level, which have been characterized as dynamic and complex (Marcus, 1997). However, the relationship of these boards and their executive officers to the institutions they oversee is equally significant. Such relationships can also be quite complicated, as institutional leaders often have mixed feelings about coordination by a statewide body (Perkins & Israel, 1972).

Complications also arise from the perspective of the state agency, as centralized boards and their staffs often find themselves "torn between the conviction that they should be institutional proponents and the realization that their statutory obligations require objectivity and a close relationship to governors and legislative bodies" (Hughes & Mills, 1975, pp. 247–248).

This space can be incredibly difficult for SHEEOs to navigate, as they essentially occupy a "no-man's-land" between institutions and state government and are expected to be effective in both environments (Hines, 1988; Tierney, 2006). This position led Tandberg (2013) to label state higher education governance structures as "boundary-spanning organizations" whose primary roles include facilitating and controlling the flow of information between various entities. This argument was further supported by earlier research, which demonstrated that governing boards and their appointed executives represent institutional interests to state government throughout the policymaking process (Bracco et al., 1999).

Because they occupy the boundary between state governments and higher education institutions, governance boards have frequently been perceived as a sort of buffer between the two entities. This viewpoint has been especially popular among higher education supporters who value institutional autonomy and who see state governing and coordinating boards as shielding institutions from state regulations and interference (Knott & Payne, 2004; Richardson, Bracco, Callan, & Finney, 1999). Others have viewed these bodies as insulating universities against direct political control that can affect university quality (Eykamp, 1995). These influences can come from a variety of state political actors, including the state legislature, the governor, and even state budget officials (Heller, 2001). From the university perspective, centralized governance boards can provide insulation from these entities and relieve public pressure for increased state control over higher education (Moos & Rourke, 1959).

It is unlikely that all university leaders share the same view of their state higher education agency, however. Leaders of different universities within a state may have differing opinions of the SHEEO and state governance board. For example, "presidents of smaller, regional component institutions may regard them very positively" due to the benefit received through use of centralized resources, whereas larger flagship universities may regard them as the source of unnecessary regulatory burdens (Flawn, 1990, p. 179). This difference reflects the privileged status many campuses enjoy within their state, which can dramatically affect the way an institutional leader views the statewide body (Perkins & Israel, 1972). Perceptions can also vary across states, depending on the level of general influence possessed by the state agency and its ability to achieve consensus from universities on its policies (Hughes & Mills, 1975).

These factors lead to a remarkable amount of variance across states in the perceptions of their governance boards. Despite this variation being well suited for empirical study, few scholars have taken this approach. This oversight has resulted in the bottom-up perspective being largely missing from the literature on higher education governance. This chapter takes this perspective by examining the role and relationships of governing boards and SHEEOs from the viewpoint of the institutions they govern.

DATA AND METHODS

Most of the data for this analysis and discussion were drawn from an original survey of public, 4-year university chief administrators, conducted in 2012.[1] The survey was sent to all chief administrators at the 565 institutions in the 50 U.S. states with Carnegie classifications ranging from Baccalaureate Institutions (both Arts and Science and Diverse Fields) to Research Universities (Very High Research), excluding institutions without undergraduate programs and institutions with specialized missions (e.g., military institutions). The response rate for the survey was comparable to similar surveys (25 percent). The 140 respondents were representative of the larger group on observable factors at the institutional level. There was no significant difference in response rates for institutions in states with a single centralized governing board and those in states with a coordinating board, but there was a slightly lower response rate for states with either no board or no single centralized board, especially California.

The survey focused on the relationships between university presidents, their institutions, and the groups and individuals involved in governance and oversight. Many of the questions asked presidents about their relationships with state actors, as well as federal, regional, and local entities. The content of these questions ranged from rating the quality of relationships among the university and state actors to the role of performance information and the role of accountability.[2] To assess the responses of university presidents to these questions, the primary methods were OLS regression models and difference of means tests between various institutions.

A key factor on which these institutions were compared was the type of governing body used in the state in which the institution is located. For this purpose, states were categorized as using either a centralized governing board or a coordinating board or having no centralized body related to higher education.[3] State categorizations were determined based on data gathered by the Education Commission of the States (ECS, McGuinness & Fulton, 2007). In those situations when the ECS data was unclear about a state's status in the year of the survey, the websites of the individual government agencies were used to make the determination. Using this process, a centralized governing board was defined as one that possessed operating authority over public institutions of higher education within the state. Coordinating boards were considered those that existed in a more advisory capacity and did not have operating authority over public higher education institutions. The remaining states had neither a governing board nor a coordinating board in 2012 and instead allowed these functions to be performed by systems of institutions or the institutions themselves.

Much of the focus of the survey centered on perceptions of the SHEEO, but it is important to note that these perceptions, as they relate to SHEEOs, were measured on the organizational level. In this format, it would be difficult to separate influences fully attributed to the SHEEO as an individual from influences that arose from the ways in which the SHEEO's decisions and leadership influenced others in their organization. For that reason, references to SHEEOs in the following analysis includes SHEEOs and their organizations.[4]

FINDINGS

The analysis focused on three core questions: (1) How do presidents view the relationships between their institutions and the SHEEO's organization? (2) How do variations in state SHEEO structures influence relationships between university leaders and other state actors (more specifically, the legislature and the governor)? (3) How do perceptions of the quality of the relationship between the institution and the SHEEO, as well as the president's characteristics, influence perceptions of state support of higher education and state influence on public higher education?

Perceptions of the SHEEO Organization

The analysis begins with a look at the two questions that capture the dual roles of the SHEEO: advocate and overseer. The "SHEEO as advocate" role was conceptualized as one in which the SHEEO is viewed as the person who represents and speaks on behalf of the state's colleges and universities, especially in legislative and budgetary arenas. In the case of an advocacy role, presidents of institutions would largely view the SHEEO as "one of us." This view would be quite different from the view of the SHEEO as the overseer. In a "SHEEO as overseer" role, the college leaders would be more likely to view the SHEEO primarily as part of the governor's team or an extension of the legislature. When presidents saw the SHEEO's role as a top-down effort to increase political oversight, the SHEEO might be seen as "one of them." It is tempting to oversimplify this distinction by pointing to career paths and methods of appointment, assuming that a SHEEO who has a history of work on a college campus or as a president would be more likely to be seen as an advocate, whereas a SHEEO who has served in elected office would be viewed as "one of them." But there were many examples where those expectations did not hold and where a SHEEO's reputation within the state might shift over time. As the person who is tasked with serving a role intended to connect colleges and political leaders, this tension is inevitable, but it is interesting to explore the variations in those perceptions and their connection to other factors.

The first question asked presidents to rate the extent to which they believe that individuals in the state's governing board, coordinating board, or planning agency "understand the challenges that [their] institution faces" on a scale of 0 to 10, with 0 representing "Not at All" and 10 representing "Completely Understand." The second question was similar in its structure, but it asked presidents to rate "how much influence [individuals in the state's governing board, coordinating board, or planning agency] have over the way you manage your institution" on a scale of 0 to 10, with 0 representing "No Influence" and 10 representing "Complete Control."[5]

Given the popular rhetoric regarding increased accountability and frustrations expressed about burdensome paperwork and oversight, the expectation was that presidents would focus more on the role of SHEEOs as overseers (level of influence) than as advocates (level of understanding). Instead, the data contained similar averages, with a mean score of 5.38 for understanding and 5.35 for influence. There was also tremendous variation. Figures 8.1 and 8.2 map the distribution of responses to these two questions. The horizontal axes of these figures represent the spectrum along which presidents gave responses, with the height of the lines showing the number of responses at a given point along the scale, relative to total respondents. With this in mind, the key takeaway from Figures 8.1 and 8.2 is that responses fell along the entire spectrum for both survey questions, rather than clustering toward one end, showing that university presidents have varying perspectives regarding the role of the SHEEO in their state.

The distributions, while similar, do have a few important differences, most notably in the way in which the "SHEEO as advocate" had both a larger percentage of respondents rating the SHEEO as 7 or higher, "but also with" a larger percentage of respondents rating the SHEEO as 4 or lower.

Figure 8.1. SHEEO as Advocate

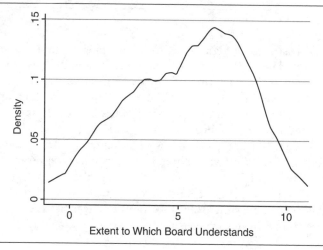

Figure 8.2. SHEEO as Overseer

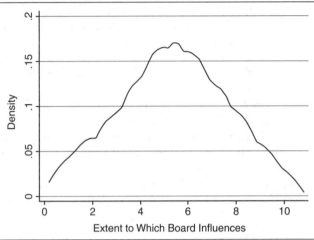

Figure 8.3. Side-by-Side Comparison of Advocate and Overseer Ratings

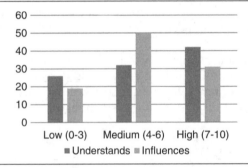

This is demonstrated in Figure 8.3, which displays the number of respondents who rated the SHEEO in terms of influence and understanding within each section of the scale. Using this figure, one can see that ratings of the SHEEO as an "overseer" were more concentrated in the middle range, while responses to the SHEEO as an "advocate" were broader to include a larger number of respondents in both the "Low" and "High" ranges. This clarifies what is harder to see in the distributions presented in these graphs, namely that presidents have somewhat different perceptions with regard to each of roles played by SHEEOs.

These dual roles of overseer and advocate are often viewed as a trade-off or a balance: In some states, SHEEOs (and the agencies they lead) have a more bottom-up role and are seen as more understanding of the institutions,

Figure 8.4. Side-by-Side Comparison of Board Level of Influence by Type

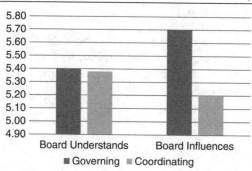

while in other states, they play more of an influential top-down role. However, from the president's perspective, these two roles may move together. The extent to which a president perceived the SHEEO's organization as having considerable influence over his or her institution was positively and significantly correlated[6] with the extent to which the president believed that the SHEEO's organization understood the challenges faced by the college or university.

These perceptions were also influenced by the structure of the state SHEEO's organization, though not as much as one might expect. As demonstrated in Figure 8.4, presidents in states with centralized governing boards rated their board's level of influence higher than the average rating of the board's influence in states with coordinating boards. Although these differences were statistically significant, the gap was not as large as expected. Interestingly, the differences in states with governing and coordinating boards in the extent to which presidents believe that the SHEEO's organization understands the challenges of their institution were neither statistically nor substantively significant, with an average of 5.40 in states with governing boards and 5.38 in states with coordinating boards.

Overall, it was a bit surprising to see such wide variation in presidents' views of their relationship with their SHEEO/board, as shown in Figures 8.1 and 8.2. However, it was more surprising to see how these views did not really trend closely with variations in state structures. This suggested state structures may not influence presidents' perceptions of their relationships with their SHEEOs as much as it may influence presidents' perceptions of their relationships with other state actors and the more general political climate. If SHEEOs are acting as buffers, differences would be expected in these other relationships as much, or more, than in the direct relationship.

SHEEO Agency Structure and Relationships Between the Campus and the Capitol

The survey also asked university presidents about their view of the political environment. For the purpose of this analysis, five measures are explored: the overall political climate for higher education, the extent to which the state legislature understands the challenges the institution faces, the extent to which the governor understands the challenges the institution faces, the extent to which the governor influences the way the president manages the institution, and the extent to which the state legislature influences the way the president manages the institution.

Political Climate. In the first measure, political climate, presidents were asked to rate "the political climate in your state as it relates to higher education and public universities" on a scale from –5 (Very Hostile) to +5 (Very Supportive). The average of the responses fell slightly into hostile territory, with a mean of –0.25 and a median of –1.00. When comparing responses for presidents in states with different board structures, expectations were uncertain. On one hand, stronger, more centralized board structures could be more effective in "keeping the peace," which would suggest more supportive climates in states with governing boards, more hostile climates in states with either a planning agency or no board at all, and coordinating boards somewhere in between. Alternatively, centralized boards could be seen as another layer of regulatory burden or as a stronger agent of the state, so that states with coordinating boards may be the most advantaged.

The basic findings support the first expectation, but only in part. Presidents in states with governing boards rated their states' political climate closer to neutral on average, at –0.02, while presidents in states with coordinating boards rated their climate at an average of –0.10. However, this difference was not significantly different. What was significantly different was the gap between presidents in states with a single, statewide governing or coordinating board and presidents in states with no statewide board or a weak planning agency, who reported a climate rating that is firmly in the hostile space, with an average of –2.30. Given how few states were in this category, the result was tested to see if it was driven by a single state (particularly, California or Michigan[7]), but it was not. Instead, there was consistent evidence that presidents in states with single, statewide SHEEO organizations viewed the political climate to more be supportive (or, at a minimum, significantly less hostile).

Legislative Understanding. This finding was consistent with the findings for presidential perceptions of the extent to which the state legislature understood the challenges faced by the institution, which can be found in

Table 8.1. Relationships with Governor and Legislature by Board Type

Board Type	Governor Understands	Legislature Understands
Governing Board	4.0	3.5
Coordinating Board	3.5	3.8
Planning Agency/No Statewide Board	2.5	2.1
Average	3.6	3.5

Note: The responses to this survey question ranged from 0 (Does not Understand at All) to 10 (Completely Understands).

Table 8.1. Overall, the presidents surveyed did not believe that their state legislature understood the mission and function of their institution, rating the legislature at an average of 3.5 on a scale of 0 to 10. There was no significant difference between the average score of presidents in states with governing boards (3.5) and of presidents in states with coordinating boards (3.8), but there was a significant difference between both groups and states without a statewide board (2.1). Again, these differences were not a function of a single state.

Gubernatorial Understanding. The findings for the relationship with the governor differed slightly and are also presented in Table 8.1. Overall, respondents' attitudes about the governor did not differ much from their attitudes about the state legislature, with an average rating of 3.6 on a scale of 0 to 10. There was no significant difference between the presidential perceptions of the extent to which the governor understands the challenges faced by presidents in states with governing boards (4.0) versus those with coordinating boards (3.5), but in this case, the absence of a state-level governing or coordinating board (2.5) was also not significant at the $p < 0.05$ level. This difference could be accounted for by the extent to which SHEEOs are part of the state's executive branch, such as being a member of the governor's cabinet, which may alter the governor's perspective of higher education policy. Alternatively, university presidents may find it easier to maintain a relationship with the governor as an individual rather than with the legislature, which encompasses a large number of actors.

Capitol Influence. The next stage of the analysis focused on whether the structure of the state SHEEO's agency could be linked to variations in the extent to which presidents believed that the governor and state legislature influence how they manage their institution the findings of which can be found in Table 8.2. Collectively, presidents rated the level of influence for

Table 8.2. Relationships with SHEEOs (Multivariate)

Independent Variables	SHEEO Understands		SHEEO Influences	
Climate	−0.121	(0.107)	0.018	(0.103)
President Tenure	0.045	(0.054)	−0.088*	(0.051)
Policy Involvement	0.196**	(0.086)	0.068	(0.084)
Think State	−0.041	(0.150)	0.309**	(0.144)
Legislature Understands	0.768**	(0.172)	0.255	(0.166)
Legislature Influences	0.021	(0.190)	0.734**	(0.192)
Governor Understands	0.136	(0.134)	0.055	(0.129)
Governor Influences	0.038	(0.172)	−0.295*	(0.165)
N	80		78	
R-squared	.43		.32	

Note: Standard errors in parentheses; Significance Levels: * $p < .10$, ** $p < .05$

both governors and state legislatures higher than they did the level of understanding, but the differences were not as stark as might be expected. Presidents rated the governor's level of influence at an average of 4.25 and the state legislature's level of influence at an average of 4.00. But once again, there were no significant differences between presidents in states with governing boards versus coordinating boards, except for California, where presidents rated both groups as significantly less influential.

What do these findings mean for our understanding of SHEEOs as buffers between state-elected officials and university leaders? At a minimum, they suggest that the differences between governing boards and coordinating boards do not seem to matter as much as might be expected, but the presence of a state-level board can matter for some of these relationships in a meaningful way. Even so, the observed effect of SHEEO agency structure was somewhat limited. Given the mixed findings on the role of organizational structure, the analysis then turned to the data on presidential perceptions of the SHEEO and their organization.

Presidents who rated their SHEEO's organization as more understanding of their institutions—the measures discussed in the first empirical section—were significantly more likely to consider their political climate to be more favorable, their governor to be more understanding, and their state legislature to be more understanding. Of course, these relationships may not have been causal, but at a minimum, they did move together. The presidents' ratings of SHEEO influence were significantly correlated with higher levels of influence for the state legislature and the governor. Again, these correlations may suggest that the balance of power and the dynamics of political support are not really trade-offs; instead, they may indicate that much of the variation is a function of the overall political climate in the state. To investigate further, we moved to multivariate analyses.

Multivariate Analysis and the Role of Institutional and Individual Characteristics

The previous discussions offered an introductory look at the dynamics of the relationships between college leaders, SHEEOs, and other state actors. Although these findings shed new light on the relationships in question, they did not offer much insight into how these dynamics differ among the diversity of colleges and universities within public higher education. In this section, multivariate analyses are presented that incorporate three key variations in college leaders: how long presidents have been in their current positions, the extent to which presidents are personally involved in the policymaking process, and the extent to which the presidents' institutions are valued or empowered in the state. The first variable, president tenure, asked how long the president had held his or her current position (in years). The second variable, policy involvement, asked presidents to rate, on a scale of 0 to 10, how involved they were in designing accountability policies. The third variable, think state, was a Likert scale response (strongly agree to strongly disagree, on a 7-point scale) to the statement "When people think of our state, they often think of my university." In earlier iterations, a dummy variable for state board structure was also included, but the differences between governing and coordinating board were not significant in any of the models. The nature of the data and the questions explored here limit our ability to speak to the more nuanced relationships for institutions in states without a single statewide board because the analysis examined relationships between presidential perceptions of elected officials and state SHEEOs and their agencies. Leaders of institutions in states with no central agency had missing data for the SHEEO relationships and as such were dropped from the analysis. Future work should explore similar dynamics for institutions in these states.

These models were also used to attempt to tease out the variation in the levels of influence and levels of understanding related to the SHEEO's organization, the governor, and the state legislature. In doing so, the goal was to better understand the strength and directionality of these state power dynamics. Empirically, these dynamics were captured by the measures of the president's perception of the extent to which the legislature (or governor) understands (or influences) the president's institution.

The multivariate portion of the analysis begins with two models that seek to explain the variation in presidents' views toward their SHEEO's organization. The first model explores the extent to which the SHEEO's organization understands the challenges faced by the president's institution, while the second considers the extent to which the SHEEO's organization influences how presidents manage their institutions. These models included a state's political climate (climate), the president's time in office (president tenure), the president's involvement in policymaking (policy involvement), the institution's link to the state's reputation (think state), the extent to which the legislature understands the institution (legislature understands), the extent to which the legislature influences the management of the institution (legislature influences), and the same two measures for the relationships with the governor (governor understands and governor influences).

Relationship with SHEEO's Organization. Table 8.2 presents the two models for the relationships between presidents and SHEEO's organizations. It shows presidents believed their SHEEO's organization to be more understanding of their challenges when the legislature was more understanding and when they were personally involved in policy development. Presidents were more likely to consider their SHEEO's organization to be influential when they believed their legislature to be influential, but they were *less* likely to see their SHEEO's organization as influential if the president had been in office for longer, if they considered their governor to be more influential, and if they were at a politically advantaged institution (those who were more likely to agree that people think of their institution when they think of their state). Before digging deeper into these findings, findings for predicting relationships with the legislature and the governor are explored.

Relationship with legislature. The models predicting the extent to which presidents perceived the state legislature to be understanding or influential were quite similar to the models predicting relationships with the SHEEOs and can be found in Table 8.3. In these models, presidents were more likely to consider the state legislature to understand the challenges faced by their institution when they perceived the SHEEO to be understanding and if they believed their governor to be understanding of the challenges they faced. Presidents of politically advantaged institutions also considered their legislature to be more understanding (or, conversely, institutions that were not as advantaged were more likely to say that the legislature did not understand the challenges they faced). Neither the state's political climate nor the president's time in office were significant predictors.

Relationship with Governors. Again, the models for presidential perceptions of their relationship with the governor were quite similar to the models for the SHEEOs and the legislatures. But the findings, which are presented in Table 8.4, were a bit different. Presidents perceived governors to be significantly more understanding when presidents perceived their state's political climate to be more favorable to higher education and when the legislature was more understanding. However, there was no relationship between the extent to which the SHEEO understands the institution and the extent to

Table 8.3. Relationships with State Legislature (Multivariate)

Independent Variables	Legislature Understands		Legislature Influences	
Climate	0.103	(0.067)	−0.069	(0.058)
President Tenure	−0.002	(0.034)	0.059**	(0.030)
Policy Involvement	−0.047	(0.058)	−0.003	(0.051)
Think State	0.206**	(0.097)	0.085	(0.085)
SHEEO Understands	0.250**	(0.069)	0.011	(0.060)
SHEEO Influences	0.075	(0.073)	0.239**	(0.063)
Governor Understands	0.265**	(0.078)	−0.147**	(0.068)
Governor Influences	0.003	(0.064)	0.660*	(0.056)
N	76		76	
R-squared	.58		.77	

Note: Standard errors in parentheses; *Significance Levels:* * $p < .10$, ** $p < .05$

Table 8.4. Relationships with Governor (Multivariate)

Independent Variables	Governor Understands		Governor Influences	
Climate	0.241**	(0.096)	0.048	(0.075)
President Tenure	−0.030	(0.048)	−0.109**	(0.038)
Policy Involvement	−0.055	(0.085)	−0.007	(0.066)
Think State	0.096	(0.147)	0.060	(0.114)
SHEEO Understands	0.160	(0.109)	0.043	(0.085)
SHEEO Influences	−0.035	(0.115)	−0.160*	(0.089)
Legislature Understands	0.571**	(0.065)	0.104	(0.128)
Legislature Influences	−0.035	(0.115)	1.022**	(0.091)
N	76		76	
R-squared	.49		.73	

Note: Standard errors in parentheses; *Significance Levels:* * $p < .10$, ** $p < .05$

which the governor understands the institution, nor were there effects for the president's individual or institutional characteristics.

The findings for the extent to which the governor was influential were somewhat different. Although there was a positive and significant relationship between the extent to which the legislature was influential and the extent to which the governor was influential, again, there was a negative and significant relationship between the governor's influence and the SHEEO's influence. We also find the governor's influence was perceived as being significantly weaker by presidents the longer the presidents were in office.

Summary of Findings from Multivariate Analyses. Two major findings emerged from the multivariate analyses that offer insight into how presidents view the role of the SHEEO in the broader political environment. First, these findings suggest that presidents may believe that SHEEOs and state legislatures exist in a similar political space. The extent to which they were perceived as understanding and the extent to which they were perceived as influential consistently and significantly moved together across models. Second, the presence of the SHEEO–legislature link was coupled with an absence of a SHEEO–governor link, suggesting that SHEEOs and governors exist in different political spaces. The extent to which presidents believed that the SHEEO's organization understood their institutions did not predict gubernatorial understanding or vice versa. Even more interesting, the influence of the SHEEO and the influence of the governor were inversely related. The more presidents perceived the SHEEO to be influential, the less the governors were perceived as influential.

To further explore why these findings matter, greater scrutiny was focused on the finding on political climate. As discussed in earlier sections, presidents varied on the extent to which they perceived the political climate to be favorable, and many presidents reported a fairly hostile (or, at best, neutral) political climate. Climate was included in all of the models, but it was only a significant predictor of the governor's influence. Of course, this relationship may run in the other direction—and additional analysis suggests that it does—but regardless of directionality, this link is important. When college leaders express frustrations over the state's political climate, it is unclear as to what, exactly, has changed. Concerns from higher education institutions often surround budget cuts. Though this is usually a function of the legislature, governors have also been shown to have significant impacts on state support of higher education, specifically through their relationship with the SHEEO (Tandberg, Fowles, & McLendon, 2017). Additionally, many higher education administrators are concerned about political intrusion into institutional matters, which may be seen through gubernatorial appointments or direct oversight. In this sense, the governor may play a large role in determining the political climate perceived by institutional leaders. Future research should continue to explore these possibilities.

Lastly, findings related to individual and institutional characteristics are presented. Presidents who were personally involved in policy design were more likely to believe that their SHEEO understood the challenges faced on campus (though this did not extend to legislatures or governors).

A president's time in office did not seem to influence the extent to which he or she perceived any of the state actors as more understanding, but tenure was related to less influential SHEEOs, less influential governors, and strangely, more influential legislatures. This was potentially due to presidents having influence on legislators who are then acting on behalf of presidents' wishes, thereby making the legislators appear more influential. However, it is more likely that university presidents perceived legislatures differently due the lack of a single individual at the head of the organization, making it more difficult for university presidents to become involved in the decision process. For politically advantaged institutions, only a couple of significant relationships were present, with more advantaged institutions reporting less influence from SHEEOs and more understanding from legislatures.

CONCLUSION

These findings present a great deal of information about the way university presidents think about the SHEEO and their organization. However, it is important to note the limitations of the present analysis as well. The main drawback was the number of respondents to the survey, leaving us with a sample size of only 140. Due to this factor, the conclusions drawn may not be as generalizable as one would hope. There was also potential for some endogeneity in the data used. The models discussed in this chapter cannot support causal claims about the relationships they suggest, meaning it is unclear whether the apparent relationships were caused by factors within the data itself. Finally, the survey was conducted toward the end of the Great Recession, at a time when higher education budgets were low due to financial strains on state governments, meaning the results may not be applicable to more prosperous economic times.

Despite these limitations, three main conclusions can be drawn from these analyses. The first is that while the SHEEO's organization serves as an intermediary between campuses and the capitol, there does not seem to be a trade-off between the role as an advocate or as an overseer. The models show presidents' views correspond in terms of how well SHEEOs and the agencies they lead understand and influence an institution, suggesting a balance between the bottom-up role of advocate and the top-down role of overseer. Instead, the trade-off may be between strong or weak authority granted to the SHEEO's organization.

The second conclusion we can draw from these models is that the structure of the SHEEO's organization may not matter in the relationship with institutional leaders. Though previous research has shown governance structure to matter in a variety of ways for higher education institutions

(Bowen et al., 1997; Lowry, 2001; Nicholson-Crotty & Meier, 2003), this analysis indicates this variable cannot be used to predict presidential attitudes toward SHEEOs and the organizations they direct, as there were no significant differences between a coordinating board and a governing board for any of the models, with one exception: College leaders in states without a single statewide board (either a planning agency or multiple system boards like California) seem to view their political climate differently. Given the limited nature of these data, one must be cautious about inferring too much about what this may mean, but it is one of the most interesting areas in this space for future research.

Finally, the models suggest that institutional leaders view the relationships between SHEEO organizations and state legislatures differently than they view relationships between the SHEEO's organization and the governor. The results displayed in Tables 8.1 and 8.2 suggest that the perceptions of university presidents toward the SHEEO's organization and the legislature trend together, while perceptions of the understanding and influence of the governor often flow in the opposite direction. This result suggests that institutional presidents seem to think of governors as occupying a very different political space than the one in which the agencies headed by SHEEOs and state legislatures exist. Presidents who view SHEEOs and their organizations as more influential also view legislatures as more influential, and the same dynamic is true for the extent to which these groups are seen as understanding the president's institution. But there is no relationship between perceptions of an understanding board and perceptions of an understanding governor, and the perceptions of influence are quite different. When presidents view the SHEEOs as more influential, they are more likely to view the governor as less influential.

This dynamic suggests that presidents may perceive SHEEOs and their organizations more as a buffer for gubernatorial power, not legislative power. Without more nuanced data on how the powers of the governor, as related to higher education, vary across states, it is difficult to say whether these relationships are a function of variations in formal power or informal influence.[8] Many governors have taken up higher education as a priority in their state and structured campaigns and initiatives around higher education reform, the adoption of certain types of policies, and rhetoric related to what should be valued in the states. And in many states, SHEEOs and their agencies are not centrally involved in either the agenda-setting process or the formulation of these initiatives, at times competing with outside organizations for space on the governors' agendas (McGuinness, 2016). Thus, for SHEEOs, building stronger relationships with the governor's office could be beneficial, but building strategic partnerships with outside groups that influence the governor's office could be even more advantageous.

Determining the drivers behind these relationships is one of several avenues for future research to pursue with regard to the organizations SHEEOs lead and their involvement in higher education at the campus level. Another path available to scholars is to investigate the role of SHEEOs and their organizations in convincing presidents of individual campuses to support state policies proposed by political actors, such as new accountability programs. The intermediary role of the SHEEO's organizations may be important for unifying higher education in order to successfully implement such policy changes in a way that is acceptable to both state government and universities. Additional research could also be used to determine in greater detail the impact of presidential characteristics such as tenure in office for relationships to various state-level actors, as the models here suggest this variable affects each of these relationships differently. Though the analysis presented here enables us to make several important conclusions about the relationships institutional leaders have with SHEEOs and their organizations, much research remains to be done with regard to these interactions.

APPENDIX 8.A: TEXT OF RELEVANT SURVEY QUESTIONS

How would you describe the political climate in your state as it relates to higher education and public universities?

Very Hostile   Neutral   Very Supportive

  –5   –4   –3   –2   –1   0   1   2   3   4   5

How well do you believe individuals in the following organizations understand the challenges that your institution faces? [Board of Regents; Coordinating/Governing Board/Planning Agency; State Legislature; Governor's Office]

Not at all   Completely Understand

   0   1   2   3   4   5   6   7   8   9   10

How much influence do individuals in the following organizations have over the way you manage your institution? [Board of Regents; Coordinating/Governing Board/Planning Agency; State Legislature; Governor's Office]

No Influence   Completely Control

   0   1   2   3   4   5   6   7   8   9   10

APPENDIX 8.B: STATE SHEEO CATEGORIZATIONS

States with Governing Boards	States with Coordinating Boards	States with No Centralized Board
Arizona	Alabama	California
Arkansas	Alaska	Michigan
Florida	Colorado	Vermont
Georgia	Connecticut	Wyoming
Hawaii	Delaware	
Iowa	Idaho	
Kansas	Illinois	
Maine	Indiana	
Minnesota	Kentucky	
Mississippi	Louisiana	
Montana	Maryland	
Nevada	Massachusetts	
New York	Missouri	
North Carolina	Nebraska	
North Dakota	New Hampshire	
Rhode Island	New Jersey	
South Dakota	New Mexico	
Utah	Ohio	
Wisconsin	Oklahoma	
	Oregon	
	Pennsylvania	
	South Carolina	
	Tennessee	
	Texas	
	Virginia	
	Washington	
	West Virginia	

NOTES

1. This sample includes various kinds of administrators, including chancellors, CEOs, deans, and executive vice presidents as well as university presidents. However, because the vast majority of our sample (88%) were university presidents, we refer to the respondents as "presidents" throughout.

2. The complete text of these questions from the survey are included in Appendix 8.A.

3. See Appendix 8.B for a list of states placed into each category.

4. Future work should explore the differences between campus relationships with the SHEEO, as an individual, and the SHEEO's organization. Unfortunately, that level of disaggregation is beyond the scope of this analysis.

5. It is important to note that some of the campus leaders did not respond to these questions, especially in states without a governing or coordinating board. For these two measures, 84–86 presidents responded, compared to approximately 135 presidents responding on other questions.

6. These two variables from the survey correlate at 0.29, with a p-value of 0.0074.

7. These two states were tested because they are the two largest states in the "no centralized board" category, meaning they could potentially have a disproportionate amount of influence over the results.

8. Some scholars have begun to work on assessing the institutional relationships between SHEEOs and governors, though more research is needed in this area. See, for example, Tandberg, Fowles, and McLendon (2017), who find that these relationships have a significant impact on state support for higher education.

REFERENCES

Berdahl, R. O. (1971). *Statewide coordination of higher education.* Washington, DC: American Council on Education.

Bowen, F. M., Bracco, K. R., Callan, P. M., Finney, J. E., Richardson, R. C., & Trombley, W. (1997). *State structures for the governance of higher education: A comparative study.* San Jose, CA: California Higher Education Policy Center. Retrieved from eric.ed.gov/?q=State+Structures+for+the+Governance+of+Higher+Education%3a+A+Comparative+Study&id=ED412866

Bracco, K. R., Richardson, R. C., Callan, P. M., & Finney, J. E. (1999). Policy environments and system design: Understanding state governance structures. *The Review of Higher Education, 23*(1), 23–44.

Eykamp, P. W. (1995). Political control of state research universities: The effect of the structure of political control on university quality and budget (Unpublished doctoral dissertation). San Diego: University of California-San Diego.

Flawn, P. T. (1990). *A primer for university presidents: Managing the modern university.* Austin: University of Texas Press.

Hearn, J. C., & Griswold, C. P. (1994). State-level centralization and policy innovation in U.S. postsecondary education. *Educational Evaluation and Policy Analysis, 16*(2), 161–190.

Heller, D. E. (2001). *The states and public higher education policy: Affordability, access, and accountability*. Baltimore, MD: Johns Hopkins University Press.

Hillman, N. W., Tandberg, D. A., & Sponsler, B. A. (2015). Public policy and higher education: Strategies for framing a research agenda. *ASHE Higher Education Report, 41*(2), 1–98.

Hines, E. R. (1988). *Higher education and state governments: Renewed partnership, cooperation, or competition?* (ASHE-ERIC Higher Education Report No. 5). Washington, DC: Association for the Study of Higher Education.

Hughes, J. F., & Mills, O. (Eds.). (1975). *Formulating policy in postsecondary education: The search for alternatives*. Washington, DC: American Council on Education.

Knott, J. H., & Payne, A. A. (2004). The impact of state governance structures on management and performance of public organizations: A study of higher education institutions. *Journal of Policy Analysis and Management, 23*(1), 13–30.

Lowry, R. C. (2001). Governmental structure, trustee selection, and public university prices and spending: multiple means to similar ends. *American Journal of Political Science, 45*(4), 845–861.

Manna, P. (2013). Centralized governance and student outcomes: Excellence, equity, and academic achievement in the U.S. states. *Policy Studies Journal, 41*(4), 682–705.

Marcus, L. R. (1997). Restructuring state higher education governance patterns. *The Review of Higher Education, 20*(4), 399–418.

McGuinness, A. C. (2003). *ECS state notes: Models of postsecondary education coordination and governance in the states*. Denver, CO: Educational Commission of the States.

McGuinness, A. C. (2016). *State policy leadership for the future: History of state coordination and governance and alternatives for the future*. Denver, CO: Education Commission of the States.

McGuinness, A. C., & Fulton, M. (2007). *50-state comparison: State-level coordinating and/or governing agency*. Denver, CO: Education Commission of the States.

Miller, G. J. (2005). The political evolution of principal-agent models. *Annual Review of Political Science, 8*, 203–225.

Millett, J. D. (1984). *Conflict in higher education: State government coordination versus institutional independence*. San Francisco, CA: Jossey-Bass.

Moe, T. M. (1995). The politics of structural choice: Toward a theory of public bureaucracy. In O. E. Williamson (Ed.), *Organization theory: From Chester Barnard to the present and beyond* (pp. 116–153). New York: Oxford University Press.

Moos, M., & Rourke, F. E. (1959). *The campus and the state*. Baltimore, MD: Johns Hopkins Press.

Ness, E. C. (2010). The politics of determining merit aid eligibility criteria: An analysis of the policy process. *The Journal of Higher Education, 81*(1), 33–60.

Nicholson-Crotty, J., & Meier, K. J. (2003). Politics, structure, and public policy: The case of higher education. *Educational Policy, 17*(1), 80–97.

Perkins, J. A., & Israel, B. B. (Eds.). (1972). *Higher education: From autonomy to systems*. New York: International Council for Educational Development.

Richardson, R. C., Bracco, K. R., Callan, P. M., & Finney, J. E. (1999). *Designing state higher education systems for a new century*. Phoenix, AZ: Oryx Press.

Tandberg, D. A. (2013). The conditioning role of state higher education governance structures. *Journal of Higher Education, 84*(4), 506–543.

Tandberg, D. A., Fowles, J. T., & McLendon, M. K. (2017). The governor and the state higher education executive officer: How the relationship shapes state financial support for higher education. *Journal of Higher Education, 88*(1), 110–134.

Tierney, W. G. (Ed.). (2006). *Governance and the public good.* Albany: State University of New York Press.

Volkwein, J. F. (1986). Campus autonomy and its relationship to measures of university quality. *Journal of Higher Education, 57*(5), 510–528.

Volkwein, J. F., & Malik, S. M. (1997). State regulation and administrative flexibility at public universities. *Research in Higher Education, 38*(1), 17–42.

Waterman, R. W., Rouse, A., & Wright, R. (1998). The venues of influence: A new theory of political control of the bureaucracy. *Journal of Public Administration Research and Theory, 8*(1), 13–38.

Part III

WHAT'S NEXT: NEW WAYS OF THINKING ABOUT THE SHEEO

Modern Era Trends in State Higher Education Coordination, Governance, and Alternatives for the Future

Implications for the SHEEO

Brian A. Sponsler and Mary Fulton

In 2005 the National Center for Public Policy and Higher Education issued a policy brief, "State Capacity for Higher Education Policy." The influential brief summarized the major postsecondary challenges facing the nation and individual states: the imperative to increase educational attainment in the face of global competition; a leaking education pipeline with too many students failing to persist through the system to successfully complete a certificate or degree; the failure to make needed progress in the success of the nation's growing African-American and Latino populations; and growing gaps between supply and demand in critical fields of science, technology, engineering, and mathematics.

The National Center (2005) called on states to improve their capacities for dealing with these challenges and for providing public policy leadership:

> States . . . need to articulate broad goals for higher education, to devise approaches to accountability that assess progress toward these goals and identify performance gaps, and use state subsidies to improve performance. States must develop the tools to look at the broad intersection between higher education and public needs in order to make judgments about how to leverage performance improvements through strategic investment of resource. (p. 3A)

The core recommendation of the National Center's statement was that states should have a broad-based, independent, and credible public entity with a clear charge to increase the state's educational attainment and prepare citizens for the workforce. The specifics would differ across states, but whatever the organizational forms, effective, sustained policy leadership for

Figure 9.1. Core Capacities for Sustained Policy Leadership in Higher Education

- Strength to counter inappropriate political, partisan, institutional, or parochial influences.
- Capacity and responsibility for articulating and monitoring state performance objectives for higher education that are supported by the key leaders in the state; objectives should be specific and measurable, including quantifiable goals for college preparation, access, participation, retention, graduation and responsiveness to other state needs.
- Engagement of civic, business and public-school leaders beyond state government and higher education leaders.
- Recognition of distinctions between statewide policy—and the public entities and policies needed to accomplish it—and institutional governance. The role of statewide policy leadership is distinct from the roles of institutional and segmental governing boards.
- Information gathering and analytical capacity to inform the choice of state goals/priorities and to interpret and evaluate statewide and institutional performance in relation to these goals.
- Capacity to bring coherence and coordination in key policy areas, such as the relationship between institutional appropriations, tuition, and financial aid.
- Capacity to influence the direction of state resources to ensure accomplishment of these priorities.

Source: National Center for Public Policy and Higher Education (2005, p. 3A)

higher education had to include the seven core capacities summarized in Figure 9.1.

The National Center's statement acknowledged that establishing such an entity would require a substantial redesign of the organizations and agencies that were already in place—cautioning that if states failed to make these changes, "traditional decision-making entities, built for other times and other public purposes and based primarily on institutionally focused issues, will crowd out attention to critical public priorities" (p. 3A).

We believe the issues unearthed in 2005 remain critical for state leadership to address today. The state policymaking context has become more complex and problematic over the ensuing years since the National Center's statement was released. State support for public postsecondary education has failed to recover from prerecession levels (State Higher Education Executive Officers Association, 2017); attainment and completion goals trail their aggressive targets (Lumina Foundation, 2017); and most of today's students draw from pools of individuals historically underserved by postsecondary institutions. Given our view that the core recommendations for the 2005 National Center statement were of an inspirational nature at the time of initial publication, we see them as critically necessary in today's higher education policy context.

Despite a general agreement that policy leadership is important to addressing the complex conditions encompassing higher education, making the kinds of changes to establish a state postsecondary policy entity as envisioned by the National Center continues to be a challenge in many states. Structures for higher education coordination and governance, commonly referred to as *SHEEO agencies*, remain encumbered by statutory mandates from earlier times and by historic norms of professional practice that are misaligned with current era needs.

Moving conceptual and practical knowledge toward a refreshed conception of a state higher education agency, and by extension those who lead such agencies, is a core purpose of this chapter. The SHEEO as an individual operates within and must respond to a broader governance structure and higher education environment that includes their agencies as well as postsecondary systems and institutional governing boards and other state policymaking entities. These structures can strengthen or constrain the role and authority of the individual SHEEO position, especially with respect to developing and advancing state higher education and workforce development policy agendas. Further, the SHEEO's influence and responsibilities may change as legislators and governors continue to reorganize their state's higher education governance systems.

Our forthcoming discussion is based on and adds to Aims McGuinness's (2016) thoughtful[1] white paper that provided a historical review of the state role in higher education, including the position of the SHEEO, and offers an organizing framework for moving forward. The framework is grounded in a firm belief in six key functions that fall within the purview of entities commonly labeled "state higher education agency," the professional habitat of the SHEEO:

- State-level planning education and workforce planning
- State finance policy linked to budgeting, appropriations, and resource allocation
- Maintenance of databases and conversion of data into information to inform policymaking
- Regulation of higher education institutions and/or academic programs
- Administration of state-level services such as student financial aid programs
- Governance of higher education systems and institutions[2]

In some states, a single entity is responsible for most or all of these functions. However, in most states, the responsibility for these functions is dispersed among policymaking entities, even as a single professional designation, the SHEEO, continues to be affiliated with and responsible for portions of these functions. This creates a dynamic where SHEEOs maintain key roles, yet those roles and corresponding responsibilities—in addition to their ability to execute against those roles and responsibilities—is in a state of flux. As will be evidenced in forthcoming sections of this chapter, state policy actors in the legislatures and governor's offices are considering and enacting a substantial number of "reforms" that impact the ability and scope of SHEEOs to do their jobs.

As will become evident, how states carry out these six functions has evolved over time. The origins of extant structures are rooted in each state's history and culture. This chapter outlines a way forward in shaping these key components of state higher education structure for the future, with the intent of supporting effective and impactful state policy creation and implementation. We are intentional in our desire to stimulate new and forward framing discussions about how state governance of higher education and the role of the individual SHEEO could be reshaped to support state goals. We do not purport to represent a consensus opinion on these questions, nor do we suggest that strong empirical evidence underlies the intended change in performance we assert revisions to governance could hold. We do, however, come to this chapter with a conviction that the evidence is less than convincing that current arrangements are sufficient to drive modern era postsecondary education to optimal and necessary outcomes.

In this chapter, we argue that states need an entity charged with leading a long-term strategy to improve the postsecondary educational attainment of the state's population. However, the concept of a single entity responsible for all six state-level functions commonly associated with SHEEO agencies may no longer be feasible nor desirable. Rather than a single entity, the responsibilities of a traditionally framed SHEEO agency of the future could comprise four distinct components located at different points in the overall state policy structure:

- Statewide policy leadership, with a focus on a redefinition of the state planning function and a more intentional link between planning and finance policy
- Statewide coordination/implementation of cross-sector initiatives, including providing staff support for planning and finance policy, maintaining databases and capacity to convert data into information that guides policymaking, and authority to regulate mission differentiation
- State service agency administration, such as student financial aid and regulation/licensure of nonstate providers
- System and institutional governance, including program approval, board leadership, and the like

Creating the "SHEEO agency of the future" cannot be achieved simply by resuscitating existing boards or agencies. It is unrealistic to expect many of these agencies to rise above their historic roles and assume the kind of statewide policy leadership role envisioned in the 2005 National Center policy statement. Observation of current practice suggests as much. It is untested, and in our view worthy of consideration and then critical examination, whether a more diffused conception of the SHEEO office would support any different policy, practice, or student-level outcomes.

While the task of bringing about the changes may seem daunting, it is in fact doable provided that state leaders and extant higher education agency leaders recognize the consequences of not acting. In some cases, these changes would involve only an updating of the mandates for existing state boards or agencies. In other cases, they would require states to establish new entities or to eliminate or significantly reconstitute existing agencies.

Although structural changes are the primary focus of our discussion, it is clear to us that structural change alone will not produce needed outcomes for states and students alike. A highly skilled, knowledgeable, and engaged professional—the SHEEO—is vital to ensuring structural changes and reallocations of responsibility are leveraged for positive ends. In their varying forms and positional roles across states, SHEEOs are critically needed professionals charged with guiding and supporting any considered structural transitions. Absent effective and dynamic leadership from SHEEOs, rearranged structures will only underperform their promise, and precious little would be done to advance our common goal of supporting a postsecondary ecosystem where all students and communities have access to necessary supports to achieve their desired educational outcomes.

We begin our discussion by highlighting modern era policy developments observed across states that exemplify a restructuring of higher education agency governance and roles. These examples illustrate the increasing diversity of powerful policy centers (legislatures, governors, and SHEEO agencies themselves) exerting influence on postsecondary governance in the states and providing ample evidence of the churn taking place in a pressurized policy environment. These governance reforms can affect decision-making channels across policymaking centers and the roles that higher agencies play with respect to the primary functions mentioned in the previous and following paragraphs.

HISTORICAL PERSPECTIVE ON THE FUTURE

In his classic analysis of the development of state higher education agencies, Berdahl (1971) distinguished between substantive autonomy and procedural autonomy. Following the principles established by the U.S.

Supreme Court's ruling in the Dartmouth College case (*Dartmouth College v. Woodward*) in 1819, states have traditionally accorded both public and private institutions a significant degree of autonomy on substantive decisions on whom to admit, what should be taught, and who should teach.[3]

From the earliest years, states have varied in the extent to which they have granted public institutions autonomy on procedural matters such as the expenditure of state funding, procurement, and capital development. Berdahl (1971) noted that with respect to autonomy, a focus should be placed not on *if* states will encroach on public institutions, but *whether* the encroachment will take place through a process and on issues of an appropriate and sustainable nature. The key is for the higher education community to recognize that it has a stake, and even a responsibility, to engage actively with state political leaders in defining the nature of the relationship. This includes defining the major societal ends toward which the academy should direct its energies and shaping the policies and other "suitably sensitive" mechanisms that will govern the relationships.

The history of state policy in the United States is one of a constant search for the appropriate "suitably sensitive" mechanisms of which Berdahl wrote. In the 19th century, there was a clear demarcation between substantive and procedural issues. At times, governors or state legislators attempted to dictate academic policy, to influence presidential and faculty appointments for partisan or ideological reasons, or to weigh in on student admissions. Nevertheless, the dominant pattern across the country was that the state governmental role was limited to deciding on the level and modes of allocation of public funding and, depending on the state, certain procedural regulations/controls (see Appendix 9.A for a fuller presentation of changes in higher education decision making over the 20th century).

Over the years, however, the boundary between substantive and procedural issues has blurred, especially as issues of the public interest focused on how institutions are responsive to public priorities such as ensuring access and equal opportunity, aligning academic programs with state workforce needs, and improving student outcomes. As governors and state legislators have become more aggressive in pressing for reform, the need for new thinking about the mechanisms to manage the interface between public priorities and the academy has become clearer and more urgent.

The need for a state higher education executive officer or, more broadly, an entity responsible for coordinating and/or governing higher education situated between the individual campus and state government can be traced to the late 19th century. The rationale for these entities has evolved over time as the nation's higher education system has become more complex and the state role has changed.

The state role in higher education is one that has evolved significantly over the nation's history in six phases, as presented in great detail in McGuinness (2016):

Phase 1: Late 19th century through end of World War II
Phase 2: End of World War II to 1972
Phase 3: 1972 through mid-1980s
Phase 4: 1980s through mid-1990s
Phase 5: Public agenda reforms mid-1990s to 2008
Phase 6: The Great Recession and economic recovery (2008 to the present)

Appendix 9.B presents a detailed description the evolution of major functions of SHEEO agencies over these six phases.

Regardless of when extant state governance structures were initiated, all currently confront a challenging and dynamic policy environment. Driven by the placement of postsecondary policy squarely in the top tier of public policy issues at the state and federal levels and the legacy of the historic economic recession of 2008, the state higher education policy environment is one that both calls for and is driving changes to state postsecondary governance.

Moving forward, we focus on Phase 6, the current era from 2008 on, as fertile ground for our discussion of elements of a forward-looking construct of the SHEEO office and the leadership skills and attributes likely to support success of individuals leading these agencies of the future.

CHANGES OVER A MODERN ERA OF HIGHER EDUCATION POLICY

The current period of state higher education governance reform differs little from prior phases with one notable exception—the sense of urgency. The economic crisis of 2008 and concerns about restoring global economic competitiveness prompted more states to adopt long-term public agenda goals for higher education. Since 2008, policy leaders in more than a dozen states proposed and enacted changes to their higher education governance systems. Factors driving the reforms include creating efficiencies, responding to circumstances within higher education (such as enrollment and funding fluctuations), and achieving statewide goals. These reforms often affect the responsibilities of and relationships among higher education agencies, state policy leaders, postsecondary systems, and institutions.

The pattern across the country has been mixed with respect to reforming postsecondary governance structures over the last decade. State leaders have taken often-divergent approaches to nudging, encouraging, or wholesale demanding reforms in the name of increased efficiency and a desire to advance educational goals and desired outcomes. California and West Virginia, for instance, reflect the turn toward decentralizing authority and responsibilities, while Connecticut illustrates an example of both decentralizing and consolidating the governance system. Oregon established a centralized statewide coordinating agency while disbanding the postsecondary system's authority and delegating power to newly created 4-year institutional governing boards. Similarly, Tennessee allowed six state universities to break ties with its multisector governing board and establish institutional boards of trustees, while it also expanded the responsibilities of its statewide coordinating agency.

In addition to efforts to restructure postsecondary governance systems, governors in several states gained more control of coordinating agencies by appointing the executive officers or tying the agency directly to the governor's office. New Jersey, Ohio, and Tennessee fall into this category, and governors in other states also appoint SHEEOs. In the short term, these changes increase the likelihood that a governor will consider the coordinating agency's advice. Nevertheless, the agencies run the risk of losing a degree of independence and ability to provide objective analysis and advice to the governor and legislature and to maintain a trusted relationship with the state's higher education institutions. Because the agency's leadership most likely will be replaced when a new governor is elected, its ability to sustain attention to long-term goals and reforms may also be weakened.

In the following section, state-level information about a range of governance changes pursued over the last several years will be explored. These examples underscore a movement toward diffusing decision making and responsibilities among key actors in the higher education landscape, including state policymakers, SHEEOs, system governing boards, and institutions. As we build toward a vision of a new future for higher education policymaking and governance, recent state policy actions provide examples of congruence or incongruence with the reforms suggested within this chapter.

California

The California governor's veto of a 2011 general fund appropriation (Assembly Bill 98) eliminated funding for and consequently shut down the California Postsecondary Education Commission. Legislative efforts (Assembly Bill 1348) to restore a statewide coordinating agency failed in 2014, and the governor vetoed a similar measure (Senate Bill 42) in 2016. Under these legislative actions, the coordinating agency would have been charged with developing and monitoring progress toward statewide higher education goals and priorities, among other responsibilities. After it was disbanded, some commission duties were transferred to the three systems—Board of Governors of the California Community Colleges, California State University Board of Trustees, and University of California Board of Regents—which expanded the authority of these governing boards. While the postsecondary systems now exercise more authority, eliminating the commission may impede the ability to coordinate and implement statewide policies, agendas, and goals. Further, it remains unclear whether the role of a SHEEO resides more prominently with one of California's systems or is shared across the leadership of all three systems.

Connecticut

Through the budget bill enacted in 2011, Connecticut eliminated the Board of Governors for Higher Education, which served as a statewide coordinating agency (Conn. Gen. Stat. Ann. § Sec. 10a-1a). The law also consolidated the public universities (which does not include the University of Connecticut), the community colleges, and a public online college under a single Board of Regents. The state retained an Office of Higher Education as an administrative and service agency that manages student aid and academic programs and regulates nonstate institutions (among other responsibilities); the office does not play a role in statewide policy planning. With the reforms, the SHEEO position is represented by both the Office of Higher Education's executive director and the chancellor of the Board of Regents. In addition, the reorganization may limit Connecticut's ability to pursue a public agenda across the state's entire system, including the Board of Regents for Higher Education, University of Connecticut, and independent sector.

New Jersey

In 2010, New Jersey created the Secretary of Higher Education role to serve as the executive director of the Commission on Higher Education, which is a cabinet-level position appointed by the governor (N.J. Stat. Ann. § 18A:3B-14). A 2010 governor's executive order (No. 26) established the New Jersey Task Force on Higher Education, which was charged with making recommendations to improve the overall quality and effectiveness of the state's higher education system, including its governance structure. In 2011, the governor followed the task force's recommendations by creating the Governor's Higher Education Council (Executive Order 52) to advise and offer recommendations to the governor and provide advice and assistance to the Secretary of Higher Education. Subsequently, the governor issued a reorganization plan (Reorganization Plan 005-2011) that abolished the Commission on Higher Education (a coordinating agency) and transferred most of its powers to the Secretary of Higher Education.

The reorganization plan furthered the governor's efforts to implement recommendations of the New Jersey Higher Education Task Force. While the Secretary's responsibilities and authority may be similar to those of the previous coordinating board's leader, the reforms established a closer structural—and perhaps personal—relationship between the SHEEO and the governor.

Oregon

Beginning in 2011, Oregon embarked on several reform efforts to create a unified preschool to postsecondary education system and improve educational outcomes, including statewide attainment rates. Lawmakers established the Higher Education Coordinating Commission (HECC) as the statewide coordinating and planning board for postsecondary institutions (Or. Rev. Stat. Ann. § 350.001). Legislation enacted in 2013 (Or. Rev. Stat. Ann. § 352.025) decentralized the governance of Oregon's state universities by authorizing each institution to establish its own governing board, and a subsequent law (Or. Rev. Stat. Ann. § 352.054) abolished the State Board of Higher Education and the Oregon University System. Together, these reforms decentralized more authority to the university governing boards while also centralizing other responsibilities for community colleges and 4-year institutions with the newly established SHEEO position and Higher Education Coordinating Commission.

Tennessee

In 2012, Tennessee enacted legislation (Tenn. Code Ann. § 49-7-205) that gave the governor authority to appoint the executive director of the Tennessee Higher Education Commission (THEC), a statewide coordinating board and agency. Previously, the commission's board members hired the executive director, defined the position's duties, and set the executive director's compensation. However, legislation enacted in 2018 returns the authority to appoint and employ the executive director back to the commission.

In 2016, lawmakers authorized (Tenn. Code Ann. § 49-8-101) the six universities that had reported to the Tennessee Board of Regents to establish and be governed by individual boards of trustees. The Board of Regents continues to govern the 13 community colleges and 27 applied technical colleges, which do not have individual boards. The legislation also expanded certain responsibilities of the executive director (the SHEEO) and the Tennessee Higher Education Commission with respect to the state university boards, the Board of Regents, and the Board of Trustees of the University of Tennessee System.

CIRCUMVENTING THE SHEEO

Beyond the structural issues addressed through policy action highlighted in these state examples, lawmakers in some states enacted legislation that has circumvented engagement of the SHEEO and placed legislators in a more direct higher education policymaking role. These shifts often draw the SHEEO and agency staff away from an agenda-setting or strategic role and into an increased regulatory role and deeper involvement in institution-level governance and management issues. For example, highly proscriptive legislative actions aimed at regulating faculty workload and promoting instructional models and academic practices have cropped up in several states in recent years. These policies affect, at least implicitly, the roles of state agencies and their relationship with systems and institutions. Decisions, that in many states, historically were considered the purview of the SHEEO, a board and/or institutional leadership are increasingly becoming a matter of state statute. Higher education policy formulated in this more direct manner, whereby the SHEEO and their staff experts may play a more secondary role to legislators, advocates, or entrepreneurial institutional leaders, has implications for how we consider the construction of the SHEEO office of the future.

Developmental Education Legislation

Turning to examples of policy formulated in such a way that circumvents the SHEEO to some degree, state legislators expanded their direct involvement in developmental education to reduce the number of students placed in noncredit bearing courses and accelerate their enrollment in college-level classes. In some cases, lawmakers specified the course placement policies and approaches that institutions may use to deliver instruction. In several instances, advocacy organizations such as Complete College America have made it common practice to directly engage legislatures in policy dialogues, with parallel or limited engagement with SHEEOs. The following state examples exemplify the types of policy considered and implemented in this area.

Connecticut. Legislation enacted in 2012 (Conn. Gen. Stat. Ann. § 10a-157a) requires institutions under the Board of Regents for Higher Education to enroll all students in entry-level college courses and, if necessary, offer supplemental academic support (known as the corequisite model). For students determined to be below this skill level, campuses must offer an intensive college readiness program before students receive the embedded remedial support. The law generally prohibits institutions from offering remediation through other approaches. In addition, institutions must use multiple commonly accepted measures to gauge students' readiness for college-level coursework.

Florida. In 2013, lawmakers enacted legislation (Fla. Stat. Ann. § 1008.30) that allows students who graduated from a state public high school in 2007 or thereafter and members of the military to bypass additional assessments and be placed directly into credit-bearing courses. Florida College System students who do not meet these criteria or who opt to enroll in remediation must take a common placement exam. Students who decide to or who must enroll in remediation can select from a list of specified instructional approaches, including corequisite, modularized, compressed, and contextualized courses.

Completion Rates Legislation

State lawmakers also proposed and enacted policies aimed at improving postsecondary student completion rates. Policymakers primarily acted in response to reports highlighting unacceptably low national graduation rates, especially at less-selective and open-access institutions. Average college graduation rates—commonly based on 6 years for a 4-year degree and 3 years for a 2-year program—show a national average of 60% and 30%, respectively (National Center for Education Statistics, 2017a, 2017b). While these percentages do not tell the full story since part-time and transfer students are mostly excluded, policy leaders will continue to pressure higher education agencies, systems, and institutions to increase completion rates in support of their state's broader agenda. The following state summaries exemplify the types of policy considered and implemented in this area, as key policy actors sought to enhance desirable outcomes of postsecondary systems in their state.

Minnesota. Minnesota's 2015 omnibus higher education legislation (Senate File 5) requires the Minnesota State Colleges and Universities Board of Trustees to develop system goals and plans for students to complete degrees or certificates. The board and institutions were directed to employ strategies that may include: (a) replacing developmental courses with corequisite courses, (b) expanding intrusive advising, (c) developing meta-majors, (d) making available alternative mathematics curriculum, (e) implementing "opt-out scheduling" by automatically enrolling students in a schedule, (f) facilitating the transfer of credits, and (g) encouraging students to enroll full-time including using financial assistance incentives. The Board of Regents of the University of Minnesota was required to develop similar goals and plans tailored toward the needs of the system's students.

Missouri. In 2016, the state enacted legislation (Mo. Ann. Stat. § 173.2515) that established the Guided Pathways to Success Act, a comprehensive approach to improving timely completion. The law required the Missouri

Coordinating Board for Higher Education, in cooperation with public 2- and 4-year institutions, to create a guided pathways pilot program. The institutional programs must include at least two of the following components: majors organized into semester-by-semester sets of courses that lead to on-time completion; degree-based transfer pathways between participating institutions; available meta-majors; student commitment to a structured schedule of courses; and clear degree maps, proactive advising, and guarantees that required courses are available when needed by students.

Gubernatorial Initiatives

Not to be outdone by their legislative counterparts, state governors also leveraged their leadership role to influence higher education policies and strategies, impacting directly and indirectly the work of higher education agencies and the SHEEOs who lead them. Several governors lead efforts, often in collaboration with higher education agencies and systems, to establish statewide attainment goals aligned with current and projected workforce demands.

Iowa. The Iowa governor signed Executive Order 88 in 2016 that set a goal for 70% of the state's workforce to have education or training beyond high school by 2025 as part of the Future Ready Iowa initiative. The executive order also created the Future Ready Iowa Alliance to develop and recommend a strategic plan to accomplish the attainment goal.

Tennessee. In 2013, the governor of Tennessee launched the Drive to 55 Initiative that established a goal of 55% of citizens holding a college degree or certificate by the year 2025. At the time, 33% of adults over 25 years old in Tennessee had earned at least an associate degree (Tennessee Higher Education Commission, 2015). Drive to 55 encompasses several programs that are administered by the Tennessee Higher Education Commission (THEC). Tennessee Promise provides recent high school graduates with last-dollar scholarships for the cost of tuition and mandatory fees not covered by other federal and state financial aid programs. Tennessee Reconnect provides a similar scholarship as well as support services to adults interested in completing a postsecondary credential.

Governance reforms in the modern era, encapsulated in part by the state examples discussed here, suggest several ways state-level decision makers, both governors and legislative bodies, have restructured higher education policymaking approaches. State leaders with varying degrees of policy authority have reconfigured their states' system for higher education policymaking, often with consequences for SHEEOs and the agencies they lead. Changes discussed reflect some actions that intentionally and unintentionally inched toward a more dispersed system of decision making that can be interpreted as touching on our four core functions of a SHEEO agency. Specific reasons for these and other policy actions at the state level have not been empirically demonstrated. Yet it is likely that a range of factors has placed increasing structural pressures on the role of the SHEEO that in most circumstances dictate professional behaviors, including reductions in state higher education agency budgets and staff; a deprofessionalization of the SHEEO position that corresponded with a rise in the professionalization of advocates in higher education fueled by philanthropic investment and interest; and the elevation of postsecondary policy to the top tier of state and federal policy dialogues.

While retail higher education policymaking on the part of legislators and governors has shifted the role of the SHEEO, one additional area of state policy has implications for how we might reimage the SHEEO role and their agency staff to meet the demands of the 21st-century public higher education systems: state budgets and financing decisions.

DISCONNECT BETWEEN STATE BUDGET PROCESS, HIGHER EDUCATION FINANCE, AND STATE GOALS

Despite the efforts to restructure and rearrange governance models, often coupled with forays into both strategic (e.g., statewide attainment plans) and operational (e.g., faculty workloads) policy areas, there has been an enduring and persistent challenge facing reconceptualization of the SHEEO agency: a disconnect between state finance policy and public agenda goals for higher education. With the disparate role of SHEEOs in budget formation, most states lack a venue where state leaders can come together to develop long-term strategic goals specific for the higher education system's performance and sustainability as well as a strategic financing plan to achieve those goals. (McGuinness, 2016).

As other areas of policy expertise developed in the governor's budget office and legislative staffs, the role of state higher education coordinating boards is perceived to be diminished, partially due to staff shortfalls that were a result of retrenchment during the 2008 financial crisis (McGuinness, 2016). In some states, a coordinating board's debate and approval of a strategic plan or budget recommendations have limited credibility in the legislative process due to relational, political, or authority issues. However, that credibility may be enhanced if the board has engaged the governor and the state legislature in the board's decision-making process. The governor's budget office and legislature may rely on the data and technical analysis of the coordinating agency staff but place less credence on the recommendations made by a group of laypeople on the board.

The states without statewide coordinating or governing entities, but likely have one or more systemwide governing boards, do not have often have an official structure to work with the state budget office and legislature to formulate state higher education policy across all sectors. The reality, then, is that most states lack a venue where state leaders can come together to develop long-term strategic goals for the higher education system's performance and sustainability as well as a strategic financing plan to achieve those goals. The absence of a statewide organization complicates decision-making efforts to achieve higher education goals, especially within the reoccurring constraints of limited public funding and concerns over affordability for students and families. Ideally, as originally discussed and detailed in McGuinness' (2016) framing paper, state higher education finance policy would:

- Frame funding decisions by relating them to clear state education and workforce goals.
- Ensure that decisions regarding state appropriations, tuition and fees, and student financial aid are synchronized. For example, if tuition and fees increased as a result of decreased appropriations, the state would ensure adequate funding for student financial aid to maintain a commitment to affordable postsecondary education for low-income students.
- Recognize that both students and institutions need a degree of predictability in financing:
  » For students and families as they plan to pay for tuition, living, and other costs.
  » For institutions to carry out their teaching and research missions (for example, academic programs and faculty must be in place as students begin the academic year).

The reality is that policymakers' decisions regarding state appropriations, tuition and fees, and student financial aid are often not aligned with and supportive of state goals, coordinated, synchronized, or in tune with the needs and schedules of students and institutions. Despite structural challenges to policy and implementation change at a systemic level, we see a need to provide more balanced, transparent, and strategic-focused bodies to design and potentially oversee longer-term higher education financial planning.

STRUCTURAL REFORM IN A TIME OF HIGHER EDUCATION POLICY DYNAMISM

There is growing concern that the current state-level policy environment is a major barrier to the changes needed to achieve long-term goals and to reshape the public higher education enterprise to remain affordable and sustainable (McGuinness, 2016). The policymaking processes and structures for system governance and regulation established for an earlier time may not be adequate for the future, but gaining support among state political leaders for the needed changes remains a challenge.

The state political scene is highly splintered, with serious divisions among opposing views about the role and efficacy of government. Turnover in political leadership, term limits, and political divisions mean that short-term agendas drive out attention to long-term reform. These conditions have led to a loss of understanding concerning the underlying rationale for higher education structures, including basic values such as the need for autonomy and a degree of independence of system-level structures from political control.

Following the 2008 economic crisis and ensuing downturn, states tightened controls in the budget process, in public employment, and in the expenditure of state funding (State Higher Education Executive Officers Association, 2017). State budget offices and legislative appropriations committees are focused on balancing the state budget, controlling expenditure of state appropriations, and reducing or containing long-term liabilities in funding pensions and health care. In this environment, there may be limited opportunities and venues to discuss and carry out long-term planning such as linking long-term strategic education goals to finance policy.

As discussed in the opening of our chapter, states need to have a broad-based, independent, and credible public entity with a clear charge to increase the state's educational attainment and prepare citizens for the workforce. This core focus is more singular in nature than the expansive responsibilities of SHEEO agencies, which appropriately have responsibility for myriad policy areas. Current evidence suggests there is some way to go to achieve this desired outcome.

As illustrated in Appendix 9.C, as of 2017, 28 states have a statewide entity that could assume the broad role suggested. Twenty of these have statewide coordinating boards, while 8 have statewide system governing boards with responsibility for essentially all the public institutions. The remaining states have one or more coordinating or governing boards for postsecondary systems and, in most cases, institutional governing boards. However, some institutions, typically community colleges, are not associated with systems and operate independently but may be affiliated with a statewide association. Some of these states have an administrative/service agency that typically maintains student data systems, administers student financial aid, and licenses certain institutions, among other responsibilities. In states without a statewide coordinating or governing entity, it is challenging to shape a public agenda or policies for the state as a whole, across all sectors and institutions. States that fall into this category include Arizona, California, Connecticut, Florida, Georgia, Minnesota, New York, and North Carolina, among others (see Appendix 9.C).

A consequence of this current state of governance organization has resulted in a shift in agency capacity away from policy leadership toward project/program management and regulation as detailed in Table 9.1. This trend is problematic. To support a more intentional system of strategic higher education policymaking, led and supported by a core enlistment of policy professionals and dedicated state leaders, we envision a SHEEO agency of the future that is crafted around four critical components, set out in the following section, and that strives to create conditions most likely to support a robust and enduring positive agenda for higher education policy.

Table 9.1. Six State-Level Higher Education Functions and State Roles in 2017

Function	Current State Role and Context
State-level planning	Continued emphasis on developing a strategic plan (public agenda) setting long-term state goals to improve the educational attainment of the state's population and postsecondary completion rates as advocated by various philanthropic foundations and policy organizations.
	Weakening of state capacity to implement long-term goals and a public agenda as states reduced staffs of existing agencies and, in some cases, eliminated state higher education agencies in the economic crisis.
	As in the prior change periods, no venue to develop and sustain attention to a long-term public agenda for the entire higher education system in many states.
State finance policy: budgeting and resource allocation	Continued expansion of outcomes-based funding overwhelmed by base-minus funding combined with concerns for affordability leading to various strategies for price controls.
	Deregulation of some fiscal policy controls countered by recentralization of state tuition controls.
	Disconnect between state budgeting in the economic crisis and state public agenda reforms.
Use of information	Continuing trends to use information to monitor progress toward state goals and to hold institutions accountable for contribution to the public agenda with new emphasis on completion.
	Increased emphasis on longitudinal student data systems to enable analysis and monitoring of student progress through the education pipeline (P–20) to the completion of a degree or certificate and into the workforce.

(Continued)

Table 9.1. State-Level Higher Education Functions and State Roles in 2017 (*Continued*)

Function	Current State Role and Context
Regulation	Continued deregulation of state procedural regulatory controls in areas such as procurement, capital development, and human resources.
	As states cut funding of state agencies in the economic crisis, continued weakening of state regulations for approval of academic programs, both new and existing, and for review and approval of changes in institutional missions.
Administration/ service agency functions	Continued strengthening of state licensure/authorization requirements to accommodate broader range of institutions to be eligible for federal student aid programs.
	Continued responsibility for administering state student financial aid and other programs/projects.
System and institutional governance	Mixed pattern of decentralization and reduced capacity for system leadership and recentralization in the establishment of a new consolidated governing system to replace a state coordinating board.
	Isolated examples of efforts to redesign the role of systems in leading change to achieve state and system goals in the face of severe economic constraints.

Source: McGuinness (2016)

FUTURE DIRECTIONS FOR STATE HIGHER EDUCATION LEADERSHIP AND GOVERNANCE

The concept of a single entity responsible for all six state-level functions commonly associated with SHEEO agencies may no longer feasible or desirable. Rather than a single entity, we posit that the SHEEO agency of the future is likely to be represented by four distinct components located at different points in the overall state governance structure:

- Statewide policy leadership
- Statewide coordination/implementation of cross-sector initiatives
- State service agency administration
- System and institutional governance

States will need to make changes to their existing structure to support effective governance and policy leadership. Creating the SHEEO agency of the future cannot be achieved simply by resuscitating existing boards or agencies. Recent state changes to higher education governance has moved some states, in some places, closer to the vision outlined by McGuinness (2016). Yet there is still work to do to build the SHEEO of the future. In particular, more direct attention is needed to understand how our reconceptualization of higher education agencies and their leadership impact the individual role of the SHEEO, a fruitful line of future inquiry we hope the ideas put forth in this chapter can support. The chapter closes with discussion of one way that the four components of tomorrow's SHEEO agency could unfold.

Component for Statewide Policy Leadership

The key component is a capacity for carrying out a statewide policy leadership process for shaping and gaining consensus around long-term goals to be enacted in state statutes and linking strategic financing policy to these goals. This capacity should be a statutorily established process, not necessarily an entity. In fact, the focus on creating an entity rather than on ensuring that a process takes place can be a major barrier to implementation. The policy leadership component might take the form of an entity with periodic rather than ongoing responsibilities. Examples include a blue-ribbon commission or an entity such as the North Dakota Higher Education Roundtable. In this respect, the process would take place for defined, periodic tasks but would not involve establishing an entity with continuing oversight, coordinating, administrative, or governing responsibilities similar to those currently assigned to statewide coordinating or governing boards.

What is important is a clear definition of what the outcomes of the process are to be, what tasks are to be performed, when in the state's budget/appropriations schedule the process is to take place, who is to be involved, who is responsible for initiating the process, who will be responsible for reporting on progress, how often the goals will be updated, and how the process is to be staffed. For example, in states with coordinating boards, the agency could provide staff support for the process, and the SHEEO could serve as an ex officio member of any process established to play this strategic role for the state. It is important to enact these specifications in state statute to ensure that the process can be sustained over changes in political leadership.

Component for Statewide Coordination/Implementation of Cross-Sector Initiatives

Statewide coordination will remain an important function. In states with a single governing board for all public higher education and a limited private sector, this function can continue to be performed by this board under the direct leadership of the SHEEO. However, in states with two or more governing boards there will continue to be a need for a coordinating entity. Our position, however, is that it is unrealistic to expect this entity, especially the members of the entity's board or council, to play the policy leadership role outlined previously. They should, of course, be involved in the process but not with the expectation that they will be the leaders. The functions of these coordinating entities will continue to include coordination across sectors through:

- Mission differentiation including review and approval of major changes in mission
- Finance policy/resource allocation among sectors
- Leadership and implementation of cross-cutting initiatives such as:
  - » P–20 coordination
  - » Links with workforce and economic development
  - » Links with adult education
- Maintenance of statewide data/information capacity, including state longitudinal data systems and, depending on the state, use of this capacity to support analysis, monitoring and reporting functions of the policy leadership component as described previously
- Issue analysis/problem solving

Component for State Service Agency Administration

States should separate these operational and regulatory functions from the entity carrying out the policy leadership component, a suggested shift from current SHEEO and agency portfolios that blend these roles. State coordinating boards could continue to carry out these functions; however, states should guard against having these dominate the coordinating agency agenda. The clearest way to ensure this separation is for the state to fund the coordinating component rather than relying on funding for the administration of student financial aid programs or funding derived from the regulatory function (for example, fees paid by nonpublic institutions for licensure/authorization).

In states with coordinating boards, the service agency/regulatory role will continue to be an important subfunction. The danger is that these functions will dominate the agency's agenda and draw its attention away from the substantive issues traditionally associated with statewide coordination (the second component). An indicator of this problem is a coordinating board agenda in which the majority of items are not related to pursuing the goals of a strategic plan but are related primarily to the administration of student aid programs or approving the licensure/authorization of nonstate institutions.

Because of this concern, coordinating boards should consider organizing the service agency/regulatory functions as a subsidiary, quasi-independent unit with delegated authority to carry out day-to-day management and regulatory tasks. The coordinating board should develop student financial aid policy (the parameters for student eligibility, etc.), but the subsidiary unit would be charged with day-to-day operations within that policy framework.

Component for System and Institutional Governance

As emphasized previously, the statewide policy leadership component should not be assigned to a statewide governing board. It can be a conflict in roles to be responsible both for governing and advocating for the interests of public institutions as well as performing the policy leadership function on behalf of the citizens of the state. On the other hand, these statewide boards will continue to have the critical responsibility for implementing the statewide goals and action plans.

In states with two or more statewide governing boards or multiple system and/or institutional boards, it is essential that the state have an independent policy leadership entity as described under the first component. Effective governing systems are critical components of a state's capacity to achieve long-term goals. Stated differently, if a state only concentrates on putting in place the policy leadership component (statewide goals, action plans and financing framework) and fails to redesign its implementation capacity encompassed in large systems, the state's plans will not come to fruition.

Many of the states with two or more large systems have no effective means to carry out either the policy leadership component or the statewide coordinating component. Without overarching state goals, these states lack the capacity to ensure the alignment of individual system goals with the overall state priorities and state finance policy.

CONCLUSION

State higher education structures have changed dramatically over the past century as the complexity of both the higher education system and state government have increased. Many of the structures now in place had their origins in earlier historical periods. In many cases, statutes defining the powers and functions of these entities have changed only marginally over the years. Often the changes have simply added new responsibilities without clearing out those that are no longer relevant. The conclusion of this chapter is that creating the SHEEO agencies of the future cannot be achieved simply by resuscitating existing boards or agencies.

And yet remarkably, over the arch of structural historic change documented herein, the necessity of highly skilled, knowledgeable, and engaged professionals—the SHEEOs themselves—remains vital. Although structural change and redistribution of authorities, responsibilities, and leadership are clearly necessary to support achievement of today's student and state higher education policy goals, what is also unquestioned from our view is the prerequisite of professionalized leadership in higher education agencies. These professionals are necessary to guide and support a period of structural transition, and perhaps more importantly, to leverage that new structure toward positive ends for states and students alike. Absent effective and dynamic professional SHEEOs, rearranged structures will only underperform.

Implementation of the components of state capacity outlined in this chapter would require changes in essentially every state and would vary depending on the existing governance structure. Although the task of bringing about the changes may seem daunting, they are in fact doable provided state leaders recognize the consequences of not acting. In some cases, these changes would involve only an updating of the mandates for existing state boards or agencies. In other cases, they would require states to establish new entities or to eliminate or reconstitute significantly existing agencies.

Few states have an entity with the characteristics outlined in the policy leadership component. This is an essential capacity if states are to be able to sustain long-term reform agendas over changes in political leadership and economic conditions, and it creates a new and potentially influential role for SHEEO agencies and the individuals who lead them.

Appendix 9.A. Change in Complexity of Major Decision Points That Affect State Higher Education Policy, Early 20th Century to Present

Decision Points		Phases 1 and 2: Late 19th Century Through End of World War II	Phases 3 through 6: 1972 to the Present
Governor		Direct relationship between governing boards and the governor; no specialized staffing	Governor's education policy advisors
	State budget office	Limited role in higher education budget	Executive branch non-higher education administrative and regulatory agencies
State legislature	House and Senate	House and Senate (except in Nebraska with its unicameral legislature); relatively simple committee structure with most higher education issues handled by appropriations/finance committees; limited legislative staff	Complex committee structures in both houses with (depending on state) specialized higher education substantive and appropriations committees
			Complex professional legislative staff structures including nonpartisan staffs, committee staffs, caucus staffs and, in some states, staffs for individual legislators

(Continued)

Appendix 9.A. Change in Complexity of Major Decision Points That Affect State Higher Education Policy, Early 20th Century to Present (*Continued*)

Decision Points		Phases 1 and 2: Late 19th Century Through End of World War II	Phases 3 through 6: 1972 to the Present
Higher education coordinating boards	Authority (depending on state) for statewide planning, review and approval of new academic programs, review and recommending funding formulas and budgets, and other administrative and regulatory functions	None	Organized in half the states
Executive branch higher education services and regulatory agencies	Institutional licensure and authorization	None, except for chartering of institutions	Agencies established in every state organized within other agencies or as independent entities
	Student financial assistance agencies	None	Agencies in each state organized within other agencies or as independent entities

	Federal higher education program administration		Organized within other agencies
System sector governing or coordinating boards for locally governed community colleges	None	None	Complex patterns of coordination and governance of community colleges and postsecondary technical institutions
System governing boards for multiple institutions		Limited number of consolidated boards for multiple universities	Most public universities within multi-institutional governing systems
Single institutional governing boards		Dominant pattern of single institutional boards; no community colleges	Limited number of public institutions with independent boards and not within systems; locally governed community colleges
State associations of universities		Informal presidents' councils of public universities	State associations of universities and community colleges

Source: Updated from McGuinness (2016)

Appendix 9.B. Six State-Level Functions: Summary of Change Over Phases

			MAJOR PHASES			
FUNCTIONS	Early 20th century to World War II	As of 1972	End of the 1970s	1980s through mid-1990s	2000s to 2008	2017
State-level planning	None	Master planning for expansion of capacity in the public sector: institutions, academic programs and facilities; limited number of agencies included the independent sector in planning	New emphasis on comprehensive planning for postsecondary education, including public, private not-for-profit, and for-profit providers reflecting provisions of Education Amendments of 1972 Centralized planning for projected retrenchment: maintaining access, quality and institutional diversity, and efficiency in a period of enrollment decline and resource constraints.	Weakening of centralized planning authority of some state agencies; beginning of shift from master planning for rational development of public institutions and systems and planning for static institutional models to strategic planning linking higher education to state priorities and planning for dynamic market models in a more decentralized and deregulated system;	More emphasis on developing a strategic plan (public agenda) setting long-term state goals to improve the educational attainment of the state's population, including goals such as narrowing gaps in access, participation, and completion between the state's majority and minority populations; maintaining affordability; linking higher education to the state's future environment for innovation and economic competitiveness.	Continued emphasis on developing a strategic plan (public agenda) setting long-term state goals to improve the educational attainment of the state's population as advocated by the Lumina Foundation and with a new emphasis on improving completion encouraged by Complete College America; weakening of state capacity to implement long-term goals and a public agenda as states reduced staffs of existing agencies and, in some cases, eliminated state higher education agencies in the economic crisis.

244

State finance policy: budgeting, appropriations, and resource allocation	Governing board staff develops consolidated budget request; state legislature appropriates funds directly to the board; no intermediary budget agency.	Development of quantitative analysis and funding formulas to ensure rational allocation of resources and curb political influences; formulas emphasize cost-reimbursement and reflect mission differences, institutional workload, and costs associated with expanding capacity.	Modification of resource allocation methods to create rationales for the distribution of reductions and provide incentives for efficient use of existing capacity (e.g., marginal cost formulas)	Beginning of shift from state subsidy of public institutions to build capacity to selective state investment on the margin to meet state priorities; finance policy to maintain existing capacity through base-plus funding; use of "plus" (incentive/competitive funding) to reward institutions that respond to state priorities; creation (and subsequent abandonment) of performance funding in a minority of states	Deregulation of fiscal regulatory controls; ties of finance policy to the state public agenda; base-plus (or minus) funding; new generation of performance funding toward outcomes-based funding; attempts to align state appropriations, tuition policy, and student financial aid	Continued expansion of outcomes-based funding overwhelmed by base-minus funding combined with concerns for affordability, leading to various strategies for price controls; deregulation of some fiscal policy controls countered by recentralization of state tuition controls; disconnect between state budgeting in the economic crisis and state public agenda reforms
				beginning of more aggressive role of governors in establishing state priorities external to the higher education system, such as contributions to workforce needs and R&D linked to state economic development	Many states, including those with two or more public governing systems, were left with no venue to develop and sustain attention to a long-term public agenda for the entire higher education system.	As in the previous period, no venue to develop and sustain attention to a long-term public agenda for the entire higher education system in many states.

(Continued)

Appendix 9.B. Six State-Level Functions: Summary of Change Over Phases (Continued)

| | | | | MAJOR PHASES | | |
FUNCTIONS	Early 20th century to World War II	As of 1972	End of the 1970s	1980s through mid-1990s	2000s to 2008	2017
Use of information	Limited as required in the budget process to institutional data on expenditures and revenues, students, human resources, and facilities	Development of state-level data/ information systems on enrollment, academic programs, human resources, and facilities; development of analytic tools for institutional management and assessing costs/benefits of alternatives for expansion	New emphasis on analysis of institutional costs, faculty/ student ratios, and academic program productivity (degrees granted by program)	New emphasis on analysis of information on student outcomes and assessment of student learning	Use of information to monitor progress toward state goals and to hold institutions accountable for contribution to the public agenda; increased emphasis on longitudinal student data systems to enable analysis and monitoring of student progress through the education pipeline (P–20) to a degree or certificate and into the workforce	Continuing trends to use information to monitor progress toward state goals and to hold institutions accountable for contribution to the public agenda with new emphasis on completion; increased emphasis on longitudinal student data systems to enable analysis and monitoring of student progress through the education pipeline (P–20) to the completion of a degree or certificate and into the workforce

Regulation	None	Focus on rational expansion of capacity and curbing unnecessary duplication primarily in the public sector; regulation of new academic programs, campuses, branch campuses, and ensuring mission differentiation between public research universities, teaching colleges/ universities, and community colleges	Strengthening state regulatory authority related to new academic programs, campuses, and branch campuses, and ensuring mission differentiation; new emphasis on state review of existing academic programs for unnecessary duplication and/or low-productivity, including in some cases state authority to discontinue programs; state mandates for external review of academic program quality	State attempts, subsequently largely abandoned, to mandate institutional accountability based on assessment of student learning; deregulation of state procedural regulatory controls in areas such as procurement, capital development, and human resources; weakening of state regulations enacted in previous decade for approval of academic programs, both new and existing, and for review and approval of changes in institutional missions	Continued deregulation of state procedural regulatory controls in areas such as procurement, capital development, and human resources; as states cut funding of state agencies in the economic crisis, continued weakening of state regulations for approval of academic programs, both new and existing, and for review and approval of changes in institutional missions	Continued deregulation of state procedural regulatory controls in areas such as procurement, capital development, and human resources; as states cut funding of state agencies in the economic crisis, continued weakening of state regulations for approval of academic programs, both new and existing, and for review and approval of changes in institutional missions

(Continued)

Appendix 9.B. Six State-Level Functions: Summary of Change Over Phases (*Continued*)

	MAJOR PHASES					
FUNCTIONS	Early 20th century to World War II	As of 1972	End of the 1970s	1980s through mid-1990s	2000s to 2008	2017
Administration/ service agency functions	None	New functions: state student financial aid program administration, state planning and administration of federal programs (e.g., facilities), and licensure/ authorization of institutions to be eligible for federal student aid programs	Modification of state authority to conform to new federal requirements: state student financial aid program administration, state planning (1202 state commissions), and administration of federal programs; strengthening of state licensure/ authorization requirements to accommodate broader range of institutions to be eligible for federal student aid programs	Continued strengthening of state licensure/ authorization requirements to accommodate broader range of institutions to be eligible for federal student aid programs; continued responsibility for administering state student financial aid and other programs/projects	Continued strengthening of state licensure/authorization requirements to accommodate broader range of institutions to be eligible for federal student aid programs; increased responsibility for regulating distance learning courses delivered across state lines through state authorization reciprocity agreements (SARA); continued responsibility for administering state student financial aid and other programs/ projects	Continued strengthening of state licensure/authorization requirements to accommodate broader range of institutions to be eligible for federal student aid programs; continued responsibility for administering state student financial aid and other programs/ projects

System and institutional governance	Limited number of consolidated governing boards that functioned more as single boards for multiple public institutions rather than as systems	Major expansion of governing systems: multiple campus universities and consolidated governing boards; for the first time, the majority of students in the public sector attend institutions within governing systems.	Strengthening of governing systems' authority to manage costs and plan for potential retrenchment	Questioning the role of systems and centralized governance; dismantling of some systems; new emphasis on decentralization within systems (e.g., delegating some authority to campus-level boards)	Governing systems continue to focus more on internal management than on aligning system priorities with long-term state goals	Mixed pattern of decentralization and reduced capacity for system leadership and recentralization in the establishment of a new consolidated governing system to replace a state coordinating board; isolated examples of efforts to redesign the role of systems in leading change to achieve state and system goals in the face of severe economic constraints

Source: Updated from McGuinness (2016)

Appendix 9.C. Authority of State Boards and Agencies of Higher Education, 2017

Type of Board	Coordinating Boards/Agencies with Authority to Coordinate all Public Higher Education		System Governing Board for All Public Higher Education Institutions (HEIs)	No Statewide Board for All Public Higher Education		Higher Education Service Agencies (student aid, private HEI licensure, data collection and reporting)
	Multiple Governing Boards for Systems and Public Institutions			One or more System Coordinating Boards or Governing Boards	Boards for Each Public HEI	
Statewide Planning Authority	Yes	Yes	Yes	No state-level entity charged with authority for statewide planning/public agenda for all higher education; planning only for individual systems or institutions	Planning only for each HEI	No authority for statewide planning or in budget process
Budget Role	Consolidated or Aggregated Budget –All Public HEIs a.	Review / and Recommend—All Public HEIs a.	Yes for public system / Limited budget role	Budget role only for governing systems and public HEIs under each board's jurisdiction	Budget role only for each HEI	
	AL AR b. CO b. IL IN KY LA	NE OR e. TX VA	WA b.f. AK HI ID g. KS h. MT i. NV ND	AZ CA j. CT k. DE FL g. m. GA o. IA l.	MI q.	AK AZ CT b. DE FL IA MN b.

MA [c]	RI [g]	ME [n, o]		NH [b]
MD [b]	DC	MN		NJ [b, r]
MO	PR	MS [l]		NY [g]
NM [b, d]		NH [o]		PA [b, g]
OH [b]		NJ		DC
OK		NY		PR
SC		NC [o]		
TN [b]		PA		
		SD [l]		
		UT [o]		
		VT [p]		
		WI [o]		
		WV [l]		
		WY [l]		
Totals 20	8, DC and PR	21	1	11, DC and PR

Source: Updated from McGuinness (2016)

(Continued)

251

Appendix 9.C. Authority of State Boards and Agencies of Higher Education, 2017 (*Continued*)

a. Coordinating boards commonly develop the formulas for allocation of state appropriations and/or make recommendations for overall system funding but do not review and/or make recommendations on individual institutional budgets.

b. The governor plays a role in the appointment or confirmation of the executive officer. Beginning in 2019, the Tennessee Higher Education Commission appoints the executive officer.

c. The Massachusetts Board of Higher Education serves as the coordinating board for all public higher education. The board also has overall state-level governing responsibilities for the state universities and community colleges, not the UMass. Each of the state universities and community colleges has a governing board which functions within the overall authority of the board of higher education.

d. The New Mexico entity is a cabinet-level department headed by a secretary of higher education. The department has authority to review, adjust and approve public university budgets prior to submission to the department of finance and administration and limited authority primarily to review and study but not to take formal action to approve academic programs or other institutional decisions.

e. In June 2011, Oregon established a Higher Education Coordinating Commission for planning and coordination of the whole postsecondary education sector, including the community colleges and the Oregon University System. In 2013, legislation was enacted strengthening the Higher Education Coordinating Commission, transferring responsibility for the community colleges to the commission, and authorizing public universities previously under the Board of Higher Education to create their own governing boards.

f. Washington Student Achievement Council makes overall recommendations on finance policy and strategic budget, but does not review and make recommendations on institutional budgets.

g. State has a board/agency responsible for coordination of all levels of education (P/K-16/20). State boards/agencies in New York and Pennsylvania have limited coordinating, not governing authority for public institutions. The Idaho State Board of Education has governing authority for public institutions and coordinates locally governed community colleges. The Rhode Island Board of Education has planning and coordinating responsibility for the P-20 system but not for governing public higher education institutions. The Florida State Board of Education has responsibility for policy direction and coordination of state's education system, P-20. A Constitutional amendment passed in November 2002 created a Board of Governors to oversee the universities. The state board of education retains overall responsibility for policy coordination for all education.

h. Kansas Board of Regents is a consolidated governing board for universities and coordinating board for locally governed community colleges and Washburn University.

i. The Montana Board of Regents serves as the governing body for state universities and the coordinating body for locally governed community colleges.

j. One system board governs state community colleges and the other two system boards govern state universities.

k. Effective July 2011, the statewide coordinating board, the Connecticut Board of Governors, was eliminated. The Board of Regents for Higher Education is a governing

Appendix 9.C. Authority of State Boards and Agencies of Higher Education, 2017 (*Continued*)

body for the community-technical colleges, the state universities formerly within the Connecticut State University System, and Charter Oak State College. The University of Connecticut retains its own governing board. The Office of Higher Education is a higher education service entity for student aid and regulatory functions.

l. One of the boards is a statewide coordinating/regulatory body for locally governed community colleges and/or postsecondary technical institutions.

m. The Florida Higher Education Coordinating Council was created by statute in 2013 to serve as an advisory board to the legislature, the state board of education, and the Board of Governors. Florida State Board of Education, through a chancellor for community colleges, coordinates locally governed community colleges.

n. Maine Maritime Academy is the only public institution with its own governing board outside a system.

o. One of the boards is a statewide governing board for community colleges and/or technical institutions.

p. Vermont has no statutory planning/coordinating entity. Vermont Higher Education Council is voluntary.

q. Michigan State Board of Education has Constitutional authority for overall planning and coordination of the state's education system. Because of the Constitutional autonomy of the state universities and local governance of community colleges, the state board does not function as a statewide higher education coordinating agency.

r. The governor's reorganization plan in June 2011 eliminated the New Jersey Commission on Higher Education and transferred its authority and duties to a secretary of higher education who is appointed by the governor and confirmed by the Senate. The Governor's Higher Education Council serves as an advisory body to the secretary and the governor.

NOTES

1. We are indebted to Aims McGuinness for his support and thought partnership in allowing us extrapolate from our prior work together on governance structures in the production of this chapter. We've attempted to contextualize and build on his good thinking and ideas; any shortcomings toward that goal are certainly ours and should not be attributed to him.

2. This paper makes a careful distinction between *governing* boards and *coordinating* boards. Coordinating boards do not have authority to govern institutions. In other words, they do not have powers to grant degrees, establish institutional policies, appoint institutional presidents/chancellors, and carry out other functions of governing boards.

3. Berdahl (1971) made an important distinction between "substantive" autonomy, meaning autonomy on matters of standards, curriculum, faculty appointments, and similar matters, and "procedural" autonomy, meaning autonomy from state procedural controls.

REFERENCES

Berdahl, R. O. (1971). *Statewide coordination of higher education.* Washington, DC: American Council on Education.

Lumina Foundation. (2017). *A stronger nation.* Indianapolis, IN: Author.

McGuinness, A. C. (2016). *State policy leadership for the future: History of state coordination and governance and alternatives for the future.* Denver, CO: Education Commission of the States.

National Center for Education Statistics. (2017a). Digest of education statistics 2016, Table 326.10. Washington, DC: National Center for Education Statistics. Retrieved from nces.ed.gov/programs/digest/d16/tables/dt16_326.10.asp

National Center for Education Statistics. (2017b). Digest of education statistics 2016, Table 326.20. Washington, DC: National Center for Education Statistics. Retrieved from nces.ed.gov/programs/digest/d16/tables/dt16_326.20.asp

National Center for Public Policy and Higher Education. (2005). *State capacity for higher education policy leadership.* San Jose, CA: Author.

State Higher Education Executive Officers Association. (2017). *State higher education finance (SHEF).* Boulder, CO: Author.

Tennessee Higher Education Commission. (2015). *Profiles and trends in Tennessee higher education, annual report.* Nashville, TN: Author.

CHAPTER 10

Theoretical Perspectives on the SHEEO

How Theory Can Inform and Improve Policy, Practice, and Research

David A. Tandberg and Jacob T. Fowles

In the hierarchy of organizational complexity, few organizations reach the level of complexity of governments. A close second, however, might be the modern-day college or university. The state higher education executive officer (SHEEO), and his or her agency, exists at the intersection of these two organizations. SHEEOs therefore face a significant challenge when trying to understand, interact with, and ultimately influence their environments to shape policy or practice. Because of the complexity of the environments in which these state higher education leaders work, scholars who wish to study the SHEEO position likewise face a daunting task. The formidable scope and critical importance of the problems faced by SHEEOs therefore both justifies not only the existence of SHEEOs and the agencies they lead but also the SHEEO position as a focus of scholarly attention. Large, complex, and important societal problems demand professional attention. In our system of government, the problem of providing accessible, efficient, and quality postsecondary education has historically been assigned to the states, and within the states, a bureaucracy of professionals has been established with the intent of helping to promote such outcomes—namely, the SHEEO agencies.

How SHEEOs go about trying to meet their responsibilities, mediate and moderate the relationships between their various and often conflicting stakeholder groups, and accomplish the outcomes assigned to them are issues of both practical and theoretical importance. In an attempt to stimulate the development of a new vein of pragmatic scholarly research focused on the SHEEO and to improve current policy and practice, this paper takes a broadly deductive approach to that exercise, seeking to apply broader theoretical lenses and frameworks drawn from the social sciences to the practice and study of the SHEEO. We first discuss the characteristics of the SHEEO position that make the application of theory so important, by applying Rittel and Webber's (1973) conceptualization of "wicked problems." We discuss what theory is and why it can be helpful before turning to the primary purpose of the chapter—to introduce several theories whose substantive application may help SHEEOs better conceptualize, contextualize, and understand their position in ways that may help them in their work. We further argue that the SHEEO is a theoretically interesting and important topic for future empirical and theoretical consideration. Accordingly, we argue that the theories discussed here may help facilitate and shape forthcoming scholarship as it engages with the wicked problem that is the SHEEO.

SHEEOs AND WICKED PROBLEMS

The complexity of both the environment and the nature of the policy issues facing SHEEOs creates ideal examples of what public policy scholars call "wicked problems." The idea of wicked problems was developed not to define an issue as evil but instead to identify those problems that are highly complex and resistant to change or resolution. Rittel and Webber (1973) first introduced the idea when they observed that some problems are impossible to understand and solve via traditional linear analytical approaches alone. These problems share several important characteristics. They need to be revisited frequently but not necessarily ever solved in the traditional sense. Proposed solutions tend to be polarizing, as there are a plurality of objectives held by a plurality of actors, which makes unitary action terribly difficult. The very nature of these problems are ill-defined and frequently debated.

Higher education is replete with these types of problems. For example, how might we solve the affordability, cost, completion gap, and access problems? Obviously, there exists no shortage of potential solutions. However, it is not the plurality of solutions that makes the problem inherently wicked; rather, it is the fact that gaining traction on how the problem itself may be solved requires a normative prioritization of the competing (and often zero-sum) elements that comprise the broader problem definition. SHEEOs and their staffs are immersed in the wicked problems of higher education. A core function (as we will argue) of the SHEEO is to function as a mediator, moderator, intermediary, and boundary spanner among the various constituencies that occupy the higher education policy space, attempting to balance the demands of each group.

Furthermore, the role and position of SHEEOs and their bureaucratic apparatus have been debated. What is the appropriate level of state engagement in institutional affairs? How far does institutional autonomy, academic freedom, and academic deference extend? How do SHEEOs balance their need to represent and advocate for higher education to state policymakers with their need to represent the desires of the public and elected officials to the individual institutions? While there has been no shortage of opinions on these matters, it is hard to identify absolute right and wrong answers to these questions. This was, in fact, another attribute of wicked problems as identified by Rittel and Webber (1973): There are no true-or-false answers; instead the answers vary, as the parties involved are diverse, have opposing or different interests, and frequently represent different ideological predilections. Therefore, the ultimate resolution is often achieved through compromise and "satisficing," with no party able to claim unilateral victory and ownership of policy and programmatic outcomes. Such is often the case for state higher education policy and governance, with 50 governance structures and a near-infinite list of solutions developed through (and sometimes outside of) these structures to solve the wicked problems of postsecondary education. Further, wicked problems become even more difficult when they are placed within a highly politicized environment, where party politics play out in polarized states, outside groups attempt to influence policymaking within states, and governors often face legislatures dominated by the opposing party (Gándara, Rippner, & Ness, 2017; Pew Research Center, 2017). Often, this culminates in a context where attempting to address wicked problems in a rational manner, with compromise serving as the logical end, seems nearly impossible when policy outcomes reflect largely zero-sum struggles for resources, influence, and control (Graber & Dunaway, 2017).

Operating within an environment defined by wicked problems, and likewise studying and evaluating wicked problems, are difficult tasks. Fortunately, the social sciences have developed various instruments to help practitioners and scholars address wicked problems. Under such circumstances, one of the most useful instruments is the application of theory. At times, individuals can have a knee-jerk reaction to the word *theory*, presuming that it is merely an abstract academic exercise with little to no utility in the real world. Furthermore, academics are prone to use the term *theory* lightly. Regardless, the application of theory to the study of the SHEEO has been almost nonexistent. It is our hope that any preconceived notions of the utility of theory might be (albeit temporarily) put to the side and that readers—whether academic or practitioner—will give serious consideration to the potential utility of theory to inform their current work.

WHY THEORY?

Strauss and Corbin (1998) defined a *theory* as "a set of well-developed concepts related through statements of relationship, which together constitute an integrated framework that can be used to explain or predict phenome" (p. 15). For more practical purposes, Johnson and Christensen (2012) suggested that a theory is an explanation or explanatory system that discusses how a phenomenon operates and why it operates as it does. These definitions presuppose and suggest utility. Put differently, a good theory is a usable theory. Johnson and Christensen also suggested that "well-developed theories explain how something operates in general and it enables one to move beyond the findings of any single research study or single case. Using a well-developed theory, you should be able to explain a phenomenon, make sense of it, and be able to make useful predictions" (pp. 18–19). In other words, well-developed theories provide understanding and explanation, potential strategies, and common language and frames. More specifically, theories should:

- lead to testable claims;
- help identify and classify things such as processes, causal relationships, and actors;
- help identify and explain patterns across observations and settings;
- avoid parochial thinking;
- make diagnoses; and
- should serve as the basis for action.

They do all of this by being based on numerous observations, settings, and evaluations, thereby providing for a greater ability for generalization. As Bess and Dee (2008) argued:

> Instead of searching for concrete solutions, we can attempt to discover organizational principles related to the problem of interest that apply across many different contexts. Theory helps leaders become aware of and sensitive to what is useful and important, and then place the important ideas into a framework that can be used to understand, predict, and allow effective and timely intervention. . . . Basically, the argument is that while some problems are unique and require unique solutions, it is more often the case that they only appear that way to those involved. Indeed, both problems and solutions, and the circumstances that surround them, usually fall into patterns or categories that persist or recur frequently. (p. 7)

A former longtime SHEEO went further when discussing his approach to teaching his students, saying, "First, I could impress upon them how important are the general models and theories they are studying, for in the beginning these will provide practically the only refuge for perspective and understanding amidst seeming chaos, uncertainty, and confusion" (Ashworth, 2001, p. xii).

Without such general understandings as provided by well-developed theories, practitioners and scholars run the risk of turning to simple and incomplete prescriptions. This is especially true when faced with wicked problems, which demand high-level and boundary-spanning perspectives. Wicked problems should not be addressed via a case-by-case approach as they are too difficult and complex. Given that the position of the SHEEO is itself a wicked problem and that the policy problems facing SHEEOs are themselves wicked problems, the application of well-developed theories must be employed practically and empirically. When properly understood and applied, relevant theories can provide current and aspiring SHEEOs with greater access to avenues for a deeper exploration and understanding of their roles and positions, general approaches to their work, and pathways to potential solutions. These same theories can illuminate the position of the SHEEO as worthy of theoretical and empirical consideration to and offer hypotheses and directions for future research. In the following sections, we review four theories that have utility both to practitioners and researchers. In so doing, two distinct veins of theoretical work were considered: theories that focus on the SHEEO position itself and theories that focus on the environments in which the SHEEO operates.

THEORETICAL PERSPECTIVES ON THE SHEEO POSITION

Here we attempt a substantive application of two theories to help SHEEOs and those who would study the SHEEO better understand the position and job of the SHEEO. The two theories we explore and apply are related to each other: Cohen, March and Olsen's garbage can theory and Kingdon's multiple streams. The former is designed to help SHEEOs understand the colleges and universities they are asked to lead, and the latter is meant to help SHEEOs understand the workings of government and politicians. Both theories provide good examples of why the position of the SHEEO might be considered a wicked problem and will also help researchers to better understand the position of the SHEEO and suggest various empirical research questions and testable hypotheses.

Garbage Can Model of Decision Making

SHEEOs are faced with the daunting task of helping steer a complex industry with unique norms, characteristics, and processes that defy traditional understandings of the way organizations ought to be organized and function. Understanding how colleges and universities function, including how best to lead and implement change within the institutions, is a necessary endeavor for any state higher education leader. One theory that attempts to provide such a perspective is the garbage can model of decision making. This classic organizational theory was developed to understand leadership and decisionmaking in colleges and universities. Cohen, March, and Olsen (1972) developed the term "organized anarchies" to describe organizations of significant complexity with problematic preferences, unclear technology, and fluid participation. As SHEEOs must understand, explain, defend, work with, influence, and lead colleges and universities, an application of this theory may help with each responsibility.

One reason SHEEOs have such a difficult, and at times frustrating, job is that the organizations they are asked to lead can be slow to change and appear to operate based on unique rules and norms. These unique characteristics led Cohen, March, and Olsen (1972) to describe colleges and universities as organized anarchies. In organized anarchies both problems and solutions as well as decisions and decision processes tend to be loosely coupled, where problems, solutions, participants, and choice opportunities flow in separate streams, disconnected from each other. Problems get attached to solutions often due to chance rather than as a true solution. This loosely coupled nature of organized anarchies is due to a number of factors:

- *highly autonomous actors* (e.g., faculty) who are difficult to manage or even influence (and often openly resistant to attempts to do so);
- *problematic goals* that are difficult to agree on, define, and attain (e.g., student learning, "excellence," prestige);
- *unclear technologies*, meaning that what the organization does is hard to understand and explain, even if it is easy to recognize (e.g., teaching);
- *fluid participation*, meaning that actors (faculty and administrators) regularly come and go, both in regard to committees and working groups within the organization and in tendencies to frequently enter and leave the organization itself, with the result that time and energy devoted to the organization or problems within the organization vary greatly among participants;
- leaders who rely on *symbolic leadership* because they often have little actual power and therefore many actions are undertaken for symbolic purposes rather than for the accomplishment of real change;
- and organized anarchies operate with a *high degree of uncertainty and ambiguity*, as problems and solutions often come together by chance.

The ambiguous characteristics merit specific attention. Four ambiguities largely define college and university environments: the ambiguity of purpose, the ambiguity of power, the ambiguity of experience, and the ambiguity of success (March & Olsen, 2010). The *ambiguity of purpose* refers to the difficulty of institutional leaders in defining in clear terms what goals are shared across the organization and how and when action is justified. Consider the multiple purposes of any one college or university. The *ambiguity of power* refers to the difficulty of identifying who has power, under what circumstances, how it might be used, and how to reasonably estimate what can be accomplished within and by the organization. Here the lack of clarity around shared governance and the purview of the president versus the purview of the faculty senate provide examples of this ambiguity. The *ambiguity of experience* refers to the difficulty of using past experience to make inferences about the present and future. Ordinary theories of learning and adaptation become problematic because the world in which college and university presidents operate is complex and outcomes depend heavily on factors other than their actions. Likewise, the world in which presidents operate changes rapidly, and therefore any learning lags the challenges they face. The *ambiguity of success* refers to the difficulty of determining when a leader and/or a college or university is successful. The multiple factors operating at any one time and the various other ambiguities make any casual argument tying a president's action to the overall goals of the institution difficult. As March and Olsen argued, the "ambiguities of purpose, power, and experience conspire to render success and failure equally obscure" (p. 82).

In this model of organized anarchy where ambiguity reigns, leaders frequently look for problems to apply to solutions. Actors within these types of organizations have preconceived solution preferences and, in an effort to implement those policies, search for problems that may justify their preferred solutions. This differs from a rational perspective that conceptualizes decisionmaking as linear where the determination of a solution would follow the problem. In addition, with organized anarchies, the complexity of some situations, and the speed at which decisions must be made, may force some actors to make decisions with incomplete information and without well-developed preferences. When an organization's technology (what it does, such as teaching with the goal of accomplishing learning) is unclear, its members may not understand the processes of the organization; thus past experience serves as the main (and highly imperfect) guide for future actions. As Cohen and colleagues (1972) described: "Organized anarchies can be viewed as collections of choices looking for problems, issues and feelings looking for decision situations in which they might be aired, solutions looking for issues to which they might be an answer, and decision makers looking for work" (p. 1). They go on to say:

> The American college or university is a prototypical organized anarchy. It does not know what it is doing. Its goals are either vague or in dispute. Its technology is familiar but not understood. Its major participants wander in and out of the organization. These factors do not make a university a bad organization or a disorganized one; but they do make it a problem to describe, understand, and lead. (p. 3)

How are decisions ultimately made within the context of organized anarchies, and how might such organizations be most effectively led? Cohen and

March (1986) explained that decisions result from an interaction between four independent streams of events: problems, solutions, participants, and choice opportunities. Change happens and decisions are made when a college or university leader takes advantage of a choice opportunity (a window of opportunity) to attach a solution to an existing problem and get buy-in from the right participants.

How is this done? Largely through the challenging work of consensus building and sense making. Cohen and March (1986) recommend that institutional leaders *spend time*, as change is slow and favors the persistent. Most leaders give up quickly, and other actors attempt to avoid extra work. Therefore, being willing to spend time and persist greatly increases the likelihood of success. Similarly, change agents ought to be willing to *exchange status for substance*. Effective leadership must be willing to do the substantive work and allow others to gain status as desired changes are sought. Leaders ought to seek the direct participation of dissident groups in the decision-making process as it decreases their dissent, and it also checks leaders' own aspirations in regard to what might actually be feasible. Leaders should also *overload the system* by creating a large inventory of potential projects and solutions for action, thereby increasing central control as other actors are occupied with the large variety of potential attention attracting issues. Leaders should also *provide garbage cans*. Garbage can situations involve any choice or decision that can provide the opportunity to raise any number of unresolved problems or issues;. In such situations, it is pointless to try to react by attempting to enforce rules of relevance, which are generally somewhat arbitrary. Instead, Cohen and March suggested providing "garbage can topics" to draw the attention of those who wish to raise extraneous issues and divert these issues away from the topic at hand. The authors suggested that low-status committees are useful garbage cans as they will not result in any real change but can be magnets for random ideas, problems, and solutions.

College and university leaders should *manage unobtrusively* as direct confrontation is unlikely to succeed in a garbage can process, where power and authority are diffused. The energy and natural tendencies of an organized anarchy cannot be suppressed, but they can be redirected to different purposes. Leaders should *interpret history* for the organization. Since most events in organized anarchies are complex and ambiguous, they are subject to various interpretations, which allows leaders to provide the official interpretation and advance their agenda. These recommendations provide insight into the processes and characteristics of organized anarchies. Leaders may reflect on and adjust them to meet their own values and goals as they attempt to lead these complex organizations.

Our hope here is that the garbage can theory of decision making can help current and future SHEEOs better understand how higher education institutions operate and how they might best work with these complex organizations. While Cohen, March, and Olsen originally directed their theory toward institutional leaders (college presidents), the strategies and perspectives may also be applied to SHEEOs as they attempt to lead multiple colleges at once. SHEEOs must reflect on the decision processes of the colleges and universities they lead. Realizing that there is not a clear command-and-control environment, that college and university actors operate with a high degree of autonomy, and that there exists a lack of clarity around actions and outcomes may help SHEEOs adjust their expectations and their strategies for motivating change. Given the nature of colleges and universities, SHEEOs ought to give special attention to policy design, implementation, and penetration. SHEEOs ought to consider how a proposed policy aligns with the characteristics of colleges and universities. Is the policy impacting those who are actually capable of causing the change the SHEEO is after? For example, is the policy impacting faculty if the SHEEO is interested in improving teaching and learning? In implementing policy, whose buy-in is essential for the success of the policy? Often this is not the president alone. Likewise, if the SHEEO wants policy to persist beyond the relative short terms of most presidents, wide and deep buy-in within the institutions will be necessary.

Researchers may use this theory as they attempt to better understand and frame the difficult responsibilities and forces facing SHEEOs. A potentially fruitful line of research might be to examine the intersection of SHEEOs and the organized anarchies they lead. The fact that SHEEOs must lead not one but multiple organized anarchies compounds the struggle. Do the recommendations, strategies, and tools provided by Cohen and March apply when leading multiple institutions? How might SHEEOs best implement and motivate change within these organizations? How do colleges and universities respond to "outside actors" like SHEEOs? These are just a few of the research questions that the garbage can model may inform.

Multiple Streams (Revised Garbage Can) Framework

Compounding the wicked problems faced by SHEEOs, they not only must work with colleges and university leaders but also be effective governmental and political actors. SHEEOs and their staffs work with governors and their staffs, legislators and their staffs, and other agency heads and their staffs. SHEEOs potentially may be involved with every aspect of the policy process with respect to higher education. While the roles vary from state to state based on laws, regulations, norms, and traditions, SHEEOs may propose new policies (legislation, rules, regulations, procedures, guidelines, etc.), play a role in advancing proposed policies, implement policies, and evaluate and revise policies. Understanding how government and the policy development process work may help SHEEOs carry out these tasks more effectively and efficiently. Kingdon's (1995) multiple streams theory may be helpful in this respect as SHEEOs often fill the role of "policy entrepreneur" and are often important actors in the agenda-setting process for state higher education policy.

Kingdon (1995) adjusted Cohen et al.'s (1972) original garbage can model to fit the federal government's policy-making process (which Kingdon also defined as an "organized anarchy") and developed the revised garbage can model, which has become more commonly known as the *multiple streams model*, theory, or approach. Kingdon developed this model to explain how issues rise to the top of a political agenda. The political agenda is the list of subjects or problems that government officials are paying attention to at any given time. Kingdon posited that three generally independent streams flow through the agenda-setting space of government: the problems stream, the policy/solutions stream, and the politics stream. When solutions flowing in the government's garbage can converge, or are coupled, with the problems and politics streams, the agenda-setting process occurs. Thus, an issue gets on the agenda when "a problem is recognized, a solution is available, and the political climate makes the time right for change" (p. 93). Kingdon defined this coupling moment as a "window of opportunity." For an issue to make the agenda, a "policy entrepreneur" must seize the window of opportunity and bring attention to the preferred problem (or solution) to get the issue on the agenda at the opportune time.

Problems are policy issues deemed to require attention. These issues are persistent and last well beyond any policy solution that is implemented to solve them. Examples might be higher education access, the cost of health care, and illegal drug use. Given the sheer number of problems, the widespread impact of problems on broad groups of citizens, and the persistent ability of problems to resist definitive resolution, there is no objective indicator to determine which problems deserve prioritization and policymaker attention. Further, attention paid to and perceptions of problems change quickly. According to Kingdon (1993), problems get attention based on external, seemingly random events occurring in the environment and the ways in which these events are framed or defined by political actors who compete for attention. In the case of the state higher education policy, the political actors may include faculty unions, student groups, the SHEEOs themselves, college and university presidents, non-higher education interest groups, and such traditional actors as governors and legislators.

Kingdon (1993) described ideas or policy solutions as existing in a "policy primeval soup" (p. 43). Solutions "float around" within communities of policy specialists (the soup) where the ideas (solutions) are modified and sometimes combined. Because it can be difficult, sometimes even impossible, to predict when a window of opportunity will open, policy solutions must be developed long before such an opening; otherwise, it will be too late to refine and suitably craft a solution. In order to deal with the apparent disconnect between shifting attention and the slow pace of policy development, policy actors, such as the SHEEO, must proactively develop solutions with sufficient bases of support to address future problems. Then they must find the right moment to exploit and encourage attention to a problem to which they can attach their preferred solution (McLendon, 2003a).

The politics stream consists of changes in administrations and legislative turnover, shifts in the partisan balance of legislatures, the ebb and flow of interest group pressure, and other cyclical and stochastic factors associated with the broader political context. This stream functions based on its own dynamics related to elections, nominations, partisan wrangling, and other functions of politics and government. Further, shifts in the public's mood and disposition can alter the politics of government and the politics of a particular problem and/or solution (Kingdon, 1993). In the case of higher education, attention to student debt, college graduation rates, and the partisan disposition of faculty members are all examples of shifts in public opinion and concern regarding postsecondary education. Policymakers, or policy entrepreneurs, must pay attention to the politics stream. In advancing their preferred solution, they may have to amend their solution and supplement their own beliefs with their perception of the "national mood" and the feedback they receive from interest groups and political parties, among others (McLendon, 2003a).

According to Kingdon (1993), policy entrepreneurs must continually push their pet proposals and try to keep the issues alive through both times when the issue receives broader attention and when it is largely ignored. The likelihood that their preferred solution will rise on the government agenda increases considerably when a policy window opens. This happens when a problem "floats by" to which they can attach their solution and/or when developments arise in the political stream that can be used to their advantage. When these moments present themselves, entrepreneurs must act quickly and decisively. Obviously, skill is needed to effectively take advantage of the politics and to effectively connect their solution to a perceived problem. Such windows do not stay open long. Things change quickly, particularly in the politics stream. Clear examples of policy entrepreneurs advancing a state-level higher education policy agenda or governance reform are provided in several of the chapters in this volume. In Chapter 6, we see this dynamic in the case of Florida legislative leaders driving governance reform. However, in the Tennessee case presented in Chapter 3, Rhoda and Linthicum show that both a SHEEO and a governor can drive a higher education agenda, while Hanna and Guilbeau in Chapter 6 show that when it came to the most recent higher education governance reform in Tennessee, the governor acted as the policy entrepreneur. Further, Kinne-Clawson and Zumeta in Chapter 5 showed in their case studies that institutional leaders, system heads, SHEEOs, and governors can all drive postsecondary policy reform.

Kingdon's model has received considerable attention and has been broadly applied to a variety of contexts, including policy innovation and diffusion, foreign policy, health policy, judicial behavior, and social movements (e.g., Baum, 1998; Durant & Diehl, 1989; Meyer & Staggenborg, 1996; Mucciaroni, 1992; Mumper, 1987; Walt, 1996; Zahariadis, 1999). More recently, it has been applied to the agenda-setting process for state higher education policy and, most recently, to evaluate the agenda-setting process for higher education governance reform (e.g., Bastedo, 2007, 2009; McLendon, 2003a, 2003b, 2003c; Mills, 2007; Tandberg & Anderson, 2012).

Kingdon's theory can help those working within government understand their environment. As SHEEOs must manage a diverse bureaucratic agency and interact with and influence lawmakers and other governmental actors, understanding how and why issues rise and fall on the agenda is critical. This is particularly true when the SHEEO wishes to drive a policy agenda. In such instances, acting as a policy entrepreneur (or recruiting someone else to do so), proactively developing solutions, identifying and taking advantage of policy windows, and actively engaging the politics stream are vital to success. Further, as the multiple streams model is a derivative of Cohen and March's garbage can model of decisionmaking, the advice regarding effectively leading an organized anarchy, described in the preceding section, may also more broadly apply in this context as well.

Kingdon's theory may also prove useful to researchers who want to better understand the SHEEO and the environment within which the SHEEO operates, leading to key insights that can inform broad and productive research agendas. In the case of policy change, was the SHEEO a critical actor? How often is the SHEEO the policy entrepreneur? How best can a SHEEO act as a policy entrepreneur and drive a policy agenda? Who are the other actors within the higher education "policy primeval soup"? Such questions and others may be illuminated by applying Kingdon's theory.

Summary

Kingdon's multiple streams model was an extension of Cohen and March's garbage can model. Nevertheless, there are some key differences in both perspective and purpose between the two models. The garbage can model's perspective is one of management and leadership. Therefore, it attempts to explain the nature and internal operations of a college and university and how, given those institutions' unique natures, an institutional leader might best manage and lead their institution. We argue that this knowledge is also critical for SHEEOs as they interact with and lead the colleges and universities in their states. Kingdon's model focuses not so much on leadership and management but on successfully advancing a policy solution, or a policy agenda, within government by taking advantage of windows of opportunities. As SHEEOs must work with and lead colleges and universities and also work within the political world, the two theories work together to help SHEEOs accomplish both responsibilities.

THEORETICAL PERSPECTIVES ON THE BROADER OPERATING
ENVIRONMENT OF THE SHEEO

Here we attempt a substantive application of principal-agent theory and boundary-spanning theory to help SHEEOs and those who would study the SHEEO better understand the broader operating environment in which the SHEEO operates. Principal-agent theory will elucidate the fundamental tensions in the relationship between state policymakers and the institutions of higher education that policy oversees and supports. Boundary-spanning theory will highlight the specific role that SHEEOs play at the boundary between the institutions and the state. As before, these efforts will not only shed some light on relevant and important aspects of the position of the SHEEO but provide some fruitful avenues for framing future empirical research on the SHEEO.

Principal-Agent Theory

Principal-agent theory (PAT) is firmly rooted in neoclassical economics. It emerged and solidified as an independent theoretical lens in the 1960s. In a broader sense, it complements economic price theory, which explores how the conditions of demand and supply determine prices in a competitive marketplace. A core tenant of that theory is that the incentive to maximize profit implies that firms face pressure to minimize costs. Principal-agent theory arose as scholars recognized that though a robust literature explored the implications of price theory for firm behaviors, comparatively little theoretical and empirical work had explored exactly how firm owners motivate, manage, and oversee their employees (workers, managers, supervisors, and contractors) within the organization to ensure that production costs are minimized (Arrow, 1964). In other words, what do supervisors do to ensure that their employees are faithfully executing the tasks to which they have been assigned? Since its inception and application to private firms, this key question has been adapted as PAT has been applied in public and not-for-profit settings where the primary mission is not monetary and the motive to generate economic return is not a primary consideration.

Accordingly, in its most basic formulation, PAT seeks to describe a situation where one party, the principal, delegates responsibility for execution of a task or set of tasks to another party, designated as the agent (Arrow, 1968). Generally, the agent is presumed to have some form of specialized expertise or other comparative advantage in execution relative to the principal, implying a potential improvement in efficiency and/or effectiveness when the responsibility for execution is delegated to the agent by the principal. Accordingly, the primary objective of the principal in this situation is to structure a contractual arrangement with the agent in order to maximize outcomes given resources invested—in other words, to design a contract that is maximally efficient (Eisenhardt, 1989). Of particular importance for the current context, contracts need not be formally written out and executed between the principal and the agent in order for PAT to be relevant. Rather, the contract itself may be metaphorical, representing the relationship (stated or unstated, formal or informal, explicit or implicit) between a party delegating work and a party performing it (Jensen & Meckling, 1976).

According to PAT, two primary factors introduce complications in the principal's ability to achieve this goal in practice. First, it is impossible for the principal to have perfect information regarding the actions of the agent; in other words, gathering information about the agent's performance cannot be done by the principal at zero cost. Second, the principal and the agent hold preferences and interests that are at least somewhat divergent. The confluence of these two factors create the opportunity for the agent to shirk, or to act opportunistically in ways inconsistent with the preferences of the principal. The primary focus of PAT, therefore, is to resolve the shirking problem by incorporating design features into the contract that yield alignment between the agent's actions and the objectives and preferences of the principal.

As this discussion makes clear, PAT is firmly rooted in the rationalist tradition, which straightforwardly presumes that, all else equal, individuals prefer the pursuit of self-interest over the interest of others. And while PAT in its simplest form describes the contractual agreement between individuals—one principal contracting with one agent—it can easily be extended in pragmatically useful ways, including where one organization contracts with another as well as moving beyond a single dyad to recognize sequential and nested layers of principals-agent relationships. Viewed from this broader perspective, Tirole (1986) argued that "organizations can [best] be seen as networks of overlapping or nested principal-agent relationships" (p. 181) between citizens and elected officials, between elected officials and bureaucratic agencies, between the managers of bureaucratic agencies and the agencies' employees, and so on.

Systematic application of PAT to the domain of the SHEEO provides a pragmatic theoretical lens through which numerous critical and unresolved questions may be addressed, and the complex, hierarchical, and nested levels of bureaucracy that exist within higher education may be organized and understood. Perhaps most fundamentally, PAT provides a theoretical justification for the existence of the SHEEO in the first place: The SHEEO occupies the space between the executive and legislative branches and the individual public institutions that ostensibly operate under government control and depend on its financial support.

A rich literature explored the various policy objectives legislatures and governors hold for colleges and universities and the functions legislatures expect institutions to perform (Florestano & Boyd, 1989; Tuckman & Chang, 1990). Given these objectives, how is the legislature and the governor to know whether the university system is meeting expectations—that is, whether (and at what level of productivity and efficiency) is it actually performing these functions? As the previous discussion makes clear, from the perspective of state lawmakers, this is a difficult question to answer with a high degree of certainty. Outputs (and especially outcomes) are notoriously difficult to measure in higher education given the complex, indirect, and nonlinear production functions that define the production of knowledge, whether in the form of educating individual students or of producing academic research. Furthermore, the long and rich traditions of academic freedom, tenure, and academic deference necessitate an arm's-length approach to the monitoring of colleges and universities. These traditions have been firmly rooted in American higher education to (among other things) explicitly keep lawmakers from getting too entwined in the central missions of the academy, the creation and transmission of knowledge. Gathering accurate, reliable, and valid information about the performance of the university and its employees is a difficult and costly enterprise from the perspective of state elected officials, who must quantify and balance the costs of shirking against the costs of gathering and evaluating performance data about university performance. Additionally, while there exists broad overlap in the objectives of the university (and its employees) and state lawmakers, there are clearly areas of divergence as well.

Lane and Kivistö (2008) argued that these divergences can be categorized into two unique types: active and passive. Active divergences are those instances in which the university intentionally chooses to pursue objectives that differ from those held by elected officials. Passive divergences are those that happen without this explicit intentionality. For instance, faculty members may simply choose not to be maximally productive and instead pursue other endeavors, thereby giving the lawmakers a lower return on its investment than it might otherwise receive.

The confluence of these factors—asymmetry of information by state leaders and divergence of preferences at the institutional level—suggest the possibility of a principal-agent problem. This potential problem has existed in principle at least since the initial creation of public institutions of higher education. From this perspective, the rise of the SHEEO agency in the 1950s, at a time in which public higher education was undergoing "massification" and significant expansion, corresponded with a dramatic increase in the potential negative social consequences of shirking due to the rise in public expenditure for higher education. Accordingly, state lawmakers at this time began experimenting with creating SHEEO agencies as intermediaries to manage, oversee, steer, and coordinate public higher education (Berdahl, 1971). While definitive answers about the most effective or efficient arrangement for the SHEEO and their agency have proven elusive, PAT nonetheless provides a pragmatic theoretical lens through which such evaluations can be conducted and the "wickedness" of the SHEEO's position within the state system of higher education may be systematically considered.

Considering the role of the SHEEO through the theoretical lens of PAT offers several direct and tangible benefits to SHEEOs and the staffs they manage. PAT first and foremost provides insights into the economic behaviors of individual universities and the individuals they employ (Kivistö & Zalyevska, 2015). Acknowledging the potential for opportunism—and proactively thinking about potential unintended consequences of policy and programmatic changes—offers SHEEOs and policymakers alike a more holistic perspective on such changes and provides a framework for scenario analysis that considers a range of potential, possible, and probable outcomes. Further, adoption of a PAT perspective necessarily introduces a more comprehensive consideration of program and policy costs, a consideration that incorporates not just the costs of program or policy adoption and administration, but also monitoring and compliance costs (Waterman & Meier, 1998). Considered within a standard benefit-cost framework, this implies a more exhaustive cost estimate that recognizes that performance information cannot be gathered for free. In other words, SHEEOs and their staffs need to be deliberate in thinking through the ways that performance objectives will be determined, implemented, and perhaps most importantly in the current climate, evaluated.

From a scholarly perspective, applying PAT to studies of the SHEEO generates a host of relevant research questions. First and foremost, it is undeniably true that a large degree of heterogeneity exists in the configuration of SHEEO offices across the states with respect to key dimensions such as degree of centralization, level of authority, and nature of staffing. PAT offers a theoretical lens to understand and explain these differences as a function of differences in not only legislative intent but also as a rational reaction by policymakers to the historical and contextual factors that explain the evolution of institutional design over time. Finally, while the application of PAT seems most obvious in the legislature/university relationship, it can be applied to other nested levels of governance as well, including university administrator/faculty and university/student. Unpacking these layers offers researchers the opportunities to explore how agents with multiple principals dynamically manage and balance such interdependencies, moving from a simple dyadic representation of state higher education policy to one that is both contextually richer and more accurately reflective of the complex reality in which the SHEEO exists. This implies a richer, more holistic exploration of the internal and external dynamics of SHEEOs and their offices than currently exists in the empirical literature.

Boundary-Spanning Theory

Boundary-spanning theory focuses on the role and impact of *boundary spanners*, defined as individuals or groups whose work happens at the nexus of organizational boundaries and who broker relationships, cultures, and norms and mediate and translate between the organizations (Cross & Parker, 2004; Williams, 2002). Boundary-spanning organizations and actors must translate and broker relationships with such outside entities as customers, competitors, funders, and those over which the primary organization has some sort of oversight or regulatory responsibility. Additionally, boundary spanners might serve such a role within a larger organization and span boundaries between offices and officials within the organization (Adams, 1976; Aldrich & Herker, 1977; Brown, 1996; Fennell & Alexander, 1987; Tushman & Scanlan, 1981). SHEEOs and state higher education governance structures may be conceptualized as boundary-spanning organizations as they sit at the boundary of higher education institutions and state lawmakers. One of the primary reasons state higher education governance structures were created in the first place was to serve as buffers between the institutions and the states (Carnegie Foundation for the Advancement of Teaching, 1982; Glenny, 1959, 1970; Hearn & Griswold, 1994; McLendon, 2003b). As Ness explained, "Regardless of the degree of centralization, the [SHEEO] agencies largely emerged in the mid-twentieth century with the primary function to buffer state government from postsecondary education institutions. This buffering (or boundary) role of state agencies best represents their function as intermediary organizations" (2010, p. 40).

The public administration literature on boundary spanning elaborates more specifically on what boundary spanners do, what risks they face, which conditions influence their decisions, and what influences their ability to achieve success. Honig (2006) identified information management as a primary role of boundary spanners in (1) the ongoing gathering of new information from outside their organizations and (2) incorporating that information into organizational routines to advance performance goals (see also Aldrich & Herker, 1977; Galaskiewicz & Wasserman, 1989; Gladstein & Caldwell, 1985; Jemison, 1984; Kanter, 1988; Tushman & Scanlan, 1981).

The entities the spanner interacts with often have different operating assumptions, values, and cultures, resulting in complex and difficult relationships that the spanner must mediate and translate. Thus, one of the primary roles of boundary spanners is identifying and collecting information and then facilitating and controlling the flow of information between the various entities and actors (Guston, 2001). This information may include organizational preferences, values, data, "insider" information, and the like. This provides boundary spanners with considerable power, as they filter and control what information gets transferred and in what form. Under these circumstances, boundary spanners often become viewed as experts on the information they routinely transfer between the various entities and on the entities themselves (Tandberg, 2013). The gathering, sharing, and use of the information is often undertaken as a continuous process of identifying conditions and ideas outside the organization, which the organization should address to improve performance (Gladstein & Caldwell, 1985; Levitt & March, 1988; Kanter, 1988). Searching activities may range from formal meetings with outside organizations to occasional informal interactions and quantitative data collection and analysis—often, a combination of efforts that may change over time. The idea is for spanners to undertake whatever activities put them in regular contact with the relevant external actors' needs and demands (Honig, 2006).

Boundary spanners have varying degrees of authority to use the information they gather to develop policy (Honig, 2006). For example, some SHEEOs and state boards have limited direct authority over the colleges and universities, while others have strong statutory and constitutional decisionmaking and policy authority. In the case of limited authority, SHEEOs still have the ability to influence behavior via their information gathering and control abilities as boundary spanners. They may help other organizational members use the information by translating it into forms the decision makers may consider accessible and actionable (examples in higher education might include state data dashboards and other performance accountability systems). This translation function serves to absorb uncertainty from the information, as the total amount of information in the environment is too massive, complex, and confusing. Therefore, boundary spanners identify only those facts perceived to be important and present them to other decision makers in a way that they can be understood and acted on (Adams, 1976; Honig, 2006; Tushman, 1977; Tushman & Katz, 1980). For example, a SHEEO, rather than deliver a large volume of complex information regarding college and university performance, would translate it into a less complex form, such as specific recommendations with a limited amount of supporting data. This reduces ambiguity and information overload (Aldrich & Herker, 1977; Honig, 2006; Leifer & Delbecq, 1978).

Boundary spanners also serve various political purposes. For example, boundary spanners often represent their organization to the outside world and vice versa (Adams, 1976; Aldrich & Herker, 1977; Honig, 2006; Leifer & Huber, 1977). In some cases, boundary spanners are the primary public face of their organizations. In these cases, the boundary spanner serves as the entry point for outside groups to have their interests represented to high-level decision makers within the organization. This function is often referred to as a boundary spanners' "political management role" (Honig, 2006). In this regard, Guston (1999, 2000, 2001) argued that governmental agencies provide an important example of boundary-spanning organizations. Such agencies often sit at the nexus of outside organizations and communities and the political world and serve to represent each to the other and to translate and share information between the various actors. These roles can be seen in the function of SHEEOs and the agencies they lead (Shakespeare, 2008). Ness explained that "although the manner in which state agencies govern higher education varies widely, state-level higher education agencies serve crucial roles in providing information to and interceding between government and colleges" (2010, p. 40).

Honig (2006) suggested that the information and political management roles may serve as a "double-edged sword" when interacting with outside organizations:

> Researchers have found that when boundary spanners operate as information managers or political brokers, they increase their contact with organizations outside their home organization, such as schools or community agencies in this case. Boundary spanners' contact with outside organizations can improve relationships and trust with those organizations and the support they provide to those organizations. . . . On the other hand, increased contact can be perceived by other organizations as regulatory rather than supportive, especially when those other organizations are dependent on the focal organization, and actually reinforce such regulatory relationships. (p. 361)

This perception may be especially likely to arise in public higher education. The campus–state relationship has always been a fraught one, with campuses seeking greater autonomy and state lawmakers seeking to establish some level of control and accountability. SHEEOs must manage this relationship. While greater engagement by the SHEEO with the institutions may satisfy state lawmakers, it may strike campuses as infringing on their autonomy and academic freedom. While a hands-off approach by the SHEEO may please the institutions, lawmakers may question whether the SHEEO is fulfilling his or her primary purpose. The right balance is likely to be constantly renegotiated and is fraught with principal–agent challenges.

Specific conditions influence the extent to which these information and political management activities may be used to improve performance of the agency and those with whom the agency interacts. We highlight several factors discussed by Honig (2006) that appear to be the most relevant to the SHEEO role. First, boundary spanners must be able to understand the language of multiple professional communities. Without this ability spanners will be unable to effectively identify and translate relevant information, nor will they be able to effectively represent their organization to others (Honig, 2006; Tushman & Romanello, 1983; Tushman & Scanlan, 1981). The language of the academy and state government are often quite different. Understanding and being able to translate the language of each is a critical skill for a SHEEO to develop.

Second, boundary spanners must develop the ability to manage role conflict. As a nature of their role, boundary spanners have responsibilities related to at least two distinct organizations (e.g., the SHEEO must work with both state lawmakers and institutional leaders). This means they will encounter conflicting demands on their attention, time, and priorities. As Honig explains: "These conflicts can lead to a lack of clarity regarding goals and rewards for performance and a limited sense of control over their own work." (2006, p. 362). SHEEOs often have a difficult time determining whether they are being successful in their roles. Potentially innumerable goals and outcomes are associated with their roles, and those goals and outcomes will likely vary depending on the audience and/or constituency. For example, colleges and universities would likely consider a SHEEO successful if they receive increased state funding. The legislature might consider a SHEEO successful if operating costs are reduced within colleges and universities. The public would likely consider a SHEEO successful if tuition is lowered (or held steady), and enrollments and completion rates are increased.

Third, boundary spanners' length of tenure and perceived organizational influence are related conditions that can impact their ability to successfully undertake their work. The longer the boundary spanners' tenure in their organizations, the more authority they may develop with those within and outside their organization. Likewise, previous research has shown that when boundary spanners have high status within their organization (i.e., their formal position within the hierarchical authority structure of the organization), they make more productive use of the information they collect than those with lower status. However, those with high status and long tenures must guard against taking a command-and-control posture to their work and remain open to new information (Honig, 2006; see also Blau, 1963; Shrum, 1990). Therefore, SHEEOs with high status and long tenures may be more likely to have strong relationships and greater clout with both institutional leaders and state elected officials.

Finally, Honig (2006) explained that when boundary spanners operate in highly complex situations that involve high levels of discretion and ambiguity and conflicting demands, they can be faced with multiple identities and unclear allegiances. In such cases they will "look for professional practice models that they associate with legitimacy or success regardless of whether following those models is actually likely to improve such outcomes" (p. 362). Further, under such circumstances, boundary spanners will, according to Honig, choose the identities that align with their individual competencies and experience and that are reinforced by others with whom they feel aligned. In other words, they will fall back on what they are most familiar with, or what they feel is their most comfortable and reinforced identity (see also Levitt & March, 1988; March, 1994; Weatherly & Lipsky, 1977). Given the wicked and highly complex and ambiguous position of the SHEEO—applying the garbage can, multiple streams, and principal-agent theories—role identity becomes a critical issue. To whom do the SHEEOs align themselves? Do they feel more comfortable within the environment of the academy or that of state government? Will a SHEEO who is a former president feel most comfortable with the academic community? Will a former legislator be more aligned with lawmakers? Gaining the knowledge and competencies necessary to operate within both environments will be essential to a SHEEO's success.

Boundary-spanning theory may help SHEEOs understand their multiple roles and identify what knowledge and competencies they ought to develop in order to effectively function as a boundary spanner. Understanding their responsibility as an information gatherer and translator will be critical to a SHEEO's effectiveness. Likewise, a SHEEO ought to understand the potential power that comes with that role (and the associated risks). Further, boundary-spanning theory clearly argues that a SHEEO must understand the languages, cultures, norms, and values of academics, policymakers, and bureaucrats. SHEEOs should be comfortable and knowledgeable enough with both government and the academy that they do not get too aligned with either, regardless of their previous professional experience. A boundary-spanning perspective suggests that there is extrinsic, underappreciated value in long tenure for SHEEOs, since it is tenure that allows the SHEEO to develop the requisite knowledge, skill, and comfort to be effective. A long tenure also allows the SHEEO to earn the status, authority, and influence that is conferred with experience and repeated interaction with various stakeholders within and beyond government, including institutional leaders.

While boundary-spanning theory has been utilized in K–12 education, public administration and management, business, sociology, and organization theory research, only two studies in higher education have applied it that we are aware of. Tandberg (2013) used this theory as a way of understanding and situating state higher education governance structures. Specifically, Tandberg hypothesized that because the structures served as boundary-spanning organizations, they might mediate the influence of various political characteristics on state funding for higher education. True to his general argument, his quantitative models revealed that the presence of a consolidated governing board significantly altered or conditioned the influence various political factors had on state funding for higher education. Nicholson-Crotty and Meier (2003) likewise found that the existence of a state coordinating board for higher education appeared to condition the effect of several political factors. Both studies, however, focused on the SHEEO agency as a boundary-spanning organization, and not the individual SHEEO as a boundary spanner. Despite these earlier discussions focused on SHEEO agencies, there remains significant potential for the application of boundary-spanning theory to the role and position of the SHEEO. This is particularly true when it comes to qualitative research. Interviews and observations focused on how SHEEOs manage their multiple identities and allegiances, use information, and influence the behavior of external actors, among other factors, would reveal important findings related to the function and influence of SHEEOs. Such investigations not only offer better empirical clarity regarding the SHEEO but also stand poised to inform boundary-spanning theory itself.

Summary

Principal-agent theory and boundary-spanning theory both situate and highlight the precarious position of SHEEO in sitting between elected officials and the colleges and universities in their states. Our application of principal-agent theory to the SHEEO tended to focus on the nested relationship of the SHEEO as an agent of legislature and the governor in monitoring the colleges and universities in their states. Boundary-spanning theory further complicates these relationships by expanding the relationship between the institutions and the SHEEO and the SHEEO and elected officials and other outside constituencies. As such, we see these theoretical perspectives as much complementary as competing. PAT reminds us of the inherent difficulty of managing, administering, and overseeing complex systems when information is costly to gather and performance difficult to measure. Boundary-spanning theory extends this challenge by drawing attention to the fact that the SHEEO is in the broader sense both a principal overseeing multiple agents and an agent who is accountable to multiple principals that hold diverging (and sometimes outright conflicting) preferences.

NEW PERSPECTIVES AND FINAL THOUGHTS

SHEEOs provide a classic example of a wicked problem. They operate in an incredibly complex environment where cause and effect are difficult to identify and potential policy solutions to persistent problems are continually and hotly debated. The four theories discussed in this chapter are meant to provide practitioners and researchers with tools to deal with the wickedness of the SHEEO position. The theories were selected because they help elucidate the specific position and job of the SHEEO and the operating environment in which the state higher education executive officer works. The first two theories (garbage can and multiple streams) are specifically applied to help SHEEOs and those who would study this position understand the operating context and the strategies SHEEOs might employ to best accomplish their role and mission within that context. The second two theories (principal-agent and boundary spanning) examine the locus of the position of the SHEEO as a critical actor between elected officials, institutional leaders, and other external actors. Taken together, these theories highlight and touch on a number of the major factors and responsibilities associated with being a SHEEO. Nevertheless, the discussions provided here only scratch the surface of how these theories might be applied to the SHEEO position.

Furthermore, while beyond the scope of this chapter, a critical reconsideration of the theories discussed here that deconstructs the underlying assumptions and considers the theories from different perspectives would be useful. For example, how might the theories be reconsidered to account for how SHEEOs' background and identities might influence their perspective on their role and purpose? We hope this chapter spurs additional thinking on these and other topics related to the application of these theories to the SHEEO.

In addition, we encourage further consideration of other theoretical frameworks, including theories of the bureaucracy, neo-institutionalism, network theory, and resource dependency theory, to name a few (Hillman, Withers, & Collins, 2009; O'Toole, 1997; Rockman, 1994; Wilson, 1989). Each of these theories may be used to elucidate critical aspects of the position and job of the SHEEO and/or the environment within which the SHEEO works. Further, other theories that have received less attention in the state higher education policy and governance literature may also prove useful. Some of these might be critical race theory, radical political theory, and other postmodern theories (Reynolds, 2000; Rhoades, 2014; Yeatman, 2014). For example, such perspectives and theories might help us answer such questions as: How might a SHEEO operate within an environment of heightened racial tension and increased inequality? How does an individual SHEEO's racial, gender, and class identities impact his or her perception of higher education and individual roles and policy preferences? Racial tension on our college and university campuses, and increased income inequality nationwide, would suggest that theories that elucidate race and class conflicts and perspectives will become increasingly important. We hope future work takes up this challenge.

Too often, practitioner and academic audiences talk past each other. The theoretical work produced by the academic community is viewed as holding little pragmatic value for the practitioner. The practical focus of the practitioner is viewed as too applied and of little value for developing a broader body of generalizable knowledge. This pervasive academic–practitioner divide persists to the detriment of both communities. It is within this broader context that this chapter should be considered. Certainly, it alone does not—and cannot—bridge the gap. Space and other constraints necessitated difficult choices about which theoretical frameworks to consider among many potentially fruitful alternatives. As such, we position this work as illustrative of the potential gains to both academic and practitioner communities by deliberately engaging each other and wrangling with the interplay between theory and practice. With state higher education leaders and researchers, all facing similar wicked problems, it would be highly inefficient if we did not develop and use shared concepts, language, and general ideas and parameters for engaging the work. This chapter is meant to be one step forward in attempting to address this issue.

REFERENCES

Adams, J. S. (1976). The structure and dynamics of behavior in organizational boundary roles. In M. Dunette (Ed.), *Handbook of organizational and industrial psychology* (pp. 1175–1199). Chicago, IL: Rand McNally.

Aldrich, H., & Herker, D. (1977). Boundary spanning roles and organization structure. *The Academy of Management Review, 2*(2), 217–230.

Arrow, K. J. (1964). Control in large organizations. *Management Science, 10*(3), 397–408.

Arrow, K. J. (1968). The economics of moral hazard: Further comment. *The American Economic Review, 58*(3), 537–539.

Ashworth, K. (2001). *Caught between the dog and the fireplug, or how to survive public service.* Washington, DC: Georgetown University Press.

Bastedo, M. N. (2007). Sociological frameworks for higher education policy research. In P. J. Gumport (Ed). *Sociology of higher education: Contributions and their contexts,* (pp. 295–316). Baltimore: Johns Hopkins University Press.

Bastedo, M. N. (2009). Convergent institutional logics in public higher education: State policymaking and governing board activism. *The Review of Higher Education, 32*(2), 209–234.

Baum, L. (1998). *The puzzle of judicial behavior.* Ann Arbor: University of Michigan Press.

Berdahl, R. O. (1971). *Statewide coordination of higher education.* Washington, DC: American Council on Education.

Bess, J., & Dee, J. (2008). *Understanding college and university organization: Theories for effective policy and practice.* Sterling, VA: Stylus.

Blau, P. M. (1963). *The dynamics of bureaucracy.* New York: Wiley.

Brown, W. (1996). Systems, boundaries, and information flow. *The Academy of Management Journal, 9*(4), 318–327.

Cohen, M. D., & March, J. G. (1986). Leadership in an organized anarchy. In M. W. Petersen (Ed.), *ASHE Reader series on organization and governance in higher education* (pp. 16–35). Lexington, MA: Ginn.

Cohen, M. D., March, J. G., & Olsen, J. P. (1972). A garbage can model of organizational choice. *Administrative Science Quarterly, 17*(1), 1–25.

Cross, R., & Parker, A. (2004). *The hidden power of social networks: Understanding how work really gets done in organizations.* Boston, MA: Harvard Business School Press.

Carnegie Foundation for the Advancement of Teaching. (1982). *The control of the campus: A report on the governance of higher education.* Princeton, NJ: Princeton University Press.

Durant, R. F., & Diehl, P. F. (1989). Agendas, alternatives, and public policy: Lessons from the U.S. foreign policy arena. *Journal of Public Policy, 9*(2), 179–205.

Eisenhardt, K. M. (1989). Agency theory: An assessment and review. *Academy of Management Review, 14*(1), 57–74.

Fennell, M., & Alexander, J. (1987). Organizational boundary spanning in institutionalized environments. *The Academy of Management Journal, 30*(3), 456–476.

Florestano, P. S., & Boyd, L. V. (1989). Governors and higher education. *Policy Studies Journal, 17*(4), 863–877.

Galaskiewicz, J., & Wasserman, S. (1989). Mimetic processes within an interorganizational field: An empirical test. *Administrative Science Quarterly, 34*(3), 454–479.

Gándara, D., Rippner, J. A., & Ness, E. C. (2017). Exploring the 'how' in policy diffusion: National intermediary organizations' roles in facilitating the spread of performance-based funding policies in the states. *The Journal of Higher Education, 88*(5), 1–26.

Gladstein, D., & Caldwell, D. (1985). Boundary management in new product teams. *Academy of Management Proceedings*, 161–165.

Glenny, L. A. (1959). *Autonomy of public colleges: The challenge of coordination.* New York: McGraw-Hill.

Glenny, L. A. (1970). Institutional autonomy for whom? In G. K. Smith (Ed.), *The troubled campus: Current issues in higher education* (pp. 153–160). Washington, DC: AAHE.

Graber, D. A., & Dunaway, J. (2017). *Mass media and American politics.* Washington, DC: CQ Press.

Guston, D. H. (1999). Stabilizing the boundary between U.S. politics and science: The role of the office of technology transfer as a boundary organization. *Social Studies of Science, 29*(1), 87–112.

Guston, D. H. (2000). *Between politics and science: Credibility on the line.* New York: Cambridge University Press.

Guston, D. H. (2001). Boundary organizations in environmental policy and science: An introduction. *Science, Technology, & Human Values, 26*(4), 399–408.

Hearn, J. C., & Griswold, C. P. (1994). State-level centralization and policy innovation in U.S. postsecondary education. *Educational Evaluation and Policy Analysis, 16*(2), 161–190.

Hillman, A. J., Withers, M. C., & Collins, B. J. (2009). Resource dependence theory: A review. *Journal of Management, 35*(6), 1404–1427.

Honig, M. I. (2006). Street-level bureaucracy revisited: Frontline district central-office administrators as boundary spanners in education policy implementation. *Educational Evaluation and Policy Analysis, 28*(4), 357–383.

Jemison, D. B. (1984). The importance of boundary spanning roles in strategic decision-making. *Journal of Management Studies, 21*(2), 131–152.

Jensen, M. C., & Meckling, W. H. (1976). Theory of the firm: Managerial behavior, agency costs and ownership structure. *Journal of Financial Economics, 3*(4), 305–360.

Johnson, B., & Christensen, L. (2012). *Educational research: Quantitative, qualitative, and mixed approaches* (4th ed.). Thousand Oaks, CA: Sage.

Kanter, R. M. (1988). When a thousand flowers bloom: Structural, collective, and social conditions for innovation in organization. *Research in Organizational Behavior, 10*, 169–211.

Kingdon, J. W. (1993). How do issues get on public policy agendas? In W. J. Wilson (Ed.), *Sociology and the public agenda* (pp. 40–50). Newbury Park, CA: Sage.

Kingdon, J. W. (1995). *Agendas, alternatives, and public policies* (2nd ed.). New York: HarperCollins.

Kivistö, J. A., & Zalyevska, I. (2015). Agency theory as a framework for higher education governance. In J. Huisman, H. de Boer, D. D. Dill, & M. Souto-Otero

(Eds.), *The Palgrave international handbook of higher education policy and governance* (pp. 132–151). London, England: Palgrave Macmillan UK.

Lane, J. E., & Kivistö, J. A. (2008). Interests, information, and incentives in higher education: Principal-agent theory and its potential applications to the study of higher education governance. In J. C. Smart (Ed.), *Higher education: Handbook of theory and research* (pp. 141–179). Dordrecht, The Netherlands: Springer.

Leifer, R., & Delbecq, A. (1978). Organizational/environmental interchange: A model of boundary spanning activity. *The Academy of Management Review*, 3(1), 40–50.

Leifer, R., & Huber, G. P. (1977). Relations among perceived environmental uncertainty, organization structure, and boundary-spanning behavior. *Administrative Science Quarterly*, 22(2), 235–247.

Levitt, B., & March, J. G. (1988). Organizational learning. *American Review of Sociology*, 14, 319–340.

March, J. G. (1994). *A primer on decision making*, New York: Free Press.

March, J. G., & Olsen, J. P. (2010). *Rediscovering institutions*. New York: Free Press.

McLendon, M. K. (2003a). The politics of higher education: Toward an expanded research agenda. *Educational Policy*, 17(1), 165–191.

McLendon, M. K. (2003b). Setting the governmental agenda for state decentralization of higher education. *Journal of Higher Education*, 74(5), 479–515.

McLendon, M. K. (2003c). State governance reform of higher education: Patterns, trends, and theories of the public policy process. In J. C. Smart (Ed.), *Higher education: Handbook of theory and research* (pp. 57–143). Dordrecht, The Netherlands: Springer.

Meyer, D. S., & Staggenborg, S. (1996). Movements, countermovements, and the structure of political opportunity. *American Journal of Sociology*, 101(6), 1628–1660.

Mills, M. R. (2007). Stories of politics and policy: Florida's higher education governance reorganization. *Journal of Higher Education*, 78(2), 162–187.

Mucciaroni, G. (1992). The garbage can model and the study of policy making: A critique. *Polity*, 24, 460–482.

Mumper, M. (1987). Understanding policy agendas. *Social Science Journal*, 24(1), 83–86.

Ness, E. C. (2010). The role of information in the policy process: Implications for the examination of research utilization in higher education policy. In J. C. Smart (Ed.), *Higher education: Handbook of theory and research* (pp. 1–49). London, England: Springer.

Nicholson-Crotty, J., & Meier, K. J. (2003). Politics, structure, and public policy: The case of higher education. *Educational Policy*, 17(1), 80–97.

O'Toole Jr, L. J. (1997). Treating networks seriously: Practical and research-based agendas in public administration. *Public administration review*, 45–52.

Pew Research Center. (2017). *The partisan divide on political values grows even wider*. Washington, DC: Author.

Reynolds, P. (2000). Post-Marxism: Radical Political Theory and Practice Beyond Marxism?. *Marxism, The Millennium and Beyond*, London: Palgrave, 257–279.

Rhoades, G. (2014). The higher education we choose, collectively: Reembodying and repoliticizing choice. *The Journal of Higher Education*, 85(6), 917–930.

Rittel, H. W., & Webber, M. M. (1973). Planning problems are wicked. *Polity, 4*, 155–169.

Rockman, B. (1994). The new institutionalism and the old institutions. In L. Dodd, and C. Jillson (Eds.), *New Perspectives on American Politics*. Washington, DC: Congressional Quarterly Press.

Shakespeare, C. (2008). Uncovering information's role in the state higher education policymaking process. *Educational Policy, 22*(6), 875–899.

Shrum, W. (1990). Status incongruence among boundary spanners: Structure, exchange, and conflict. *American Sociological Review, 55*(4), 496–511.

Strauss, A., & Corbin, J. (1998). *Basics of qualitative research: Grounded theory procedures and techniques* (2nd ed.). Thousand Oaks, CA: Sage.

Tandberg, D. A. (2013). The conditioning role of state higher education governance structures. *Journal of Higher Education, 84*(4), 506–543.

Tandberg, D. A., & Anderson, C. K. (2012). Where politics is a blood sport: Restructuring state higher education governance in Massachusetts. *Educational Policy, 26*(4), 564–591.

Tirole, J. (1986). Hierarchies and bureaucracies: On the role of collusion in organizations. *Journal of Law, Economics, & Organization, 2*(2), 181–214.

Tuckman, H. P., & Chang, C. F. (1990). Participant goals, institutional goals, and university resource allocation decisions. In S. Hoenack & E. L. Collins (Eds.), *The economics of American universities: Management, operations, and fiscal environment* (pp. 53–76). Albany: State University of New York Press.

Tushman, M. L. (1977). Special boundary roles in the innovation process. *Administrative Science Quarterly, 22*, 587–605.

Tushman, M. L., & Katz, R. (1980). External communication and project performance: An investigation into the role of gatekeepers. *Management Science, 26*(11), 1071–1985.

Tushman, M. L., & Romanello, E. (1983). Uncertainty, social location and influence in decision making: A sociometric analysis. *Management Science, 29*(1), 12–23.

Tushman, M. L., & Scanlan, T. J. (1981). Boundary spanning individuals: Their role in information transfer and their antecedents. *The Academy of Management Journal, 24*(2), 289–305.

Walt, G. (1996). *Health policy: An introduction to process and power*. London, England: Zed.

Waterman, R. W., & Meier, K. J. (1998). Principal-agent models: an expansion? *Journal of Public Administration Research and Theory, 8*(2), 173–202.

Weatherly, R., & Lipsky, M. (1977). Street-level bureaucrats and institutional innovation: Implementing special education reform. *Harvard Educational Review, 47*(2), 171–197.

Williams, P. (2002). The competent boundary spanner. *Public Administration, 80*(1), 103–124.

Wilson, J. Q. (1989). Bureaucracy: What government agencies do and why they do it. New York: Basic Books.

Yeatman, A. (2014). *Postmodern revisionings of the political*. New York, NY: Routledge.

Zahariadis, N. (1999). Ambiguity, time and multiple streams. In P. A. Sabatier (Ed.), *Theories of the policy process* (pp. 73–93). Boulder, CO: Westview Press.

CHAPTER 11

Data, Measures, Methods, and the Study of the SHEEO

T. Austin Lacy and David A. Tandberg

Much of this volume has focused on the relatively underappreciated, yet critically important, role of the SHEEO in state policy and politics. However, we also acknowledge that these arguments are mainly based on anecdote, personal experience, and a smattering of qualitative research. When the SHEEO is not a meaningful actor in the development of state postsecondary policy, there is typically no story to tell so understanding the influence of these individuals is often based on observations of the affirmative. While the role of the SHEEO is meaningful, we encourage more systematic and empirical investigations of these positions, including quantitative analyses that attempt to better document the role and influence of the SHEEO in state higher education policy and politics.

This chapter introduces several quantitative measures of the SHEEO that might be implemented in empirical models meant to predict state higher education policy adoptions, state higher education spending decisions, and other similar outcomes. We propose that these important measures can be generated for all 50 states and, with effort, across time. These examples highlight critical characteristics of the SHEEO, encourage new thinking about the position from an empirical perspective, attempt to show how future research may examine the role and function of the SHEEO, and highlight for practitioners factors that may be impacting their positions and functions. Beyond measures surrounding SHEEOs, there are other meaningful dimensions that define the space in which they operate. These too should be measured and will promote new research questions, approaches, and studies that we believe, if undertaken, might add useful knowledge about SHEEOs and the work they do. We offer a number of potential such measures for consideration. While the most obvious use of measurement is for academic research purposes, delineating the differences among SHEEOs has potential benefits for state policymakers, advocacy organizations, interstate compacts, and other intermediary organizations. Understanding the differences inherent in SHEEO positions may inform the manner in which they interface with those individuals and other actors in a given state.

QUANTITATIVE STUDIES RELATED TO THE SHEEO

Over the past decade, a vein of research emerged within the field of post-secondary education that tended to borrow heavily from the political science literature. Broadly speaking, this work examined the intersection between politics, organizational theory, and postsecondary policy. Much of this research centered on analyses where the state was the unit of analysis, frequently examining the correlates of postsecondary policy adoption and levels of public funding.

While this work has employed both qualitative and quantitative techniques, the latter borrow heavily from other fields in both their theory and methods, frequently using time-series cross-sectional (i.e., panel) data and estimators such as event history analysis and fixed effects regression, among other techniques. In part through the appropriation of these theories and methods, inquiry has been driven by available state-level political science indicators such as partisan balance and longstanding indicators of various state-level postsecondary attributes (e.g., state postsecondary governance structures and state appropriations to postsecondary education). Beyond using the more familiar measures of partisanship, indicators of economic conditions, demographic compositions, and so forth, political scientists studying state policy have created measures of so-called "latent variables."

Latent variables are typically measures of constructs that are not read-ily observed but believed by theory and anecdote to exist. For example, one could measure how conservative a congressional representative is by his or her party affiliation. However, some Republicans are more conservative than others in their party while some Democrats are more liberal than other Democrats. One way political scientists recover the individual ideolo-gies of lawmakers, judges, and other public officials is through examining their voting records and allowing for certain issues (e.g., abortion) to more greatly differentiate people on an ideological continuum than other votes (e.g., naming a park).[1] At the state level, latent variables measuring citizen ideology (Berry, Ringquist, Fording, & Hanson, 2007) and legislative pro-fessionalism (Squire, 1992) have been used in postsecondary studies with mixed findings. This chapter looks to this tradition of measurement with the attempt to extend these analyses to the position of the SHEEO.

Recently we, with other colleagues, began to examine indicators associ-ated with the SHEEO and their relationship to other structures and actors in state government and the effect they have on state funding. While moving in an important direction, our early works were crude (Tandberg, Fowles, & McLendon, 2017; Lacy, Fowles, Tandberg, & Hu, 2017). This chapter seeks to explore additional avenues through which future research may refine these measures and, in turn, further the understanding of these individuals and their role in shaping postsecondary policy. Prior to these examinations of the SHEEO as the unit of analysis, studies of state postsecondary policy focused on their agency, resulting in the use of a binary measure of post-secondary governance. Largely drawing on the work of Aims McGuinness (1985, 1988, 1994, 1995, 1997, 2001, 2003, 2005) but owing an often-overlooked debt to Paltridge (1965), these studies frequently delineate between states that have a consolidated governing board and those that do not. Across these studies, the relative influence of these arrangements was mixed, which led our research to begin considering the influence of the SHEEO in more direct ways.[2]

The field of political science grounds our initial thinking surrounding how researchers might measure various characteristics of the SHEEO, specifically the work of Thad Beyle (e.g., 1968, 2004) and his effort to measure of the powers of another chief executive, the governor.[3] Beyle identified several powers of the governor, collected indicators where appropriate, and then aggregated them to form a total "Gubernatorial Power Ranking." The dimensions identified by Beyle included a governor's tenure, the number of elected officials in a state, a governor's budgetary power, and his or her party's control of state government. Additional dimensions were identified over the years, such as a governor's institutional power, comprising different observed characteristics. Most recently, the institutional power of governors has been measured by criteria including the existence of separately elected executive branch officials and the governors' tenure potential, appointment powers, budgetary powers, veto powers, and party control. These constructs relied on observable characteristics that are part of statute and constitutional provisions. While developed by political scientists, these measures and other gubernatorial indicators have found their way into postsecondary research, particularly in the micro-field of studies that examined the adoption of certain higher education policy innovations and degree of state support of higher education (see Hearn, McLendon, & Linthicum, 2017, for a recent review).

In our own work, we have taken initial steps to incorporate measures surrounding the SHEEO into analyses of postsecondary state policy. Our past efforts to measure characteristics related to the SHEEO have used binary measures of particular relationships SHEEOs have in respect to the governor and state government.

In Tandberg et al. (2017), three indicators were used: (1) if the governor had the power to appoint the SHEEO, (2) if the SHEEO served at the pleasure of the governor, and (3) if the SHEEO made budgetary recommendations. The first two indicators were closely related in that they measured the explicit relationship between the SHEEO and the state chief executive. This study found that state appropriations were significantly impacted by the two indicators surrounding the SHEEO and governor's relationship but not the third regarding the budget. Specifically, the results revealed that the governor's ability to dismiss the SHEEO correlated to lower spending on higher education. However, the indicator variable capturing the governor's appointment powers with respect to the SHEEO was positive and significant, suggesting the opposite effect.

Separately when Lacy et al. (2017) examined volatility in state funding for higher education, two of these indicators were employed: whether the governor appointed the SHEEO and whether the SHEEO was able to recommend a budget. In recognition of the dynamic interplay between these two indicators, this study then created an interaction term. The authors found that the interaction term was negative and significant with the model demonstrating that, when SHEEOs were closely aligned with governors but have little authority themselves over budgets, they were better able to capture volatility in state funding for higher education.

Taken together, these early findings suggest that the SHEEO's formal relationship to the governor—or lack thereof—is a domain that merits both further research and refinement in concept and measure. This nests neatly with the evidence pointing toward the importance of governors in educational policy formation, with the suggestion that "education governors" can influence certain outcomes (Mokher, 2010). While the nuances between governors who focus on K–12 and postsecondary education is outside the scope of this chapter, several studies have shown that particular attributes of the governor that extend beyond partisanship influence postsecondary policy formation and funding. For example, McLendon, Hearn, and Mokher (2009) found that as a governor's institutional power increased, state appropriations to postsecondary education decreased. Using a different mix of variables, Tandberg (2010) found no statistically significant effect of governor's budgetary power on the same outcome. Consistent, positive effects of a governor's budgetary powers have been found in relation to the adoption of economic development policies involving universities, with the same influence on the adoption of state R&D tax credits (Hearn, Lacy, & Warshaw, 2014) and a positive relationship between a governor's budgetary powers and state eminent scholars policies, an effect that is dynamic and becomes more pronounced over time (Hearn, McLendon, & Lacy, 2013). In contrast, no statistically discernable relationship was found between a governor's budgetary powers and the adoption of a broad conceptualization of postsecondary finance innovations (Lacy & Tandberg, 2014).

In light of these findings, the study of the SHEEO cannot be completely decoupled from the governor. The "closeness" between the SHEEO and the governor, as measured by the latter's ability to hire and fire the former, is a theoretically defensible construct for measurement. However, despite our clear interest and investment in this research, this relationship is a rare occurrence. Currently only five states—Arkansas, Colorado, New Jersey, Pennsylvania, and Tennessee—have arrangements where the governor appoints the SHEEO and the governor has the power to remove the SHEEO from office. While in the past more states have had either one or both of these arrangements, from a quantitative research standpoint, measures that are more broadly applicable are needed.

The ability of the SHEEO to make budgetary recommendations closely mirrors Beyle's (2004) conception of gubernatorial budgetary power in that it, albeit crudely, measures their ability to formally set agendas through the budgetary process. In contrast to the gubernatorial data, research on states where a SHEEO recommends a budget has the opposite challenge, with only six states (Delaware, Minnesota, New Hampshire, Texas, Vermont, and Wyoming) having SHEEOs without this power in our data (that we are aware of as of this writing).

MEASUREMENT CONSIDERATIONS

Before continuing, it is essential to note two somewhat basic, but important, considerations for measurement.

First, the measure needs to conform to either some theoretical construct or often-cited (unmeasured) characteristic that is used by experts to describe and/or interpret findings. One example is the conception of "financial literacy," wherein social scientists measure a purported theoretical construct that captures individuals' understanding of financial concepts (e.g., Lusardi & Mitchell, 2011). For a postsecondary example, we turn inward and look to one of our attempts to develop a measure of centralization for postsecondary governance. This effort emerged from the field's frequent interpretation of the presence of a consolidated governing board as states' degree of governance "centralization." Yet the blunt measure did not differentiate levels of centralization both within governing boards and outside of them.

The second consideration of measurement is that the measure needs some degree of variance within it. This is a practical consideration in that an attribute without variance is of little use to attempt to measure quantitatively. As an extreme example, if all—or nearly all—states possess the same attribute, then the measure is of little utility as there is little predictive power. Past measures of the SHEEO suffer from this dilemma, and as much, if not more, knowledge could be gleaned on these rare events via rigorous qualitative case studies.

Nevertheless, we believe that better measures that align to both characteristics are possible. It is also important to acknowledge that the types of data and the arrangements we are proposing to measure are not static. They change over time, so the data need to be reevaluated and updated over time. Likewise, concepts like power and authority can play out in unpredictable or unmeasurable ways. For example, while a governor may not have the formal authority to directly dismiss a SHEEO, for all intents and purposes, he or she may have the power to remove the SHEEO. These nuances are difficult to capture in quantitative measures but are nonetheless important to acknowledge.

PROPOSED MEASURES RELATED TO THE SHEEO

We now turn to the SHEEO and discuss what we could measure across states and over time that would have utility to researchers and analysts interested in making cross-state comparisons as well as comparisons within states and that, when employed, might provide useful new knowledge regarding the SHEEO. Like states and state agencies, the circumstances surrounding any particular SHEEO position is unique. Important characteristics associated with individual SHEEOs that are challenging or impossible to measure must be thrown out. No doubt charisma factors into SHEEOs' ability to perform their duties, but such characteristics are beyond the scope or ability of this sort of endeavor. In other words, we acknowledge that every SHEEO and SHEEO office is unique like a snowflake, but here we discuss attributes that can be legitimately measured.

To extend the snowflake metaphor, can we measure along the lines of temperature, whiteness, and wetness? We see two broad, conceptual approaches that we will measure for the SHEEO: A politicization index and a power index would be beneficial and promote new research uncovering the influence, or lack of influence, these actors have on state postsecondary policy. These two broad characteristics are among the most important, measurable characteristics shaping the role, function, and influence of a SHEEO; therefore, they are relevant to both practitioners (e.g., SHEEOs, SHEEO agency staff, college and university leaders, lawmakers) and to researchers.

SHEEO Politicization Index

While the SHEEO office itself may not be inherently political, SHEEOs operate in a political space, and many SHEEOs themselves have identifiable careers and associations with particular political parties. If a politicization measure is statistically associated with various postsecondary policy outcomes, we can better understand a form of influence associated with an important structural characteristic of the SHEEO. Conceptually, the SHEEO politicization index would capture both the position of these state officials and their formal ties to government. In all practicality, a partisanship component of a SHEEO politicization measure would perhaps be the most challenging dimension to measure, as in many situations SHEEOs can be incentivized to obscure their partisanship in efforts to more effectively perform their duties. In fact, overt partisanship can be seen as a liability, particularly for SHEEOs who are appointed by boards and may outlast gubernatorial administrations (Ashworth, 2001). Nevertheless, we include a partisan component as part of our larger attempt to uncover such political characteristics of the SHEEO. In that regard, we propose a six-indicator measure where one point is ascribed for SHEEOs who have the following relationships and attributes surrounding their office:

1. Has the SHEEO ever held a publicly elected or appointed office?
2. Is the SHEEO appointed by the governor?
3. Does the governor have the ability to fire the SHEEO?
4. Is the SHEEO a formal member of the governor's cabinet?
5. Has the SHEEO in the past been a member of the same party that controls the legislature?
6. Has the SHEEO in the past been a member of the same party that controls the gubernatorial branch of government?

These measures may have both empirical and theoretical implications.

Public Service. A SHEEO who is a former elected or appointed official may have personal and professional relationships with current elected officials and may be more disposed toward the concerns of elected officials and be better able to work with them. In many cases, these data would need to be collected directly from the state agencies or the SHEEOs themselves; however, in many states both are a matter of public record.

Hiring and Firing. In some states governors have formal power over the SHEEOs, with the ability to hire and fire them at will. Conceptually, this relationship raises the governor's institutional power and lowers that of the SHEEO. In other states, agency boards and legislatures are the bodies that have the ability to hire and fire a SHEEO, making the governor institutionally weaker. Where the governor is stronger, the SHEEO may be expected to advance the governor's agenda. As Lingenfelter, Novak, and Legon (2008) observed, when the governor appoints the SHEEO, "the governor has great leverage over the actions and the decisions made by the state's higher education agency" (p. 10). Gubernatorial appointment is a tool through which the office can exert control over state agencies (Beyle, 1968; Dometrius, 1979; Wright, 1967), a finding also supported by surveys of governors themselves (Beyle & Muchmore, 1980). That said, the true politics of this relationship can materialize in ways that are challenging to measure quantitatively. For example, in many states where boards hire and fire the SHEEO, board members in turn can be appointed by legislators and/or governors. In these scenarios, boards often can serve as agents for politicians, and these phenomena would benefit from qualitative inquiry.

Cabinet Seat. While the heads of the other major state agencies are generally assumed to be part of the governor's cabinet, it is not as common for SHEEOs to serve in this capacity. This service may be important for a number of reasons, one of which is the potential for such service to increase the influence of the governor over the SHEEO. As Berdahl (2004) observed: "For the board CEO [the SHEEO] to sit with the [governor's] Executive Cabinet or some other senior body could . . . further increase the power of the governor and lessen the appearance of the board's theoretical independence" (p. 4). Historical appointment and cabinet service data are available via McGuinness's (1985, 1988, 1994, 1997, 2003) profile/handbooks and are easily coded for use. Researchers would be able to update and collect these data directly from state documents and websites.

Partisan Alignment. Regarding the final two indicators, partisan alignment may mean greater commitment on the part of the SHEEO to the dominant party's political platform and increased pressure on the SHEEO to align with the party's goals. That said, the data for these measures may be difficult and in some cases impossible to collect as our conceptualization of partisanship requires some assumptions of ideology being static across time. It is unfair to assume that SHEEOs such as Erskine Bowles, Janet Napolitano, and Margaret Spellings, who have strong historical ties to parties have maintained partisan positions. However, any error surrounding this measurement is likely small. As indicated, data for these final two indicators would likely be difficult to collect, however potential sources include voter registration records, media/news reporting, and various online resources, among other public sources. Despite the difficulty in collecting the data and the potential for missing data, the practical and theoretical implications of the potential role of partisanship in the SHEEO job make these measures worthy of consideration.

We find support for our notion of the importance of accounting for the politicization of the SHEEO is rooted in the work and observations of Leslie and Novak (2003). These researchers used case studies to examine governance restructuring in Florida, Kentucky, Maryland, Minnesota, and New Jersey. Also borrowing theories from the political science and public policy fields, they too found politics to be at the center of debates on restructuring, though in some cases of restructuring, actual policy change was made in order to accomplish certain instrumental goals. Rather than a purely political process, they suggest that reform is a result of an interaction between politics and the instrumental goals and levers of influence. For example, they describe the interaction as "governors and legislators constantly [playing] the levers available to them as they seek to achieve both the control of the governmental apparatus and their own party objectives" (Leslie & Novak, 2003, p.117).

SHEEO Power Index

In contrast to the SHEEO politicization index, the SHEEO powers index attempt to measure the control and personal power the SHEEO may have in functions that involve running postsecondary education.[4] Here again, this measure attempts to identify important structural characteristics associated with the SHEEO. This measure may help researchers and practitioners identify important forms of influence that may be associated with the SHEEO's ability to influence other actors and postsecondary policy and finance outcomes. In constructing institutional measures we acknowledge that the line between the individual SHEEO and the agency or board can be blurred. For example, tuition setting authority can exist at multiple levels including with the SHEEO agency, however, we do not include it in this measure as it is often treated as an attribute of the agency or board (Deaton, 2006; Warne, 2008). The dimensions for this are authority over the budget and authority over the institutions' presidents and chancellors with this measure ranging from zero to eight points:

1. Does the SHEEO have authority over the budget? (Max 6 points)
   a. 1 point if the SHEEO recommends the state budget for higher education
   b. 2 points if the SHEEO allocates the state appropriation to the institutions
   c. 3 points if the SHEEO approves institutional budgets
2. Does the SHEEO have authority over presidents and chancellors of the institutions under his or her purview? (Max 2 points)
   a. 1 point if the SHEEO can only either hire <u>or</u> fire presidents and chancellors
   b. 2 points if the SHEEO can hire <u>and</u> fire presidents and chancellors

The Budget. Regarding SHEEO budgetary authority, previous research has shown agency head budget recommendations have the potential to influence governors' recommendations (e.g., Sharkansky, 1968). A similar effect is expected when a SHEEO makes budgetary recommendations to the governor. In some instances, particularly when the SHEEO heads a governing board or state system, the state appropriation is made to the SHEEO agency, which then determines and makes the allocation to the institutions. Similarly, some SHEEOs have the ability to approve institution operating budgets. Both of these final two authorities place the SHEEO in a particularly powerful position relative to the institutions and other entities associated with higher education in the state. In such circumstances, the institutional leaders become dependent on the SHEEO for a major portion of their budget and may therefore be more inclined to please the SHEEO and support a SHEEO's policy and finance agendas and positions. Likewise, such powers may provide the SHEEO with political capital to enact other, nonfinance agendas. Historical budget recommendation data are available via McGuinness's (1985, 1988, 1994, 1997, 2003) profiles/handbooks.

Researchers would also be able to collect the data directly from state documents and websites and update accordingly. The other two data points would need to be collected via state documents and websites.

Institutional leaders. The SHEEO's authority over institution presidents and chancellors as a component of the SHEEO power index is scaled so the instances where a SHEEO can both hire and fire presidents and chancellors receive 2 points and 0 if the SHEEO can do neither. As in the logic applied to the governor's ability to hire and fire the SHEEO, the hiring and firing power of an executive is particularly potent in its ability to garner the attention of those who work under the executive's direction (Beyle & Ferguson, 2008). When the SHEEO has greater hiring and firing authority of the presidents and/or chancellors, those institutional leaders may be more likely to support the SHEEO's agenda and positions and less likely to actively oppose the SHEEO. Therefore, policy outcomes the SHEEO supports would be more likely to be realized when the SHEEO has the ability to hire and fire the institutional leaders. These data points would need to be collected via state documents and websites.

For both the SHEEO politicization index and the power measures, we have proposed additive measures that mirror Beyle's work (e.g., Beyle, 2004), measures that are relatively simplistic compared to other efforts. A priori, more sophisticated latent variable modeling would not produce a more elegant measure as these typically depend on the collection of a larger number of indicators that can be used to differentiate the units of study. While it is perfectly possible to create a model that generates measures and provides the ability for different attributes to contribute different weights to the measure, the limited qualities that we believe are readily observable across SHEEOs would generate a measure with a large degree of uncertainty.

EMPLOYING THE MEASURES IN INFERENTIAL RESEARCH

Simply reporting these metrics and submetrics by state and SHEEO agency would provide much needed descriptive information. Knowing how states and state agencies compare to each other regarding the powers and politicization of the SHEEO may benefit practitioners, policymakers, and researchers. Further, the changes of these measures within states and across time merit study. Over time, have SHEEOs become more politicized in certain states? Have SHEEOs become imbued with more power or has the power once afforded to them been eroded over time?

However, such measures as those we propose here may also allow researchers to provide deeper and nuanced analyses regarding the role, function, and influence of the SHEEO on perennial state policy questions. For example, would greater politicization result in lower tuition and fees?

One reason to expect this type of relationship might be that governors and legislatures must appeal to the broadest possible swath of the likely voter population in their state/district (Soss, Schram, Vartanian, & O'Brien, 2001). The governors and the general state population tend to support lower tuition and fees, and the same is true for the state legislature (Mulhere, Stratford, & Rivard, 2014). Therefore, economic conditions being held constant, we could expect that a highly politicized SHEEO would be more likely to support and to provide greater support for lower tuition and fees. For similar reasons, highly politicized SHEEOs would be expected to provide greater support for state merit-aid programs, ceteris paribus, as merit aid programs tend to benefit the active and influential segments of a state's voting population—middle- and upper-income students and their families (Heller & Marin, 2002).

Further, our work on the factors associated with states adopting market-based approaches to financing higher education (Lacy & Tandberg, 2014) ought to be reconsidered with the addition of our proposed measures of the SHEEO. Would the presence of a highly politicized SHEEO and/or a powerful SHEEO increase the likelihood of a state adopting a market-based approach (e.g., performance-based funding, merit aid, a student voucher program, etc.)? What is the interaction between a SHEEO's politicization and partisanship? On one hand, we can envision a scenario where a politicized SHEEO and certain ideologies could hasten particular reforms. On the other, there are likely scenarios where SHEEOs who are not politicized may be able to buffer and oppose the adoption of the preferred policies of a particular party.

Similarly, previous research focused specifically on the likelihood of states adopting various accountability programs (performance reporting, budgeting, and/or funding) (Li, 2017; McLendon, Hearn, & Deaton, 2006) may need reconsideration to account for the potential influence of a highly politicized and/or powerful SHEEO. In this regard, there may be reason to believe that SHEEOs who are highly politicized would be more likely to support accountability policies and that the presence of a powerful SHEEO would significantly increase the likelihood of a state adopting an accountability policy. Previous research has examined the role of other state political, demographic, economic, and higher education system characteristics in determining state higher education finance and accountability strategies (e.g., Doyle, 2010; Lacy & Tandberg, 2014; Li, 2017; McLendon et al., 2006; McLendon et al., 2009; McLendon, Tandberg, & Hillman, 2014), but the potential influence of the SHEEO, and particularly the politicization and power of the SHEEO, has yet to be examined.

As mentioned earlier, our nascent research used blunt measures to understand the relationship between the SHEEO and outcomes of revenue volatility (Lacy et al., 2017) and the SHEEO–governor relationship's effect on appropriations (Tandberg et al., 2017). While it is obvious that these works would benefit from a refined measure, the SHEEO's role in many state outcomes was overlooked simply due to a lack of a convenient measure. While we do not suggest revisiting the corpus of state-level postsecondary research, reviewing many studies with these useful measures would contribute to our understanding of state postsecondary policy.

OTHER MEASURES RELATED TO THE SHEEO

Although in this chapter we have focused on measuring the SHEEO as an individual, we would be remiss not to note that additional measurement endeavors should be made to further understand the context in which they operate. Adopting a neo-institutional perspective, which argues that governmental and political institutions influence both the behavior of individuals and the outcomes of public policymaking (McLendon, 2003), we can anticipate that there may be an interactive relationship between the two measures of the SHEEO and between the measures of the SHEEO and characteristics of the agencies they lead. Regarding the potential interactive relationship of the SHEEO and the agency, neo-institutional theory argues that the structures individual actors operate within impact their decision making and potentially condition the influence they have on associated outcomes. The most immediate structure to the SHEEO is the agency they lead. Accordingly, one could assume that a highly politicized SHEEO leading a highly centralized and powerful agency would function differently than a highly politicized SHEEO leading a highly decentralized agency with little statutory authority. To examine these potential differences, we could interact the two measures of the SHEEO and/or we could interact the politicization measure with a measure of agency centralization.[5] One such measure of SHEEO agency centralization was developed by Lacy (2011). This measure placed all state structures on a "continuum of centralization," thereby permitting a higher degree of variance and precision in measurement than is possible with the traditional binary variable (i.e., 1 if the agency is a consolidated governing board, 0 if not).

A potential important aspect of agency authority or power might be whether the agency has tuition setting authority. Prior research has shown that locus of this authority (whether with the institution, the SHEEO agency, or with state lawmakers) significantly impacts tuition rates (e.g., Kim & Ko, 2015; Kramer, Ortagus, & Lacy, 2017). Therefore, the ability to control institutional tuition rates would be a powerful tool for SHEEO agencies as tuition rates significantly impact college and university budgets. If the agency has this authority institutions may be more willing to go along with and appease the SHEEO's preferences. Including such an indicator in inferential models, and perhaps interacting the indicator with the measures proposed earlier, may help researchers better understand the SHEEO's interactions with, and influence over, institutions. These data are available from the State Higher Education Executive Officers Association *Tuition Surveys* and state documents and websites.

Beyond SHEEO agency centralization and authority, we might consider agency capacity. To begin accounting for this concept, one might consider agency operating budget and/or agency staff. Such measures might include full-time equivalent (FTE) agency staff, FTE agency staff per public institution, agency operating budget per FTE agency staff, and/or agency operating budget as a percent of state higher education appropriation. Again, these measures could be interacted with the SHEEO measures to examine how they might magnify or buffer the impact of the SHEEO measures. Historical counts of professional and supporting staff (occasionally disaggregated by full- and part-time) and agency budgets are also available from McGuinness's (1985, 1988, 1994, 1997, 2003) profile/handbooks. Staff salaries, which are publicly available for many states, would be another valuable measure that could help develop a measure approximating the analytic and political capacity of the staff.

While increasingly complex, one could also imagine a three-way interaction of SHEEO politicization, agency centralization, and agency capacity. Measures of agency centralization and capacity can be refined to further recognize the multiple agencies that exist within many states.

Returning to the idea of the SHEEO as an individual, the path to "SHEEOship" may also matter. For example, if the SHEEO was a former college president, would he or she be more disposed to institutional concerns and/or better able to work with institutional leaders? As indicated in our politicization measure, perhaps a former elected official may be more disposed toward the concerns of elected officials and/or be better equipped to navigate the political side of the SHEEO's work. Someone with neither governmental/political nor higher education experience (say someone from business) may come into the job with different perspectives, loyalties, and preferences. Would these distinctions impact how a SHEEO might approach the job or policy preferences? Would they influence the SHEEO's effectiveness? Again, interaction variables may be important to explore here. For example, would greater SHEEO powers magnify the potential influence of these indicators?

Another potential measure future researchers may consider is the tenure of the SHEEO. Beyle (2004) argued that gubernatorial tenure is one component related to governors' power, a measure that has been frequently employed in state-level postsecondary research (e.g., McLendon et al., 2006). Likewise, Honig (2006) (see also Blau, 1963; Shrum, 1990) argued that the longer an individual serves in a boundary-spanning role (like the SHEEO), the greater his or her power or influence.[6] Therefore, one might want to employ number of years or months as a SHEEO in various predictive models.

CONCLUSION

While the utility of such measures and quantitative research efforts may be obvious to researchers, such efforts may also have utility to SHEEOs and others working in state higher education governance and policy. As Layzell and Lyddon (1990) referred to state budgeting for higher education: "You have got to know the system to beat the system" (p. xix). The measures proposed here may provide indicators of factors important to the role and function of a SHEEO. For sitting SHEEOs, they may help identify potential levers, constraints, strategies, and warnings, all of which may provide for a better understanding of their working environments and hopefully facilitate improvement in their effectiveness. For example, SHEEOs have a dual obligation to lawmakers and to higher education institutions. If being appointed by the governor draws them closer to the governor and impacts their actions and policy outcomes in systematic ways, attention to their orientation may be needed.

Likewise, individuals considering working as a SHEEO generally or considering an opportunity to work as a SHEEO in a specific state may want to consider the characteristics identified in this chapter, namely their formal relationship with state lawmakers, their budgetary powers, and their power over institutional leaders. We contend that these characteristics are some of the most important structural characteristics shaping a SHEEO's role and influence.

It is difficult to argue that the study of state policymaking could be complete without recognition of governors' influence on the process. We argue that the same holds true for studies of postsecondary policy and finance: Ignoring one of the primary actors in the process obfuscates our understanding of the underlying mechanism at work. There exist few passable measures, but a better empirical understanding of the SHEEO is needed to advance both research and practice regarding the position and state higher education policy and finance generally. The measures discussed here, if developed and utilized, may help in developing such understandings. In fact, our own empirical work would be vastly improved if these measures existed at the time, and many of the works referenced in this chapter would be enhanced if rigorous, publicly available measures of the SHEEO had existed when the authors began their work. Likewise, for those who believe that the position is important and worthy of support and advancement, documenting the role and influence of the SHEEO is necessary to make supportable arguments and conclusions. We hope that this piece can begin the conversation and result in the systematic measurement of these individuals.

NOTES

1. For an overview of this approach see Poole (2005) and Clinton, Jackman, and Rivers (2004a, 2004b). For a postsecondary application, see Doyle (2010).

2. In full disclosure, both authors of this chapter have worked at a state higher education agency under SHEEOs who, between the two, had large differences in their structural powers. Currently one author is employed by the membership organization of these chief executives, and both frequently interact and work with individuals from SHEEO agencies. Our perspectives from our work led us to believe that there were identifiable structural characteristics of the SHEEO office and individual that would be related to state higher education policy and finance outcomes.

3. Prior to Beyle, others have catalogued and measured powers of the governor (e.g., Schlesinger, 1965, 1971; Dometrius, 1979).

4. This is very similar to Beyle's institutional powers. The term *institution* has been removed as to avoid confusion among postsecondary researchers and policymakers who tend to use this word to refer to colleges and universities.

5. Formally speaking, interacting is allowing one variable to be conditional on another through including a term that multiplies the two.

6. See Chapter 10 by Tandberg and Fowles in this volume for a discussion of boundary-spanning theory and the SHEEO.

REFERENCES

Ashworth, K. (2001). *Caught between the dog and the fireplug, or how to survive public service*. Washington, DC: Georgetown University Press.

Berdahl, R. O. (2004). *Strong governors and higher education*. Boulder, CO: SHEEO.

Berry, W. D., Ringquist, E. J., Fording, R. C., & Hanson, R. L. (2007). The measurement and stability of state citizen ideology. *State Politics and Policy Quarterly, 7*(12), 111–132.

Beyle, T. L. (1968). The governor's formal powers: A view from the governor's chair. *Public Administration Review, 28*(6), 540–545.

Beyle. T. L.(1980). Governors. In V. Gray, H. Jacob, & K. N. Vines (Eds.), *Politics in the American states* (4th ed., pp. 180–221). Boston, MA: Little, Brown.

Beyle, T. L. (2004). Governors. In V. Gray & R. L. Hanson (Eds.), *Politics in the American states* (8th ed., pp. 194–231). Washington, DC: CQ Press.

Beyle, T. L., & Ferguson, M. (2008). Governors and the executive branch. In V. Gray & R. L. Hanson (Eds.), *Politics in the American states* (9th ed., pp. 192–228). Washington, DC: CQ Press.

Beyle, T. L., & Muchmore, L. (1980). The governor as party leader. *State Government, 53*(3), 121–124.

Blau, P. M. (1963). *The dynamics of bureaucracy*. New York, NY: Wiley.

Clinton, J. D., Jackman, S., & Rivers, D. (2004a). The statistical analysis of roll call data. *American Political Science Review, 98*(2), 355–370.

Clinton, J. D., Jackman, S., & Rivers, D. (2004b). The most liberal senator? Analyzing and interpreting Congressional roll call. *PS: Political Science and Politics, 37*(4), 805–811.

Deaton, S. B. R. (2006). *Policy Shifts in Tuition Setting Authority in the American States: An Events History Analysis of State Policy Adoption*. (Unpublished doctoral dissertation). Vanderbilt University: Nashville, TN.

Dometrius, N. C. (1979). Measuring gubernatorial power. *The Journal of Politics*, 41(2), 589–610.

Doyle, W. R. (2010). U.S. senator's ideal points for higher education: Documenting partisanship 1965–2004. *Journal of Higher Education*, 81(5), 619–644.

Hearn, J. C., Lacy, T. A., & Warshaw, J. B. (2014). State research and development tax credits: The historical emergence of a distinctive economic policy instrument. *Economic Development Quarterly*, 28(2), 166–181.

Hearn, J. C., McLendon, M. K., & Lacy, T. A. (2013). State-funded "eminent scholars" programs: University faculty recruitment as an emerging policy instrument. *Journal of Higher Education*, 84(5), 601–639.

Hearn, J. C., McLendon, M. K., & Linthicum, K. C. (2017). Conceptualizing state policy adoption and diffusion. In M. B. Paulsen (Ed.), *Higher education: Handbook of theory and research* (pp. 309–354). New York, NY: Springer.

Heller, D. E., & Marin, P. (2002). *Who should we help? The negative social consequences of merit scholarships*. Cambridge, MA: The Civil Rights Project.

Honig, M. I. (2006). Street-level bureaucracy revisited: Frontline district central-office administrators as boundary spanners in education policy implementation. *Educational Evaluation and Policy Analysis*, 28(4), 357–383.

Kim, M. M., & Ko, J. (2015). The impacts of state control policies on college tuition increase. *Educational Policy*, 29(5), 815-838.

Kramer, D. A., Ortagus, J. C., & Lacy, T. A. (2017). Tuition-setting authority and broad-based merit aid: The effect of policy intersection on pricing strategies. *Research in Higher Education*, 1–30. Retrieved from link.springer.com/article/10.1007/s11162-017-9475-x

Lacy, T. A. (2011). Measuring state postsecondary governance: Developing a new continuum of centralization (Doctoral dissertation, University of Georgia).

Lacy, T. A., Fowles, J. T., Tandberg, D. A., & Hu, S. (2017). U.S. state higher education appropriations: Assessing the relationships between agency politicization, centralization, and volatility. *Policy and Society*, 36(1), 16–33.

Lacy, T. A., & Tandberg, D. A. (2014). Rethinking policy diffusion: The interstate spread of "finance innovations." *Research in Higher Education*, 55(7), 627–649.

Layzell, D. T., & Lyddon, J. W. (1990). *Budgeting for higher education at the state level: Enigma, paradox, and ritual*. Washington, DC: George Washington University, School of Education and Human Development.

Leslie, D. W., & Novak, R. J. (2003). Substance vs. politics: Through the dark mirror of governance reform. *Educational Policy*, 17(1), 98–120.

Li, A. Y. (2017). Covet thy neighbor or "reverse policy diffusion"? State adoption of performance funding 2.0. *Research in Higher Education*, 1–26.

Lingenfelter, P. E., Novak, R. J., & Legon, R. (2008). *Excellence at scale: What is required of public leadership and governance in higher education?* Washington, DC: Association of Governing Boards of Universities and Colleges.

Lusardi, A., & Mitchell, O. S. (2011). Financial literacy around the world: An overview. *Journal of Pension Economics & Finance*, 10(4), 497–508.

McGuinness, A. C. (1985). *State postsecondary education structures handbook*. Denver, CO: Education Commission of the States.

McGuinness, A. C. (1988). *State postsecondary education structures handbook.* Denver, CO: Education Commission of the States.

McGuinness, A. C. (1994). *State postsecondary education structures handbook.* Denver, CO: Education Commission of the States.

McGuinness, A. C. (1995). *Restructuring state roles in higher education: A case study of the 1994 New Jersey Higher Education Restructuring Act.* Denver, CO: Education Commission of the States.

McGuinness, A. C. (1997). *State postsecondary education structures handbook.* Denver, CO: Education Commission of the States.

McGuinness, A. C. (2001). *ECS policy brief: Reflections on postsecondary governance changes.* Denver, CO: Education Commission of the States.

McGuinness, A. C. (2003). *Models of postsecondary education and governance in the states.* Denver, CO: Education Commission of the States.

McGuinness, A. C. (2005). The states in higher education. In P. G. Altbach, R. O. Berdahl, & P. J. Gumport (Eds.), *American higher education in the twenty-first century: Social, political, and economic challenges,* (2nd ed., pp. 198–225). Baltimore, MD: Johns Hopkins.

McLendon, M. K. (2003). The politics of higher education: Toward an expanded research agenda. *Educational Policy, 17*(1), 165–191.

McLendon, M. K., Hearn, J. C., & Deaton, R. (2006). Called to account: Analyzing the origins and spread of state performance-accountability policies for higher education. *Educational Evaluation and Policy Analysis, 28*(1), 1–24.

McLendon, M. K., Hearn, J. C., & Mokher, C. G. (2009). Partisans, professionals, and power: The role of political factors in state higher education funding. *Journal of Higher Education, 80*(6), 686–713.

McLendon, M. K., Tandberg, D. A., & Hillman, N. W. (2014). Financing college opportunity: Factors influencing state spending on student financial aid and campus appropriations, 1990 through 2010. *The ANNALS of the American Academy of Political and Social Science, 655*(1), 143–162.

Mokher, C. G. (2010). Do "education governors" matter? The case of statewide P–16 education councils. *Educational Evaluation and Policy Analysis, 32*(4), 476–497.

Mulhere, K., Stratford, M., & Rivard, R. (2014). Higher ed in the governors' races. *Inside Higher Ed.* Retrieved from www.insidehighered.com/news/2014/10/31/higher-ed-especially-tuition-issue-governors-races

Paltridge, J. G. (1965). *Organizational forms which characterize statewide coordination of higher education.* Berkeley, CA: Center for Research and Development in Higher Education, University of California, Berkeley.

Poole, K. T. (2005). *Spatial models of parliamentary voting.* New York: Cambridge University Press.

Shrum, W. (1990). Status incongruence among boundary spanners: Structure, exchange, and conflict. *American Sociological Review, 55*(4), 496–511.

Schlesinger, J. A. (1965). The politics of the executive. In H. Jacob & K. N. Vines (Eds.), *Politics in the American states* (pp. 207–238). Boston, MA: Little, Brown.

Schlesinger, J. A. (1971). The politics of the executive. In H. Jacob & K. N. Vines (Eds.), *Politics in the American states* (2nd ed., pp. 210–237). Boston, MA: Little, Brown.

Sharkansky, I. (1968). Agency requests, gubernatorial support and budget success in state legislatures. *American Political Science Review*, 62(4), 1220–1231.

Soss, J., Schram, S. F., Vartanian, T. P., & O'Brien, E. (2001). Setting the terms of relief: Explaining state policy choices in the devolution revolution. *American Journal of Political Science*, 45(2), 378–395.

Squire, P. (1992). Legislative professionalization and membership diversity in state legislatures. *Legislative Studies Quarterly*, 17(1), 69–79.

Tandberg, D. A. (2010). Interest groups and governmental institutions: The politics of state funding of public higher education. *Educational Policy*, 24(5), 735–778.

Tandberg, D. A., Fowles, J. T., & McLendon, M. K. (2017). The governor and the state higher education executive officer: How the relationship shapes state financial support for higher education. *Journal of Higher Education*, 88(1), 110–134.

Warne, T. R. (2008). *Comparing theories of the policy process and state tuition policy: Critical theory, institutional rational choice, and advocacy coalitions.* (Unpublished doctoral dissertation). University of Missouri–Columbia.

Wright, D. S. (1967). Executive leadership in state administration. *Midwest Journal of Political Science*, 11(1), 1–26.

Final Thoughts

David A. Tandberg, Brian A. Sponsler,
Randall W. Hanna, and Jason P. Guilbeau

As Janus was capable of looking into the past and into the future, we have attempted to do the same with the SHEEO, our modern-day Janus of sorts. We hope the reader has come away with a new appreciation of the role and position of the SHEEO in advancing the public interest and in mediating between institutional leaders and state elected officials. As the authors in this volume have articulated so well, the job of the SHEEO is critically important. We have addressed this importance from both an applied and a scholarly perspective. In this regard, we have attempted to follow the advice of Pat Callan, who argued, "Emerging social and political conditions affecting higher education in America will require scholars and leaders who understand the complexities of developing and implementing sound public higher education policies from both the academic and practical perspectives, and someone should think about this" (Chance, 2009, p. 1). We hope this volume has created a space for scholars and practitioners to come together to think about these issues, and we hope the engagement continues.

While the role of the SHEEO is important, the chapters in this volume have also made clear how difficult it is. SHEEOs are at the front lines of some of society's most important and fierce battles. In fact, those who choose to enter the profession deliberately position themselves where the battles are the thickest and the lines are the thinnest. SHEEOs, unlike campus presidents and elected officials, have no natural constituency. The positions they take are often unpopular and the terrain they travel is always contested. Yet, the difficulty of their job is one indication of its importance—which leads us to our final points: Collectively, we need to turn our attention to developing resources and tools to help our current SHEEOs do their jobs better and to developing the next generation of leaders.

Regarding helping the current generation of leaders, there is no shortage of organizations and individuals suggesting potential policy solutions to the problems facing higher education in the United States. This is important and should continue. However, there is less attention paid to informing state higher education leaders on how best to operate in their positions. We need thinking, research, and writing focused on state higher education leadership. This volume can be seen as an effort in advancing such work. We hope others will pick up where we have left off.

There is also an urgent need to attract and retain bright, energetic, and talented individuals into our SHEEO agencies. The staff of today may very well become the SHEEOs of tomorrow. And more immediately, SHEEOs will only be as effective as the staff they employ. Highly knowledgeable and skilled state higher education policy professionals are critical for thoughtful and well-conceived policy development and implementation and higher education coordination and governance. Responding to what they saw as a dearth of up-and-coming higher education leaders, Munitz and Breneman (1998) argued:

> We firmly believe that higher education needs young, vital leaders for the years ahead, regardless of the vicissitudes of growth or development that the enterprise experiences. . . . Perhaps the most important issue to discuss is whether some extraordinary activity needs to take place to ensure that higher education secures its necessary share of leadership talent for the years ahead. If we conclude that action is warranted, today's leaders must discuss exactly what type of action might be effective. (p. 13)

We argue that such action is, in fact, needed. Far too often, talented staff in our SHEEO agencies are recruited away from their positions to work in other organizations. These departures may shortchange the SHEEO agencies that are responsible for the development, implementation, and evaluation of new policies and programs. These agencies have the legal responsibility for higher education and will be held accountable if something goes wrong. Outside organizations bear no such responsibility or accountability. How can we make a career in state higher education leadership attractive to young people leaving our graduate schools? We need to find answers to this question.

Similarly, and particularly at the SHEEO level, the profession lacks diversity. There is a critical demographic divergence between state higher education leaders and the students they serve. Currently, women make up only 23% of SHEEOs, and racial/ethnic minorities make up only 18%. Without deliberate efforts, these statistics are not likely to change in any significant way as the current baby boom generation of SHEEOs retires. Increased attention from policy organizations, current SHEEOs, and the scholarly community may help in recruiting and retaining new and diverse talent to the profession.

It is also important to acknowledge that more could be done to diversify the state higher education policy research community. While there are critical female and racial/ethnic minority voices, we believe more could be done to attract and support diverse communities to this area of scholarship. Furthermore, additional research on the SHEEO, and state higher education governance and policy topics generally, ought to focus specifically on issues related to diversity and equity. Recruiting more diverse graduate student communities, focusing our research efforts on the connections between state higher education policy leadership and issues of diversity and equity, and supporting young diverse scholars may help in improving the representation of researchers in this area of scholarship. Furthermore, more diverse researchers and research topics may potentially increase the interest of young people in state higher education policy and leadership, and they may be more likely to work in our state agencies and become our future state higher education leaders.

We hope that the chapters in this volume have given readers a new and more informed appreciation of the SHEEO and state higher education leadership in general. We appreciate you joining us on this journey, and we especially appreciate the authors for lending us their vast knowledge, wisdom, and talents. We believe they have been put to a good and important purpose. Here is to the past, current, and future SHEEOs and their good fight.

REFERENCES

Chance, W. (2009). *The National Center for Public Policy and Higher Education's associates program.* San Jose, CA: National Center for Public Policy and Higher Education.

Munitz, B., & Breneman, D. W. (1998). The 1997 leadership poll. *Change: The Magazine of Higher Learning, 30*(1), 12–13.

About the Editors and Contributors

David A. Tandberg is vice president for policy research and strategic initiatives at the State Higher Education Executive Officers Association. Tandberg's interests center on state higher education policy, finance, politics, governance, and economics. Previously he served as an associate professor of higher education and an associate director and cofounder of the Center for Postsecondary Success at Florida State University. Before that, Tandberg served as a special assistant to the Deputy Secretary for Postsecondary Education and later to the Secretary of Education in Pennsylvania. He holds a PhD from Penn State University, and his research has appeared in a variety of peer-reviewed outlets.

Brian A. Sponsler is vice president of policy at Education Commission of the States. His professional experiences include large-scale, high-visibility, and high-stakes project development, management, and execution in nonprofit and higher education settings. Prior to joining ECS, Sponsler served as the vice president for research and policy at the National Association of Student Personnel Administratorsand (NASPA) and as associate director for research at the Institute for Higher Education Policy. His research interests include college access for disenfranchised student populations, structural and geographic impediments to college-going, and policy-adoption theory. He holds a doctorate in higher education administration from The George Washington University.

Randall W. Hanna is the dean and chief executive officer of Florida State University Panama City. In addition, he serves as the dean of the University's College of Applied Studies. Hanna previously served as chancellor of the Florida College System, on the governing boards of two universities in the state and one community college, and as the chairman of the State Board of Community Colleges. Hanna was the managing shareholder of Bryant Miller Olive, a multistate law firm from 1998 to 2011. He received his doctorate of education from the University of Pennsylvania and his Juris Doctorate from Florida State University.

Jason P. Guilbeau is a doctoral candidate in the higher education program at Florida State University. His dissertation research explores the relationship between alumni engagement and institutional diversity. Guilbeau's broad research interest lie at the intersection of higher education policy and social justice. Prior to joining Florida State, he successfully led volunteer and fundraising efforts for the University of New Orleans' Alumni Association and the American Cancer Society. He holds a master's of education in educational administration from Texas A&M University and a bachelor of arts in political science from the University of Louisiana.

Robert E. Anderson serves as president of the State Higher Education Executive Officers Association. Previously, Anderson served as the vice chancellor for Academic Affairs & Policy at the University System of Georgia. Prior to his appointment at the University System of Georgia, Anderson served as executive vice chancellor for administration at the West Virginia Higher Education Policy Commission in Charleston, West Virginia. He previously served as vice chancellor for policy and planning at the same agency, director of research and planning for the Tennessee Higher Education Commission in Nashville, Tennessee, and as an administrator and instructor at Montreat College.

Tracey Bark is a doctoral candidate in political science at the University of Oklahoma. Her research interests are broadly concerned with public policy and its administration. Specifically, much of her work lies at the intersection of state politics, education policy, and bureaucratic institutions. Bark is also a graduate research assistant at the Center for Risk and Crisis Management at the University of Oklahoma, where she works on a variety of projects related to regulatory politics and the federal bureaucracy.

Jacob T. Fowles is an associate professor in the School of Public Affairs and Administration at the University of Kansas. He teaches graduate courses on public finance, policy analysis, program evaluation, and quantitative research methods. Jacob's broader research agenda involves the application of organizational theories developed in public administration, economics, and political science to the study of public education finance and policy. He received his PhD in public administration in 2010 from the Martin School of Public Policy and Administration at the University of Kentucky.

Alisa Hicklin Fryar is an associate professor of political science at the University of Oklahoma. Her work focuses on the politics of higher education, bureaucratic structures, higher education policy, student access and success, and issues of race and ethnicity. She received her PhD in political science at Texas A&M University in 2006.

Mary Fulton is a senior policy analyst with Education Commission of the States and has been with the organization for more than 20 years. Fulton leads the organization's project activities related to higher education governance; she has specialized in development education and college completion policies and serves as a generalist on higher education topics. Fulton has authored several reports and policy papers, provided assistance to state leaders on higher education and K–12 policy issues, tracked and analyzed state and postsecondary system policies and reform efforts, and managed projects related to higher education policies.

James C. Hearn is professor and associate director in the Institute of Higher Education at the University of Georgia. His research and teaching focus on postsecondary education organization, finance, and policy. He has recently examined marketization and performance accountability in postsecondary institutions and systems; the shifting ecology of state higher education policymaking; the growing use of contingent faculty labor; and institutions' organizational adaptations to shifting economic, demographic, and political conditions. Hearn's research has been published in sociology, economics, and education journals as well as in several books.

Neal Holly serves as the assistant director for Postsecondary and Workforce at the Education Commission of the States. Prior to joining ECS, he served as vice chancellor for policy and planning for the West Virginia Higher Education Policy Commission and the West Virginia Council for Community and Technical Education. He has also served multiple staff roles at public and private colleges and universities throughout North Carolina, South Carolina, and Virginia. He is a graduate of Wingate University, Appalachian State University, and the College of William and Mary.

Alicia Kinne-Clawson is the committee coordinator and lead policy analyst for the Washington State Senate Higher Education and Workforce Development committee. She earned her undergraduate degree in political science at Eastern Washington University, a master's degree in public affairs from the Daniel J. Evans School of Public Policy and Governance at the University of Washington, and her PhD from the College of Education at the University of Washington. Her research primarily focuses on regional comprehensive universities, higher education governance, and higher education finance.

T. Austin Lacy is a researcher and analyst at RTI International, where his principal duties involve the design of the National Center for Education Statistics' National Postsecondary Student Aid Study (NPSAS), the Beginning Postsecondary Students Longitudinal Study (BPS), and the Baccalaureate and Beyond Longitudinal Study (B&B). Before joining RTI in 2014, he was a researcher and policy analyst for the University of North Carolina system.

Lacy's current research interest lies at the intersection between state and federal postsecondary policy.

Thomas D. Layzell served 24 years as a SHEEO or multicampus system head in Illinois, Mississippi, Kentucky, and Louisiana in both permanent and interim positions. Layzell has served as president of SHEEO, president of the National Association of System Heads, a member of the National Commission on Accountability in Higher Education, a member of the Illinois Legislative Study Commission on Higher Education Finance, and a member of the AGB Council of Presidents. Layzell received a BA degree in history from Millikin University and JD and MAPA degrees from the University of Illinois.

Paul E. Lingenfelter was president of the association of State Higher Education Executive Officers from 2000 to 2013, where he convened the National Commission on Accountability in Higher Education and launched the annual study, *State Higher Education Finance*. Previously he was vice president of the Program on Human and Community Development at the John D. and Catherine T. MacArthur Foundation and deputy director for fiscal affairs at the Illinois Board of Higher Education. He holds a PhD from the University of Michigan and is the author of *"Proof," Policy, and Practice: Understanding the Role of Evidence in Improving Education*.

Kristen C. Linthicum is a doctoral candidate at the Institute of Higher Education at the University of Georgia. Her research examines state policies and politics related to public research universities.

Erik C. Ness is associate professor and graduate coordinator in the Institute of Higher Education at the University of Georgia. He conducts research on higher education politics and policy. His current research projects examine research utilization—the extent to which policymakers rely on research evidence to craft policy—in the adoption and implementation of various state higher education policy initiatives, including an examination of the distinct role of intermediary organizations on college completion policies.

Richard G. Rhoda is executive director emeritus of the Tennessee Higher Education Commission, having served 17 years as the Tennessee SHEEO. His entire 40-year career was dedicated to Tennessee higher education. He served on the senior staff of Tennessee State University and the Tennessee Board of Regents. He fulfilled interim appointments as president of Nashville State Community College and Austin Peay State University and as chancellor of the Tennessee Board of Regents. He also taught at Vanderbilt University. Rhoda earned a BA in history, MA in education, and PhD in higher education administration, all from Vanderbilt University.

Paul G. Rubin serves as a 2017–2018 American Educational Research Association (AERA)/American Association for Advancement of Science (AAAS) Congressional Fellow after completion of his PhD from the University of Georgia's Institute of Higher Education. His research focuses on higher education policy, governance of the postsecondary sector, and the impact of research on the policymaking process.

William M. Zumeta is professor in the Evans School of Public Policy & Governance and the College of Education at the University of Washington in Seattle, where he teaches and writes about public policy with an emphasis on higher education policy and finance. He is a TIAA Institute Fellow and was president of the Association for the Study of Higher Education. He is coauthor of *Financing American Higher Education in the Era of Globalization*.

Index

References followed by the letter *f* are figures, those followed by the letter *t* are tables, and references with "n" indicate reference is in the end note.